TRASH *to* CA$H

New business opportunities in the post-consumer waste stream

SUSAN WILLIAMS

Landfill   CLOSED

INVESTOR RESPONSIBILITY RESEARCH CENTER

The Investor Responsibility Research Center compiles and impartially analyzes information on the activities of business in society, on the activities of institutional investors, on efforts to influence such activities, and on related public policies. IRRC's publications and other services are available by subscription or individually. IRRC's work is financed primarily by annual subscription fees paid by some 400 investing institutions for the Social Issues Service, the Corporate Governance Service and the South Africa Review Service. This report is a publication of the Social Issues Service. The Center was founded in 1972 as an independent, not-for-profit corporation. It is governed by a 21-member board of directors who represent subscribing institutions.

Executive Director: Margaret Carroll
Director, Social Issues Service: Carolyn Mathiasen

ISBN 0-931035-84-8

TABLE OF CONTENTS

List of Tables, Figures and Boxes

ACKNOWLEDGEMENTS

The author would like to thank a number of individuals who assisted in the preparation of this report. Teresa Opheim, Scott Fenn and Douglas Cogan of IRRC's Environmental Information Service and Carolyn Mathiasen of IRRC's Social Issues Service served as reviewers for this report and offered many helpful comments. Charine Adams and Shirley Carpenter prepared this report for publication, and Mike Davis designed the cover.

The author also wishes to thank a number of outside reviewers for their time and insight, including the Aluminum Association Inc.; the Council for Solid Waste Solutions; J. Rodney Edwards, vice president, American Paper Institute Inc.; Austin Fiore, regional manager of recycling and public affairs, Owens-Brockway Glass Containers; William Heenan Jr., president, Steel Can Recycling Institute; Stephen Katz, New England CRInc.; Jonathon V.L. Kiser, manager of resource recovery and combustion programs, National Solid Wastes Management Association; Ron Kofmehl, plant manager, Ravenswood Aluminum Corp.; Ellen M. Kosty, communications coordinator, National Polystyrene Recycling Co.; Chaz Miller, director of recycling, Glass Packaging Institute; Randall B. Monk, director of operations, Solid Waste Composting Council; Robert Morris, director of facility development, Waste Management Inc.; James F. Ordendorff, director of used can plants, AMG Resources Corp.; John Phillips, Ogden Projects Inc.; and Brian Sturgell, director of market planning, Alcan Rolled Products Co.

Lastly, the author would like to thank the more than 100 companies and trade associations that provided information on their operations and shared their viewpoints on the evolving municipal solid waste disposal industry.

Susan Williams
Senior Analyst
September 1991

INTRODUCTION

Business opportunities abound in municipal solid waste disposal. The United States is dramatically transforming the way it handles that waste, providing openings for many new players to enter the field and for existing players to expand their services. For decades, the nation has depended heavily on landfills, which in 1988 swallowed nearly three-quarters of the nation's municipal garbage.[1] Many of these landfills are now nearing capacity, however, and still others will close soon rather than meet increasingly stringent federal and state standards. The Environmental Protection Agency projected in 1988 that nearly half of the nation's 6,000 landfills will close by the end of 1991.[2] But the prevalence of the NIMBY (Not In My Backyard) syndrome and the rising costs associated with new landfills have precluded the siting of new landfills in many locations. As a result, EPA estimates that only slightly more than half of the nation's municipal solid waste, at best, will be landfilled by 1995.[3]

The growing shortage of permitted solid waste disposal capacity in many parts of the country has sent municipalities scrambling in search of alternative waste disposal methods. The shortage also has contributed to skyrocketing waste disposal costs, making many waste disposal alternatives that had been unable to compete with inexpensive landfills in the past economically viable today.

A multitude of companies are seizing this opportunity to offer municipalities a broad array of waste disposal alternatives, which fall under three general categories: recycling, incineration and composting. Companies marketing these services range from traditional waste disposal and recycling operations to completely new start-up companies. All intend to generate a profit from their waste disposal services, essentially turning "trash to cash."

Yet the economic underpinnings of "trash to cash" in the 1990s differ markedly from those of the 1970s, when municipalities mistakenly hoped to find "gold in garbage" by retrieving and selling recyclable materials from the waste stream. In the 1990s, municipalities have themselves become the source of cash as they pay companies to process their solid waste and reduce the amount being landfilled. As in the 1970s, the markets for most recyclables remain insufficient to cover fully the costs of recovering them from the waste stream. Nevertheless, many municipalities are finding it more cost-effective to subsidize recycling efforts than to pay high landfill disposal fees. Still other communities are paying more for recycling today in the belief that this strategy will pay off in the long run as landfill fees continue to rise. Moreover, recycling enjoys wide public support in the environmentally conscious 1990s, and many programs are driven as much by public sentiment as by economics. As such, the primary reason for recycling's success in the 1990s—as well as the characteristic that distinguishes it from recycling in the 1970s—is that heightened environmental awareness is coupled with limits on traditional waste disposal practices.

Companies profiting from processing recyclables are not the only ones turning trash to cash. Waste-to-energy developers also have attracted the interest of municipalities running out of landfill space. Orders for modern waste-to-energy projects surged in the 1980s. By the end of the decade, the nation's waste-to-energy industry was disposing of approximately 15 percent of the nation's trash, while generating electricity for sale to electric utilities.[4] Although the market for new waste-to-energy facilities has been flat for the last five years, the industry shows signs of regaining momentum later in the 1990s.

Composting is yet another business that has emerged in response to the nation's shortage of permitted solid waste disposal capacity. Composting companies process both mixed municipal waste and source-separated components of the waste stream, such as yard and food waste. A fledgling industry today, composting also is poised for tremendous growth in this decade.

Trash to Cash reviews each of these three main waste disposal alternatives to landfilling—recycling, incineration and composting. It also highlights the companies taking the lead in turning the nation's discards into commodities—whether they are recycling waste material into industrial feedstock, using it as fuel or producing compost.

Of the three main waste disposal alternatives, recycling is in the limelight today. "The waste industry is on a recycling 'high,'" William Hulligan, president of Waste Management of North America Inc., said recently. "We are not just involved—we are committed! Recycling is...not just the passing

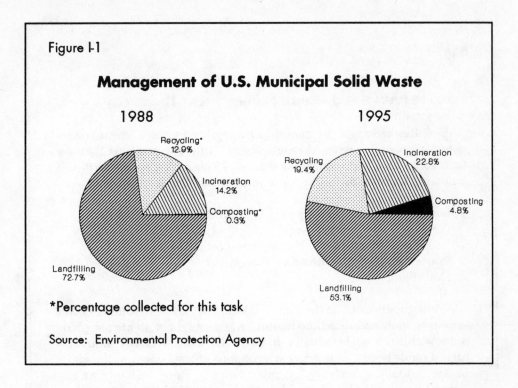

Figure I-1

Management of U.S. Municipal Solid Waste

1988

Recycling*
12.9%

Incineration
14.2%

Composting*
0.3%

Landfilling
72.7%

1995

Recycling
19.4%

Incineration
22.8%

Composting
4.8%

Landfilling
53.1%

*Percentage collected for this task

Source: Environmental Protection Agency

fad that it has been in the past. It is here and now."[5] Recycling has been spurred on by federal support, and more importantly, by state and local legislation that mandates recycling, provides tax incentives, and requires the procurement of products with recycled content. The recycling industry has blossomed into a $1 billion to $2 billion business and is now one of the nation's fastest growing industries.[6] One estimate placed the amount of post-consumer recyclables collected for recycling in 1990 at 75 million tons, an increase of almost 5 percent from 1989. However, the value of the recyclables shipped to domestic and foreign mills was estimated at $14 billion in 1990, down from 1989 levels because of depressed markets.[7] Even so, some analysts are predicting that more than $2 billion will be spent across the nation for recycling equipment between 1990 and 1995.[8]

Given the current emphasis on recycling, and the fact that the recycling process creates myriad business opportunities, the first six chapters of *Trash to Cash* are devoted to companies involved in various aspects of recycling. The first five chapters of the report review recycling initiatives within the five major industries producing the consumer products commonly collected in curbside recycling programs: aluminum, glass, steel, paper and plastics. In addition, these chapters review the efforts of emerging companies that are producing products from items collected at curbside, such as plastic lumber from milk jugs. (Many view these efforts as reusing, rather

Box I-1

EPA'S Solid Waste Management Hierarchy

EPA has endorsed the concept of integrated solid waste management—managing wastes through several different practices that are tailored to fit a community's needs. In 1989, EPA also set forth the following four-tier hierarchy for managing municipal solid waste[9]:

- Source reduction (including reuse of products and backyard composting of yard wastes)
- Recycling of materials (including composting)
- Waste combustion (with energy recovery)
- Landfilling

While governments at the state and local level and environmentalists appear to have embraced the hierarchy generally, not all are satisfied. Some within the waste industry, in fact, believe the hierarchy should be turned on its head. "This approach contains at least one component to rankle virtually everybody," commented Ben Rose, manager of the Central Vermont Solid Waste Management District. "Waste-to-energy proponents tend to dismiss calls for re-examinations of lifestyles. Recyclers, on the other hand, resist the notion that large high-tech facilities will be necessary even after reduction and recycling are fully implemented."[10] Some environmental groups specifically oppose including composting as a form of recycling, arguing that recycling should be given a clear preference over composting, particularly for products such as paper.[11]

Despite the criticisms, EPA believes the solid waste management hierarchy is a key to managing the nation's solid waste. EPA's goal is for the United States to recover and recycle 25 percent of its municipal solid waste by 1995 and 35 percent by 1996, up sharply from 13 percent collected for recycling in 1988. Estimating that the United States will produce nearly 200 million tons of municipal solid waste in 1995, EPA has projected recovery and composting rates ranging from 20 to 27.7 percent of municipal solid waste in that year. EPA also projects that the nation will combust 45.5 million tons, or nearly 23 percent, of its waste in 1995. Accordingly, if mid-range recovery projections are used, EPA estimates the nation will landfill about 53 percent of its waste in 1995.[12] (See Figure I-1 for EPA's estimate of municipal solid waste management methods in 1988 and in 1995.)

than recycling, materials, arguing that the term recycling should be reserved for product-to-same-product recycling.)

Industry's willingness to reprocess recyclable material into new products is a critical link in the recycling process. A driving force behind industry's interest in recycling is growing consumer demand for "environmentally friendly" products. Many companies have come to realize that if they want to keep their products on the supermarket and department store shelves, those products must contain recycled content and their industries must have a visible recycling infrastructure. This realization is based, in part, on polls such as one conducted for the Glass Packaging Institute that found that nearly three-quarters of American consumers say they would purchase food or beverages in containers that are recyclable over nonrecyclable containers.[13]

In some instances, public pressure has moved beyond clout in the marketplace to state and local legislation requiring recycled content or even banning nonrecyclables outright. In the newspaper industry, for example, most newspapers have had low recycled content, yet old newspapers collected for recycling piled up in warehouses in 1989. This situation translated into legislation in several states requiring recycled content in newsprint. Similarly, the plastics industry has encountered bans of its products in some locales, largely because the lack of a recycling infrastructure resulted in all plastics being sent to landfills. Other industries fear their products may be targeted next and are boosting recycling rates to head off similar recycled content legislation or bans.

Still another reason industries are pursuing recycling is that companies generally save money when they use recycled materials in place of virgin materials, although the savings vary by industry. Yet until recently, few industries were presented with a reliable supply of recycled materials that warranted the reorientation of their production lines. Municipal recycling programs are now providing that steady supply, prompting industries to reexamine their feedstock.

The five industries producing the consumer products commonly collected through curbside recycling programs are not equally prepared to boost their use of recycled materials. Based on their respective industrial processes, each industry has distinct incentives and obstacles to using recycled materials in place of virgin materials. As a result, the recycling infrastructure in each of these industries is at a different stage of development. (Figure I-2 shows the recycling rates and goals for several consumer products, and Figure I-3 lists the price industries pay for several recyclables.)

The aluminum industry is motivated by the extremely favorable economics of aluminum recycling (primarily the result of capital investment avoidance and energy savings). It established a comprehensive collection

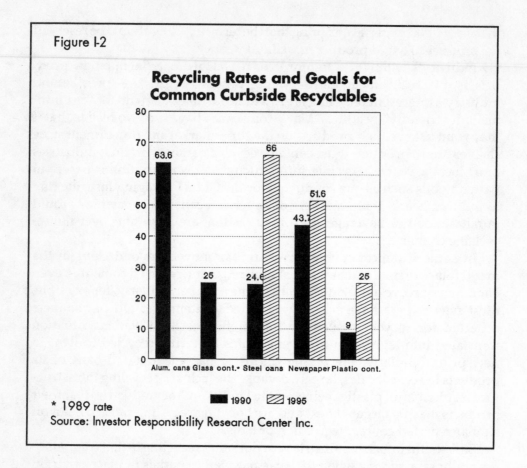

Figure I-2

Recycling Rates and Goals for Common Curbside Recyclables

* 1989 rate
Source: Investor Responsibility Research Center Inc.

network for aluminum cans long before the latest recycling frenzy swept the nation. Today, the aluminum beverage can has the highest recycling rate of any post-consumer product. In contrast, the plastics industry has the most immature recycling infrastructure, but it is mounting one of the most publicized recycling drives. The steel industry has an extensive collection network to reclaim scrap metal, but it was not until the late 1980s that it launched a full-scale campaign to funnel tin cans—a common curbside recycling item—into that network.

While the barriers to recycling in some industries are large capital investments for processing equipment, others are vulnerable to contaminants in the recycled material resulting in the production of inferior products, or worse, extensive damage to their industrial plants. Although all industries need to make capital investments to use recycled materials, the paper industry faces the greatest capital requirements—estimated in the billions of dollars—and new paper recycling capacity also takes the longest to build. Indeed, the lack of existing industrial capacity to use old newspa-

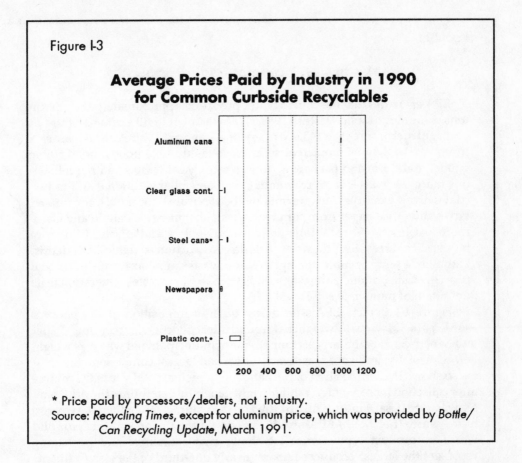

Figure I-3

**Average Prices Paid by Industry in 1990
for Common Curbside Recyclables**

* Price paid by processors/dealers, not industry.
Source: *Recycling Times*, except for aluminum price, which was provided by *Bottle/
Can Recycling Update*, March 1991.

pers, and the inability of the paper industry to move quickly to build new
capacity to head off criticism that it was stymying recycling efforts, were
major factors leading to recycled content legislation for newsprint in several
states.

The glass industry does not face major capital investments to incorporate used glass into the glassmaking process. On the other hand, contaminants in used glass, such as aluminum and steel, can damage glass furnaces.
In addition, noncontainer glass, such as ceramics, mixed in with used glass
containers can create weak spots in new glass containers. Austin Fiore of
Owens-Brockway Glass Containers, the nation's largest glass container
producer and recycler, summed up the importance of a quality recycled
feedstock to his industry by noting that a market for used glass (cullet)
exists, but "we are not going to become your second landfill. We want
quality cullet free of contaminants."[14]

The glass industry also does not have the potential to reap the large cost
savings associated with recycled materials that the aluminum industry

Box I-2

What's in U.S. Municipal Solid Waste?

EPA estimates that the United States produced approximately 180 million tons of municipal solid waste in 1988.[15] The waste could fill a convoy of 10-ton garbage trucks more than 145,000 miles long—enough to circle the equator six times.[16] EPA defines municipal solid waste as durable goods, nondurable goods, containers and packaging, food wastes, yard wastes and miscellaneous inorganic wastes from residential, commercial, institutional and industrial sources. Examples include cans and bottles from households, corrugated boxes and office paper from commercial establishments, cafeteria and classroom wastes from institutions, and wood pallets and plastic film from industrial sources. EPA does not include construction or demolition debris, automobile scrap, mining and agricultural wastes, nonhazardous industrial process wastes, municipal sewage sludge or ash from waste incineration in its definition of municipal solid waste.[17]

Figure I-4 depicts EPA's estimates of the composition of the nation's municipal solid waste by weight before and after collection for recycling. Paper and paperboard are the largest components of municipal solid waste by weight before recovery, and yard wastes are the second largest component. Figure I-4 also shows the composition of the nation's municipal solid waste by volume after collection for recycling. (While weight generally determines the price paid for waste disposal, landfills fill up based on the volume, rather than the weight, of the waste they hold.) EPA also breaks down the nation's municipal solid waste by product type. Figure I-4 shows that containers and packaging represent the largest product segment, nearly one-third of the waste stream.

enjoys. Glass, however, is the only type of container that can be recycled in a true closed-loop, product-to-same-product system, whereby a container is made into a new container with no loss, no waste and no by-products. Hoping to capitalize on the shift in consumer attitudes, the glass container industry is aggressively publicizing this characteristic in an attempt to regain market share lost over the years to plastic and aluminum manufacturers.

Beyond a commitment by industry to use recycled materials, an infrastructure needs to be developed that reliably delivers recycled material in a form useful to industry. This critical link in the transformation from discard to commodity is examined in Chapter 6 of *Trash to Cash*. Chapter 6 highlights companies involved in the materials handling side of the waste industry—those that collect, process, market and ship source-separated material from the nation's waste stream to industry. Once the domain of Scout troops and church groups attempting to raise money, the collection of recyclables has

Not all experts concur with EPA's estimates of the amount of municipal solid waste. EPA arrived at these figures using a "materials flow" methodology, which is based on production data (by weight) for the materials and products in the waste stream. Adjustments are made for imports and exports, lifetimes of products, and diversions from municipal solid waste, such as paper products used as building materials. Food and yard wastes and a small amount of miscellaneous inorganic wastes are accounted for by compiling data from a variety of waste sampling studies.[18] Critics believe EPA's adjustments are faulty, and some argue that a site-specific approach, which would involve sampling, sorting and weighing the individual components of the waste stream, would be more accurate. (Regional and even site-specific variations in sampling studies could provide misleading national data, however.) Still others fault EPA for not including materials such as automobile scrap or demolition debris as municipal solid waste.

The lack of a standard definition of municipal solid waste or standard procedures for calculating and reporting amounts of municipal solid waste is a serious impediment to monitoring growth within the evolving waste disposal industry. Without standards, compiling accurate aggregate figures from state and local data or making comparisons between state or local recycling programs is nearly impossible. Often, apples-and-oranges comparisons are made that mislead the public and municipal officials. Local officials need to be cognizant, though, that the makeup of the local waste stream is the most important factor in determining an appropriate waste management strategy.

become big business. Curbside recycling programs are sweeping the nation, increasing by almost 80 percent in 1990 alone. Curbside programs, now the most popular recycling collection method, served more than 37 million people, or nearly 15 percent of the U.S. population, by the end of 1990. Alaska and Delaware were the only states with no curbside recycling programs. About 41 percent of the more than 2,700 curbside recycling programs in existence are mandatory.[19]

These curbside recycling programs are changing the dynamics of traditional commercial recycling operations. It used to be that scrap dealers offered the only recycling game in town. Now they often find themselves in direct competition with new municipal recycling programs that threaten to drive them out of business. In some instances, municipalities and waste haulers are beginning to sign long-term contracts, or even form partnerships, with manufacturing companies, bypassing the existing network of waste dealers and brokers altogether.

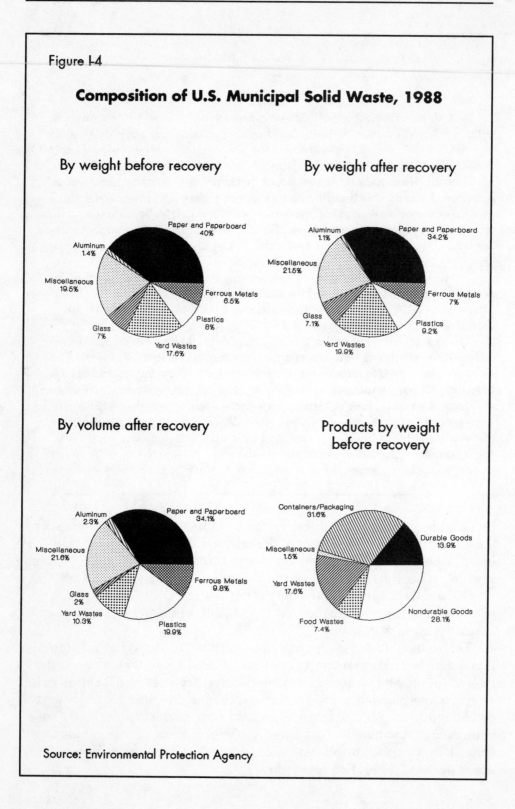

Figure I-4

Composition of U.S. Municipal Solid Waste, 1988

By weight before recovery

Paper and Paperboard 40%
Aluminum 1.4%
Miscellaneous 19.5%
Ferrous Metals 6.5%
Plastics 8%
Glass 7%
Yard Wastes 17.6%

By weight after recovery

Aluminum 1.1%
Paper and Paperboard 34.2%
Miscellaneous 21.5%
Ferrous Metals 7%
Glass 7.1%
Plastics 9.2%
Yard Wastes 19.9%

By volume after recovery

Aluminum 2.3%
Paper and Paperboard 34.1%
Miscellaneous 21.6%
Ferrous Metals 9.8%
Glass 2%
Yard Wastes 10.3%
Plastics 19.9%

Products by weight before recovery

Containers/Packaging 31.6%
Durable Goods 13.9%
Miscellaneous 1.5%
Yard Wastes 17.6%
Nondurable Goods 28.1%
Food Wastes 7.4%

Source: Environmental Protection Agency

The final two chapters of *Trash to Cash* discuss the two other significant waste disposal alternatives to landfilling—composting and incineration. Chapter 7 reviews mixed waste processing firms, which are primarily composting companies. The chapter also includes companies that produce a transportable fuel from mixed waste, known as densified refuse derived fuel, as well as companies that recover recyclables from mixed waste and process them to industrial specification. The final industry chapter, Chapter 8, focuses on waste-to-energy projects and players.

Overall, the solid waste disposal industry is a dynamic and growing industry. Kidder, Peabody & Co. Inc. Senior Vice President Marc Sulman estimates that over the last several years the number of solid waste management companies has grown from only five publicly traded companies to between 80 and 100. Nearly 30 Wall Street analysts now track these companies.[20] These companies bear close watching by investors interested in growth industries as well as by decisionmakers confronted with a shortage of permitted solid waste disposal capacity in their communities.

Information for *Trash to Cash* was drawn from a wide range of sources, including interviews with more than 100 companies and their respective trade associations, presentations at a number of resource recovery and recycling conferences, and an extensive literature review. The solid waste disposal industry is a fast-paced market, though, and companies discussed in *Trash to Cash* are continually adapting their plans to reflect newly gained experience and information. This rapidly evolving market promises to be a major source of business opportunity and innovation in the 1990s.

Chapter I
POST-CONSUMER ALUMINUM

The aluminum beverage can is consumer recycling's biggest success story. It has achieved the highest recycling rate of any post-consumer recyclable—more than 60 percent—and the aluminum industry believes its recycling rate could reach 70 percent by 1995.[1] This rate appears achievable: New York already has reported recovering 80 percent of the aluminum beverage cans sold in that state in 1988,[2] and California reported reclaiming 75 percent of its aluminum cans in 1990.[3]

Because of significantly reduced capital costs and substantial energy savings associated with recycling aluminum, the aluminum industry has strong economic incentives to use post-consumer aluminum as a feedstock. To ensure that the cans find their way back to aluminum companies for melting, the aluminum industry has developed a comprehensive collection and processing infrastructure that is the envy of other industries. The high economic value of aluminum scrap to industry has enabled aluminum companies to offer lucrative prices—the highest for any post-consumer recyclable—that motivate consumers to return the aluminum can. The high price also is spurring newer municipal recycling programs to include aluminum, and aluminum cans often wind up subsidizing the recovery of other waste stream components. Indeed, because of the value of aluminum scrap, interest in used aluminum beverage cans is out of proportion to its low percentage—less than 1 percent—of the waste stream.[4]

The aluminum can is a high quality, highly engineered product. Almost all of the used aluminum beverage can scrap is used to make new beverage cans, primarily because the alloys used to make aluminum can sheet differ from the alloys used to make other aluminum products, from foil to screen doors. Accordingly, the 10 U.S. aluminum can sheet manufacturers are the primary market for used beverage cans. This market is quite strong and appears capable of absorbing increases in aluminum can recycling rates. The aluminum can has captured more than 95 percent of the beverage can market that was once dominated by steel, and the market is growing in most regions of the country.[5]

Aluminum is 100 percent recyclable. The production of aluminum, however, is not quite a closed loop system; there is melt loss of approximately 5 to 15 percent when aluminum scrap is melted.[6] Aluminum cans are easily collected and, for the most part, easily separated from other waste stream components. While most aluminum cans are still hand-sorted by residential recyclers, automated processes have been developed that can separate aluminum from other recyclables or from the rest of the waste stream.

Recycling proponents invariably point to the aluminum can as the shining example of what aggressive recycling programs can achieve. The aluminum can also will be the first recyclable to test the limits of recycling. Despite the industry's impressive track record of reclaiming aluminum cans, experts within the industry predict that the nationwide aluminum can recycling rate will be difficult to push beyond 80 percent, largely because not all people will recycle.

Aluminum in the Municipal Waste Stream

Although aluminum has been produced in commercial quantities for less than 100 years, it now ranks second only to iron in world metal consumption. In 1989, the United States consumed approximately 7.5 million tons of aluminum.[7] Relatively light in weight yet yielding a high strength-to-weight ratio, aluminum is ideally suited for aircraft, missiles, automobiles and trucks, and marine vessels.[8] Aluminum is found in the municipal solid waste stream primarily in the form of beverage cans, but also as foil wrap, pots and pans, pie plates, frozen food and dinner trays, food cans and pudding and meat containers. Aluminum siding, gutters, storm doors, window frames, lawn furniture tubing, power lawnmower housings and barbecue grills also are common examples of durable aluminum products that eventually are discarded as waste.[9]

As worldwide consumption of aluminum has steadily increased, so has the amount of aluminum in the nation's municipal waste stream—a trend that analysts believe will continue. The total amount of aluminum in the waste stream is still quite small, however. Aluminum grew from just one-half of 1 percent of municipal waste by weight in 1960 to 1.4 percent in 1988. In 1988, 2.5 million tons of aluminum were added to the waste stream, and approximately 800,000 tons were recycled, bringing aluminum's share of total discards down to 1.1 percent. Because aluminum weighs about one-

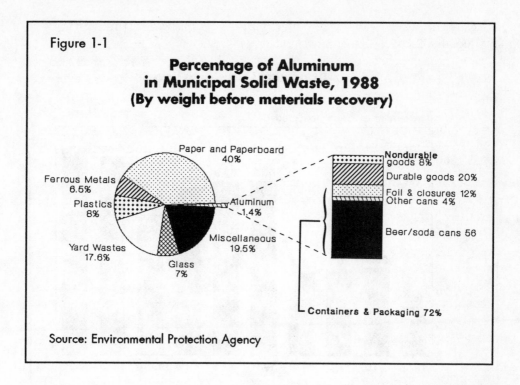

Figure 1-1

**Percentage of Aluminum
in Municipal Solid Waste, 1988
(By weight before materials recovery)**

Paper and Paperboard
40%

Ferrous Metals
6.5%

Plastics
8%

Aluminum
1.4%

Yard Wastes
17.6%

Glass
7%

Miscellaneous
19.5%

Nondurable goods 8%

Durable goods 20%

Foil & closures 12%
Other cans 4%

Beer/soda cans 56

Containers & Packaging 72%

Source: Environmental Protection Agency

third as much as steel, its percentage of the waste discards by volume is higher, at 2.3 percent.[10]

Aluminum beer and soft drink cans, which represent 56 percent of the aluminum in the solid waste stream, are the only aluminum products in the municipal waste stream that are being recycled in measurable amounts.[11] (Scrap auto parts, another source of used aluminum, are not considered a part of the municipal waste stream for the purposes of this report.) Figure 1-2 depicts the steady rise in the rate of aluminum can recycling, which reached 63.6 percent in 1990, representing approximately 55 billion aluminum cans, or more than 1.9 billion pounds of aluminum.[12] Over the last decade, more than 50 percent of aluminum beverage cans were recycled.[13] The adoption of container deposit legislation in nine states in the late 1970s and early 1980s, as well as the aluminum industry's attempts to head off similar legislation in other states by increasing aluminum can recycling rates, account for the jump in aluminum can recycling in the 1980s.

Recycled aluminum represents more than a quarter of the U.S. aluminum industry's total supply.[14] About 60 percent of the aluminum scrap is used beverage cans,[15] which have been and remain the fastest growing component of aluminum scrap.[16] The Aluminum Association estimates that the recycled content of aluminum cans themselves was 52 percent in 1989 and projects that it will rise to between 59 and 63 percent by 1995.[17]

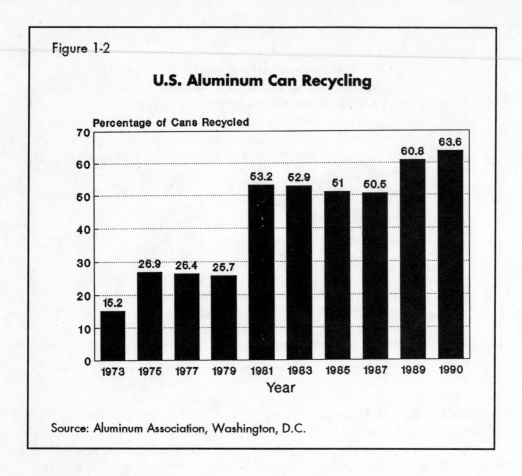

Figure 1-2

U.S. Aluminum Can Recycling

Source: Aluminum Association, Washington, D.C.

The Post-Consumer Aluminum Recycling Process

Producing manufacturing-grade aluminum from post-consumer scrap is not a difficult process, although freedom from contamination is a key concern. High levels of contaminants can render a load of used beverage cans unsuitable for reuse as new can stock, and the aluminum must be recycled into less economically valuable aluminum products.[18] Used beverage cans are sometimes contaminated with broken glass, plastic, steel and food as a result of commingling with other waste stream components. Moisture content also is a problem. Because payment is based on weight, end-users may reject a load of used beverage cans with more than 8 percent moisture content or reduce the amount paid.[19] In addition, recyclers sometimes deliberately contaminate a load of aluminum with lead, hoping to collect more by boosting the weight of the load.

Another challenge for the industry is the growing amount of aluminum packaging in forms other than beverage cans, primarily aluminum cans containing pet foods, soup and snack foods. Today, aluminum cans hold only 5 to 10 percent of the non-beverage container market,[20] but the aluminum industry hopes to capture a third of the food can market, which is dominated by steel, over the next 10 years.[21] One of the nation's largest food companies, Campbell Soup Co., made the switch to aluminum containers for its Juice Bowl and V-8 juices in the spring of 1990.[22] The metallurgical content of these non-beverage aluminum cans is not the same as beverage can stock, but the industry often has allowed them to be included in used beverage can collection programs because their volume has been so low. Now that their numbers are growing, aluminum companies are reassessing their position.[23]

Preparing used beverage cans for recycling requires little effort on the part of residential recyclers. Aluminum beverage cans have no labels, caps or tops that must be removed. They often are separated manually from other waste stream components at the home or at central processing facilities. Cans that are manually separated usually still pass an electromagnet either at a central processing facility or at the aluminum recycler's plant to ensure that all ferrous material, especially look-alike steel cans, has been removed.

Aluminum processors also are gaining experience with more advanced mechanical processes that separate aluminum from mixed recyclables or the rest of the waste stream. At some material recovery facilities, sorting processes based on weight, size and magnetization are able to isolate aluminum from mixed recyclables. At New England CRInc.'s materials recovery facility in Johnston, R.I., for example, the plant uses eddy current separators to separate aluminum that has been isolated with plastic materials. Electrodes on either side of a conveyor belt induce a positive charge in aluminum cans. The belt pulls the cans a few inches farther into a second positively charged electric field that repels them off of the belt.[24] National Recovery Technologies Inc., a waste processing firm, also has developed technology to remove aluminum from mixed waste. Air nozzles, activated by detectors, eject aluminum cans along with adjacent materials into what the firm calls an aluminum-rich concentrate. A pulsed eddy current sorter then recovers aluminum from the concentrate.[25] (See Chapter 6 for a fuller discussion of New England CRInc. and Chapter 7 for more information on National Recovery Technologies Inc.)

Once the aluminum cans are separated, they are flattened and sometimes baled, and then shipped to a larger processing facility where the cans are shredded into popcorn-sized chips. The chips are sent to a melting plant where the outer labels and inside-coating, which prevent beverages from coming into contact with bare metal, are burned away in a special process. The cans are then melted at around 1,200 degrees Fahrenheit in furnaces the size of a small house.[26] Generally, the principal materials added to the furnace during melting of aluminum cans are primary aluminum and other

Box 1-1

The Plastic Can

The burning of even small quantities of plastic in aluminum smelting furnaces can cause fires and severe damage. Without the use of an eddy current separator, plastic is difficult to separate from aluminum, particularly plastic cans that are nearly identical in appearance to aluminum cans. Although plastic cans are not currently on the U.S. market, they have been test marketed in the past amid widespread controversy because of the implications for recycling.

In the mid-1980s, aluminum companies began receiving both plastic and aluminum cans as a result of The Coca-Cola Co.'s test marketing of a plastic beverage container. The president of Alcoa Recycling Co. wrote a letter to the recycling community asking it to remove all plastic cans, warning that otherwise entire railcar loads of beverage cans could be rejected. Environmental groups led by the Environmental Task Force (which subsequently merged with Environmental Action) mounted a campaign against the plastic can, arguing that the plastic can would never reach the recycling rates of the aluminum can and would adversely affect existing recycling infrastructures.[27]

Coca-Cola stopped selling its soft drink in plastic cans less than a year after their introduction. Petainer S.A., a Swiss firm whose U.S. affiliate had patented the plastic can, began pursuing other markets for the plastic can in the United States. In 1987, the beverage manufacturer Original New York Seltzer Co. agreed to test market its product in Petainer's transparent plastic can, saying that it valued a container that allowed consumers to see its product. Confronted by another campaign against the plastic can led by the Environmental Task Force, that company also discontinued use of the plastic can within a year.[28]

Propects for resurrection of the plastic can appear slim. Nearly two dozen states have banned the plastic can,[29] and Jerry Powell, editor-in-chief of *Resource Recycling*, asserts that the "plastic beverage can with an aluminum top in the United States is dead."[30]

alloying agents, which are added to provide the proper alloy and specifications for the final product.[31]

The melted metal is cast into ingots—rectangular slabs of aluminum—which are rolled into large coils of aluminum sheet, known as can sheet, from which new aluminum cans are stamped out.[32] One rolling ingot can weigh as much as 60,000 pounds and can provide enough metal to produce more than 1.5 million beverage cans.[33] The turnaround time from collection of a used aluminum beverage container to production of a new aluminum container can be as short as six weeks.[34]

While it is technically possible to make a new aluminum can out of 100 percent recycled aluminum,[35] most aluminum cans are composed of three different alloys. The alloys are needed to accommodate mechanical differences in manufacturing the can body, lid and tab, each of which has a specific chemical composition. Accordingly, there may be limits to the amount of recycled cans that can be used to produce each one of these alloys. Most used beverage cans are used to produce can bodies, which comprise more than 75 percent of a can. Far fewer used beverage cans are used in the production of can ends, which account for roughly 20 percent of a can, and a minimal amount is used in the production of can tabs, which comprise about 3 percent of a can.[36]

Economics of Aluminum Recycling

The greatest economic advantages of using recycled aluminum rather than virgin materials to produce new aluminum are the savings in both capital expenditure and energy. Producing aluminum from scrap results in savings when production capacity is expanded. Building a primary smelter costs about $4,000 per ton of annual capacity—eight times the cost required to construct the equivalent aluminum used beverage can melting facility.[37]

Producing aluminum from recycled aluminum also requires a whopping 95 percent less energy than producing aluminum from virgin materials.[38] For each pound of aluminum recycled, the aluminum industry conserves approximately 7.5 kilowatt-hours of electricity. In 1989, recycling aluminum cans conserved more than 12 billion kilowatt-hours[39]—enough energy to supply the annual power needs of a city the size of Boston, or the energy equivalent of 20 million barrels of oil. The aluminum industry achieves these savings by eliminating the most electricity-intensive portion of the aluminum manufacturing process, which involves bauxite ore—the primary ore of aluminum. One ton of bauxite ore, which is found predominantly in tropical and sub-tropical regions, produces only 500 pounds of pure aluminum. Once the ore is mined and shipped to a refining plant, it is crushed and chemically treated to produce a white powdery oxide called alumina, a combination of aluminum and oxygen. To separate the aluminum from the oxygen, a high-voltage electrical current must pass through the chemical mixture.[40]

The aluminum industry is a major consumer of electricity, with electricity costs generally accounting for roughly one-third of the total cost of producing aluminum from virgin materials.[41] No new virgin capacity is planned in the United States, largely because all new primary aluminum production capacity is being constructed in countries that have lower electricity, labor and materials costs than the United States. In addition, passage of the Clean Air Act amendments may substantially boost electricity costs for some members of the aluminum industry.

Although the Aluminum Association does not gather data on any differences in air emissions when using recycled and virgin materials in aluminum production, the Worldwatch Institute, a research organization in Washington, D.C., estimates that using recycled aluminum would cut air pollution by 95 percent. Worldwatch adds that "one ton of remelted aluminum eliminates the need for four tons of bauxite and 700 kilograms of petroleum coke and pitch, while reducing emissions of air polluting aluminum fluoride by 35 kilograms. By doubling worldwide aluminum recovery rates, over a million tons of air pollutants—including toxic fluoride—would be eliminated."[42] Recycling aluminum, however, also creates some toxic emissions, requiring anti-pollution devices.[43] The melting of outer painted labels and inside-coatings produces air emissions with particulate matter as well as acid gases.[44]

Used aluminum beverage can prices: Used aluminum beverage cans are the most valuable recyclable collected in curbside recycling programs. (See Figure I-3 on p. 7 for a comparison of prices.) They are often the single largest material revenue source in community recycling programs and almost always the only material generating revenues that exceeds the cost of collection and processing. As Figure 1-3 shows, while aluminum comprised 1 to 3 percent of the total tonnage of recyclables in Rhode Island's and Seattle's multi-material curbside recycling programs, it generated as much as 50 percent of the revenues from the sale of materials.[45]

The average price end users paid for used beverage cans in 1990 was $1,000 a ton, a 22 percent decline from the 1989 average price of $1,280 a ton.[46] Addressing a recycling conference in March 1990, Brian W. Sturgell, director of market planning for the Alcan Rolled Products division of Alcan Aluminum Corp., an aluminum can sheet manufacturer, noted that prices paid for used beverage cans have never dipped below $600 a ton, asserting that used beverage cans "are not subject to the volatility and severe price collapses that have affected other secondary materials." Sturgell attributed the relative price stability to fundamental economics, strong markets and a comprehensive recycling infrastructure.[47]

Industry analysts say that two regional markets are emerging to replace a nationwide market for used beverage cans. In the spring of 1991, for instance, the Aluminum Co. of America was paying $40 more per ton for cans delivered east of the Rockies. Whereas West Coast demand is influenced by the export market, the market east of the Rockies is "driven by too

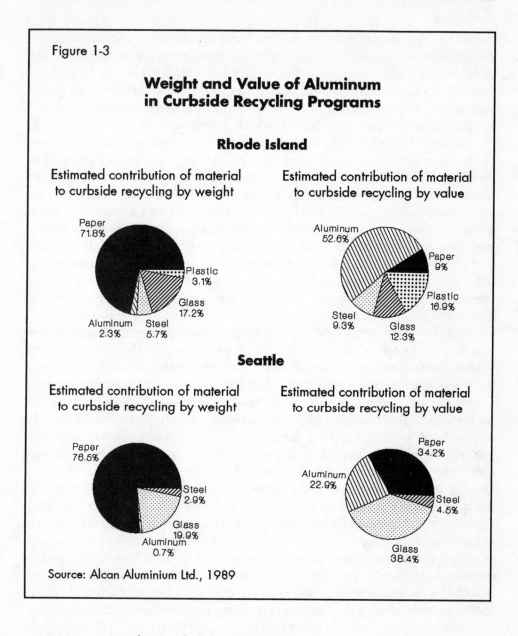

Figure 1-3

**Weight and Value of Aluminum
in Curbside Recycling Programs**

Rhode Island

Estimated contribution of material
to curbside recycling by weight

Estimated contribution of material
to curbside recycling by value

Paper
71.8%

Plastic
3.1%

Glass
17.2%

Aluminum
2.3%

Steel
5.7%

Aluminum
52.6%

Paper
9%

Plastic
16.9%

Steel
9.3%

Glass
12.3%

Seattle

Estimated contribution of material
to curbside recycling by weight

Estimated contribution of material
to curbside recycling by value

Paper
76.5%

Steel
2.9%

Glass
19.9%

Aluminum
0.7%

Paper
34.2%

Aluminum
22.9%

Steel
4.5%

Glass
38.4%

Source: Alcan Aluminium Ltd., 1989

many processors for too few cans," analysts say.[48]

U.S. Aluminum Industry's Recycling Initiatives

With 10,000 aluminum buy-back locations nationwide, including mobile recycling units, the aluminum industry oversees the most extensive
collection network for any recyclable commodity commonly collected in

recycling programs. Processing facilities, transportation systems and secondary smelting operations are geared to handle recycled aluminum, and the network continues to expand.[49] In 1990, the industry paid close to $900 million for used beverage cans,[50] and since aluminum can recycling got its start 20 years ago, Americans have reaped more than $4 billion recycling 360 billion aluminum cans, or about 7 million tons of aluminum.[51]

Cleveland and Chicago hosted the first aluminum recycling plants in 1904, about 16 years after the first commercial production of aluminum in the United States. By the 1950s, recycled aluminum accounted for more than one-fifth of the supply of the U.S. aluminum industry, but post-consumer scrap represented only 20 to 25 percent of the recycled aluminum. Once aluminum began penetrating the beverage can market in the late 1960s, post-consumer aluminum began claiming a larger share of industry's feedstock. Reynolds Metals Co. opened a pilot used beverage can recycling plant in southern California in 1968, and the entire aluminum industry stepped up its recycling efforts in the 1970s in response to the oil crises and the resulting rapid escalation in energy prices.[52] Also during the 1970s, the aluminum industry embraced post-consumer recycling as a weapon in the war over the beverage can market. Aluminum companies used recycling as a counterattack against the steel industry's criticism that aluminum cans were less durable than bimetallic steel cans (cans with steel bodies and aluminum lids), which dominated the market in the early 1970s, and lacked the biodegradability of steel cans, the bodies of which eventually rust. In addition, the aluminum industry promoted recycling as an alternative to state laws springing up in the 1970s and early 1980s that required the payment of deposits on aluminum beverage cans.[53]

The industry continued to expand its recycling network during the 1980s, and in the 1990s, Sturgell of Alcan Rolled Products asserts that "the aluminum industry is in a strong position to utilize all the secondary aluminum that can be recovered. The industry is committed to expanding recycling systems and improving recovery rates, and the long-term market outlook is positive."[54] The Aluminum Association maintains that collection is the key to boosting recycling rates further, claiming that "barriers to even higher aluminum can recycling rates involve the collection of cans—not the industry's need and ability to recycle and reuse this metal."[55] (The Aluminum Association represents about 85 percent of domestic aluminum ingot production and a similar percentage of U.S. aluminum mill product shipments, as well as nine of the 10 domestic producers of aluminum can sheet and seven aluminum foil producers.)

End users of used beverage cans: Virtually all of the metal recovered from aluminum cans is used to make new aluminum cans. The 10 U.S. companies making aluminum can sheet melt between 90 and 95 percent of the used beverage can scrap. The balance is melted by secondary aluminum producers or scrap processors and foundries; sold for metallurgical and destructive uses, such as steel deoxidizing and chemical applications; or exported.[56] In 1989, only 77 million pounds of the 1.69 billion pounds of collected used beverage cans were exported.[57]

The 10 U.S. aluminum can sheet manufacturers are: Alcan Aluminum Corp., a subsidiary of Alcan Aluminium Ltd.; Alumax Inc., a subsidiary of Amax Inc.; Aluminum Co. of America (Alcoa); Arco Aluminum Co., an operating company of Atlantic Richfield Co.; Commonwealth Aluminum Corp., a subsidiary of the Australian firm Comalco Ltd.; Consolidated Aluminum Corp., a subsidiary of Alusuisse of America Inc.; Golden Aluminum Co., a subsidiary of Adolph Coors Co.; Kaiser Aluminum and Chemical Corp., a subsidiary of Maxxam Inc.; Ravenswood Aluminum Corp.; and Reynolds Metals Co. Data on the percentage of used beverage cans these companies use in the manufacture of can sheet, including can body sheet, can ends and can tabs, are shown in Table 1-1. The industry average was 52 percent in 1989.[58]

Alcoa, Reynolds Metals Co. and Alcan Aluminum, the three largest U.S. can sheet manufacturers, are also the clear leaders in aluminum beverage can recycling. **Alcoa** is undisputedly the world's largest recycler of aluminum cans, recycling 712 million pounds of used beverage cans, or 36 percent of the total recycled in the United States, in 1990.[59] It is also the world's leading supplier of aluminum can sheet for beverage containers and food packaging.[60] Alcoa has spent hundreds of millions of dollars to increase its use of recycled feedstocks, including used beverage cans.[61] Alcoa Recycling Co. reached a major milestone in this effort in June 1990, striking a landmark agreement with Browning-Ferris Industries Inc. to purchase all of the aluminum beverage and food cans that the waste industry giant collects through its U.S. and Canadian curbside recycling programs.[62]

Alcoa's primary source of aluminum scrap has been its 2,400 independent suppliers, which are served in part by 70 processing sites either owned or contracted by the company. Alcoa also operates about 35 buy-back trailers and 85 reverse vending machines. In a marked departure from the past, however, Alcoa reportedly has set aside $20 million to establish company-owned buying facilities, following the lead of Reynolds Metals Co., which has the most comprehensive company-owned collection system in place. This move has angered some used beverage can processors who claim they are being driven out of business. George Cobb, president of Alcoa Recycling, counters that Alcoa receives just 5 percent of its used beverage cans through company-owned retail buying sites, and that it operates fewer than 30 such centers. Alcoa planned to open an additional four or five retail buying sites in 1990 and is considering expanding services at these centers by buying other non-used beverage can aluminum scrap and newspapers.[63]

Alcoa also manufactures recycling equipment—the only primary aluminum processor to do so. In April 1989, Alcoa created a new subsidiary, Alcoa Recycling Machinery Services, to manufacture and sell aluminum beverage can recycling equipment, including a portable recycling center.[64] Reaction to the new venture has been mixed and is somewhat similar to response to the company-owned collection centers: Some equipment manufacturers complain that they are being squeezed out of the market.[65]

Reynolds Metals Co. is a pioneer of used aluminum beverage can recycling. In 1967, the company began experimenting with post-consumer aluminum in Miami where it purchased cans from charitable organizations. Because the project was only moderately successful, Reynolds tried a new approach the following year in Los Angeles, opening a permanent recycling plant that paid any individual or organization cash on the spot for aluminum cans or other household aluminum products.[66] Today, Reynolds Aluminum Recycling Co. has the country's largest consumer aluminum recycling network with 725 buy-back locations nationwide, 100 of which are reverse vending machines. Approximately 80 percent of the remaining locations are trailers that accept many types of post-consumer aluminum, including foil and pie plates. In addition to buying directly from the public, the company purchases used beverage cans from 2,000 independent collectors and processors.[67]

In 1990, Reynolds Metals says it reclaimed 219,000 tons of consumer-generated scrap, including 17 percent of the used cans collected in the United States.[68] To date, Reynolds has recycled more than 4 billion pounds of aluminum, the equivalent of more than 100 billion aluminum beverage cans, and has paid the public more than $1 billion.[69] Reynolds also touts the fact that over the last decade it has recycled more cans than its can manufacturing division has produced. (Reynolds's can manufacturing division is distinct from its can sheet manufacturing division; the can sheet manufacturing division provides can sheet to outside customers as well as to Reynolds's can manufacturing division.) The company melts the cans at two plants in Sheffield, Ala., that Reynolds's Andrew McCutcheon says are essentially dedicated to used beverage can melting. The plants are located near the company's rolling mill that produces can sheet, and they have the ability to process a combined capacity of 761 million pounds a year.[70]

Canada-based **Alcan Aluminium Ltd.** is the world's largest marketer of primary aluminum and the second largest producer of aluminum cans in North America.[71] Although Alcan may have less incentive than other aluminum can sheet manufacturers to recycle, given its substantial supply of low-cost hydroelectric power, Alcan continues to build on its recycling efforts begun in the late 1970s.

In 1979, Alcan's U.S. subsidiary, Alcan Aluminum Corp., added a 35,000 ton per year can processing unit to its rolling mill in Oswego, N.Y., which can now handle twice that amount of used beverage cans and other

Table 1-1

Recycling at the 10 U.S. Aluminum Can Sheet Manufacturers

Company	1990 Estimated Can Sheet Production (millions of lbs.)	Average Percentage of Recycled Cans in Can Sheet
Aluminum Co. of America	1,480-1,560[a]	50+
Alcan Aluminum Corp. (subsidiary of Alcan Aluminium Ltd.)	700-800	50-60
Reynolds Metals Co.	750	68-72
Kaiser Aluminum and Chemical Corp. (subsidiary of Maxxam Inc.)	400	55
Arco Aluminum Co. (operating company of Atlantic Richfield Co.)	350[b]	50+
Ravenswood Aluminum Corp.	300[c]	33
Consolidated Aluminum Corp. (subsidiary of Alusuisse of America Inc.)	125-175	75+
Commonwealth Aluminum Corp. (subsidiary of Comalco Ltd.)	110	75
Golden Aluminum Co. (subsidiary of Adolph Coors Co.)	60	d
Alumax Inc. (subsidiary of Amax Inc.)	NA	NA

[a] IRRC calculated figure using 1989 estimates of total can sheet production and Alcoa's estimate that its market share generally averages in the high 30s.

[b] Arco Aluminum manufactures can body sheet and can ends only; it does not manufacture can tabs.

[c] Ravenswood Aluminum manufactures can body sheet only; it does not manufacture can ends or tabs.

[d] Golden Aluminum uses up to 95 percent recycled products, primarily used beverage cans, in its patented alloy for the production of can body sheet and can ends; it does not use used beverage cans in the manufacture of can tabs.

Source: Investor Responsibility Research Center Inc.

aluminum scrap. The following year, Alcan opened its first dedicated scrap processing plant in Greensboro, Ga., which can process 100,000 tons per year of used beverage cans, and in October 1989, Alcan opened its second dedicated used beverage can melting facility—a $50 million, 120,000 ton per year plant in Berea, Ky. Overseas, Alcan plans to open a $34 million, 60,000 ton per year used beverage can processing plant near Manchester, England, in late 1991. To supply the die-cast industry with aluminum scrap such as used lawn chairs, foil, sheet, cast and automotive scrap (post-consumer scrap not in the form of used beverage cans), the company also invested $7 million in 1990 to purchase and improve a 70,000 ton per year mill in Shelbyville, Tenn., that had opened the previous year.[72]

In 1990, Alcan reported it held an 18 percent share of the U.S. used beverage can recycling market.[73] Unlike Reynolds, Alcan does not have a company-owned collection network in the United States. Instead, it relies on its can sheet customers and independent used beverage can collectors to supply its processing facilities. Alcan is developing a collection network in Canada, however, purchasing five Canadian can buyers and processors with a combined processing capacity of nearly 75 million pounds per year.[74]

Golden Aluminum Co., a subsidiary of Adolph Coors Co., will become a larger player in the used beverage can market when it opens a new $155 million rolling mill in San Antonio, Tex., in late 1991. The new plant will be capable of producing 130 million pounds of can body sheet annually and will more than triple Golden Aluminum's can sheet production. The company's patented continuous casting process and patented alloy enables it to produce up to 95 percent of its can bodies and ends from recycled products, primarily used beverage cans. Coors has been marketing its products in aluminum cans for several decades. The company was the first major beverage packer to introduce aluminum cans in the late 1960s and the first to switch entirely to aluminum cans. In 1980, Coors formed Golden Aluminum to reclaim and recycle used beverage cans, and in the mid-1980s it expanded its mission to manufacture aluminum sheet products at its rolling mill in Fort Lupton, Colo. Today, Golden Aluminum Co. produces can sheet not only for Coors but also for other beverage and food can manufacturers.[75]

Melting capacity: Given the existing comprehensive collection infrastructure for used aluminum beverage cans, some of the more important developments for expanding recycling within the aluminum industry have been the recent and planned expansions of used beverage container melting capacity. The industry says it already has more melt capacity for used beverage containers than supply, and more capacity is scheduled to come on-line in the early 1990s.[76] In fact, Chuck Rayfield of Reynolds Metals Co. projected in the fall of 1990 that used beverage can recycling would have to reach an 88 percent recovery level for all the smelters to operate at capacity.[77]

Table 1-2

U.S. Can Sheet Manufacturers' Dedicated Used Beverage Can Melting Facilities

Company	Location	Capacity
Alcan Aluminum Corp.	Greensboro, Ga.	200 million lbs.
	Berea, Ky.	240 million lbs.
Aluminum Co. of America	Alcoa, Tenn.	not available
	Warrick, Ind.	not available
Kaiser Aluminum and Chemical Corp./Imsamet	Hauser, Idaho	120 million lbs.
Ravenswood Aluminum Corp.	Bedford, Ind.	150 million lbs.
Reynolds Metals Co.	Sheffield, Ala.	551 million lbs.
	Sheffield, Ala.	210 million lbs.

Source: Investor Responsibility Research Center Inc.

Aluminum companies can melt used beverage cans at their secondary smelters and through independent processors, but a number are dedicating plants specifically to melting used beverage cans. The U.S. can sheet manufacturers' dedicated used beverage can recycling plants are shown in Table 1-2.

Tolling companies: The majority of used beverage can scrap is processed and melted directly by the can stock producer. In some cases, however, the material is melted through a tolling arrangement, whereby an independent company melts the used beverage cans and then ships ingot to the can stock producer for final processing into new can sheet. **IMCO Recycling Inc.** of Dallas, Tex., a publicly traded firm, is the country's largest independent recycler of used aluminum beverage cans, can scrap and dross (an aluminum-oxide byproduct from melting aluminum). IMCO had the capacity to process 430 million pounds of aluminum and magnesium in 1990. The company earned 84 percent of its revenues from tolling, down from 91 percent in 1989.[78] IMCO does not purchase any used beverage cans itself, but melts them under contract for its customers, including Alcoa, which accounted for approximately 26 percent of the company's revenues in 1989. Additional customers include Kaiser Aluminum and Chemical, Consolidated Aluminum, Logan Aluminum and Reynolds Metals.[79]

IMCO delivers some aluminum within a 100-mile radius of its plants in molten form, saving the aluminum company the energy, expense and melt loss associated with reheating the aluminum. This service, however, requires that a melting plant be in close proximity to a mill. Much of IMCO's reclamation operations focus on recycling dross, which the primary aluminum producers have discontinued processing yet continue to produce as a byproduct of aluminum melting activities. The company's aluminum scrap reclamation operations have been and remain on a high growth track. In September 1989, IMCO increased its annual production capacity by more than 40 percent when it opened an $8 million plant in Morgantown, Ky. The company plans to expand the plant's capacity by an additional 15 percent, as well as to boost capacity by 20 percent at its Rockwood, Tenn., facility. IMCO also operates a third aluminum scrap reclamation plant in Sapulpa, Okla.[80]

Imsamet, another independent aluminum reclamation and recycling company, delivers molten aluminum metal to Kaiser Aluminum and Chemical's can sheet manufacturing operations in Spokane, Wash. In 1989, Imsamet began operating a $15 million, 60,000 ton per year used beverage can and dross recycling plant that melts baled used beverage cans delivered by Kaiser. (Kaiser also uses used beverage cans collected and melted in southern California in its can sheet production. Secondary smelters melt the cans in the Los Angeles area and deliver ingot to the plant.[81])

Imsamet is a division of publicly traded **EnviroSource Inc.**, a company offering specialized industrial services for the steel, aluminum and utility industries. Imsamet plans to expand its activities in the recycling area by pursuing new strategic alliances with producers and by acquiring or developing technology that will advance and expand its aluminum processing capabilities. Imsamet also has a 70 percent-owned joint venture, Imsalco, that recovers aluminum from dross at a facility in Goodyear, Ariz. Imsalco began a program in 1989 designed to procure oversized scrap aluminum materials for its large capacity melting furnace and to negotiate tolling contracts with key customers.[82]

Additional collection methods: Container Recovery Corp., established in 1978 as a subsidiary of **Anheuser-Busch Inc.**, the world's largest brewer and a major user of aluminum cans, operates one of the country's largest used beverage can recycling collection programs. The company has collected more than two billion pounds of aluminum to date, and it collected 375 million pounds of used cans in 1989 alone. CRC sends the cans to an aluminum producer in exchange for a discounted price on the finished can stock, which Metal Container Corp., another Anheuser-Busch subsidiary, manufactures into beverage cans. Container Recovery is expanding into the collection of additional materials, offering communities assistance in developing and operating municipal recycling systems.[83]

In addition to the aluminum industry's own network, other collection methods also feed aluminum beverage cans to industry. The highly valued aluminum can is invariably included in a variety of recycling programs, including municipal drop-off and buy-back centers, curbside recycling and bottle-deposit systems. (See Chapter 6 for a fuller discussion of collection methods.) The industry welcomes aluminum through all methods, but some companies are concerned that curbside collection programs and mandatory deposit systems may have an adverse effect on the industry's existing collection infrastructure. The industry is particularly opposed to aluminum subsidizing the cost of recycling other containers, but it also has expressed concern that other recyclables will contaminate aluminum collected in curbside collection programs. Lee Benbenek, head of Kaiser Aluminum and Chemical's recycling efforts, told a recycling industry meeting in 1990, "there is no uniform industry position on curbside recycling, but such programs raise UBC [used beverage cans] quality concerns."[84]

Another aluminum can collection method gaining favor in the United States is the reverse vending machine, designed to increase access for recyclers. At least 7,000 of these machines are operating in the United States.[85] Recyclers insert used aluminum cans into the automatic machines, which weigh the can and pay on the spot. The machines can be sited almost anywhere consumers travel, including supermarkets, drug and convenience stores, and shopping center parking lots.

A variation on this theme has been developed by Egapro Management of Zurich, Switzerland, which designed a combination can-crushed/slot machine for steel and aluminum cans. The Egapro machine is promoted in the United States by the advertising firm Saatchi and Saatchi. The machine gives a recycler a lottery ticket for each can dropped in. In addition, the can deposit sets a series of wheels spinning in the face of the machine, which resembles a Las Vegas slot machine, for possible instant wins.[86]

Envipco of Fairfax, Va., has introduced a reverse vending machine that allows a beverage producer to woo consumers who buy competing brands. If, for example, Pepsi purchased the rights, a recycler who puts a Coke can in the vending machine would receive a coupon that says "Switch to Pepsi and get 30 cents off a six-pack."[87]

Future Market for Post-Consumer Aluminum

The aluminum can will undoubtedly retain its position as the king of recyclables for years to come. The sound economic basis for aluminum can recycling—namely, the metal's value to the 10 U.S. aluminum can sheet manufacturers—ensures a strong future market for used beverage cans. Despite the fact that aluminum companies have dropped their prices substantially for used beverage cans, the price still is unmatched in post-consumer recycling, and it provides ample incentive for recyclers to continue funneling cans into the aluminum industry's comprehensive recycling network. In turn, the Aluminum Association is confident that demand and melting capacity within the industry are more than sufficient to keep pace with increased aluminum can recycling efforts.

Strong industry demand for recycled aluminum is coupled with strong industry concern about contamination of the recycled product. Moisture, food, plastics, lead, dirt and mixed alloys all pose obstacles to providing industry with a quality stream of recycled aluminum cans. The greatest challenge to boosting overall post-consumer aluminum recycling rates further, however, is development of an infrastructure and technologies to recover and recycle the other 44 percent of post-consumer aluminum that is not in the form of used beer and soft drink cans. The primary constraints to recycling additional aluminum in the waste stream are that most other aluminum products can be found only in small quantities, and even similar products manufactured by different companies can contain different alloys. Both of these conditions adversely affect the economics of identifying alloys—an essential step if industry is to make the best use of post-consumer aluminum. An additional constraint is that recycling some aluminum products can be a cumbersome task for the residential recycler. It is much easier to put out cans at the curb than to dismantle the aluminum housing to a power lawnmower and find a scrap dealer who will take it. While these obstacles are not insurmountable, they have deterred both industry and municipalities from tackling additional forms of post-consumer aluminum. The increase in aluminum packaging of pet foods, snacks and soups, however, is prompting the aluminum industry to re-examine the ability of its existing collection infrastructure to incorporate additional post-consumer aluminum. This may spur the industry to broaden its collection net.

Chapter II
POST-CONSUMER GLASS

"Glass...The 'Ideal' Environmental Package...100% Recyclable" headlines a brochure from Owens-Brockway Glass Containers, the nation's leading manufacturer and recycler of glass containers. "Only The Best Comes in Glass," it adds. The brochure hammers home that the only type of container that can be recycled in a true closed-loop system—a process that recycles a bottle into an entirely new container with no loss, no waste and no by-products—is glass.[1]

Owens-Brockway is not alone in stressing recyclability. As the marketplace becomes ever more environmentally conscious, recyclability becomes the key to gaining a market share advantage. After watching lighter-weight plastics and aluminum eat away its market share during the 1980s, the glass container industry has come out swinging—touting the virtues of glass and assailing the plastics industry for its low recycling rate. After plastics companies ran ads portraying glass as unsafe and as a product of the 1950s, the Glass Packaging Institute launched a counterattack ad: "Plastics Recycling Is in the Dumps." The ad juxtaposes a 2 percent recycling rate for plastics with the average glass container that contains about 30 percent used glass.[2]

The glass industry may be on to something. After nearly a decade of declining demand for glass, in 1990 analysts predicted modest growth in the glass container industry and cited the recyclability of glass as a major reason. The U.S. Department of Commerce attributed projected growth in part to "the soft drink industry's sensitivity to solid-waste issues and the public's perception of glass as 100-percent recyclable material."[3]

U.S. glass container manufacturers are the primary market for crushed recycled glass, or cullet, and representatives of the top three told IRRC they hoped to boost the cullet percentage of containers to 50 percent by 1995.[4] Integrating higher rates of cullet in the manufacturing process does not appear to pose problems, although consistently high rates of cullet have never been tested for any great length of time in the United States. It most likely will take years, however, before industry approaches any projected limits to cullet usage. Industry's use of cullet would have to more than double before it would represent 70 percent of industry's feedstock for new containers—the bottom range of potential cited by glass container manufacturers.

While the recyclability of glass may create an advantage in the marketplace, used glass containers provide few economic advantages in the glass production process. Although each ton of cullet melted in a glass furnace extends the life of the furnace and produces some energy savings, the 1.2 tons of virgin materials the cullet replaces[5]—sand, limestone and soda ash—are relatively inexpensive. In addition, the job of processing cullet to remove contaminants often falls on the glass container industry and represents an added, and often unwelcome, step not usually required for the industry's other raw materials. As one glass container company representative told IRRC, "Corporate goodwill to reclaim material is the major reason for recycling glass."

Glass in the Municipal Waste Stream

The emphasis on glass container recycling bodes well for removing glass from the waste stream. On average, each American uses approximately 85 pounds of glass a year.[6] In 1988, about 12.5 million tons of glass worked its way into the municipal solid waste stream, representing about 7 percent of the total waste stream by weight. Given that glass is a relatively dense and compact material, its percentage of the volume of materials discarded in 1988 was significantly lower, measuring only 2 percent. Glass containers, primarily beer and soft drink bottles, represent a whopping 90 percent of all glass in the nation's municipal garbage.[7] Durable glass products, such as flat glass (window and auto glass), pressed and blown glass (light bulbs) and fiberglass, constitute the remainder of the waste stream glass.[8]

The amount of glass in the solid waste stream grew steadily until the early 1980s, when aluminum and plastic containers gained favor. Glass accounted for 6.7 million tons, or 7 percent, of municipal solid waste in 1960, rose to 15 million tons and 10 percent of waste generation in 1980, and then fell to 12.5 million tons and 7 percent of waste generation in 1988. The Environmental Protection Agency projects that the percentage of glass in the waste stream will continue to decline, decreasing to 9.5 million tons and

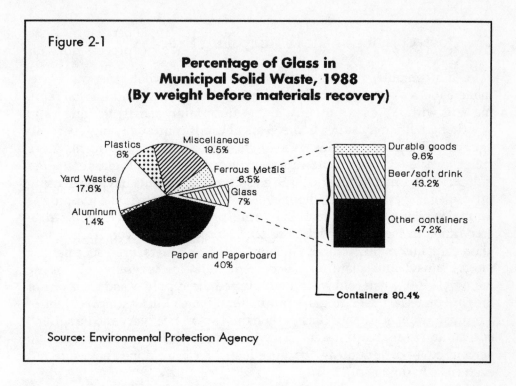

Figure 2-1

**Percentage of Glass in
Municipal Solid Waste, 1988
(By weight before materials recovery)**

Plastics
8%

Miscellaneous
19.5%

Yard Wastes
17.6%

Ferrous Metals
8.5%

Glass
7%

Aluminum
1.4%

Paper and Paperboard
40%

Durable goods
9.6%

Beer/soft drink
43.2%

Other containers
47.2%

Containers 90.4%

Source: Environmental Protection Agency

less than 4 percent of total waste generation by 2010.[9]

Estimates of the recovery rate of glass from the post-consumer waste stream vary. EPA estimates that 1.5 million tons of glass were recovered from the post-consumer waste stream in 1988, representing a 12 percent recovery rate for all glass and a 13 percent recycling rate for glass containers.[10] The congressional Office of Technology Assessment estimates a slightly higher 1988 post-consumer glass recovery rate of 15 percent.[11]

The Glass Packaging Institute's recycling estimate is nearly double EPA's—at 25 percent in 1989.[12] Instead of using the amount of glass recovered from the waste stream as a yardstick to measure the success of recycling, however, the glass container industry prefers to use the amount of cullet that serves as a feedstock for new glass containers. The industry believes it has made great strides to use more cullet, pointing out that the 30 percent cullet average in new glass containers is up from 25 percent in 1988 and no more than 15 to 20 percent in the 1970s. More importantly, post-consumer glass has claimed an increasing share of the cullet. Most cullet fed into glass container furnaces 15 years ago was generated from the manufacturing process. Today, because of technological improvements, the manufacturing process is a source for far less than 10 percent of overall cullet usage.[13]

The Post-Consumer Glass Recycling Process

Glass container industry representatives report that glass can be remelted and reused an indefinite number of times without additional refining and without loss of quality. Some uncertainty exists, though, as to whether quality may suffer in the years ahead if continually high percentages of cullet comprise new finished glass products. High percentages of cullet have never been consistently used throughout the U.S. glass container industry.[14] A small number of U.S. glass container plants have been using up to 70 or 75 percent cullet, though, and their experience is encouraging as no major changes in the manufacturing process have been required to accommodate these high levels of cullet.[15] Moreover, the second largest U.S. glass container manufacturer, Anchor Glass Container Corp., successfully ran a Pennsylvania plant on 100 percent cullet for several weeks in the winter of 1990, when cold weather disrupted the supply of soda ash, one of the raw materials used in glass production. James Luci, vice president of administration for Anchor Glass, called this experience "very encouraging," but cautioned that still the industry is unsure if it is possible to run 100 percent cullet continuously "because it's never been done and we're not even close to doing so."[16]

As the growing numbers of recycling programs funnel more glass back to the manufacturing process, industry will be better able to estimate the optimum level of cullet. Today, estimates of the optimum level vary. While some assert that continual use of 100 percent cullet is achievable, pointing to glass furnaces in Europe that reportedly use 100 percent cullet, the Dutch glass container industry claims the upper limit for cullet usage is around 70 percent. U.S. glass industry representatives say the optimum level is somewhere in between, most likely between 80 and 85 percent. Chaz Miller, director of recycling for the Glass Packaging Institute, maintains that because of the need to maintain a consistent quantity and quality of cullet supply, 70 percent is probably the maximum feasible cullet level.[17] Miller added that the U.S. glass container industry is averse to becoming dependent on one raw material source.[18]

Glass container industry representatives also say it is critical to maintain consistent levels of cullet in the manufacturing process. The need for consistency was the primary reason that Anchor Glass chose to use 100 percent cullet at one glass manufacturing plant, rather than increase cullet usage at several plants. Industry representatives say it becomes inefficient and counterproductive to change the mix of raw materials constantly. Thomas McKnight, recycling director for Ball-Incon Glass Packaging Corp., explains that "when the percentage of cullet changes, the batch mix must be changed. This requires recalculating the furnace temperature and the amount of raw materials....[Changes in furnace temperature] cause wear and tear on the furnace. The greatest efficiency is to run the furnace at the same temperature."[19] In addition, fluctuations in furnace temperature can affect both the color and the density of the new glass being produced, unless chemical compositions and furnace pressures and temperatures are carefully monitored and controlled. To avoid these complications, furnace operators prefer to run a lower percentage of cullet to ensure a steady supply rather than run a higher level of cullet and risk the chance of running out. The furnace operator's goal is a sustainable, long-term percentage of cullet.[20]

Cullet preparation: Industry cites the inability to obtain a steady supply of quality cullet as the major limiting factor in greater cullet usage, and as the percentage of cullet in the glass container industry's feedstock grows, quality will become increasingly important. High quality cullet requires that the glass be separated by color and the contaminants removed.

Separating glass from other components of the waste stream is perhaps the most difficult quality control step. Because glass has no magnetic properties and equipment does not exist that can efficiently color-sort it, the glass must be hand-sorted by color. Glass broken before it is separated by color is nearly impossible to sort by hand and most often winds up as a mixed-colored cullet that is of little or no use to the glass container industry. Color-sorting laser equipment is operating in Holland, but its sorting ability is too slow for use in the United States at present. In addition, the lasers can sort only pieces three-eighths of an inch or greater—sizes that are larger than most pieces of broken glass.[21] Additional research on the use of lasers or optical sensors to separate glass by color is underway and will benefit other recyclables as well; glass shards created during collection and processing of commingled recyclables are a common contaminant in other recyclables.

Once the glass is sorted, operators run the collected glass containers through a mechanical processor that crushes the bottles into half-inch pieces of cullet. Cullet processing equipment also is designed to remove contaminants that have the ability either to destroy a glass furnace or to produce imperfect glass. Contaminants such as iron, steel and lead, for instance, will settle to the bottom of a furnace and attack its refractory lining. Aluminum, on the other hand, will melt into small balls called "stones" or bubbles called "seeds" that can appear in the containers being made, causing both structural and aesthetic problems.[22] New cullet processing equipment has become quite effective at removing these metal contaminants as well as labels, plastic rings and caps through magnetic separation and air blowing processes. In addition, paper labels, small amounts of plastic and food contamination will burn in the furnace if not removed by the processing equipment.

The only contaminants that the newest processing equipment is incapable of removing are noncontainer glass, dirt and stones.[23] The composition of noncontainer glass (such as ceramic glasses, light bulbs, dishes or plates, windows, windshields and eyeglasses) is different from that of glass bottles, and it must be removed from glass container cullet or it will interfere with the manufacturing process. Light bulbs, for instance, have a high level of soda ash, leaded crystal contains lead, and window glass often contains borax. Heat resistant glass, such as pyrex and laboratory glass, which melts at much higher temperatures, creates weak spots in new glass containers.[24] A few companies are marketing ceramic detection systems but, as with the color-sorting laser equipment, it remains to be seen whether the equipment can detect small pieces at a sufficient speed. At present, public education and quality hand sorting are the only viable means of keeping noncontainer glass out of cullet.

Economics of Glass Recycling

Because the virgin materials used in glass container production are relatively inexpensive, the major economic incentives for using cullet— furnace-life extensions and energy savings—stem from the fact that cullet has a lower melting temperature than do virgin materials. Industry estimates that using 100 percent cullet instead of virgin materials would reduce energy usage in the manufacturing process by roughly 25 percent,[25] because each percentage of cullet saves an estimated one-quarter of a percent of energy. The U.S. Department of Energy estimates potential energy savings in the manufacturing process at around 30 percent;[26] the congressional Office of Technology Assessment's estimate is 15 percent. OTA also estimates another 16 percent in energy savings because mining and transporting virgin materials would be avoided, bringing its estimate of overall energy savings to 31 percent.[27]

Remelting cullet, rather than producing glass from raw materials, also reduces particle emissions, which in turn reduces air pollution control operation and maintenance costs. EPA estimates that recycling glass cuts air pollution by 20 percent and water pollution by 50 percent.[28] Austin Fiore, regional manager of recycling and public affairs for Owens-Brockway, believes that some California glass plants probably could not meet the state's stringent air emissions standards without using cullet.[29]

The refillable glass bottle, which is common in Europe and Japan,[30] offers even greater energy and virgin materials savings than using cullet to produce new bottles. Although the refillable bottle has lost favor in the American marketplace, there are signs that it is making a comeback in the environmentally aware 1990s, albeit a small one so far. Anchor Glass, a major producer of refillable bottles, reported 1990 sales were up 25 percent over 1989 levels.[31] In 1989, 9 billion refillable glass bottles were sold, accounting for 8.7 percent of the packaged soft drink market. The number of times these bottles are refilled has declined considerably, however, dropping from as many as 50 round-trips in 1950 to an average of 8.5 today.[32]

Used glass container prices: In order to compete with virgin materials used in glass container production, the cost of cullet must remain in a similar price range. Although prices vary throughout the country, in 1990 the cost of delivered virgin materials averaged between $45 and $47 per ton,[33] while the price end-users paid for clear used glass containers averaged between $45 and $50 per ton.[34] The average price paid for glass cullet ranks toward the lower end of prices paid for recyclables commonly collected at curbside. (See Figure I-3 on p. 7 for a comparison of prices.) Some glass manufacturing plants have a two-tiered price structure for glass, paying substantially more for used glass containers from buy-back centers than for curbside-collected material, which tends to have a greater percentage of contaminants.[35]

Between 1986 and 1990, Owens-Brockway raised its cullet prices as part of a special promotional program designed to increase glass recycling. In an attempt to offset the start-up costs of new collection and processing programs, the company was paying brokers $70 per ton, with the understanding that the public would be paid 2 cents per pound. Early in the summer of 1990, however, the company reduced its glass buy-back prices to $50 per ton, saying it was going "back to proper value pricing."[36] From time to time, Anchor Glass also offers promotional incentives to help start new recycling efforts.[37]

Transportation—Because of the relatively heavy weight of glass, transportation costs can significantly affect the economics of glass recycling. As a result, the price paid for reclaimed glass containers is more dependent on the dynamics of regional, as opposed to national, markets. The importance of regional markets will only become more pronounced in the future, as the U.S. glass container industry continues consolidating and further reduces the number of glass manufacturing plants across the country. Figure 2-2 identifies the approximate location of the country's 79 plants, which are in 27 states. As Figure 2-2 shows, the bulk of the glass plants are in the East.

With the exception of California, which hosts 13 glass manufacturing plants, and Oklahoma, which hosts six, states west of the Mississippi River have far greater distances to transport their cullet. Unless these states face high waste disposal fees, the cost of transporting the cullet to a manufacturing plant may deter glass recycling programs. In the Pennsylvania/New Jersey corridor, however, elements are in place to produce highly successful glass recycling programs. While a scarcity of landfill capacity has resulted in skyrocketing disposal fees, the heavy concentration of glass manufacturing plants significantly reduces the transportation costs for glass recycling programs.

To attract cullet to its more remote plants, Owens-Brockway pays an extra $5 per ton for glass shipped more than 50 miles and an extra $10 per ton for glass shipped more than 300 miles.[38] Glass plants owned by Ball-Incon that need to attract cullet from great distances also have the option of offering incentives.[39] Anchor Glass does not offer such incentives; it bases its prices on virgin material costs and then factors in energy savings only.[40] Chaz Miller of the Glass Packaging Institute also points out that identifying local materials that can be sent back on the trucks delivering cullet, rather than sending them back empty, can help defray transportation costs and improve the economics of a glass recycling program.[41]

Color sorting—The glass container industry generally requires that used glass containers be sorted by color. The quality of color separation influences the value of glass and can limit potential purchases if a manufacturer is producing new containers with strict color specifications. At least 66 percent of all glass containers produced in the United States are clear, at least one-quarter are brown, and the remainder are green.[42] Clear used glass is the most valuable because it has many domestic uses. The supply of green used glass, however, often exceeds the local manufacturing demand, particularly in non-wine-producing states on the East Coast. While most imported beer and wine are packaged in green bottles, domestic use of green glass is limited to wine bottles and a small amount of beer and soft drink containers. Given the large supply of green and brown bottles in relation to domestic demand, brown and green containers made in the United States have higher percentages of cullet—an average of 50 percent and 70 percent, respectively—than clear bottles, which contain an average of 25 percent cullet.[43]

Not all glass container plants will accept all three colors of bottles. Because a glass plant that manufactures clear glass can use only limited or no colored cullet, it may not accept colored cullet, or it may pay less in order to offset reshipping costs to other glass plants. In the spring of 1991, Anchor Glass, Owens-Brockway and Central New York Bottling Co., which produces bottles for Miller Brewing Co., notified glass processors in the Northeast that they planned to discontinue purchasing green glass. Because these companies do not make green glass containers in the Northeast, they had been shipping green glass to Pennsylvania and points further south.[44]

Glass container companies are experimenting to determine how stringent their color separation requirements need to be. Owens-Brockway, for example, has used a feedstock with 5 percent brown glass to make clear bottles at one plant with no adverse effects. The company used separated brown glass that could be measured precisely, however; the same precision could not have been achieved with mixed-color cullet.[45]

Contamination—Contaminants in cullet can render a load of cullet worthless for bottle reproduction. The glass industry will accept only cullet that meets specifications, rejecting outright loads that are contaminated. In

Figure 2-2

U.S. Glass Container Manufacturing Plants

Source: Glass Packaging Institute, Washington, D.C.

most cases, the only recourse for rejected loads is a landfill, resulting in the payment of disposal fees rather than the receipt of payments. The rejection of loads was described as an acute problem in California in 1989 and 1990. Recyclers accused manufacturers of rejecting loads of glass for even a single piece of ceramic, saying the manufacturers were looking for excuses not to purchase the high-priced California cullet. (See Box 6-3 on p. 178 for more information on California pricing.) Industry says that the claims are overblown and that the percentage rate of rejections has remained steady at under 5 percent.[46] Industry also says the state lowered its final estimate of the amount of rejected and landfilled cullet to less than 1,000 tons—a small amount compared with the 350,000 tons of cullet recycled in California in 1990.[47]

Consumers Packaging Inc., the only Canadian glass manufacturer, is tackling the ceramic contamination problem by finely grinding up contaminated glass it obtains from curbside recycling programs. After experimenting with 500 tons of contaminated mixed-color cullet, the company determined that it can safely use at least a 10 percent ratio of the finely ground contaminated glass. Its use is limited to the production of green bottles, however, and the additional processing costs, although not available, were described as "quite high" by Allen Newfeld of Consumers Packaging. Newfeld added that the company is "philosophically opposed to landfilling glass" and that, although it is not profitable to grind up the contaminated glass, it is "the least-cost alternative," given the high cost of waste disposal. Newfeld estimates the company will be able to handle up to 15,000 to 20,000 tons per year of contaminated glass.[48]

Bassichis Co., a national waste glass processor, also is testing a powder ground from ceramic-contaminated, mixed-color cullet in cooperation with a U.S. glass container manufacturer. Although it costs more to process mixed cullet in this fashion, Roger D. Hecht, president of Bassichis Co. and Allwaste Resource Recovery, told IRRC it can be a cost-effective process because the company pays less for the cullet in the first place.[49]

U.S. Glass Container Industry's Recycling Initiatives and Secondary Markets

Since glassmaking was discovered more than 5,000 years ago, glassmakers have funneled unusable bottles and other glassmaking waste back into the glass production process. In the late 1960s, however, technological developments reduced the amount of glass waste generated in the manufacturing process, and glass manufacturers began looking outside their plants for new sources of glass. Owens-Illinois pioneered this effort in 1968, scheduling a "Glass Day" and urging residents to bring in used glass containers to its Bridgeton, N.J., glass plant. By 1970, all of the company's glass container plants had recycling centers, and in that same year Owens-Illinois expanded its public buy-back campaigns to encompass communities without glass plants. In cooperation with an environmental group, the company led a two-day collection drive in Ann Arbor, Mich., which then became the first community to host a permanent public collection station. By the end of 1970, public collection programs had netted nearly 25,000 tons of used glass containers.[50]

Beginning in the 1980s, the nation's solid waste disposal crisis spurred the glass container industry to reexamine and expand its collection infrastructure. Today, glass container manufacturers accept cullet at all of their glass plants, and in cooperation with state and local governments they have set up voluntary collection centers in 30 states and the District of Columbia.[51] The solid waste disposal crisis also has provided glass container manufacturers with a new marketing tool that appeals to the growing number of environmentally aware consumers—the recyclability of glass. "We see great potential for glass, a 100 percent recyclable material, as the solid waste crisis worsens and Americans take action to curb the crisis," said Lewis D. Andrews Jr., president of the Glass Packaging Institute (GPI), the trade group representing the nation's glass container manufacturers, in February 1990.[52]

The GPI is spearheading the industry's recycling efforts, having realigned its goals in 1985 to place a new emphasis on glass recycling.[53] With a full-time national recycling director, the GPI oversees eight regional glass recycling organizations. The GPI funds its recycling programs through the Nickel Solution Trust, a $6.5 million trust workers and management formed in 1983 to counter inroads made by plastic containers in the soft drink container industry and to fight container deposit legislation. The trust acquired its name because it originally was funded by employee contributions of a nickel per man-hour (which have since been upped to 10 cents per man-hour) and matching employer donations.[54]

The glass container industry has devoted a portion of the more than $15 million that it has spent over the last three years on recycling programs to alert consumers to the recyclability of glass.[55] One such project was the creation of a recycling "G" symbol that appears on glass containers to remind consumers that glass is 100 percent recyclable. Pepsi, Heinz, Kraft and Prego are using the logo, and All Bamma Food Products, Borden, Maxwell House, Mountain Valley Spring Water and Vintage Wines reportedly plan to add the logo to their glass containers.[56]

End-users of used glass containers: The U.S. glass container industry—the primary end market for used glass containers—annually produces 11 million tons of containers for food, beer, soft drinks, wine, liquor, cosmetics and medicines.[57] The five leading U.S. glass container producers, which accounted for 90 percent of industry sales in 1989,[58] are Owens-Brockway Glass Containers, a unit of Owens-Illinois Inc.; Anchor Glass Container Corp., which along with Latchford Glass Co. is owned by the Mexican conglomerate, Vitro S.A.; Ball-Incon Glass Packaging Corp., a wholly owned subsidiary of Ball Corp.; Foster-Forbes Glass Co., a division of American National Can Co.; and Kerr Glass Manufacturing Corp. Kerr Glass and Ball Corp. are the only publicly traded companies. Table 2-1 identifies the numbers and tons of glass containers each company recycled in 1990 and the average percentage of cullet used in their feedstock.

Other U.S. glass container manufacturers include Arkansas Glass Container Corp.; Carr-Lowery Glass Co.; Central New York Bottling Co.; Coors Brewing Co.; Gallo Glass Co.; Glenshaw Glass Co.; Hillsboro Glass Co.; Leone Industries; Liberty Glass Co.; Tropicana Products Inc.; and Wheaton Industries.[59]

The industry leader, in terms of both glass container production and glass container recycling, is **Owens-Brockway Glass Containers**. The company recycled 4.5 billion glass bottles and jars in 1990, an increase of 18 percent from the previous year. As Table 2-1 shows, in 1990 the company made approximately 35 percent of its glass containers and 55 percent of its beverage containers with cullet.[60] Owens-Brockway continually worked more cullet into its glass production process during the 1980s, increasing the amount of recycled glass it used at an annual rate of more than 16 percent. During the decade, the company recycled more than 18 billion used glass containers, paying approximately $250 million for the glass.[61] The ability of Owens-Illinois, the nation's 29th largest private business with annual sales of $3.6 billion,[62] to continue breaking recycling records has been called into question by a Federal Trade Commission ruling that its acquisition of Brockway violates antitrust laws.[63]

Following close behind Owens-Brockway is **Anchor Glass**, which recycled 3.9 billion bottles in 1990, more than double the amount it recycled in 1986. Between 1986 and 1989, the company remelted more than 10 billion bottles.[64] Vitro S.A., a corporation in Monterrey, Mexico, took the publicly traded Anchor Glass private in November 1989 in what was billed as the largest takeover of an American company by a Mexican company.[65] Formed in April 1983, Anchor achieved much of its own growth through acquisitions. In May 1983, it acquired the glass container division of Anchor Hocking Corp. through a leveraged buyout, and the following year it acquired Midland Glass Co. Four years later, Anchor acquired Diamond-Bathurst, which was the fifth-largest domestic manufacturer of glass containers. Anchor had its initial public offering in June 1986, trading on the NASDAQ National Market System until April 1987, when it moved to the New York Stock Exchange.[66]

All of the U.S. glass container manufacturers purchase reclaimed glass containers from the public at the country's 79 glass container manufacturing plants depicted in Figure 2-2.[67] Whether plants purchase all three colors of bottles, however, depends on what color bottles the plants are producing. Cullet specifications also vary from plant to plant, depending on the ability of individual glass container manufacturing plants to process cullet. To improve its processing capabilities, the glass container industry has installed cullet processing equipment, called beneficiation systems, at 27 glass plants, with costs running between $500,000 and $1 million each.[68] Chaz Miller of the Glass Packaging Institute expects that glass container companies will continue to assume responsibility for cullet processing, doubling the number of beneficiation systems at their plants within the next five years.[69]

Table 2-1 identifies the number of plants with cullet processing equipment at each of the top five U.S. glass container manufacturers. In addition to processing cullet at seven of its plants, Anchor Glass operates two 150 ton

Table 2-1

Recycling in the U.S. Glass Container Industry

Company	# of Glass Manufac- turing Plants	# of Plants with Cullet Processing Equipment	Glass Containers Recycled in 1990	Cullet as Average % of Feedstock
Owens-Brockway Glass Containers	24	14	4.5 billion (1,100,000 tons)	35%
Anchor Glass Container Corp.	19	7[a]	3.9 billion[b] (876,441 tons)	33%
Ball-Incon Glass Packaging Corp.	12	1	4.8 million[b] (110,000 tons)	30%
Foster-Forbes Glass Co.	8	NA	NA	NA
Kerr Glass Manu- facturing Corp.	4	0	NA	18-30%

[a] Anchor Glass operates two additional cullet processing plants in California.
[b] Calculated using conversion rate of 2.2 bottles/lb.

Source: Investor Responsibility Research Center Inc.

per day glass beneficiation facilities in California in partnership with New England CRInc., a company that designs and builds materials recovery facilities.[70]

While most glass companies view operating their own beneficiation systems as a necessary means of quality control, Austin Fiore of Owens-Brockway envisions the day when the glass container industry will be able to phase out its beneficiation systems and purchase cullet from an industry of third-party cullet processors, just as it does its other raw materials. Fiore believes that many glass container manufacturers would welcome such an industry, because it would allow them to concentrate fully on their primary business of manufacturing containers.[71] There are signs that a cullet processing industry is developing. Ball-Incon, for example, relies on Fibres International's new $2 million, 30,000 ton per year beneficiation plant near Seattle to supply cullet to its Seattle and Okmulgee, Okla., glass container manufacturing plants.[72] American National Can Co., the parent of Foster Forbes, has formed a national partnership with Waste Management Inc. that plans to build a glass beneficiation facility in the Chicago area in 1991. Created primarily to market glass and metal collected through Waste Management's curbside recycling programs, the partnership says it plans to use the Chicago glass beneficiation system as a model for future plants.[73]

Secondary markets: Secondary markets for used glass containers are weak, falling into two categories—markets for color-sorted glass containers and markets for mixed-color cullet. Given the glass container industry's strong demand for color-sorted glass, few industries are eager to engage in a bidding war for these containers, and as a result, few new markets have been created. Fiberglass companies, which produce 1 million tons of glass annually, are a potential market, however. Although no U.S. fiberglass insulation manufacturing firms use container cullet on a regular basis, interest is growing because federal procurement guidelines on building insulation, which oversee the purchase of about $150 million of building insulation annually, give preference to insulation containing recovered materials. The fiberglass industry fears losing market share to cellulose and foam insulators, which use recycled paper, in the $3 billion building insulation industry. Near-term interest by fiberglass manufacturers, however, will most likely focus on the more than 1 million tons of available waste plate glass, rather than container cullet, to avoid competition with glass container manufacturers.[74] Owens-Corning Fiberglas Corp., a leading fiberglass manufacturer, says that 3 to 4 percent of its feedstock is already composed of plate or auto glass.[75]

Catamount Inc., a Bennington, Vt., manufacturer of oven-proof cookware, is in the market for post-consumer, color-sorted glass containers. The company plans to build what it believes is the first manufacturing plant in the United States designed to use 100 percent recycled glass. The $2 million plant, scheduled to be operational by the summer of 1991, will process 10 tons of primarily clear glass per day to produce decorative housewares, including plates, bowls, goblets and candle holders.[76]

Breakage during the collection and processing of glass containers inevitably occurs, making color separation quite difficult, if not impossible. In fact, industry analysts estimate that 10 to 25 percent of glass coming from curbside collection programs is mixed-color cullet.[77] Mixed-color cullet also typically has a high number of contaminants, and there is minimal demand for it at present. In addition, as collection rates of green and brown glass increase, supply is overwhelming demand in some regions of the country, and marketers are exploring these same secondary markets to unload green and brown glass containers.

Products that can be made from mixed-color and colored cullet include glass containers, glasphalt (similar to asphalt), reflective beads for paint, landfill cover, clean fill and drainage material. One company also is reportedly using mixed cullet to polish metals, and another is using it to encapsulate hazardous waste.[78] With these markets representing relatively small outlets for cullet, each will need to be pursued to its fullest in order to utilize contaminated and mixed-color cullet.

As processors develop means to improve the quality and consistency of mixed-color cullet, additional markets may emerge. Roger D. Hecht, president of Allwaste Resource Recovery and Bassichis Co., cites the U.S. glass container industry as one example of a market that will expand as technology develops to upgrade mixed-color cullet. Although the glass industry does not routinely accept mixed-color cullet, Hecht told IRRC that the glass container industry is already his company's largest market for the product, albeit a small one, and that he believes the U.S. glass container industry will accept more mixed-color cullet in the future.[79]

In the meantime, glasphalt is the most promising market for mixed-color cullet. Its use is on the rise as municipalities attempt to find local uses for the mixed-color cullet generated through their recycling programs. New York City is paving the way, laying the sparkling glasphalt on more than 400 miles of streets,[80] including Times Square, where the embedded glass reflects the flickering neon lights. Noting that the city plans to use glasphalt in all of its boroughs, Department of Transportation Commissioner Lucius Riccio remarked that "this year, the tree in Rockefeller Center won't be the only thing that glitters."[81] Virginia, New Jersey and Pennsylvania also are experimenting with glasphalt,[82] and Waste Aggregate Recycling Co., a privately owned company formerly named Ecosphere Recycling Systems, has recycled more than 20,000 tons of mixed glass for asphalt and road base over the last four years.[83]

New York City is using up to 20 percent cullet to replace sand in its conventional asphalt mix,[84] and other analysts say crushed glass can replace as much as 30 percent of the stone and sand used in asphalt. With the nation using approximately 1 billion tons of asphalt each year, the potential for glasphalt is tremendous. In addition, the only processing requirements are removal of metal, plastic and labels. Because of the low cost of sand and gravel, however, the revenue potential of this market is limited, and cullet is used only when the quality of the cullet is low or the distance to a glass plant is great.[85]

In addition to sparkling pavement, the highway industry has discovered that adding finely ground glass spheres, or beads, to its road paint gives it a reflective quality that aids motorists. Additional construction applications include filling in pot holes or serving as drainage material around storm drains, and some say glass aggregate is superior to dirt in these uses because it is nontoxic, it is cleaner than soil, and it does not create air pockets. The potential for glass aggregate is perhaps best summed up by Richard Menkes, a glass broker and president of Menkes Municipal Services of West Orange, N.J.: "New Jersey is full of holes."[86]

Although a small amount of cullet is exported to Canada, the market for cullet is essentially a domestic one. Export markets for green bottles may be developed in the future, however. The New Jersey Glass Association reports it received a phone inquiry from an anonymous broker interested in exporting cullet overseas to an unidentified European country.[87]

Additional collection methods: In addition to the collection network established by glass container manufacturers, thousands of independent reclamation centers and commercial recyclers around the country purchase reclaimed glass.[88] Glass also is a popular recyclable nearly always included in additional collection programs, including curbside recycling, municipal drop-off and buy-back centers, and bottle-deposit systems. (See Chapter 6 for a fuller discussion of collection methods.) The glass industry prefers curbside separation as the collection method, developing education materials for municipalities and actively promoting the concept to local and state decision-makers, and strongly opposes container deposit legislation. (See Box 6-2 on p. 174 for information on container deposit legislation.) In fact, the Glass Packaging Institute applauds New Jersey's mandatory recycling program, saying it should serve as a model for all states and the federal government.[89]

One notable independent collector and processor of glass containers is **Allwaste Inc.**, a publicly traded environmental services company. Allwaste collects used glass and processes it for resale not only to the glass container industry but also to companies engaged in the production of fiberglass, reflective highway paints, ceramics and industrial abrasives.[90] In 1990, the company processed about 400,000 tons of container and industrial cullet.[91] Allwaste became involved in glass recovery in April 1989, when it merged with The Bassichis Co., and it further bolstered its glass recycling operations in October 1989 when it acquired Circo Glass Co. of California, the largest glass processor in the western United States.[92]

Future Market for Post-Consumer Glass

Post-consumer glass has one characteristic that distinguishes it from other municipal waste stream commodities—nearly all of it is in the same form, namely glass containers. The advantage of this characteristic is that it makes identification a snap, particularly in comparison with post-consumer plastics, which are made from numerous and often indistinguishable resins, and post-consumer aluminum products, which contain a variety of alloys that are difficult to identify. The downside is that large quantities of the same material can quickly swamp undeveloped markets. While the U.S. glass container industry represents a strong primary market, not all used containers can be recycled into new containers, primarily because of their color or level of contamination.

Demand by glass companies for clear used glass containers appears quite strong, and in some areas there are steady markets for all colors of glass. Ben Davol, executive director of the Mid-Atlantic Glass Recycling Program, told recycling conference attendees in June 1990 that glass companies in his region would purchase "all the color-separated, contaminant-free cullet that can be delivered to our plants."[93] In some locales, however, the supply of green and brown cullet simply overwhelms local demand, and the high cost of transporting glass limits the geographic extent of most markets. In addition, glass container companies are reluctant to purchase mixed-color cullet, which is often interspersed with contaminants. Further advances in cullet processing, as well as continued industrial experimentation to determine how strict color specifications must be, will allow the glass container industry to use higher quantities of colored cullet in the future. Nevertheless, development of local secondary markets for colored and mixed-color cullet is essential to avoid landfilling these types of glass, particularly as the growing number of recycling programs exacerbate regional distortions.

The greatest near-term challenge for increased recycling in the primary market is for the glass container industry to expand its existing collection infrastructure while maintaining quality control. The major obstacle to industry's use of more cullet is the difficulty of obtaining a "good quality supply of cullet and a sustainable supply," says Thomas McKnight, recycling director for Ball-Incon Glass Packaging Corp.[94] Unless glass furnace operators are assured of a steady supply, they are averse to increasing the percentage of cullet in their feedstock. More importantly, damage to the furnace resulting from contamination far outweighs any economic incentives associated with using cullet. Therefore, glass container manufacturers will readily reject loads of cullet if they are not free from contamination.

Chapter III
POST-CONSUMER FERROUS METALS

With almost 200 years at it,[1] the U.S. steel industry has considerable experience in recycling, and steel—the primary ferrous, or iron-containing, metal found in the nation's garbage—has the highest recycling rate of any material in this country. Most of the industry's experience, though, has been with ferrous scrap outside the municipal solid waste stream, not with post-consumer packages and containers. Only recently, and largely because of the nation's solid waste disposal crisis, has the steel industry taken aim at the "tin" can, a very high-profile steel product in the garbage pile. It hopes to expand the recycling rate of tin cans, now 25 percent,[2] to match the rate for all steel materials today, 66 percent.[3]

The tin can is actually a steel can with a thin layer of tin on the interior and exterior to stabilize flavors and prevent rusting. Americans have been using tin cans for more than 150 years;[4] today approximately 90 percent of the nation's food cans and about 5 percent of its beverage cans are tin cans.[5] Charles G. Carson, general manager of marketing, development and technology of Tin Mill Products at the USS Division of USX Corp., the nation's largest steel maker, believes "it will take two or three years for the steel industry to get its [steel can] recycling system up to speed,"[6] but the industry remains confident it can achieve significantly higher recycling rates. Elizabeth H. Olenbush, director of marketing at the Steel Can Recycling Institute, said a 66 percent steel can recycling rate "sounds ambitious, but we think it is highly achievable because of the network that is in place for steel. Our job is to get cans funneled into that network."[7]

Like the glass container industry, the steel industry is spurred on by the belief that the steel can's recyclability will make it attractive to consumers. This belief is reflected in the fact that the industry members taking a leadership position in steel recycling initiatives are the steel can manufacturers—the major domestic tin mill products producers. However, the entire steel industry, which along with detinners constitute the primary market for steel cans, shares both the political pressures and the public relations advantages associated with recycling. The steel industry also has the added incentive of high scrap purchase requirements, and ferrous metals from the post-consumer waste stream, particularly detinned steel cans and bimetallic cans (cans with steel bodies and aluminum lids), represent a high quality source of ferrous scrap.

Steel has many characteristics that lend themselves to the recycling process. All steel products, including tin-coated, tin-free and bimetallic cans, are 100 percent recyclable, and steel made from detinned scrap is chemically and metallurgically equivalent to steel manufactured from virgin iron ore.[8] In addition, the magnetic properties of ferrous scrap provide it with an advantage over other recyclables. Because automated processes capitalizing on its magnetism can easily separate ferrous metals from other recyclables or the rest of the waste stream, recyclers can reclaim ferrous scrap regardless of the collection system used. Moreover, contamination of the feedstock is less of an issue with this waste stream component, because the high furnace temperatures required for steel manufacturing burn contaminants that processing equipment has failed to eliminate.

The potential amount of steel to be recovered from the residential waste stream is dwarfed by the amount of steel already being recovered from other sources, making it impossible for post-consumer steel cans to flood the scrap markets. Recycling all steel cans, for instance, would yield only 3 million tons of scrap—a small amount compared with the approximately 60 million tons of ferrous scrap recycled in 1989.[9] Some steel mills and detinners are taking the lead, however, in targeting purchases of steel cans and other ferrous scrap recovered from the municipal waste stream.

Ferrous Metals in the Municipal Waste Stream

The Environmental Protection Agency and the steel industry have different estimates of the amount of steel in the municipal waste stream and the amount that is recycled. EPA estimates that ferrous metals in the municipal waste stream comprised 6.5 percent of the total waste stream by weight, at 11.6 million tons, before recovery, and 9.8 percent by volume, after recovery, in 1988. EPA also estimates that more than three-quarters of the ferrous metals in the municipal waste stream are found in durable goods, such as appliances, furniture and tires; slightly less than a quarter are beverage, food and other tin cans; and the remaining 2 percent are other types of steel packaging.[10] Some steel industry representatives contend that

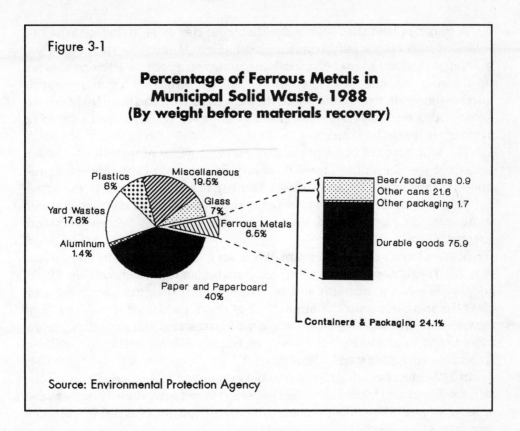

Figure 3-1

**Percentage of Ferrous Metals in
Municipal Solid Waste, 1988**
(By weight before materials recovery)

Plastics 8%
Miscellaneous 19.5%
Yard Wastes 17.6%
Glass 7%
Aluminum 1.4%
Ferrous Metals 6.5%
Paper and Paperboard 40%

Beer/soda cans 0.9
Other cans 21.6
Other packaging 1.7
Durable goods 75.9

Containers & Packaging 24.1%

Source: Environmental Protection Agency

EPA's estimate seriously understates the amount of ferrous material in the municipal solid waste stream by excluding junked automobiles, office equipment and worn out fixtures from commercial and institutional establishments.[11]

Industry analysts also dispute EPA's estimated 1988 recovery rate of 5.8 percent of ferrous metals in the municipal waste stream, which represents around 700,000 tons of scrap. EPA estimates that 400,000 tons of steel cans and another 300,000 tons, or 3.4 percent, of durable steel goods, primarily major appliances, were recovered in 1988.[12] Steel industry representatives say this conclusion is far too modest,[13] estimating that 75 percent of major appliances—representing 2.1 million tons—are collected and delivered to auto-shredders for processing.[14] Industry representatives also estimate that at least 400,000 tons of miscellaneous ferrous scrap were recovered from waste-to-energy plants in 1989, and that roughly 60 percent of it was in the form of cans.[15] In addition, the Steel Can Recycling Institute reports that more than half a million tons of steel cans were recycled in 1989,[16] bringing the total amount of recycled post-consumer ferrous materials closer to 3 million tons.[17]

A major reason that such large discrepancies exist is that all types of ferrous scrap are usually commingled before delivery to steel furnaces, making it difficult to measure post-consumer scrap. In an attempt to clear up the most significant discrepancy—the recycling rate for major appliances—the appliance industry and the American Iron and Steel Institute are joining forces to develop a program to improve tracking methods once appliances leave the home.[18]

The total amount of scrap used in the production of new steel is easier to calculate—52.6 million tons, or nearly 54 percent of the raw steel produced in the United States, in 1989. (Another 12 million tons were exported to foreign mills.)[19] Most steel products contain an average recycled content of at least 25 percent, and many products have 100 percent recycled content.[20]

EPA estimates that the amount of ferrous metals in the waste stream has remained fairly constant over the years, but began to drop during the 1960s and 1970s when aluminum and plastics began displacing both steel and glass. In addition, with the amount of garbage produced growing every year, ferrous metals as a percentage of the waste stream have declined from more than 11 percent in 1960 to 6.5 percent in 1988, according to the EPA. Analysts expect this trend to continue.[21]

In 1990, steel cans, both food and beverage, had a 24.6 percent recycling rate, up 37 percent from 1989. Steel beverage cans had a slightly higher rate of recycling in 1990—33.4 percent, up 55 percent from 1989, and steel food cans had a 25.6 percent recycling rate.[22]

The Post-Consumer Steel Recycling Process

Preparing steel cans for reuse by industry is a simple process. Residential recyclers need only rinse them for cleanliness; they do not have to be delabeled or flattened.[23] (Many processors will flatten steel cans recovered from the waste stream to reduce transportation costs, however.) After employing magnetic separation to ensure that nonferrous materials are removed, the processor or end-user may shred the cans to remove paper labels and other materials. Most contaminants not removed during this process will burn at the high furnace temperatures required to melt steel. Steel cans are detinned or fed directly into the steel furnace. While the aluminum lids of bimetallic cans have been found to be a beneficial heat source for steel production,[24] the aluminum lids of bimetallic cans slated for detinning are magnetically separated. The cans are then detinned in processes that remove tin chemically and electrolytically.[25]

The steel can's magnetic properties provide an advantage over other recyclable products by greatly enhancing the separation process. Magnetization allows automated processing to replace hand sorting, the most common technique for sorting recyclables. Magnetic separation also enables steel products to be easily separated not only from other recyclables, but also from unsorted trash, such as that delivered to waste-to-energy plants. In many instances, ferrous scrap is the only waste steam component being reclaimed at waste-to-energy facilities, both pre- and post-combustion. Magnetic separation at waste-to-energy plants can even enhance the overall steel recovery rate because it pulls out additional steel products not commonly collected in curbside recycling programs. Some waste-to-energy plants, for instance, have reported steel recycling rates of more than 90 percent.[26] There are concerns, however, that steel recovered from waste-to-energy plants before combustion is dirtier and steel recovered after combustion is of lower quality than steel collected through curbside collection programs.[27] One waste processing company reported that nearly half of 24 waste processing plants that separate ferrous metals from the waste stream landfilled the material either because the product was too contaminated or because customers were not available.[28]

While nearly all U.S. steel mills technically are capable of utilizing ferrous scrap from the post-consumer waste stream,[29] until recently most steel mills were reluctant to accept steel cans. The steel industry recently determined, however, that tinned steel can scrap can be used directly by steel mills when blended with other ferrous scrap, particularly when the percentages of steel cans in the feedstock are kept low. One major reason for the increasing acceptance of steel cans is that technology has reduced the average tinplate coating to about 6 pounds per ton, down from pre-World War II levels of about 50 pounds a ton.[30] Steel cans also are now marketed as a separate commodity that can be measured precisely, rather than being hidden in a bale of steel scrap.[31] And lastly, furnace operators have discovered that aluminum lids of bimetallic cans actually enhance the steel manufacturing process.[32]

As mill operators gain experience with steel cans, and with chrome on the rise as a less problematic replacement for the tin in steel cans, mills will continue to increase their consumption of unprocessed steel cans.[33] In contrast to the unlimited number of detinned steel cans that steel mills can accept, however, there still are limits to the number of unprocessed steel cans that mills can consume. These limits, however, are yet to be defined, and a study at the American Iron and Steel Institute is tackling this issue.[34] The appropriate amount is highly dependent on the steel product being manufactured. Richard Jordan, director of municipal recycling for the David J. Joseph Co., the country's largest ferrous scrap broker, estimates that some steel mills will buy unprocessed ferrous scrap recovered from the municipal waste stream for up to 3 percent of their needs in the short term, but that in the long term, ferrous scrap recovered from the waste stream will require processing.[35] Florida Steel Corp. foresees using even greater amounts of unprocessed steel cans, estimating that it will be able to use a minimum 10 percent ratio of "properly processed," but not detinned, ferrous material from the post-consumer waste stream. Today, post-consumer ferrous scrap represents only 1.5 percent of Florida Steel's overall use of ferrous scrap.[36]

Economics of Steel Recycling

Steel is the most recycled material in the country today because the economic benefits associated with using ferrous scrap in the steelmaking process are great. According to the steel industry, using recycled materials in place of virgin materials cuts overall energy usage by three-quarters.[37] (As for the bimetallic soft drink can specifically, the National Soft Drink Association estimates that it takes about half as much energy to manufacture with recycled materials as with virgin materials.[38]) Generally, every ton of steel recycled would save 1,000 pounds of coal and 40 pounds of limestone through lower energy requirements, as well as 2,500 pounds of virgin iron ore. The steel industry also calculates that for every pound of steel recycled, 5,450 Btus of energy are conserved, an amount capable of lighting a 60-watt bulb for more than 24 hours. Through all of its steel recycling efforts, both pre- and post-consumer, the steel industry says it saves an average of 600 trillion Btus each year, enough energy to electrically power more than 18 million households or enough energy to meet the electrical power needs of Los Angeles for more than eight years.[39] The congressional Office of Technology Assessment cautions, however, that these estimates may no longer reflect more efficient industry conditions, given that the Department of Energy developed the basis for them during the 1970s.[40]

EPA also has identified some additional benefits when scrap iron and steel are used instead of virgin materials: 90 percent savings in virgin materials use; 86 percent reduction in air pollution; 40 percent reduction in water use; 76 percent reduction in water pollution; 97 percent reduction in mining wastes; and 105 percent reduction in consumer waste generated.[41]

Used steel can prices: The average price that ferrous scrap processors, who in turn sell the cans to steel mills or detinners, paid for steel cans in 1990 ranged from $64.80 per ton to $71.10 per ton.[42] The price paid for steel cans ranks toward the middle of prices for recyclables commonly collected at curbside. (See Figure I-3 on p. 7 for a comparison of prices.)

In late 1990, steel companies raised the price paid for steel cans. Steel companies had mixed steel cans in with #2 steel scrap but broke out steel cans as a separate product category, which commanded a higher price.[43] Weirton Steel Corp., whose West Virginia steel mill accepts steel can scrap from the public, was the first to boost the price it paid for used bimetallic steel cans by 36 percent to $150 a ton.[44] USX Corp.'s USS Division and Bethlehem Steel Corp. followed suit.[45] Ultimately, however, the potential market for ferrous scrap, including steel cans, depends on the worldwide demand for steel. Analysts expect planned capacity expansion abroad to put downward pressure on U.S. scrap prices and the steel market in general.[46]

Because ferrous scrap has a relatively low value per ton, transportation costs play a pivotal role in the economics of ferrous scrap recycling. Close proximity to an end-user translates into a cost advantage. The locations of the end-users of steel cans are depicted in Figure 3-3.

U.S. Steel Industry's Recycling Initiatives

Steel cans represent a $500 million market for the steel industry,[47] which says it is committed to recycling all of the steel cans it produces.[48] Proclaiming that "there is no logical reason for any steel product to find its way to landfill," the industry has pledged to the public that "the market [for steel cans] will remain strong."[49] The industry also is confident that residential recyclers will participate in steel can recycling programs, noting that Americans demonstrated their ability to recycle steel cans as part of America's defense effort during World War II.[50]

In 1988, the major U.S. tin mill products producers—Bethlehem Steel, LTV Steel Co. Inc., National Steel Corp., the USS Division of USX, Weirton Steel and Wheeling-Pittsburgh Steel Corp.—and two Canadian members, Dofasco Inc. and Stelco Inc., formed the Steel Can Recycling Institute.[51] In what it calls "an unprecedented show of industry-wide unity,"[52] the coalition has committed $30 million through the next four years to promote the steel can.[53]

The steel industry has two primary reasons for promoting steel can recycling: to woo consumers and to service its high scrap purchase requirements. Like the glass container industry, the steel can producers view recyclability as a key factor in regaining market share. The steel can once dominated the entire can market; now it reigns only over the food can market. Steel's domination of the beverage can market began eroding in the 1970s with the advent of the aluminum can, which eventually stole away the market. Competitive pricing and an aggressive marketing campaign by aluminum companies, as well as passage of beverage container deposit acts, contributed to the steel can's decline, with retailers opting for high quality and lighter-weight aluminum containers.

However, the steel industry says that it is well-positioned to rechallenge the aluminum can, maintaining that recent cost reductions are making the steel can more attractive to the beverage industry[54] while "recycling will increase the appeal of steel cans among consumers."[55] To increase public

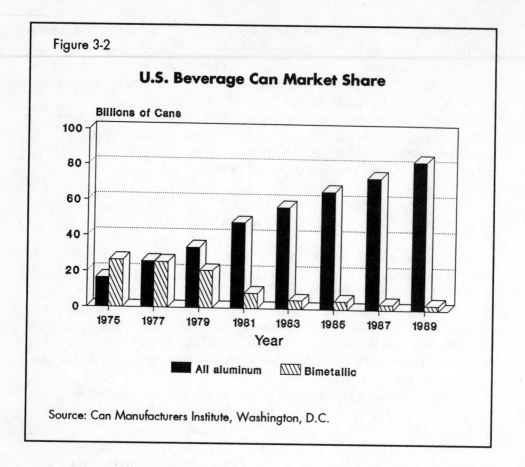

Figure 3-2

U.S. Beverage Can Market Share

Source: Can Manufacturers Institute, Washington, D.C.

awareness of steel's viability as a recyclable material, the Steel Can Recycling Institute and several companies, including Dole Packaged Foods Co., Hormel & Co. and Stokely U.S.A., have begun using the logo "Steel—*the recycled material*" in their advertisements and on their steel can labels.[56] The institute also is labeling steel as "the most environmentally compatible packaging material available,"[57] and the Steel Manufacturing Association is chiming in with its own public relations campaign for the steel can, saying its member companies purchase them whenever possible "to make a significant environmental contribution to their communities."[58]

The other major reason the steel industry welcomes steel can recycling is that improved steelmaking technologies, such as continuous casting, yield less scrap to be funneled back to the production process. During the last 10 years, the steel industry's use of self-generated scrap has decreased from 60.5 percent to 28 percent of the total scrap feed used in mills.[59] As a result, demand for purchased scrap has increased by more than 50 percent during the last decade.[60]

Table 3-1

U.S. Steel Companies Purchasing Steel Can Scrap

Company (Parent)	Private*	Number of Mills Accepting Steel Can Scrap
Acme Steel Co.	NAS	1
Atlantic Steel Co. (Ivaco Inc.)	TOR	1
Auburn Steel Co. Inc. (Sumitomo Corp. & Kyoei Steel Ltd.)	PVT	1
Bayou Steel Corp.	ASE	1
Bethlehem Steel Corp.	NYSE	4
Birmingham Steel Corp.	NYSE	4
Chaparral Steel Co.	NYSE	1
Florida Steel Corp. (FLS Holdings Inc.)	NAS	5
LTV Steel Co. Inc. (LTV Corp.)	NYSE	2
Lukens Steel Co. (Lukens Inc.)	NYSE	1
National Steel Corp. (NII Capital Corp. & NKK USA Corp.)	PVT	2
Newport Steel Corp. (NS Group Inc.)	ASE	1
North Star Steel (Cargill Corp.)	PVT	5
Nucor Steel Corp. (Nucor Corp.)	NYSE	6
Republic Engineered Steels Inc.	PVT	1
Roanoke Electric Steel Corp.	NAS	1
Structural Metals Inc. (Commercial Metals Co.)	NYSE	2
The Timken Co.	NYSE	1
USS Division (USX Corp.)	NYSE	6
Weirton Steel Corp.	NYSE	1
Wheeling-Pittsburgh Steel Corp.	NYSE	1

U.S. Detinning Companies Purchasing Steel Can Scrap

Company	Public/ Private*	Number of Detinning Plants
AMG Resources Corp.	PVT	4
MacLeod Metals Corp.	PVT	1
Proler International Corp.	NYSE	2

* If public, exchange on which company (or parent company) stock is traded.

Sources: Steel Can Recycling Institute, Pittsburgh, Pa., and Investor Responsibility Research Center Inc.

End-users of used steel cans: Steel can recyclers have the advantage of being able to sell steel cans to two primary end-use markets that sometimes find themselves bidding against one another[61]: steel mills, more than 120 of which have operating furnaces throughout the country, and detinners.[62] At least 48 U.S. mills and seven detinning facilities purchase steel cans or the ferrous fraction of the municipal solid waste stream from the public. Approximate locations of these facilities are shown in Figure 3-3. The three detinning companies and 21 steel companies that operate these plants are identified in Table 3-1. The number of end-users continues to increase, as new detinning facilities are opened and additional steel mills establish a policy of purchasing post-consumer ferrous cans and packaging.

U.S. detinning companies have recycled tinplate scrap from tin mills and can manufacturers for decades. With secondary recovery of tin representing the only domestic source of tin in the United States,[63] detinning companies sell reclaimed tin to can manufacturers, the electronics industry and solder manufacturers and for dental applications. These companies also provide detinned scrap to steel mills for new production and, in fewer instances, to copper producers in the Southwest, who use it to precipitate copper from copper sulfate solutions. The copper producers market, however, may decline with the advent of new copper recovery technologies.[64]

AMG Resources Corp. of Pittsburgh, Pa., a privately owned company, is the world's largest detinner and the country's leading processor of ferrous scrap cans. Operating primarily in the East and Midwest, the company operates detinning facilities in Gary, Ind., Baltimore and Pittsburgh, and recently opened the world's first detinning plant dedicated to post-consumer ferrous scrap. While municipal ferrous scrap composes only 6 to 7 percent of the feedstock for the company's first three detinning facilities, a 40,000 ton per year facility opened in St. Paul, Minn., in late October 1990 that is designed to process only used steel cans and other ferrous scrap derived from the municipal waste stream. AMG plans to open a second detinning facility dedicated to post-consumer ferrous scrap in Elizabeth, N.J., at the end of 1991. With the plant sited across from New York City and within reach of the New England market, the company is confident that the 60,000 ton per year plant will have no difficulty finding an adequate amount of feedstock. AMG also is exploring opportunities in California and Florida. Overseas, the company operates two detinning plants in the United Kingdom that accept post-consumer ferrous scrap and recently purchased a 60,000 ton per year detinning facility in Calahorra, Spain, which will add equipment in the near future allowing it to process post-consumer scrap. AMG also has licensed its technology for plants in Greece and Czechoslovakia.[65]

Proler International Corp., traded on the New York Stock Exchange, is the second largest U.S. detinner, and along with its joint venture partners

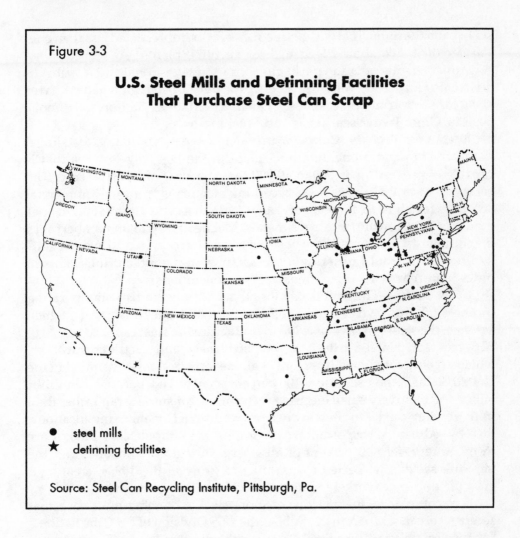

Figure 3-3

U.S. Steel Mills and Detinning Facilities
That Purchase Steel Can Scrap

● steel mills
★ detinning facilities

Source: Steel Can Recycling Institute, Pittsburgh, Pa.

it is the country's largest exporter of ferrous scrap. Proler pioneered the
continuous detinning process in 1975. In the spring of 1991, Proler closed an
18-month-old Houston facility designed to process the equivalent of 2.5
billion tin cans per year, with all feedstock derived from can companies and
municipal waste. Proler reported $2.9 million in losses at the plant, citing
price competition with steel mills. "The use of recycled tin cans and tin-
plated clippings as a feedstock for steel mills...has adversely affected the
Houston facility," said Herman Proler, Proler's chairman of the board.[66]
Before the Houston plant closed, Proler had announced that "solid waste
recycling is anticipated to be a significant long-term activity" for the
company, maintaining that it had the capacity to recycle "a significant
share" of the tin cans discarded each year in the United States. Proler
operates two other detinning plants, in Seattle and Randolph, Ariz. Ferrous

scrap from the municipal waste stream, however, represented less than one-quarter of the combined feedstock of all three plants. To acquire post-consumer ferrous cans and packaging, Proler International and its subsidiaries, MRI Corp. and Prolerized Steel Corp., developed regional markets for steel cans covering nine states: Alabama, Arizona, California, Illinois, Kansas, Ohio, Tennessee, Texas and Washington.[67]

MacLeod Metals Corp., a privately owned company, is a third detinner. It operates one detinning plant in the Los Angeles area that is capable of processing 36,000 to 40,000 tons per year of ferrous scrap. The company says that it has been accepting steel cans from its commercial accounts for eight to 10 years and that it now accepts up to 600 tons per month of post-consumer ferrous metals. MacLeod's William Lambert says the company will take "all [the post-consumer ferrous metals] we can get," adding that it would turn down can scrap from manufacturing plants in order to purchase the less expensive post-consumer scrap.[68]

Steel mills—The country's more than 120 steel mills with operating furnaces fall into two categories: the older major integrated mills, which produce the steel can sheet used to manufacture the steel can, and use 20 to 30 percent scrap infeed in the basic oxygen furnace; and electric arc furnaces, which account for about 60 percent of all the ferrous scrap consumed in the United States,[69] and use close to 100 percent scrap infeed. Because minimills, which use relatively small electric arc furnaces, consume scrap rather than iron ore, they can be located away from traditional steelmaking locations, thereby reducing transportation costs for ferrous scrap dealers. Electric arc furnaces represent 40 percent of all steel production nationally, and the minimill sector is expected to continue to grow in the 1990s, creating a growing domestic market for steel cans collected by recyclers.[70]

Five companies operate four or more steel producing mills each that accept steel can scrap from the public: the USS Division of USX, the nation's largest steelmaker; Nucor Steel Corp., a subsidiary of Nucor Corp.; Florida Steel Corp., a subsidiary of FSL Holdings Inc.; North Star Steel, a subsidiary of Cargill Corp.; Bethlehem Steel; and Birmingham Steel Corp. All five of the steel producing mills owned by **USS** purchase steel can scrap, as does its joint venture with Kobe Steel in Lorain, Ohio. USS's largest plant in Gary, Ind., has recycled 30,000 tons of steel cans over the last three years, yet ferrous metal from the post-consumer waste stream represents less than 1 percent of scrap usage at all six of the USS mills.[71] USS also is involved in the Coinbak program, a reverse vending machine program that collects steel and aluminum beverage cans.

Florida Steel's five mills accepted a total of 17,000 tons of post-consumer ferrous scrap in 1989. The company's two steel mills in Florida—a state with a high number of waste-to-energy projects that are capable of pulling ferrous metals out of the waste stream—purchased nearly all of the scrap—14,000 tons.[72] All five of **Nucor Steel**'s steel mills accept steel can scrap.[73] **Bethlehem Steel**, which in late 1989 recycled its one billionth steel can at its Sparrows Point, Md., plant, has four of its five steel producing mills accepting steel can scrap. Although Bethlehem Steel does not keep statistics specifically on post-consumer ferrous metals, it does report that in the first seven months of 1990 it recycled roughly 76,000 gross tons of used steel cans and detinned scrap from manufacturing plants. In 1989, the company recycled 141,000 gross tons of used steel cans and detinned scrap, which represented 36 percent of its total tin mill product shipments.[74]

The 2,000 iron and steel foundries across the United States constitute an emerging market for used steel cans. Foundries fabricate cast and molded parts for industrial use, using 30 to 40 percent purchased scrap. Only a handful have bought steel products derived from the municipal waste stream to date, but the Steel Can Recycling Institute says many are beginning to view steel cans as a valuable raw material source. Given that foundries are more geographically dispersed across the country than steel mills or detinning facilities, they represent a potentially widespread market for steel cans.[75]

In addition to domestic uses, some steel cans are being exported overseas, but only when mixed in with other metal scrap.[76] Because the U.S. supply of ferrous scrap far outweighs domestic demand, a well-developed international market for steel scrap exists. Consistent demand for the scrap comes from industrialized but still less-developed nations, such as India or Korea, that do not generate enough scrap domestically to meet their own needs.

Additional collection methods: In addition to selling steel cans directly to a detinner, steel mill or export market, a large infrastructure of scrap dealers already is in place. Located close to population centers, scrap dealers frequently help to shorten shipping distances between recyclers and end users. Many of the more than 1,500 ferrous scrap dealers throughout the country are beginning to expand their traditional services and serve as intermediate processors for steel cans. David J. Joseph Co., for instance, the country's largest broker and processor of ferrous scrap, formed a municipal recycling division in late 1989 to handle scrap collected from materials recovery facilities, curbside programs and waste-to-energy plants.[77]

One of the most comprehensive collection systems for steel beverage cans has been implemented by Bev-Pak of Monticello, Ind., a steel can production company that produces about 1.5 billion beverage cans a year—nearly 40 percent of the steel beverage can market. Established in 1987 by a former general manager of the tin plate division of USX Corp., Bev-Pak created a recycling division—Recycle Indiana Resources—and now has two mobile scrap units and 830 buy-back centers throughout the Midwest. The division also has formed a partnership with an Indianapolis affiliate of Keep

America Beautiful to form a citywide "Cash for Trash" recycling program.[78]

Additional collection systems for post-consumer ferrous materials in the municipal waste stream include curbside recycling, municipal drop-off and buy-back centers and reverse vending machines. (See Chapter 6 for a fuller discussion of collection methods.) The Steel Can Recycling Institute endorses curbside recycling as the most effective method of residental recycling and favors commingled recycling collection over source separated pick-up service.[79] The steel industry reports that 97 percent of materials recovery facilities, which process curbside recyclables, process steel cans.[80] As for reverse vending machines, the Coinbak program, a cooperative effort of EMRO Marketing Co., Marathon Oil Co., Nationwide Recyclers, Crown Cork & Seal Co. and USX Corp.'s USS Division, placed reverse vending machines at 218 convenience stores in the eastern United States. Coinbak machines return one penny for every can, steel or aluminum, deposited.[81]

Future Market for Post-Consumer Ferrous Metals

The key to increasing post-consumer ferrous metals recycling rates lies in creating an ancillary collection infrastructure that will feed ferrous materials from the municipal waste stream into the vast steel scrap collection network already in place. The steel can is the primary focus of the steel industry's post-consumer recycling efforts even though durable steel goods, primarily major appliances, represent more than three-quarters of ferrous metals in the post-consumer waste stream, according to EPA.[82] The steel industry believes that major appliances are already recycled at the high rate of 75 percent—a claim disputed by EPA.[83] Nonetheless, the industry believes that most ferrous materials in the United States are being recycled at high rates and that the steel can represents one of the few sources of ferrous scrap that has the potential to increase its rate of recycling significantly. William Heenan Jr., president of the Steel Can Recycling Institute, told IRRC that the steel can is the "only one [type of ferrous material] with a great opportunity to get new scrap."[84]

The Steel Can Recycling Institute has its work cut out for it. The steel can typically has been among the last of the waste stream components to be included in community recycling programs; most communities have begun with the traditional trio of paper, glass and aluminum, which had the first established markets. The institute is banking on the future inclusion of steel cans in commingled curbside recycling to boost their recycling rate. The substantial price increase for steel cans is a real boost to this effort, enticing municipalities to add steel to their recycling programs.

Unlike used aluminum cans, the bulk of which are remade into aluminum cans, can sheet producers are not targeting the purchase of used steel cans. (Given that steel can sheet is produced at integrated steel mills, which use only 20 to 30 percent ferrous scrap, all steel cans could never be made back into steel cans.) Instead, steel cans generally are mixed in with other ferrous scrap to produce a variety of steel products.

The Steel Can Recycling Institute is confident that U.S. steelmakers are prepared to recycle "each and every steel can sold in America," describing steel cans as the "new raw material 'mine' for steel production."[85] Heenan says that efficiency improvements within the industry are reducing the amount of scrap generated in-house and are forcing mills to look outside industry to meet their scrap requirements. Saying that steel cans are "material we really need," Heenan added that the decline in internal scrap "opens up more doors for post-consumer scrap."[86] The institute also says that as mill operators gain experience with unprocessed steel cans, some advantages associated with using them in place of other types of ferrous scrap are coming to light. When steel cans are delivered in large bundles, for instance, mills view the uniform nature of these deliveries as a benefit. The steel industry also values the high quality of the metal found in steel cans.[87]

A larger question for the U.S. steel industry is whether increasing post-consumer steel recycling will eventually produce an increase in the country's overall steel recycling rate, or whether steel cans and other ferrous scrap from the municipal waste stream will simply replace other scrap in the manufacturing process. In an editorial in *Iron Age*, George McManus, the journal's steel editor, questions whether there is "some inherent ceiling on scrap usage." Noting that the U.S. steel industry is already failing to recycle as much scrap as it is generating each year, and that the scrap portion of steel melt has been constant over the last 50 years despite dramatic changes in steel technology, McManus questions whether the additional supply of steel cans actually will translate into increased scrap consumption domestically. McManus concludes that "there doesn't seem to be any basic reason for a rigid ceiling on scrap usage. It's a fact, however, that the scrap rate hasn't exceeded a certain maximum for the last half century."[88]

Chapter IV
POST-CONSUMER PAPER
AND PAPERBOARD

Waste paper is the number one U.S. export by weight[1]—a fact that has earned the United States the title "the Saudi Arabia of waste paper."[2] Even though the United States recovers only about one-third of the paper it consumes each year and exports only 22 percent of the amount it recovers, the sheer volume of waste paper produced in this country catapults it to the top of the list of U.S. exports. Although other materials commonly found in the waste stream have higher rates of recycling than paper, the vast amount of paper used makes it the most recycled material in the United States and in the world. In the United States, paper accounts for more than 80 percent of all post-consumer material recovered for recycling.[3]

The paper industry's goal is to raise the overall waste paper collection rate from nearly 34 percent in 1990 to 40 percent, or 40 million tons, by 1995. Achieving this goal requires a 50 percent increase over 1988 paper recovery levels, and the industry says that nearly 90 percent of the increased tonnage will need to come from the post-consumer waste stream.[4] Paper usage continues to grow, though, leading some analysts to predict that the 40 percent recycling goal is unlikely to eliminate even a single ton from the 60 million tons of paper now landfilled or incinerated each year.[5]

Integrating post-consumer waste materials into the production process is a more costly proposition for the paper and paperboard industry than for other industries. While all industries encounter costs in preparing a recycled feedstock for industrial use, paper and paperboard mills have to add capital-intensive waste paper repulping and cleaning equipment. In the case of paper production, industry also needs to remove ink from waste paper, and the limited number of U.S. de-inking facilities already are operating at full capacity. The American Paper Institute (API) estimates that a multi-billion investment in recycling facilities, including de-inking projects, will be needed to reach the 40 percent recycling goal; newsprint mills alone have spent or committed $1.5 billion dollars on recycling projects.[6]

Because the paper industry has to commit large amounts of capital in order to boost its use of recycled paper, the industry waited to be convinced that the nationwide recycling fervor was not a passing trend. Moreover, whereas the aluminum, glass and steel industries readily can integrate reclaimed materials into existing facilities, permitting and building new de-inking facilities takes between 18 months and three years, creating a delay before paper mills can use more waste paper. Ira Stone, senior vice president of Stone Container Corp., explained that "timing alone leads to inevitable [market] dislocations."[7] The resulting delays in its ability to use more waste paper, however, have made the paper industry the target of criticism by those eager to step up recycling efforts. In 1989, dislocations in the market for used newspapers gained nationwide attention as newspapers collected through curbside recycling programs began piling up in warehouses with nowhere to go. Public attention translated into mounting political pressure for newspaper publishers to increase the amount of recycled fiber in their papers. In fact, many of the newsprint industry's recycling projects are an effort to comply with a spate of newsprint recycling legislation at the federal, state and county levels and to head off similar initiatives elsewhere. Calling newsprint "the nation's No. 1 recycling problem," Rep. Richard Schulze (R-Pa.) introduced a bill in September 1990 to provide economic incentives for recycling newsprint and stiff penalties for newspapers that failed to boost recycled content.[8] At the state level, specific percentages of recycled content in newspapers have been mandated in California, Connecticut, Maryland, Missouri, Wisconsin and Suffolk County, N.Y. Voluntary agreements have been struck with newspaper publishers in Iowa, New York, Pennsylvania, Massachusetts, Michigan and Vermont.[9]

The need to build new de-inking and recycling capacity in order to use waste paper as a feedstock for papermaking comes at an inopportune time for the U.S. paper industry. The industry has been struggling with overcapacity, largely the result of a round of construction of virgin paper plants, that is not scheduled to wind down until the end of 1991. Development of these plants began in the mid-1980s when paper prices were rising steadily and before municipalities began supplying a steady stream of waste paper. In the case of newsprint, the market for recycled newsprint had been flat for a decade. Today, the newsprint industry also faces the added obstacle of decreased revenues resulting from a slump in the number of advertising pages.[10]

In addition to the capital costs involved, substituting waste paper for virgin fiber requires major changes in the way paper companies operate. Characterized by large and costly plants, the U.S. paper industry tends to adapt to change slowly. Moreover, the major paper companies are vertically integrated, growing the trees they make into paper in rural areas. Mills that are older, too small to make de-inking cost effective or located far from the new supplies of used waste paper will have difficulty staying in business. Siting new mills in urban areas closer to the growing feedstock of waste paper poses its own problems, including higher land values, stricter environmental regulations, higher energy costs and potential citizen opposition to proposed plant sites.[11]

Canadian newsprint mills, which supply about 53 percent of the newsprint consumed in the United States[12] and are located in remote areas near virgin forests, face the greatest challenges in boosting the use of waste paper. Not only will it cost them more to import old newspapers from large metropolitan areas, but also Canadian newsprint producers are building most of the virgin pulp newsprint capacity in the current expansion boom.[13] Other older Canadian mills, with less than 25 more years of life expectancy, make the huge capital investment required for using recycled materials difficult to justify economically.[14]

Despite all of these obstacles, building de-inking plants is simply becoming a cost of doing business. API says that the growth in virgin capacity is slowing and that waste paper consumption in domestic mills is expected to grow at a rate more than twice that of virgin fiber in the near future.[15] "Even if it's unprofitable, we have to get into recycling," says Charles-Albert Poissant, chairman and chief executive office of Donahue Inc., a Canadian newsprint company. Poissant says he regrets spending $70 million on a recent upgrade of a virgin pulp mill, explaining that if the company's newsprint machine uses de-inked pulp from newspapers, the virgin pulp mill would have to operate at a lower capacity, raising costs. Donahue also faces the extra costs of getting the de-inked pulp to Canada.[16]

Keith Winrow, vice president of corporate development at Canadian Pacific Forest Products, says there may be some return on investment in a de-inking plant in the form of lower raw material costs for those newsprint mills that pay higher-than-average costs for wood pulp. But otherwise, says Winrow, "there's no payback, it's just money out of your pocket."[17] Carl Landegger, chairman of the Black Clawson Co., one of the nation's largest manufacturers of recycling equipment, sees the situation differently. "Some newsprint producers may see this [spending money on a de-inking facility] as an investment with zero return, but the payoff on the recycling investment can be measured in terms of protecting or increasing market share in a changing environment."[18]

Consumer demand has a greater ability to play a role in paper recycling than it does in the recycling of other waste stream materials. Because paper is sold as a product, and is not limited to packaging material, consumers can signal an unmistakable preference for recycled content by purchasing recycled paper products rather than virgin paper products. (In the case of packaging material, such as aluminum cans or glass bottles, consumers generally lack information on the recycled content of these containers. Moreover, purchasing decisions generally are based on the product within the container, not on the recycled content of its packaging.)

Consumers are increasing their purchases of recycled paper products, and the Environmental Protection Agency is attempting to use the government's clout as a major paper consumer by setting guidelines on the waste paper content of paper products. (EPA's efforts, however, have drawn mixed reviews. See Box 4-2 for more information on EPA's paper procurement guidelines.) Paper consumers are discovering that many concerns about the substandard quality of recycled paper are outdated; technological improvements have made recycled and virgin paper virtually indistinguishable in many instances. The American Newspaper Publishers Association completed a three-year test project in the fall of 1990 that concluded there are no significant differences between recycled and virgin newsprint.[19]

Paper and Paperboard in the Municipal Waste Stream

Americans use an average of 600 pounds of paper per person each year.[20] Paper's total share of the municipal waste stream grew from 34 percent, or 30 million tons, in 1960 to 40 percent in 1988.[21] In 1988, paper products represented the largest portion of the waste stream—40 percent by weight, or 71.8 million tons. EPA classifies more than half of the waste paper as nondurable goods, including newspapers, books and magazines, and nearly 46 percent as containers and packaging, such as boxes and milk cartons. As for individual products, nearly one-third of the waste paper in the municipal waste stream is corrugated, or cardboard, containers. Newsprint comprises the second largest amount of waste paper in the waste stream, representing 18.5 percent of all waste paper. Office papers rank third, representing more than 10 percent of all waste paper.[22]

API reports that the overall recovery rate of waste paper, including waste paper recovered from manufacturing and converting processes, reached a record level of 33.5 percent in 1990, representing 28.9 million tons. (About 22.4 million tons were used in the United States, and 6.5 million tons were exported.[23]) The overall recovery rate was 32.4 percent in 1989, representing 27.3 million tons[24], up from 29.9 percent, or 26 million tons, in 1988.[25] Of the nearly 30 million tons recovered in 1990, about 75 percent, or 22 million tons, was post-consumer paper.[26]

About one-quarter of the raw material used to manufacture paper and paperboard in the United States is waste paper, including paper that never leaves the mills or processing facilities.[27] API estimates that by 1993 waste

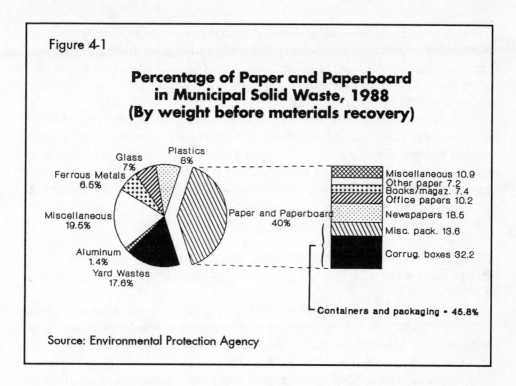

Figure 4-1

**Percentage of Paper and Paperboard
in Municipal Solid Waste, 1988
(By weight before materials recovery)**

Glass 7%
Ferrous Metals 6.5%
Plastics 8%
Miscellaneous 19.5%
Aluminum 1.4%
Yard Wastes 17.6%
Paper and Paperboard 40%

Miscellaneous 10.9
Other paper 7.2
Books/magaz. 7.4
Office papers 10.2
Newspapers 18.5
Misc. pack. 13.6
Corrug. boxes 32.2

Containers and packaging - 45.8%

Source: Environmental Protection Agency

paper could climb to 29.3 percent of all fiber used in production.[28] Today, the paperboard segment uses the greatest volume of waste paper, approximately 34.1 percent of total fiber requirements in 1986, compared with 13.8 percent for the paper segment.[29] Another 30 percent of the paper and paperboard industry's raw material usage is waste wood from manufacturing processes and forest residues, bringing the total amount of industry's raw materials derived from waste materials to about 55 percent.[30]

Recycling goals: API's goal is for the U.S. paper and paperboard industry to recover 40 percent of the nation's waste paper, or 40 million tons, by 1995. API estimates that 70 percent or more of the waste paper recovered will be consumed by U.S. mills, and the remainder will be exported to foreign recycling mills.[31] The U.S. paper and paperboard industry recognizes 49 grades of waste paper and 31 other specialty grades,[32] all of which can be classified into five major categories. Specific recycling goals for the five major categories are shown in Table 4-1, along with API's estimates of 1988 recycling rates. Corrugated refers to old corrugated containers used to ship merchandise, cuttings generated from the manufacturing process, and other kraft paper, such as grocery bags. Newsprint is old newspapers, and pulp substitutes are a combination of paper and paperboard trimmings from paper mills and converting plants that offer the highest quality fiber to recyclers. High-grade de-inking paper generally requires de-inking before it is reused in papermaking and is composed primarily of bleached paper that has been discarded from data processing centers, printing and converting operations and office recycling programs. Mixed papers is a "catch-all" category including colored papers, envelopes, magazines and food packaging generally collected from offices.[33]

API believes that once the overall 40 percent goal is achieved, further growth in paper recycling (with the exception of mixed waste paper) will be limited by the ability to collect sufficient quantities of the grades producers demand. API attributes the small increase between the 1988 and 1995 recovery rates of mixed paper primarily to the technological difficulties of recycling mixed papers, not to the ability to collect it.[34]

The Post-Consumer Paper and Paperboard Recycling Process

In contrast to glass recycling, paper recycling is not generally, and cannot in the long-term, be a closed-loop process. While a select group of paper and paperboard manufacturers use 100 percent recycled fibers, most paper manufacturers continually infuse virgin fiber to upgrade the quality of the end product. Each time paper is repulped, the cellulose fiber is weakened and shortened, degrading its quality. Eventually the paper is no longer recyclable.[35] Estimates of the maximum number of times paper can be recycled range from four to eight.[36] Currently, about 10 percent of the paper that goes into a mill is lost in processing.[37]

The difference between manufacturing paper from recycled paper or from virgin materials lies in the fiber preparation; otherwise, the manufacturing process is the same. To recover the fiber in waste paper in the municipal solid waste stream, the paper first needs to be separated from other materials in the waste stream. For the most part, paper is sorted manually; mechanizing the separation process has had limited success so far. (In 1990, Waste Management Inc. began using technology at a Florida materials recovery facility that mechanically separates paper from heavier recyclables. See Chapter 6 for more information.)

Separating scrap paper by grade is as important to the paper industry as separating glass by color is to the glass industry or plastic by resin type is to the plastics industry. The various waste paper grades do not easily lend themselves to making different types of new products. Old newspapers, for example, are used primarily to make new newsprint and recycled paperboard; old corrugated containers to make recycled containerboard or packaging papers; high-grade de-inking papers and pulp substitutes to make tissue and printing or writing papers, and mixed papers to make recycled construction board, other buildings products, and paperboard.[38] If waste

Table 4-1

Recycling Rates and Goals
for the
Five Principal Grades of Waste Paper

Grade of Waste Paper	1988 Recycling Rate % (millions of tons)		1995 Goal % (millions of tons)	
Corrugated	50.0%	(12.4)	66.0%	(15.98)
Newsprint	34.8%	(4.8)	51.6%	(8.0)
Pulp substitutes	100.0%	(3.6)	100.0%	(4.3)
Mixed papers	13.0%	(2.9)	15.0%	(4.1)
High grade de-inking paper	37.0%	(2.5)	50.0%	(4.3)

Source: "Key Questions and Answers on Paper Recycling," American Paper Institute Inc., New York, N.Y.

paper is not separated, it will qualify only as the lowest grade of paper within the mix.

As with other recyclables, contamination of the paper degrades the value of the product to industry. Jefferson Smurfit Corp. and Sonoco Products Co. have publicly complained about the quality of paper collected from municipal recycling programs.[39] As a result of commingling recyclables picked up at curbside, waste paper can become contaminated with broken glass, metals and plastic. In addition, waste paper that comes into contact with food waste can become soiled with odor and bacteria. Additional contaminants include non-water soluble adhesives, rubber bands, asphalt, string and carbon paper. Plastic coated and laminated papers also can cause serious problems in the recycling process. Waste paper dealers focus on removing non-fibrous materials called "tramp" materials, such as metals and plastic, but other contaminants that are an integral part of the paper, such as staples, inks and coatings, are removed during the repulping and cleaning processes in the recycling mill.[40] Paper bales usually are allowed to contain between 1 and 10 percent of outthrows (papers of a lesser grade than the bale as a whole) and contaminants.[41]

Once separated by grade, the paper is sometimes shredded and baled and then shipped to mills for manufacture into new paper or paperboard. Some recycling mills are equipped to receive loose waste paper from nearby sources, eliminating the cost of baling. Waste paper that arrives at the mill is ground up and then transferred by conveyor belt to a beater, or hydra-pulper, where the paper is immersed in water and torn apart by rotating steel blades. The resulting slurry is run through a series of screen and gravity separation devices known as cyclones to remove impurities. If the resulting mixture, known as stock, is to be made into paperboard, it is ready to be manufactured. If the stock is to be made into paper, it then must be de-inked.[42]

There are two de-inking methods: wash and flotation. The wash method fires the stock at a rapidly moving wire screen, which traps the fibers. Much of the ink is carried off in the water forced through the screen. Flotation technologies hold the stock in a tank in which chemicals are added. The ink particles adhere to air bubbles, which are injected from the bottom, rise to the surface, and are skimmed off. Because neither de-inking process effectively removes all inks used today, most new installations will employ both types.[43]

A welcome discovery for municipalities hard-pressed to find markets for old magazines is that magazines are a useful raw material in flotation de-inking technologies. Magazines have a high clay content, and the ink clings to clay particles that float in the batch, making it easier to skim the ink off.[44] Flotation cleaning systems appear to work best when coated papers repre-sent about 20 to 30 percent of the fiber feedstock.[45] In contrast, wash flotation technologies consider the high clay content of magazines a contaminant and use 100 percent paper.[46]

De-inking technologies typically can remove a maximum of 90 to 95 percent of the ink from pulp. To meet consumer demand for bright, white paper, most processes bleach the pulp following the de-inking stage, often using chlorine or hydrogen peroxide. Because chlorine is associated with dioxin emissions, more papermakers are shifting to hydrogen peroxide.[47] In addition, recycling mills use 75 percent less bleach than mills using virgin feedstock, and there is less opportunity for dioxin formation in the recycling paper process overall because virtually all of the lignin (an ingredient in wood that interacts with chlorine to produce dioxin) has been removed.[48]

Sludge created during the manufacturing process of recycled paper contains not only ink residues, but also fillers, clays, fiber fragments and other materials.[49] Because clay coatings become part of the leftover sludge, more material is lost during processing when magazines are included in the feedstock; the loss of material increases to around 35 percent from the approximately 10 percent noted earlier.[50] Moreover, the clay coating can contain heavy metals, as can the ink, which also ends up in the sludge. In the past, inks have contained high concentrations of lead, chromium, cadmium and other heavy metals that produce color. Recently, however, toxic agents in inks have been reduced because of new EPA standards for ink-manufac-turing air emissions and water effluents. If the sludge contains toxic levels,

---

Box 4-1
Technological Innovations in the Recycling Process

Chesapeake Corp., a Richmond, Va., papermaker, and Stake Technologies, a Toronto firm, have joined forces to pursue a new method of recycling paper. The joint venture—Recoupe Recycling Technologies—is marketing a steam explosion system that recycles newsprint, office waste and corrugated cardboard. An influx of oxygen joins waste paper under high pressure in a chamber, creating an explosion that produces pulp that can be made into bags, towels and tissues. Stake Technologies developed the technology in the 1970s to process biomass, such as wood chips and straw. A system costs about two-thirds the amount of conventional paper recycling alternatives—$40 million versus $60 million—and can be set up in six to eight months, versus 18 months to two years for competing technologies. The process also reduces water, energy and chemical use, according to the joint venture. The technology's first commercial application will be in a Canadian mill, and Recoupe Recycling Technologies also plans to build a U.S. pilot plant in 1991. Consumers Paper Corp. of Calgary will use the process to produce 100 percent recycled tissue paper and toweling from office grade waste paper. The venture also hopes to market the technology to municipalities, which could produce pulp for sale to paper companies.[51]

Other technological innovations, including new chemical processes, are enabling the industry to undertake more recycling efforts. Mills are currently addressing problems associated with de-inking laser-printed and xerographic-printed papers.[52] With some conventional de-inking systems, 25 percent of the ink removed from laser-printed paper still slips through the screens at a paper mill and contaminates the end product. PPG Industries Inc. of Pittsburgh, Pa., a $5 billion company that has been supplying chemicals to the paper industry for 50 years, recently introduced a proprietary mix of chemicals that it says cleans up as much as 96 percent of the ink in laser-printed computer printouts.[53]

---

it is required to be disposed of in a hazardous waste landfill. Sludge from many de-inking facilities has tested non-toxic even under strict state regulations and is prized by farmers as a clay-heavy soil conditioner. Many tout waste paper recycling as the most ecologically safe way to handle potential toxic materials in waste paper.[54]

Environmental groups also support waste paper recycling because producing paper from waste paper creates less air and water pollution than producing paper from virgin timber. EPA projects that one ton of recycled paper results in 74 percent less air pollution and 35 percent less water pollution.[55]

The papermaking process reaches temperatures of 350 degrees Fahrenheit, so recycled boxboard is considered reasonably safe from normal contamination and can be used in food packaging—a significant market for paper products. The Food and Drug Administration has approved the use of recycled paper for all packaging provided that it does not contain poisonous or deleterious substances.[56]

Economics of Paper and Paperboard Recycling

The U.S. paper and paperboard industry manufactures a number of products with recycled waste paper. The paperboard segment of the industry uses the bulk of the waste paper consumed by the industry—nearly 70 percent—to make products such as corrugated boxes; recycled paperboard (cereal and soap boxes); cushioning material for packaging and shipping merchandise; and molded products, such as egg cartons and flower pots.[57]

Table 4-2 lists the amount of waste paper used to produce four main categories of paperboard in 1986: unbleached kraft, which is used as the outer facing to make corrugated and solid fiber boxes; semi-chemical, which is used primarily as corrugating medium—the fluted, middle layer in corrugated cardboard; bleached paperboard, which is converted into packages such as milk cartons for moist or oily foods and liquids; and recycled paperboard, which is used to make folding cartons and rigid boxes, other packaging and what are commonly referred to as "cardboard" products. As Table 4-2 shows, recycled paperboard is the largest consumer of waste paper, accounting for nearly half of all waste paper consumption in 1986.[58] Recycled paperboard also is the largest user of mixed waste paper and the second largest user of old newspapers.[59]

Paper products made from recycled waste paper include newspapers; printing and writing papers; kraft paper, a category that includes brown grocery bags and shipping sacks used to package bulk products; and tissues, including toilet and facial tissues, towels, napkins, diapers and other sanitary products. Tissue production uses a substantial amount of waste paper. As Table 4-2 shows, tissue consumed approximately 45 percent of the waste paper made into paper products in 1986.[60]

In addition to the products already mentioned, nearly a million tons of waste paper, primarily old newspapers, are used annually as raw material for construction products, including insulation, gypsum wallboard, roofing paper, flooring, padding and sound-absorbing materials,[61] as well as for animal bedding and mulch.

As mentioned previously, the various paper grades cannot produce

Table 4-2

Waste Paper Used as Raw Material
in Paper and Paperboard Mills
1986 Data Thousands of Short Tons[a]

End Product	Total U.S. Production[b]	Total New Supply[c]	Total Waste Paper Consumption[d]
TOTAL ALL GRADES	72,908	80,122[d]	17,800
TOTAL PAPER	35,443	45,203	4,900
Newsprint	5,630	12,994	1,400
Printing, Writing & Related	19,601	21,989	1,000
Unbleached Kraft Pkg. Ind.			
Conv. Special Industrial & Other	5,117	5,076	300
Tissue	5,095	5,144	2,200
TOTAL PAPERBOARD	35,419	32,873	12,000
Unbleached Kraft	17,689	15,689	1,600
Solid Bleached	4,271	3,862	0
Semi-Chemical	5,376	5,264	1,700
Recycled	8,083	8,058	8,700
CONSTRUCTION PAPER & BOARD & OTHER	2,046	2,046	900

[a]2,000 lbs = 1 ton
[b]Preliminary
[c]Total production plus imports less exports
[d]Includes imports less exports of products

Source: American Paper Institute Inc., New York, N.Y.

paper and paperboard products interchangeably. Specific grades are best utilized for specific products. A brief description of four principal grades of waste paper, as well as old magazines, and the products for which they can serve as a raw material follows. (Pulp substitutes, the fifth principal grade of waste paper, has a 100 percent recycling rate and is not discussed.)

Old corrugated containers: Old corrugated containers are the largest single source of waste paper. (See Table 4-1.) These containers primarily are used to produce new corrugated containers but also are recycled into paperboard, hand towels and industrial wipes, and insulation.

For years, retail stores, supermarkets and factories have separated and sold used corrugated boxes for profit. In 1990, more than half of these boxes, or 13 million tons, were recycled. The bulk, around 10.5 million tons, was consumed in the United States.[62] Moreover, an additional 1.6 million tons per year of old corrugated container recycling capacity is scheduled to come on-line in the United States between 1990 and 1993.[63] If all of the announced capacity comes on-line and the export market stays strong, analysts are predicting a shortfall of old corrugated containers in the next three to five years and expect to see the containerboard, boxboard and export markets fighting for a limited amount of old corrugated containers. In order to meet projected demand, the old corrugated container recycling rate will have to increase to 60 percent by 1994.[64]

Old newspapers: The more than 13 million tons of newspaper discarded in 1988 represented 7.4 percent of the municipal waste stream, making newspapers one of the waste stream's largest single components.[65] In 1990, collection of old newspapers reached a record high of almost 6 million tons, increasing the recycling rate to nearly 45 percent. Figure 4-2 depicts the major uses of old newspaper in 1990, which included newsprint; paperboard, such as folding cartons; paper, such as tissue; construction paper and board, such as wallboard; and other products such as insulation, molded egg cartons and animal bedding.[66] (An additional unknown amount of old newspapers were burned in fireplaces or wood stoves and were not available for recycling.) Other potential uses for recovered old newspapers include roadside mulch, panels for car doors, cat litter, fire logs, hand towels and industrial wipes and computer printouts. Research also is underway to make fuel pellets from old newspapers as a new energy source and to convert newspapers into ethanol.

As Figure 4-2 shows, newsprint is the primary market for old newspapers. But all uses of old newspapers must be explored in the short-term in order to utilize the amounts that Americans are willing to collect. A significant increase in the supply of old newspapers in 1988 and 1989 led to a glut of newspapers, particularly on the East Coast.[67] Yet despite limitations on the amount of old newspapers that industry can use, community recycling programs fear adverse publicity and a drop in participation rates if they stop collecting newspapers. Moreover, new curbside recycling programs beginning operation during the newspaper glut invariably included newspapers despite the glut. Accordingly, the number of newspapers being collected will continue to climb along with the number of new curbside recycling programs, but any new recycling programs collecting newspapers without first having identified markets will only further saturate the overall used newspaper market.[68]

Over the longer term, analysts are predicting dramatic changes in the used newspaper market. They say that if all the planned capacity to utilize old newspapers comes on-line, demand for old newspapers could exceed supply by the mid-1990s.[69]

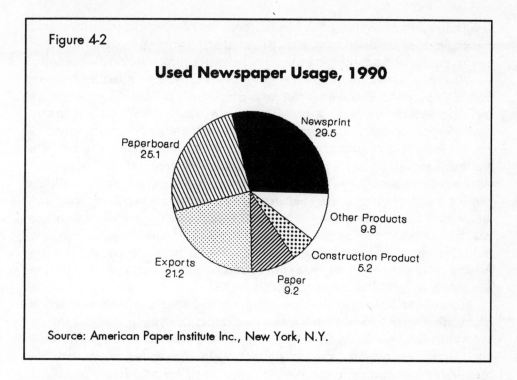

Figure 4-2

Used Newspaper Usage, 1990

Newsprint
29.5

Paperboard
25.1

Other Products
9.8

Construction Product
5.2

Exports
21.2

Paper
9.2

Source: American Paper Institute Inc., New York, N.Y.

Newsprint—Newsprint is and will remain the major market for old newspapers. "If any headway is made in old news, it will be in making new news," remarked Terry Grist, an EPA project manager.[70] Newsprint is relatively easy to recycle since it contains little or no fillers or chemicals.[71] The primary constraint to producing more newsprint from old newspaper is the scarcity of newsprint de-inking facilities.

About 30 key North American newsprint executives surveyed in the spring of 1990 for the Black Clawson Co. predicted that the 1990 newsprint-to-newsprint recycling rate of 11 percent will rise to 33 percent by 1995 and to 41 percent by the year 2000. The executives predicted the recycling rate then will level off because of supply constraints.[72]

On Earth Day, April 22, 1990, the American Newspaper Publishers Association set a goal of increasing recycled newsprint to 28 percent of the total by 1992.[73] Also in the spring of 1990, the National Solid Wastes Management Association estimated that the recycled content of newsprint will rise from 9 percent in 1988 to 16 percent in 1992, to 25 percent in 1995 and to 40 percent by the year 2000.[74]

Paperboard—The use of old newspapers in paperboard and packaging materials has remained fairly constant in the last several years and is expected to grow 2 percent annually through the decade.[75] The amount of old newspapers that can be used in the manufacture of linerboard (the outer facing used to make boxes) is limited because of strength considerations. Newspaper's fibers are too short to provide the strength needed for linerboard, but small amounts can be used without affecting the board's strength.[76]

Paper—Tissue manufacturers say tissue products must be soft and bright to please consumers—characteristics that are not old newspapers' forte. It is technically possible to produce tissue from old newsprint, however, particularly if major purchasers were to adjust product specifications.[77] Nearly all commercial tissue, which is used outside the home at stadiums and other public places, is made from 100 percent recycled paper.[78]

Construction products—The use of old newspaper in building products is declining, in part because of competition from fiberglass insulation and the substitution of other grades of waste paper.[79] Few technical constraints exist to using additional old newspapers in construction materials, but quality requirements can be a major obstacle. Most recycling programs in metropolitan areas fail to remove sufficient amounts of contaminants to meet building specifications.[80]

Just under 80 U.S. plants produce paper-based cellulose insulation, consuming some 335,000 tons of recycled paper per year. Cellulose insulation typically is made up of 99.1 percent waste paper, including as much as 60 to 70 percent old newspapers and some old corrugated cardboard. The remainder is borax, which is coated onto the paper as a flame retardant. Cellulose holds only 3 percent of the building insulation market, which is dominated by fiberglass manufacturers, but cellulose insulation manufacturers are banking on federal recycled content guidelines to boost their market share. In February 1989, EPA issued procurement guidelines for building insulation products for all federal, state and local agencies using federal funds that encourage these agencies to purchase products made from recycled materials. The guidelines led Ed Stoary of Insul-Tray Inc., which uses post-consumer old corrugated cardboard to manufacture panels that serve as borders in houses filled with cellulose insulation, to remark, "I think the market is going to go bonkers as people get into actual buying of recycled material."[81]

Animal bedding—Shredded newsprint as bedding material for animals is gaining acceptance. Farmers using newsprint in this manner say it is clean, inexpensive and more absorbent than straw, woodchips or sawdust.[82] In addition, it can be plowed into the ground after use. Soybean-based inks, which are on the rise at newspapers across the country, break down naturally, and research shows newsprint contains fewer heavy metals than straw.[83] Research on animal bedding made from old newsprint is underway at several universities, including Pennsylvania State, the University of Wisconsin and Cornell.[84]

The animal bedding market could provide a significant outlet for old newspapers in rural communities where it is expensive to ship old newspapers to newsprint mills. Vermont sent most of its recovered newspaper to dairy farmers in the winter of 1989,[85] and John Reindl, of Dane County, Wisconsin's, department of public works, commented in late 1989 that "Potentially, in Wisconsin, animal bedding could use more old newspaper than we have available."[86] Each cow needs 1,000 pounds of bedding a year, and alternative straw bedding was selling for $50 to $120 per ton in Wisconsin in the spring of 1990.[87] In New Hampshire, sawdust, the dairy farmer's traditional bedding, is becoming more difficult and more expensive to acquire, largely because farmers are competing with wood-fired electric power plants for the supply of sawdust.[88]

Mulch products—Mulch products include grass seeding cover made from old newspapers, water, fertilizer and grass seed that is often used along highways. Proponents say it is superior to straw because it suspends the seed, allows for better germination, and contains no weed seeds. Mulch made from 20 percent old newspaper, 20 percent ground wood and 60 percent chemicals, primarily non-toxic clay and polymer glue, also can serve as a final cover for landfills and strip mines. The mulch occupies less space than traditional soil cover.[89]

Ethanol—Researchers also are exploring converting newsprint into ethanol. One ton of waste paper has the potential to yield 100 gallons of ethanol. Assuming the cost of old newspapers is zero, the price per gallon of ethanol could be as low as 35 cents, compared with the estimated $1 or more per gallon when making ethanol from corn, its traditional source. Even at a price of $50 per ton of old newspapers, the price per gallon could be as low as 85 cents.[90]

FSC Paper Corp. is making computer printout from old newspapers that is estimated to cost about 10 percent less than that made from virgin materials. The printout is not as bright, however, and will yellow after a month or two if left outside its box. These are not considered crippling limitations, though, as many computer printout users discard printouts after a relatively short time.[91]

High grade de-inking paper: In 1990, more than 6 million tons of high grade paper were recycled.[92] Products that use high-grade waste paper and pulp substitutes include towels, tissues and printing, writing and copying papers. Tissue products, printing paper and export markets show the greatest growth potential for these high grade fibers. Although some offices are instituting paper recycling programs, the quantity of high grade waste paper being collected for recycling is small. Moreover, because much of it is collected in cities with major ports, such as New York, some of it is being exported.[93]

API says a "massive movement" toward office paper recovery will be needed to satisfy the future demand for these high-grade waste fibers. Analysts are predicting that computer printout paper, for instance, which

Box 4-2

EPA'S Paper Guidelines Under Fire

Because the federal government alone accounts for 2 percent of all paper purchased nationwide,[94] proponents of greater waste paper usage believe the government could prove to be a powerful force in establishing a market for waste paper. In June 1988, using authority derived from the Resource Conservation and Recovery Act, EPA issued paper procurement guidelines for all federal, state and local agencies receiving federal funding. EPA established minimum waste paper contents for a variety of paper products, including a 50 percent minimum for high-grade paper—office and bond paper, envelopes, offset printing paper and cover stock—a 40 percent minimum for newsprint and an 80 percent minimum for paperboard. EPA directed agencies to purchase papers meeting these guidelines if prices for recycled paper matched the lowest bid for virgin paper. In the summer of 1990, the U.S. Joint Committee on Printing, which writes specifications for all paper sold to the U.S. Government Printing Office, added a 50 percent minimum waste paper content for computer forms and xerographic paper.[95]

Criticisms of EPA's paper procurement guidelines are multifold. Some argue that not including a price preference for recycled paper limits agencies' abilities to buy recycled products. The National Recycling Coalition, a coalition of private and public agency recyclers, and the Environmental Defense Fund, which had jointly sued EPA to force it to issue its June 1988 guidelines, unsuccessfully mounted a legal challenge to EPA's guidelines over the issue of price preference. Critics also assert that no effective monitoring system exists to ensure that agencies are adhering to the guidelines.[96]

Perhaps the most controversial aspect of the EPA guidelines, though, is that they do not require any percentages of *post-consumer* waste paper. EPA's definition of waste paper includes both post-consumer and pre-consumer waste paper. Pre-consumer waste paper, which is generated after the paper-making process but never reaches the consumer, includes manufacturing waste, such as envelope cuttings and bindery trimmings, as well as overruns on printing and obsolete inventories of paper. (EPA's waste paper definition does not include mill broke, which is paper waste generated in a paper mill before the completion of the papermaking process, or fibrous by-products and other forest residue from the manufacturing or wood cutting processes.)[97]

Advocates of post-consumer content standards contend that paper companies are increasing only the amount of pre-consumer waste paper in paper products, and are not using post-consumer waste paper, to meet EPA guidelines. Conservatree Paper Co. of San Francisco, the largest U.S. wholesaler of recycled printing and writing paper, says paper qualifying under EPA's procurement guidelines is "phony recycled paper."[98] "The truth is that all the paper purchased by government could meet EPA's definition for 'recycling' and still not reduce the nation's solid waste problem by one garbage truck full," said Alan Davis, president of Conservatree.[99]

Industry argues there is no need for a post-consumer content standard. "The argument regarding the issue of 'post-consumer' versus 'pre-consumer' is ridiculous at best," said George Elder of Southeast Paper Manufacturing Co. in Atlanta, Ga. Elder added, "There are those in our industry which need to consider that efforts to force 'post-consumer' material recycling can displace 'pre-consumer' material and send the latter to the dump. When one recyclable is displaced by another, nothing has been accomplished."[100] Other opponents of post-consumer standards say that the recycling rate for pre-consumer waste is greater than 90 percent and that industry will have to include post-consumer paper to meet waste paper content requirements.[101]

In the spring of 1990, EPA issued a controversial decision allowing printing and writing paper made from sawdust at two Maine paper mills to qualify as a recycled product. EPA says it based its decision on the fact that the digester process that turns sawdust into pulp is a specialized papermaking process and that there were no alternative uses for sawdust in the state.[102] Critics say the Maine paper mills are circumventing the original intent of Congress, which was to stimulate the market for recycled paper.

Because of the controversy surrounding EPA's paper procurement guidelines and the growing supply of waste paper, EPA solicited public comment in the fall of 1990 on several proposed changes, including post-consumer and de-inked waste paper content standards in high grade printing and writing papers.[103] De-inked waste paper could include post-consumer waste paper as well as printed pre-consumer waste paper.

EPA is not alone in tackling these issues. The Recycling Advisory Council (RAC), which EPA and the National Recycling Coalition established in 1989, is working on its own recommendations for paper recycling. "There is no single issue that has been a larger barrier [to paper recycling] than the lack of uniform guidelines," Jeffrey Eves of Fort Howard Corp. and a RAC member. To avoid the "post-consumer" controversy, the RAC is considering a two-step standard that would establish waste paper percentage requirements based on overall recycled content (including pre- and post-consumer) and de-inked fiber content.[104] The American Society of Testing and Materials (ASTM), a nonprofit group of 134 technical committees and 32,000 volunteer members, expects to issue its own standard definitions for waste paper and pre-consumer and post-consumer content by January 1992.[105] Arguing that because "EPA has used its regulatory authority to undermine paper recycling, Congress must pass laws to stimulate recycling when it tackles reauthorization of RCRA in the coming session,"[106] Conservatree advocates a multilevel recycling standard based on three terms: post-mill material, de-inking material and post-consumer material.[107]

Controversy surrounding the definition of waste paper is not limited to the federal procurement arena. Critics object to paper product manufacturers advertising their consumer products on supermarket shelves as "recycled" when they contain only mill scrap or paper reclaimed from print shops.

needs little processing to be used directly as pulp substitute, will be in short supply unless recycling activity increases. Pointing out that "most of the 10 percent recycled printing and writing paper now gets fiber from impact-printed CPO [computer printouts]," Thomas Norris of P.H. Glatfelter Co., a major producer of recycled printing and writing paper, said the supply of computer printout is "totally inadequate to supply a major increase in recycled printing and writing paper."[108] API also says that expansions at tissue mills are dependent on an increasing supply of high grade waste paper.[109]

Mixed paper: In 1990, around 3.6 million tons of mixed waste paper was recycled. About 2.5 million tons were consumed in the United States; the remainder was exported.[110] Mixed waste paper's traditional market has been paperboard and roofing products, which require no bleaching. Mixed waste paper is used to produce roofing products and some containers. Mixed paper often is mixed with old corrugated containers and old newspaper; the corrugated containers provide strength while mixed paper and old newspapers provide the bulk. Using mixed paper, as opposed to old newspapers only, historically saved about $20 per ton until the market for old newspapers collapsed. In comparison with mixed waste paper, old newspaper is often cleaner, readily available and, in some areas, cost competitive.[111]

The use of mixed waste paper has declined over the last 10 years, primarily because of the collapse of the organic roofing materials industry.[112] Unable to compete with the popularity of fiberglass-based shingles and other competing roofing products, 44 organic roofing product mills closed, reducing the industry's operational capacity 41 percent from levels of the early 1980s. Moreover, given the low price of old newspapers, many remaining mills are substituting old newspapers for some or all of their feedstock. Fiberglass shingles, however, have not performed as well as organic ones in cold climates, and organic shingles may be making a comeback in northern areas.[113]

Given the collapse of the roofing market, the greatest market today for mixed waste paper is recycled paperboard, primarily recycled boxboard, which is used to make products such as shoe boxes, but also composite cans, cores and tubes. The increased use of mixed paper in recycled paperboard from 1986 to 1988 accounted for half of the market recovery for mixed paper. In the last year, however, mills producing recycled boxboard also have replaced mixed paper with old newspapers. Growth in recycled paperboard is expected, which either will increase consumption of mixed waste paper in its manufacture or will increase consumption of old newspapers, which in turn may prompt roofing mills once again to use more mixed waste paper.[114]

The fate of mixed waste paper, which is the "bottom of the barrel" of waste paper grades, is somewhat dependent on the fate of higher grades of waste paper—when the supply of higher grades tightens, industry turns its attention to mixed waste paper. If analysts are correct in predicting a shortfall of old corrugated container in the next three to five years, new markets may open up for mixed waste paper. Integrating mixed waste paper in the production of corrugated containers is already a common practice in Europe. In the United States, however, where old corrugated containers have always been plentiful, there has been no incentive to use mixed paper. In addition, using mixed paper reportedly slows down the production process, increasing costs. Analysts project that if the price for old corrugated containers hits $70 to $80 per ton and if mixed waste paper were free, then U.S. producers might find it worthwhile to integrate it.[115]

Another market with room for increased amounts of mixed waste paper consumption is linerboard manufacturing. In late 1989, a representative of International Paper Co. told an industry meeting that only 3 percent of U.S. linerboard is made from recycled fiber, compared with some 54 percent in the rest of the world. He predicted that "we may not see a new virgin liner mill built in the '90s."[116]

One bright spot in the mixed waste paper market is the increasing separation of certain papers traditionally considered part of the mixed paper grade, such as magazines or file stock paper generated from office paper collection programs. Initiated by Fort Howard Corp., tissue and toweling mills, as well as recycled paperboard manufacturers, are increasingly using file stock.[117]

Collecting mixed waste paper does not appear to present any obstacles even though old newspaper is most often the largest source of paper collected in a municipal recycling program. In Seattle, which has a successful recycling program, mixed paper is the largest single item collected, representing 35 percent of all materials households placed at the curb.[118] Some specialty papers in the mixed waste paper category, such as fax paper and carbonless copy paper, cannot be recycled. Others, such as envelopes with plastic windows in them, pose problems at some mills.

Magazines and coated inserts: Roughly 6.4 million tons of coated paper is produced each year in the United States. Of that amount, about 4 million tons is made into magazines.[119] Municipalities eager to divert heavy magazines from the waste stream to avoid tipping fees (disposal fees based on weight) have had a difficult time finding markets. The future appears much brighter, however, largely because newsprint manufacturers have discovered that old magazines are a useful raw material in flotation de-inking technologies, which are used to manufacture newsprint from waste paper.[120] (See section on the post-consumer paper and paperboard recycling process for more details.) An informal survey undertaken by *Recycling Times* in late 1990 estimated that newsprint mills will buy at least 942,920 tons of post-consumer magazines within the next two years.[121]

A study released by the Magazine Publishers Association (MPA) in December 1990 predicted that by 1992 demand for old magazines from newsprint mills using flotation de-inking technology will equal between 17 percent and 24 percent of the magazines printed in the United States. MPA projected that demand could rise to 40 percent of the magazines printed by 1995 and up to 60 percent by the year 2000. The initial supply of old magazines will come from newsstand returns (magazines consumers did not purchase). MPA believes, however, that demand will exceed the supply of returns by the mid-1990s and that post-consumer collection will become necessary to supply these mills. Currently, less than 10 percent of the magazine wholesalers are selling their wastes.[122]

Old magazines also can be used to manufacture containerboard, combination folding boxboard and industrial packaging. Inexpensive mixed waste paper usually supplies these markets, however.[123]

Exports: Unlike glass, waste paper is a world commodity. While only 22 percent of recovered U.S. waste paper is exported, the export market is the "largest single factor affecting waste paper supply, demand and pricing," according to Edward Sparks, Browning-Ferris Industries Inc.'s manager of marketing and operations. Most analysts agree, ranking municipally sponsored curbside collection programs second to the offshore market in terms of its effect on the supply and price of old newsprint.[124]

The export market has been growing at a rate of 16 percent a year since 1970, compared with a 4 percent growth rate for the domestic waste paper market.[125] Analysts expect the export market to continue to increase sharply. API estimates that exports could reach 10 million tons by 1995 and that it is "highly unlikely" the foreign waste paper markets will soften.[126] Foreign purchasers of waste paper include South Korea, Mexico, Taiwan, Japan, Canada, Italy, Spain and Venezuela. The Far East is a major market where paper is reprocessed into paper products, and in some cases, imported back to the United States as value-added products.[127]

Some analysts are concerned that the United States has become too reliant on exports, leaving waste paper recycling programs at the mercy of a host of factors outside of its control. (In 1990, the export value of bulk waste paper grades collectively declined 27 percent.[128]) The offshore market has had a notoriously erratic effect on the waste paper market, which Sparks and other industry analysts primarily attribute to a history of panic buying by foreign purchasers, but also to volatility in the availability of shipping containers, freight rate increases and the value of the U.S. dollar overseas.[129] Recently, a shortage of shipping containers particularly has contributed to the soft market for waste paper in the Northeast. The shortage is the result of the diversion of many containers to the Persian Gulf for military cargo, as well as to a slowdown in the shipment of goods from the Far East and other areas. Less space has been available on vessels returning to their original port of departure.[130]

While analysts are wary of the effect of the offshore market on the U.S. waste paper market, the U.S. waste paper glut also has been wreaking havoc with the European waste paper market. Analysts say that increased exports of U.S. waste paper to Europe have created a glut there, reducing prices to close to zero and disrupting existing reclamation systems.[131]

Liaisons between foreign buyers and U.S. paper dealers or municipalities are increasing. In the last several years, several offshore mills have purchased or opened waste paper plants and brokerage offices on the East and West Coasts.[132] In addition, a subsidiary of Norcal Solid Waste Systems, one of the country's largest solid waste management firms, reportedly has explored sending waste paper collected in San Francisco to China, and the city already is sending waste paper to South Korea.[133] Getting into the export market is not an easy proposition for U.S. waste paper dealers, though. Bales of waste paper to be exported must meet certain size and density specifications, and export balers cost more than $500,000. Adding in the costs for power, a building, storage space and operating area, analysts estimate a minimum investment for export trade of about $1 million.[134]

Waste paper grades—Old newspapers, old corrugated containers and mixed papers are the primary bulk wastepaper grades exported.[135] In 1989, the strongest export growth was in old newspapers, spurred on by demand from Pacific Rim countries. Old corrugated containers also showed a strong increase in exports, with more than half of the increase attributed to a growing Mexican market. Mixed paper exports grew only slightly, and high-grade paper and pulp substitutes dropped, in large part because of the shrinking supply available for export.[136]

Shipments of old newspapers from the United States to Canadian mills are expected to increase dramatically by 1993. Canadian newsprint recycling mills are planning more than 2.4 million tons of old newspaper capacity in 1991 and 1992. (See Table 4-6.) Exports of old newspaper to countries other than Canada are expected to rise from 1 million tons in 1988 to 1.6 million tons by 1995, with the bulk going to the Pacific Rim.[137]

A concern of the North American newsprint industry is the positioning of offshore producers, such as Japan and Korea, to sell recycled newsprint made from old U.S. newspapers back into the North American market. Taking advantage of the two-to-five-year time frame North American producers need to start producing substantial quantities of newsprint, several offshore producers have set up offices and packing plants on both the East and West Coasts and in the Midwest "ostensibly to buy waste paper, but they are also conveniently located to sell new recycled newsprint," Edward Sparks, BFI's manager of marketing and operations, warned recycling conference attendees in April 1991.[138]

Waste paper prices: The editor and publisher of *The Paper Stock Report*, a weekly update on the paper recycling market, commented that "after experiencing historically good paper stock markets during the late 1980s, paper stock dealers are sure to remember 1990 as the year the good times disappeared."[139] Because waste paper has so many varied end uses, the domestic market is affected by changes in a number of areas, including the inconsistent export market, labor and production problems at major end-user mills, increases in supply, interest rates, recessions and the level of housing starts. Edward Sparks of BFI says the reason for the downturn in paper recycling markets was that negative influences from all of the above factors hit the waste paper market at the same time.[140]

Old newspapers—Because the newspaper is one of the most easily collected items in municipal recycling programs, the majority of people jumping on the recycling bandwagon begin with newspapers. Newspaper recycling increased 37 percent between 1983 and 1988.[141] The result was an explosion in the supply of old newspapers, particularly on the East Coast, that combined with labor problems at a major U.S. mill and cyclical swings in the export market,[142] swamped the market for old newspapers and led to a price collapse. Prices dropped from an average of $25 to $30 per ton in early 1989 to zero by mid-1989, and some cities in the Northeast were paying paper dealers $5 to $25 per ton to take away their old newspapers.[143] In 1990, the average price end-users paid for old newspapers ranged from $11.20 per ton to $22.90 per ton,[144] although many communities still had difficulty locating markets.

Old corrugated containers—In 1990, the average price paid by end-users for old corrugated containers ranged from $23.80 per ton to $38.60 per ton.[145] The price for this paper grade is expected to rise because of a significant increase in industrial capacity to use old corrugated containers.

High grade de-inking papers—In 1990, the average price paid by end-users for laser-free computer printouts ranged from $204.20 per ton to $313.60 per ton, while the average price end-users paid for sorted white ledger ranged from $161.10 per ton to $215.50 per ton.[146] Because computer printouts can be used as a pulp substitute, their price is influenced by the price for pulp. In the spring of 1990, for instance, a drop in pulp prices prompted South Korea, the largest waste paper market overseas, to buy pulp in place of the computer printouts it had been purchasing.[147]

Mixed waste paper—In 1990, the average price end users paid for mixed waste paper ranged from 10¢ per ton to $11.30 per ton, with the higher prices paid at the beginning of 1990.[148]

Transportation: Transportation is a major factor in the economics of recycling, particularly for old newspapers. Transporting used newspapers to Canadian mills is an expensive proposition, which has prompted Canadian companies to search for the most cost-effective ways to acquire old

Box 4-3

Government Assistance for Paper Recycling Investments

States including New Jersey, New York, West Virginia and Michigan are making special funding available to assist companies investing in paper recycling equipment.[149]

Examples are plentiful. The New Jersey Department of Environmental Protection provided **Marcal Paper Mills Inc.** with $3 million toward a $27 million project to improve and expand its de-inking and pulpmaking facilities. The company, which recycles 150,000 tons per year of old magazines, mixed office paper and junk mail, also will receive $13 million in tax-exempt bond financing.[150] In New York, the economic development office reserved $500,000 as part of a financial package to lure the **Jefferson Smurfit Group** into building a recycled newsprint mill in upstate New York.[151]

West Virginia has allocated tax-free bonds to help finance a mixed office waste paper project scheduled to begin operation in 1993. The plant, developed by **American Power Corp.** of Bala Cynwyd, Pa., will process 500 tons per day of unsorted paper into market pulp that will be sold to other companies for manufacture into tissues, toweling and high-grade communication paper.[152] Michigan provided **James River Corp.** with a $5.4 million recycling grant to help finance a $97 million expansion project at its Kalamazoo, Mich., paperboard mill. The mill produces 100 percent recycled boxboard from old newspapers, old corrugated cardboard and trimmings from the manufacturing process.[153]

The Canadian government and a Canadian utility also are providing financial assistance for recycled paper projects. Ontario Hydro, a province-wide public utility, approved an energy conservation grant of more than $6 million to assist **Abitibi-Price Inc.** in financing a $50 million expansion at its Thunder Bay, Ontario, mill that includes a de-inking plant.[154] British Columbia provided **Newstech Recycling** with a $14 million loan to build an $83 million Canadian de-inking facility that will supply de-inked pulp to **Fletcher Challenge Canada Ltd.** and **MacMillan Bloedel Ltd.**, British Columbia's two largest newsprint companies.[155] In addition, the Quebec government is providing $18 million—$7 million in market rate loans and $11 million by acquiring preferred shares of **Kruger Inc.'s** stock—to assist Kruger Inc. in adding de-inking capacity at its Bromptonville, Quebec, mill that will cost more than $40 million.[156]

newspapers.

The railroad industry recently responded by revamping its rate structure to make transporting old newspapers back to Canada by rail more attractive. With at least 90 percent of the railcars that had carried paper to the United States returning to Canada empty, the railroad industry had compelling reasons to provide incentives. "We can offer lower rates than trucks, and we are looking at savings of 60 percent off usual rail rates," said Herman Berkenbosch, Canadian National Railroad's senior market manager for paper. Berkenbosch added that the railroad industry hopes to fill 25 percent of its empty cars with waste paper by 1994.[157]

Other railroad companies including Conrail of Philadelphia, Canadian National Rail of Montreal and CSX of Baltimore also are pursuing customers to fill empty railcars heading back to Canada. The railroad cars carrying paper into the United States historically have returned empty because the specialized cars are limited in terms of what materials they can haul. Paper carrying cars have cushioned underframes and smooth interior walls that easily could be damaged by other types of cargo.[158]

Within the United States, Stone Container Corp. struck a deal on freight costs to ship newsprint and old newspapers between its Arizona newsprint mill and Wisconsin. Under an agreement with the *Wisconsin State Journal*, Stone Container agreed to ship back a ton of used newspaper from the area for every ton of paper sold to the newspaper. FSC Paper Corp. of Chicago has a similar agreement with the *Journal*.[159]

Stone Container also reached an agreement with Burlington Northern Railroad whereby the railroad will deliver 145,000 tons annually of old corrugated containers to Stone's Missoula, Mont., mill. Grocery store chains and paper brokers in six midwestern metropolitan areas will supply the old corrugated containers, which Stone will make into linerboard and eventually new corrugated containers. Before the deal was struck, Burlington Northern hauled linerboard to market and returned to the mill with empty cars.[160]

Kruger Inc., a Canadian newsprint producer, which sells more than 90 percent of its newsprint in the Northeast, Florida and Midwest, has begun transporting waste paper back to Canada on the same trucks that carry its newsprint to the United States.[161]

Costs of de-inking facilities and repulping equipment: In the spring of 1991, John Burke of James River Corp., the nation's largest packaging manufacturer, estimated that the cost of building a de-inking facility ranged from $50 to $100 million.[162] One year earlier, the Black Clawson Co. had placed the average cost of a de-inking facility to process old newspapers at $60 million, with the most sophisticated units costing upwards of $80 million.[163] Construction time for a de-inking facility is 18 months to two years.[164] J. Rodney Edwards, vice president of API's paperboard group, told IRRC that the cost of adding repulping equipment to a paperboard mill (which does not need to remove ink from waste paper) is about 25 percent less than adding a de-inking facility at a paper mill. Edwards added that construction time is similar.[165]

A 1990 study by Resource Information Systems Inc. (RISI) of Bedford, Mass., found that the best returns on investment in de-inking capacity are generated by expansion of existing U.S. mills that limit the recycled fiber content to 40 percent. "New mills based on 100 percent recycled fiber are generally characterized by long payback periods and—at best—limited profit margins....Investment in 40 percent de-inking capacity generates modest cost savings for U.S. producers, but provides little or no gains for the average Canadian newsprint supplier," concludes the report. "Canadian producers will add de-inking capacity simply to stay in the U.S. market, since the investment will provide little or no return to the majority of Canadian suppliers," says RISI.[166]

The trade publication *Pulp & Paper* published an article in March 1990 listing the typical capital costs per ton of daily capacity for a 200 ton per day deinking mill facility: $195,000 for newsprint; $180,000 for tissue; and $265,000 for fine paper. In comparison, the capital cost of expanding papermaking capacity to use virgin timber is $500,000 to $1 million per ton of daily capacity.[167]

Cost of producing recycled paper: Paper and paperboard mills are gearing up to use more waste paper not only to meet recycled content standards but because using waste paper can cut costs—if they can find a steady supply. The cost of producing recycled paper varies from mill to mill, though, and once capital investments are made in recycling equipment, the economics of producing recycled paper are highly dependent on the cost of waste paper and whether a mill is idling virgin papermaking equipment to produce recycled paper.

A study released by the National Solid Wastes Management Association (NSWMA) in the spring of 1990 estimated that a new 600 ton per day de-inking newsprint mill could pay up to $58 per ton for old newspaper and produce lower cost newsprint than an existing plant using virgin timber. (The NSWMA estimated it cost $180 per ton, on average, to produce newsprint from virgin timber at existing plants.) The economics become even more favorable for used newspapers when compared with newly built pulping capacity. A recycling facility could pay up to $95 a ton for old newspaper and still produce lower cost newsprint than a newly built facility, according to the NSWMA.[168]

A spring 1991 study presented by Duncanson Investment Research Inc. of Toronto to the American Newspaper Publishers Association also found that both Canadian and southern U.S. mills could cut costs by using waste paper. The report concluded that mills would save on raw material and energy costs, but that southern U.S. mills would save more because their costs of acquiring recycled paper would be lower. Duncanson estimated that by using recycled paper for 25 percent of the feedstock, the manufacturing cost per finished metric ton would drop by $24 for the average Canadian newsprint mill and by $30 for the average southern U.S. mill.[169]

Cost savings are not limited to newsprint production. A spring 1990 article in *Pulp & Paper* reported that an efficient de-inking mill that has an economical supply of waste paper could produce de-inked fiber for fine writing and printing paper at a cost of $300 to $400 per ton. In comparison, the article placed the cost to produce virgin kraft fiber at about $300 to $500 per ton and placed the market price for kraft pulp at as high as $700 per ton. Other typical operating costs ranged from $140 to $170 per ton to produce newsprint and $275 to $375 per ton to produce tissue.[170]

Estimates of energy savings resulting from waste paper recycling range from the Department of Energy's 20 percent to Greenpeace's 50 percent to EPA's 64 percent. DOE also estimates that recycling saves 50 percent of the water required to make paper and paperboard from virgin fiber.[171] A disadvantage to recycling waste paper is that it often requires a greater use of fossil fuels, since the process does not generate wood waste byproducts often used as fuel in the production of paper from lumber.

Given that it can cost less to produce paper from recycled paper than from virgin paper, the fact that recycled paper costs the consumer more than virgin paper in some cases largely can be attributed to economies of scale and an immature distribution system. Machines in recycling mills typically are much smaller than machines in virgin mills. As the industry produces more recycled paper, prices should continue to drop. In the case of newsprint, the cost of recycled paper already is comparable to the cost of virgin paper in many instances.[172] Proponents of recycled paper also say that subsidies for virgin paper production, including sales by the U.S. Forest Service of national forest timber at below market value and government loans for power plant construction and pollution control equipment, unfairly mask the real cost of virgin paper production.

U.S. Paper and Paperboard Industry's Recycling Initiatives

U.S. paper and paperboard production capacity stood at approximately 82 million tons in 1990. API estimates capacity will increase by 2.3 percent, or 1.9 million tons, to reach 84 million tons by the end of 1991. Moreover, from 1991 through 1993, 18 additional paper machines are scheduled to add another 7.5 million tons of capacity.[173] Although exact figures are not available on the amount of new capacity that will be recycled capacity, API says that the growth in virgin capacity is slowing and that the use of waste paper is expected to grow twice as fast as the use of virgin fiber in the near future.[174]

Recycling was an integral part of the U.S. paper industry at its start. The country's first paper mill, built in 1690 near Philadelphia, recycled rags to manufacture paper. It was not until the 1850s that the paper industry began using trees in place of rags and wastepaper to make paper. By early this century, paper companies were de-inking waste paper commercially on a large scale.[175]

Today, the paper and paperboard mills are the major consumers of U.S. waste paper.[176] Approximately 200 of the 600 U.S. mills depend exclusively on wastepaper, including pre-consumer waste paper, for their raw material. Another 300 mills use between 10 and 35 percent waste paper in their operations.[177] Some 131 paper and paperboard mills, 114 in the United States and 17 in Canada, use old newspapers as part of their feedstock.[178]

"Additions to capacity to produce newsprint, tissue, kraft and recycled linerboard and recycled paperboard from recovered paper will continue to come on stream in 1991 and 1992, with a corresponding increase in demand for all grades of recovered paper," predicted J. Rodney Edwards of API in the spring of 1991. Edwards added that "the collection system will be challenged again this year and next to expand to meet total demand."[179]

Table 4-3 lists publicly announced plans by API's member companies to expand facilities or build new mills capable of consuming recovered waste paper as a raw material source. Table 4-3 lists 88 U.S. projects ranging from projects with firm commitments to projects undergoing feasibility and engineering studies. Eighteen of the projects would produce recycled newsprint; 20 would provide recycled containerboard or would increase the recycled fiber content of unbleached kraft linerboard; 14 would manufacture recycled tissue products; 12 would make recycled paperboard; 10 would produce printing and writing papers containing recycled fiber; and 14 would manufacture de-inked pulp for further conversion into a variety of recycled paper products.

A number of company recycling initiatives stand out. **Jefferson Smurfit Corp.**, for example, a U.S. subsidiary of the Jefferson Smurfit Group of Ireland, a printing, paper and paperboard packaging company, is the nation's largest reclaimer and recycler of waste paper. In 1989, the company recovered more than 3.7 million tons of old newspapers, old corrugated containers and other paper products. Operating 32 waste paper processing centers, the company processes paper for its own use and also markets waste paper to third parties.[180]

Jefferson Smurfit is the nation's largest producer of recycled paperboard, followed by **The Newark Group Inc.**, which consumes more than 1 million tons of waste paper each year at its 11 mills.[181] Table 4-4 lists the leading U.S. producers of recycled paperboard, which represent a market

Table 4-3

U.S. Expansion Plans for Increased
Use of Recovered Waste Paper, 1990-1995

Company	Location	Product Grade	Est. Annual Waste Paper Consumption (thousands short-tons)
Alabama River Newsprint Co.	Claiborne, Ala.	Newsprint	140
American Power Corp.	Barrackville, W. Va.	De-inked market pulp	175
Augusta Newsprint Co.	Augusta, Ga.	Newsprint	115
Bear Island Paper Co.	Ashland, Va.	Newsprint	45
Boise Cascade Corp.	W. Tacoma, Wash.	Newsprint	105
	Ashland, Va.	Newsprint	45
	Vancouver, Wash.	Printing/writing papers	NA
Bowater Inc.	Calhoun, Tenn.	Newsprint	125/130
Brownsville Specialty Paper Products Inc.	Brownsville, N.Y.	Recycled paperboard	32
Caithness King Inc.	Pejepscot, Maine	De-inked market pulp	235
	Midland, Mich.	De-inked market pulp	235
Cascade Niagara Falls Inc.	Niagara Falls, N.Y.	Printing/writing papers	125/130
Champion International Corp.	Sheldon, Tex.	Newsprint	175
Chesapeake Corp.	Menasha, Wis.	Tissue	95
	Stockton, Calif.	Recycled linerboard	385
Daishowa America Co.	Port Angeles, Wash.	Newsprint/directory paper	75

Company	Location	Product	
Evergreen Pulp & Paper Co.	Redrock, Ariz.	Newsprint	310
Fairfield Paper Co.	Baltimore, Ohio	Recycled paperboard	18
Federal Paper Board Co.	Sprague, Conn.	Recycled paperboard	20/25
Fort Howard Corp.	Rincon, Ga.	Tissue	100
	Muskogee, Okla.	Tissue	90/100
	Green Bay, Wis.	Tissue	100
Fox River Fiber Co.	Kaukauna, Wis.	De-inked market pulp	100
FSC Corp.	Alsip, Ill.	Newsprint	NA
Gaylord Container Corp.	Bogalusa, La.	Linerboard	105
Georgia Pacific Corp.	Cedar Springs, Ga.	Linerboard	15
	E. Millinocket, Maine	Newsprint	100
Green Bay Packaging Co.	Green Bay, Wis.	Recycled linerboard	240
Howard Paper Mills Inc.	Urbana, Ohio	Printing/writing papers	NA
Inland Empire Paper Co.	Millwood, Wash.	Newsprint	43
International Paper Co.	Mobile, Ala.	Printing/writing papers	NA
	Unknown	De-inked pulp	NA
James River Corp.	Old Town, Maine	Tissue	NA
	Kalamazoo, Mich.	Recycled paperboard	160
	Halsey, Ore.	De-inked pulp	110/120
	Green Bay, Wis.	Tissue	NA
Jefferson Smurfit Corp.	Fernandina Beach, Fla.	Linerboard	230/240
Kenaf of North America Inc.	Muskogee, Okla.	Recycled linerboard	300
Kieffer Paper Mills	Brownstown, Ind.	De-inked market pulp	NA
Kimberly-Clark Corp.	Coosa Pines, Ala.	Newsprint	45
	Loudon, Tenn.	Tissue	NA
Kruger Inc.	Albany, N.Y.	NA	110
Longview Fibre Co.	Longview, Wash.	Linerboard	NA
MacMillan Bloedel Ltd.	Pine Hill, Ala.	Linerboard	80/90

Company	Location	Product	Capacity
Macon Kraft Inc.	Macon, Ga.	Linerboard	115
Manistique Papers Inc.	Manistique, Mich.	Newsprint	NA
Manville Forest Products Corp.	W. Monroe, La.	Recycled paperboard	NA
Marcal Paper Mills Inc.	Elmwood Park, N.J.	Tissue	NA
Mead Corp.	Mahrt, Ala.	Recycled paperboard	70/80
Menasha Corp.	Ostego, Mich.	Corrugating medium	45
Mi Ho Paper Co.	St. Joseph, Mo.	Printing/writing papers	70/75
Mississippi River Corp.	Natchez, Miss.	De-inked market pulp	60
Mosinee Paper Corp.	Middletown, Ohio	Tissue	140
North Pacific Paper Co. (Weyerhaeuser Corp.)	Lonview, Wash.	Newsprint	200/210
Northhampton Paperboard Co.	Northhampton, Pa.	Recycled paperboard	340
Orchids Paper Products Inc.	Flagstaff, Ariz.	Tissue	20
Paperboard Specialties Inc.	Paterson, N.J.	Recycled paperboard	38
Papyres Newton Falls Inc.	Newton Falls, N.Y.	Printing/writing papers	125/130
Patriot Paper Co.	Hyde Park, Mass.	Printing/writing papers	95
Pentair Inc.	W. Carrolton, Ohio	Printing/writing papers	NA
Ponderosa Fibres of America Inc.	Augusta, Ga.	De-inked market pulp	NA
	Augusta, Ga.	De-inked market pulp	50
	S. Bronx, N.Y.	Newsprint	130
	Memphis, Tenn.	De-inked market pulp	50
	Oshkosh, Wis.	De-inked market pulp	35
	Tomahawk, Wis.	De-inked market pulp	NA
Prime Fibre Corp.	Appleton, Wis.	De-inked market pulp	NA
Putney Paper Co.	Putney, Vt.	Tissue	3
Recycled Paperboard Co.	Clifton, N.J.	Recycled paperboard	100/140
Recycling Systems Corp.	Gaffney, S.C.	Recycled paperboard	100

Company	Location	Product	Capacity
Riverside Paper Co.	De Pere, Wis.	De-inked pulp	NA
Scott Paper Co.	Owensboro, Ky.	Tissue	NA
Seaman Paper Co.	Otter River, Mass.	Printing/writing papers	NA
Seminole Kraft	Jacksonville, Fla.	Recycled linerboard	425
(Stone Container Corp.)			
Shelby Tissue Co.	Memphis, Tenn.	Tissue	NA
Simpson Paper Co.	W. Linn, Ore.	Printing/writing papers	170/180
Smurfit Newsprint Co.	Upstate New York	Newsprint	330
Stone Container Corp.	Missoula, Mont.	Linerboard	144
Tagsons Papers Inc.	Mechanicville, N.Y.	Tissue	NA
Temple-Inland Inc.	Ontario, Calif.	Recycled linerboard	80
	Newport, Ind.	Recycled corrugating medium	50/60
	Maysville, Ky.	Recycled linerboard	240
	Savannah, Ga.	Paperboard and paper	NA
Union Camp Corp.	Menasha, Wis.	Recycled paperboard	40
U.S. Paper Mills Co.	Harford City, Ind.	Recycled corrugating medium	65
VISY Board Packaging Co.	Terre Haute, Ind.	Corrugating medium	40
Weston Paper & Mfg. Co.	Springfield, Ore.	Linerboard	160
Weyerhauser Corp.	Dunkirk, N.Y.	Recycled paperboard	290

NA

Source: American Paper Institute Inc., New York, N.Y., July 1991

for nearly half of all the waste paper consumed by the paper and paperboard industry.

Stone Container Corp. is the nation's largest recycler of brown waste paper grades, converting it into cardboard and paper containers.[182] The company consumes primarily old corrugated containers and newspaper at 16 of its 24 mills worldwide, and by 1993 plans to use 3 million tons per year of recyclable paper around the world. Some 1.7 million tons of waste paper are scheduled to be recycled at Stone's 12 U.S. mills by 1992. Stone estimates it will spend $200 million to reach its worldwide recycling goal. In the United States, Stone is spending $16 million to rebuild a linerboard mill in Missoula, Mont., and $24 million to upgrade and expand waste paper usage at its Uncasville, Conn., corrugating medium (the fluted middle layer in corrugated cardboard) mill. In 1989, the company introduced computer printout made from old newspapers, and it is making grocery bags and carry-out bags for McDonald's restaurants from old newspapers. Stone also is the leading producer of unbleached paper products and newsprint, and it says it plans to produce recycled newsprint at one of its Canadian mills by 1993.[183]

James River Corp. is the largest maker of packaging in the country. According to API's database *PaperMatcher: A Directory of Paper Recycling Resources,* James River consumes waste paper (other than pulp substitutes) at six of its mills and plans to use waste paper at three additional mills.[184] *PaperMatcher* also identified 11 mills owned by **Georgia Pacific Corp.** that consume waste paper (other than pulp substitutes) as well as a planned de-inking facility at Georgia Pacific's East Millinocket, Maine, newsprint mill.[185]

Recycling Systems Corp. of Covington, Ga., is building two new mini-mills in Gaffney, S.C., and Ashland, Ky., that each will consume 250 tons per day of old corrugated containers. Scheduled to begin operation by January 1992, the mills will produce linerboard and corrugated medium. RSC also is planning to switch the feedstock of an existing mill in Harriman, Tenn., from wood chips to 100 percent old corrugated cardboard.[186]

Newsprint mills: In 1990, the 25 U.S. newsprint mills had 6.8 million tons of capacity, and API estimates U.S. newsprint capacity will expand to 7.4 million tons by 1993.[187] The 44 Canadian newsprint mills have the capacity to produce approximately 11.5 million tons.[188] As mentioned before, in recent years the ability to collect old newspapers outpaced the ability of the existing infrastructure to reclaim them. The newsprint industry is responding by adding de-inking facilities at its mills to remove ink from old newspapers or by purchasing de-inked pulp from independent de-inking facilities.

In mid-1991, 10 U.S. and two Canadian mills had the capacity to produce around 3.6 million tons of recycled newsprint.[189] Table 4-5 lists the mills' owners, their location, their capacity to produce recycled newsprint and the

---

Box 4-4

Trade Associations Promoting Paper Recycling

American Paper Institute (API): API, whose more than 175 member companies represent more than 90 percent of U.S. paper production,[190] has a paper recycling committee that has undertaken the following to promote paper recycling: encouraged investment in expansion; compiled a national database called *MatchMaker* to put cities in contact with waste paper dealers and mills; developed a public education program; and expanded the industry's current recycling awards program. The paper industry also has designed two symbols so that consumers can easily recognize recycled and recyclable paper products.[191]

Paper Recycling Coalition (PRC): Formed in June 1990, PRC consists of 10 recycled paper and paperboard producers that consume approximately 4 million tons of waste paper annually: Field Container Corp., Garden State Paper Co. Inc., Halltown Paperboard Co., The Newark Group Inc., Newman & Co. Inc., Rock-Tenn Co., Sonoco Products Co., Southeast Paper Manufacturing Co., Waldorf Corp. and White Pigeon Paper Co. Member companies employ 21,000 people in 35 states at 39 mills and 271 plants nationwide. PRC is lobbying government to "ensure that accurate information specifically concerning the paper recycling industry is ably presented to government forums, particularly at the federal level."[192]

Inter-Association Council on Paper Recycling: Formed in July 1990, the council's members include 25 trade associations representing paper and print communications companies. The council focuses on recycling newspapers, magazines, catalogs, direct marketing materials, books and office materials. The council is working on three major projects: developing key definitions and a glossary of frequently asked questions; developing an information center and resource guide; and drafting model legislation.[193]

---

recycled content of their newsprint. **Manistique Papers Inc.**, which **Kruger Inc.** of Montreal, Quebec, acquired in the spring of 1991, makes newsprint from 100 percent old magazines.[194] The other mills use either old newspapers or a combination of old newspapers and magazines to produce recycled newsprint.

Garden State Paper Co. Inc. of Garfield, N.J., which is owned by newspaper publisher **Media General Inc.**, was the first to produce recycled newsprint, in 1961. By 1989, another seven U.S. newsprint mills and one Canadian mill were producing recycled newsprint that met EPA's 40 percent waste paper content guideline for newsprint. (See Box 4-2 for

Box 4-5

The Supermarket Dilemma

"Paper or plastic?" the supermarket clerk asks. There are a lot of strong opinions on the subject but no simple answers. At first glance a more mature recycling infrastructure appears to favor paper. Studies examining the full range of environmental impacts, however, make the choice more difficult. The National Audubon Society's studies, for instance, show that virgin paper production produces more pollution and consumes more energy than does the manufacture of polyethylene, the material in plastic grocery bags.[195] Today, most paper grocery bags are made from virgin paper, although the recycled content is increasing.

Papermaking is a dirty and energy-intensive process. Paper mills regularly emit sulfur and chlorine, and coal, which contributes to the greenhouse effect and acid rain, provides about half of paper mills' energy. The National Audubon Society assails the U.S. Forest Service's harvesting and replanting techniques and also says that the pulp production process clogs streams and lakes with silt by-products and robs water of the oxygen needed by fish. In addition, the bleaching process used to whiten paper creates dioxins as a by-product. Once discarded, paper bags take up more room in a landfill, being two to six times more bulky than plastic bags. Moreover, when the paper bags decompose in a landfill, they generate methane gas, a potent greenhouse gas.[196]

Plastic grocery bags have made significant inroads at the supermarket, growing from 5 percent of bags used in grocery stores in 1982 to 60 percent today.[197] Plastic grocery bags are not without their own adverse environmental impacts, however. Few plastic grocery bags are presently recycled, although the number is growing as the major plastic grocery sack manufacturers and grocery store chains have launched recycling programs. Plastic bags are made from natural gas or oil. Additives used to produce the bags, such as cadmium or lead, can be toxic pollutants, and volatile hydrocarbons, benzene and particulate matter often are released into the atmosphere during the manufacturing process. (Some paper bags also are printed with inks containing heavy metals.) Because plastic does not decompose, plastic litter can be an eyesore and also harm fish and wildlife. If discarded properly, however, plastic bags take up less space in a landfill, and their failure to decompose is a plus if the landfill leaks.[198] If incinerated, plastic provides a greater heat value than paper, and the recycling process requires less energy and produces fewer emissions, according to the Council for Solid Waste Solutions.[199]

With as many as 34 billion bags distributed by the grocery industry each year,[200] how to have your groceries bagged is not an easy decision. Many environmentalists suggest avoiding the dilemma altogether through the use of reusable canvas or vinyl bags.

Table 4-4

Top U.S. Producers of Recycled Paperboard

Company	Annual Capacity (000 tons/year)	Market Share (percentage)
Jefferson Smurfit Corp.	1,330	13.3
The Newark Group Inc.	875	8.7
Sonoco Products Co.	850	8.5
Caraustar Industries Inc.	550	5.5
Rock-Tenn Co.	532	5.3
Inland Container Corp.	475	4.7
Waldorf Corp.	395	3.9
U.S. Gypsum Co.	332	3.3
National Gypsum Co.	220	2.2
Packaging Corp. of America	210	2.1
TOTAL	5,769[a]	57.5

[a]Total U.S. capacity in 1990 was estimated at slightly more than 10 million tons.

Source: *Pulp & Paper*, June 1990

further information on EPA's paper procurement guidelines.) These mills represented 14 percent of U.S. newsprint supplies in 1989.[201] Since 1989, three additional mills owned by **Augusta Newsprint Co.**, which is owned by **Abititi-Price** of Toronto; **Atlantic Newsprint Co.** and **North Pacific Paper Co.**, which is 90 percent owned by **Weyerhaeuser Corp.** and 10 percent owned by **Jujo Paper Co.** of Tokyo, have begun producing recycled newsprint.[202] **Southeast Paper Manufacturing Co.**, an equal partnership of newspaper publishers **Media General, Cox Enterprises Inc.** and **Knight-Ridder Inc.**, is the nation's largest producer of 100 percent recycled newsprint.[203]

Newspaper publishers are business partners in several of the mills producing recycled newsprint[204] and also are entering the collection business. In the summer of 1990, *The Washington Post* acquired 90 percent of a new company, **Capitol Fiber Inc.**, that processes and markets old newspapers. Although the company estimated it initially would lose $10 to $20 per ton processing old newspapers, it believes it will become a profitable venture in the long run.[205]

Planned recycled newsprint projects—The American Newspaper Publishers Association reports that since October 1988, the newsprint industry has spent or committed approximately $1.5 billion on newsprint recycling projects.[206] By 1993, the 18 planned newsprint recycling projects listed in Table 4-6 are projected to raise North American newsprint recycling capacity to 7.3 million tons. Nearly 60 percent of the existing and planned recycled newsprint capacity is in the United States.

A survey of about 30 key North American newsprint executives conducted in the spring of 1990 for the Black Clawson Co. found that by 1995 nearly everyone expected to produce some recycled newsprint. About 30 percent of those surveyed said they currently were producing recycled newsprint, and another third predicted they would produce nothing but recycled newsprint by 1995. The newsprint executives voiced concern, though, about poor quality, high costs and an inadequate supply of old newspapers, estimating that as much as 20 to 40 percent of newspapers picked up through curbside recycling programs contained contaminants, such as rubber bands, chewing gum or plastics.[207]

Tissue mills: Nine major companies make up the tissue industry, which uses about 51 percent recycled paper and plans to use 57 percent recycled paper by 1992. Three companies—**Fort Howard Corp., Chesapeake Corp. and Pope & Talbot Inc.**—use 100 percent recycled paper, including both post-consumer and post-industrial waste paper. One firm uses none. Most private label tissue is made of 100 percent recycled tissue.[208] Fort Howard Corp. is the world's largest manufacturer of tissue products made with recycled waste paper and is one of the largest U.S. consumers of mixed waste paper. Each year, the company uses more than 1 million tons of waste paper.[209] API has identified nine publicly announced planned waste paper de-inking projects at tissue mills, two of which are at Fort Howard mills. The planned projects will boost the total number of tissue mills with de-inking facilities to 40.[210]

Printing and writing papers: Several years ago, two dozen high-grade de-inking mills were making printing and writing paper.[211] Today, API reports there are only nine mills with de-inking facilities that produce printing and writing paper. P.H. Glatfelter Co. operates the largest facility, which has an estimated annual de-inking capacity of 90,000 short tons.[212] In some instances, paper companies purchased the de-inking mills and converted them into virgin paper mills.[213] Reasons cited for closing the de-inking facilities included the difficulty of removing inks developed from new laser printing and xerographic processes, an increasing amount and variety of contaminants and increasing competition for pulp substitutes and high grades of waste paper.[214]

New initiatives are underway in the writing and printing paper industry to increase the use of recycled paper, however. API identified seven publicly

Table 4-5

Operating U.S. and Canadian
Newsprint Recycling Mills

Company	Location	Recycled Capacity (000 tons)	Recycled Content (%)
Atlantic Newsprint Co.	Whitby, Ont.	150	100
Augusta Newsprint Co.	Augusta, Ga.	400	23
FSC Paper Corp.	Alsip, Ill.	134	100
Garden State Paper Co. Inc.	Garfield, N.J.	222	100
Manistique Papers Inc.	Manistique, Mich.	62	100
North Pacific Paper Co.	Longview, Wash.	772	40
Quebec & Ontario Paper Co. Ltd.	Thorold, Ont.	337	55-62
Smurfit Newsprint Co.	Pomona, Calif.	134	100
	Newberg, Ore.	394	up to 60
	Oregon City, Ore.	243	up to 60
Southeast Paper Manufacturing Co.	Dublin, Ga.	417	100
Stone Container Corp.	Snowflake, Ariz.	303	65

Source: American Newspaper Publishers Association, Reston, Va., Spring/Summer 1991

announced de-inking facilities for mills that produce printing and writing papers.[215] In addition, **Fox River Fiber Co.** in Kaukauna, Wis., a new company formed by several paper companies, is building a de-inked pulp mill that will convert high grade office paper, electrostatic printed paper and mixed waste paper into fine printing and writing paper.[216]

One of the largest U.S. paper manufacturers, **International Paper Co.**, which operates 25 U.S. mills producing various grades of paper, recently signed a licensing agreement with Steinbeis Temming Papier GmbH & Co. of Brannenburg, Germany, that will allow it to make printing and writing paper from 50 percent post-consumer waste paper, including old newspapers and magazines. Before reaching the licensing agreement, which gives International Paper exclusive rights to the German technology in North America, Central America and the Caribbean, the company had been using pre-consumer waste paper in some of its printing and writing papers.[217]

Table 4-6

Planned U.S. and Canadian Newsprint Recycling Mills

Company	Location	Recycled Capacity (000 tons)	Recycled Content (%)	Year
Abitibi-Price Inc.	Thunder Bay, Ont.	154	40	NA
Alabama River Newsprint Co.[a]	Claiborne, Ala.	243	40-45	1991
Boise Cascade Corp.	Steilacoom, Wash.	195	40	NA
Bowater Inc./Advance Publications	Calhoun, Tenn.	260	Variable 40	1991
Canadian Pacific Forest Products Ltd.	Gatineau, Que.	485	40	1991
	Thunder Bay, Ont.	265	Maximum 40	1991
Champion International Corp.	Sheldon, Tex.	473	40	1992
Daishowa Forest Products Ltd.	Quebec, Que.	331	40	1992
Donohue Inc.	Clermont, Que.[b]	276	10-15	NA
Fletcher Challenge Canada Ltd.	Campbell River, B.C.[b]	165[c]	40	1991
	Crofton, B.C.[b]		40	
Inland Empire Paper Co.	Millwood, Wash.	79	40	1991
James Maclaren Industries Inc.	Masson, Que.	206	20	NA
Kruger Inc.	Bromptonville, Que.	55[c]	40	1991
	Trois-Rivieres, Que.[b]		40	
MacMillan Bloedel Ltd.	Port Alberni, B.C.[b]	165[c]	40	1991
	Powell River, B.C.[b]		40	
Spruce Falls Power	Kapuskasing, Ont.	336	11	NA

[a] Joint project of Abitibi-Price Inc. and Parsons & Whittemore Inc.
[b] Purchasing de-inked pulp
[c] Total for two mills

Source: American Newspaper Publishers Association, Reston, Va., Spring/Summer 1991

Collection: API believes municipal collection programs, which now supply more than 65 percent of old newspapers, will replace volunteer or commercial collection programs for old newspapers. For the remaining paper grades, API is urging communities to rely on the existing private infrastructure of roughly 1,500 paper dealers that collect, sort, bale and ship waste paper throughout the country.[218]

Waste paper dealers are concerned that municipal collection efforts will adversely affect the existing infrastructure. New York City, for example, was considering becoming its own waste paper broker, setting up long-term supply contracts directly with recycled newsprint mills. The city said that it would continue to market the amount it currently recycles through waste paper dealers but that it would handle additional amounts of waste paper directly. The city also is considering setting up its own processing facility.[219]

Joint ventures with waste management companies—Paper companies also are forming alliances with a number of the leading solid waste management companies to ensure a steady flow of waste paper. Chapter 6 provides additional information on these alliances.

Future Market for Post-Consumer Paper and Paperboard

The entire U.S. paper and paperboard industry is coming under increasing pressure to boost its use of waste paper, particularly in products, such as newsprint and printing and writing paper, where waste paper content is low. (See Table 4-2 for a listing of waste paper usage by end product.) The paperboard segment of the industry uses the most waste paper today, but the greatest projected growth in waste paper usage is in the paper segment of the industry. The grades of waste paper that will be in greatest demand in the near term appear to be old corrugated containers and high grade paper fiber, such as computer paper, and in the longer term, old newspapers.

The ability of the paper and paperboard industry to meet its goal of recovering 40 percent of all waste paper by 1995 hinges on a number of factors. Industry says achieving its goal "will require the investment of billions of dollars over several years by U.S. paper and paperboard producers, sufficient marketplace demand for the resulting recycled materials, and continued growth in foreign demand for U.S. waste paper."[220]

Because the paper and paperboard industry is sensitive to broad economic trends, uncertainty about the strength of the economic recovery from recession brings into question the industry's ability to follow through with all of its expansion plans and invest billions of dollars in recycling capacity by the middle of the decade. Meanwhile, it is likely that the industry will continue to consolidate as larger and better capitalized companies squeeze smaller companies unable to make the transition into recycled paper production from the marketplace.

If the paper industry is unable to keep pace with the growing number of collection programs, there is the potential for further market dislocations. Paper collection, particularly newsprint, lends itself very easily to municipal recycling programs, and as large cities such as Philadelphia, Los Angeles, New York and Chicago expand or start up their citywide recycling programs, these programs could add almost 1 million tons of old newspapers to the market each year.[221] The ability of several large cities to implement or expand recycling programs also is uncertain, however, because of the fiscal constraints many are facing.

The uncertainty surrounding both industry's ability to use more waste paper and the ability of large cities to gear up recycling programs that have the potential to swamp waste paper markets indicates that dislocations in waste paper supply and demand are likely to continue in the near term. The marketing challenge for municipalities will be to supply a clean material that is sorted by grade. Recyclers will need to determine the grades of paper nearby mills need and structure the collection and processing system to supply the quality needed. Over the longer term, demand and supply should even out as industry, spurred on by political and consumer pressure and potential cost savings, continues to invest in recycling capacity, and experience with recycling programs provides a better gauge as to how much paper realistically can be recovered. Eventually, the paper and paperboard industry foresees the day when the "challenge will be generating a sufficient raw material supply to meet demand."[222]

Chapter V
POST-CONSUMER PLASTICS

After decades of research produced plastics heralded for their inde-structibility, plastics are now under fire for that very ability to endure. Concerned about landfills that are rapidly reaching capacity, environmentalists and those responsible for solid waste disposal are scrutinizing materials taking up landfill space. Because of their advertised longevity, and also because their use has become so prevalent, plastics have become an obvious target for those attempting to divert materials from landfills. First introduced in the commercial marketplace in the late 1930s, U.S. plastic production has skyrocketed over the last 30 years, jumping from 3 billion pounds in 1958 to 57 billion pounds in 1988—an annual average growth rate of 10.3 percent.[1] Since the 1970s, plastic has become the most widely used material in the United States, outpacing aluminum, steel and copper combined.[2]

Post-consumer plastics recycling is in its infancy, however, posting the lowest recycling rate among the major recyclables in the municipal solid waste stream—a barely measurable 1.1 percent in 1988. Perhaps because of this low recycling rate, the industry may boast the largest number of new recycling initiatives. Proposals to establish large-scale plastics recycling facilities surface frequently.

A driving force behind this scramble to establish plastics recycling has been legislation. In 1990 alone, 33 states adopted laws singling out plastics in the waste stream.[3] Outright bans of certain plastic packaging have been passed in Suffolk County, N.Y.; Newark, N.J.; Berkeley, Calif.; and Minneapolis and St. Paul, Minn. Competing industries and environmentalists also have launched campaigns to dissuade consumers from buying plastic because of its low recycling rate. The glass container industry, for example, ran an ad in an October 1990 issue of *USA Today* that said: "Plastic recycling is in the dumps. Forget all those pretty ads you've seen about plastic recycling. Instead, think garbage."[4] Some within the plastics industry are combatting these ads with their own ad campaigns highlighting recycling initiatives. Amoco Chemical Co. produced a two-page spread that headlines, "We'd like to recycle the thinking that plastics can't be recycled,"[5] while Lever Brothers Co., producer of Wisk detergent, which is marketed in plastic bottles, boasts, "Now you can enjoy the benefits and convenience of our plastic bottles knowing they can find new life far from landfills."[6]

Although industry argues that attention focused on plastics in the waste stream is inappropriate given that plastic represented only 8 percent of the waste stream by weight in 1988, industry also recognizes it must respond with recycling initiatives. Indications are that the plastic industry's initiatives have made inroads with the public—early legislation banned plastics, while more recent plastics legislation focuses on recycling. In fact, some analysts project that plastics recycling programs will actually expand markets for new plastic resins by appeasing environmentalists' concerns and eliminating restrictions against plastics.[7]

The glass industry and environmentalists are attacking the plastic industry for its limited ability to recycle in a closed-loop system. (A closed-loop system means the same products are produced out of used ones.) Plastics often are recycled into "throw-away items that also end up in the trash," such as flower pots or carpeting, say ads from the glass container industry. Another glass industry brochure uses the term "cascading" to describe plastics recycling, saying that turning plastics into disposable items merely delays the day when plastics end up in a landfill.[8]

Despite these criticisms, many within the plastics industry view multiple uses for plastics products as an adequate response to calls for recycling. Edmond Carreras of Day Products Inc., a firm that recycles plastic bottles, said that "ideally, the life cycle of plastic packaging would include: six months as a package, five years as an auto part, and then 10 years as [plastic] lumber."[9] General Electric Co. foresees a similar future for plastics and is developing a nationwide recycling network to fulfill its slogan, "Bottles to Bumpers to Buildings." The company envisions that after its new returnable plastic milk bottle is refilled more than 100 times, it will be remanufactured into automotive parts and then, years later, into building panels and systems with a service life of many decades.[10]

Others within the plastics industry, however, see a need to establish a closed-loop recycling system. While some used plastic containers are being made into new nonfood containers with up to 50 percent recycled content, a major obstacle to closed-loop recycling has been that beverage containers—the most recycled plastic product—as well as plastic films, coatings and many other packaging applications, require resins with tightly controlled technical specifications. As a result, most post-consumer plastics are recycled into products that make fewer physical and chemical demands on the plastics.[11] Coca-Cola Co., however, recently introduced soda bottles made from 25 percent recycled plastic resins, and Pepsi-Cola Co. says it plans to follow suit this year. (See Box 5-1 for additional information.) The U.S. Food and Drug Administration's approval of the new Coke bottle marks only the second type of plastic food packaging that has a federal stamp of approval, the other being egg cartons. Given that food packaging is a major source of plastics in the waste stream, lack of FDA approval for other packaging severely limits the establishment of closed-loop recycling systems. Successfully producing large quantities of new soft drink bottles from old ones would open substantial markets for recycled plastics and pave the way for other types of food packaging, but it remains to be seen whether processing used plastics to meet the strict specifications of food packaging is cost-effective.

Given the industry split over the importance of creating closed-loop recycling systems, the plastics industry is pursuing two major routes to reuse plastics: separating plastic resins into homogeneous or pure resins that can be used in some of the same applications as virgin resins, or creating new markets for mixed plastic resins, often called commingled plastics. The second route requires less processing but produces a lower-grade product with limited uses, such as plastic lumber.

Regardless of which avenue is pursued, the major constraint to boosting the plastics recycling rate is the lack of a reclamation infrastructure. Establishing a steady supply of used plastics poses a much greater challenge than any technical limitations to recycling plastic. The nine states with beverage container deposit legislation are the largest source of plastic bottles at present, supplying a steady and reasonably clean stream of bottles.[12] For the most part, the plastics industry is banking on curbside collection systems as the primary means of funneling additional plastics back to manufacturers or to entrepreneurs creating new products from used plastics.

Plastics in the Municipal Waste Stream

Plastics offer a number of advantages over other materials, including design flexibility, high resistance to corrosion, shatter resistance and low weight. Moreover, plastics meet U.S. consumers' demands for convenience and speed, particularly in food preparation.[13] The largest category of plastics in the municipal waste stream is undoubtedly containers and packaging. Roughly 39 percent of all plastic wastes fall into this category, which includes condiment and beverage containers, bags and protection for

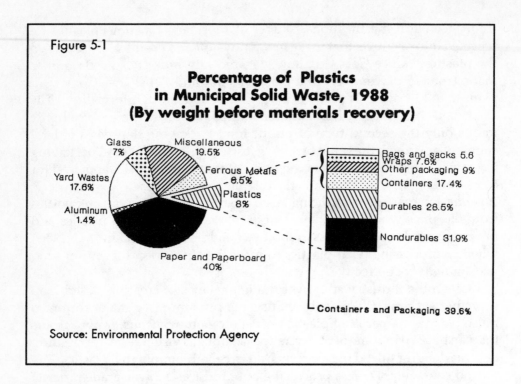

Figure 5-1

**Percentage of Plastics
in Municipal Solid Waste, 1988
(By weight before materials recovery)**

Source: Environmental Protection Agency

electronic equipment and computers. Other plastics in the waste stream include durable goods, such as appliances, furniture and casings of lead acid batteries, and nondurable products, including disposable diapers, plates and cups, clothing and footwear.[14]

In 1988, Americans discarded 14.4 million tons of plastic, which represented 8 percent of the total municipal solid waste stream. Because there is minimal recycling of plastics, virtually all plastics remained in the waste stream, raising its percentage of total discards to 9.2 percent, or 14.3 million tons. A light-weight material, plastics represent a much larger portion of waste discards when measured by volume—19.9 percent of the total.[15]

Corresponding with the rise in plastics production, the percentage of plastics in the municipal solid waste stream has escalated over the last three decades. In 1960, plastics represented only 400,000 tons of municipal solid waste generation, or less than 1 percent of the total. The Environmental Protection Agency projects that plastics in the municipal waste stream will increase to 25.7 million tons in 2010, at which time plastics will represent 10 percent of the waste stream by weight.[16]

Although there are more than 10,000 types of plastic on the market today, more than 90 percent of plastics in the waste stream are composed of six resins. Product examples of the six resins are shown in Table 5-1, along with their percentages of plastics in the waste stream and their percentages

Table 5-1

Six Plastic Resins in the Municipal Waste Stream

Resin	Product Examples	% of Plastics in Waste Stream	% of Plastic Bottles
Low-density polyethylene (LDPE)	Wrapping films, grocery bags	27%	5-10%
High density polyethylene (HDPE)	Milk jugs, detergent bottles, toys	21%	50-60%
Polystyrene (PS)	Coffee cups, "clam-shells," utensils	16%	5-10%
Polypropylene (PP)	Syrup bottles, yogurt tubs, diapers	16%	5-10%
Polyvinyl chloride (PVC)	Pipe, meat wrap, cooking oil bottles	6.5%	5-10%
Polyethylene terephthalate (PET)	Soft drink bottles, medicine containers	5%	20-30%

Sources: % of plastics in the waste stream: Franklin Associates Ltd., 1990
% of plastic bottles: "1989 Plastics Recycling Directory," Society of the Plastics Industry Inc., Washington, D.C., 1989

of all plastic bottles, which are the most recycled plastic products. As Table 5-1 shows, although polyethylene terephthalate (PET) has the highest recycling rate among plastics, it represents the smallest of the six major resin groups in the waste stream.

Recycling rates: The plastics recycling rate of 1.1 percent is the lowest among the five major waste stream recyclables. Besides durable plastic goods, which have a 1.5 percent recovery rate,[17] the only plastic products with measurable recovery rates are containers. The Council for Solid Waste Solutions estimates that 9 percent of all plastic bottles were recycled in 1990, yielding 360 million pounds.[18] In 1989, roughly 20 percent of all containers made of PET were recycled—more than 190 million pounds of the roughly

1 billion pounds produced.[19] In that same year, PET soft drink bottles posted a recycling rate of 28 percent, which rose to 30 percent in 1990.[20] First introduced in 1978,[21] PET bottles are the plastic bottle market's fastest-growing item, holding more than 30 percent of the market for soft drink containers in 1989. The popularity of the two-liter PET bottle is the major reason for PET's growth in the market, accounting for about 80 percent of all plastic soft drink containers sold.[22]

Efforts also are underway to recycle HDPE containers, namely milk jugs, juice and water containers. Approximately 7 percent of milk jugs were recycled in 1990, up substantially from 1.4 percent in 1989. Roughly 2.5 percent of other uncolored HDPE containers were recycled in 1990, and another 3 percent of colored HDPE containers were recycled in 1990, with both recycling rates up from less than 1 percent in 1989.[23] In 1989, about 85 million pounds of post-consumer HDPE were recycled in the United States,[24] up from 72 million pounds in 1988.[25] (Approximately 8.3 billion pounds of HDPE resins were produced in 1990, 8.1 in 1989 and 8.4 billion in 1988.[26])

The Council for Solid Waste Solutions has set a 50 percent recycling goal for PET and HDPE bottles and a 25 percent recycling goal for all plastic bottles and containers by 1995.[27] Market research sponsored by the Plastics Recycling Foundation and the state of Ohio determined that the potential market for recycled PET could grow to a substantial 600 million pounds by 1993 and that the market for recycled HDPE could grown even higher to 660 million pounds by 1993.[28] Darrell Morrow, former director of the Center for Plastics Recycling Research at Rutgers State University, predicts that the overall recycling rate for all types of plastics will reach 25 percent in about five years, eventually reaching 50 to 60 percent.[29]

The Post-Consumer Plastics Recycling Process

Industry representatives say there are no technical obstacles to reclaiming plastics, and they note that most plastic producers have been routinely recycling their own plant scrap for decades. Dr. Sidney Rankin of the Center for Plastics Recycling Research at Rutgers asserts that "relatively low-investment, low-cost technology exists to reclaim and reuse all packaging plastic wastes (if they were collected)—all of them. The entire remainder of the wastes can be made into saleable articles using commingled processing technology."[30] Wayne Pearson, executive director of the Plastics Recycling Foundation, agrees that if plastics "are collected and sorted, they are easy to recycle."[31]

In order to understand the plastics recycling process, it is important to understand the origin of plastic products. Plastics are resins derived from

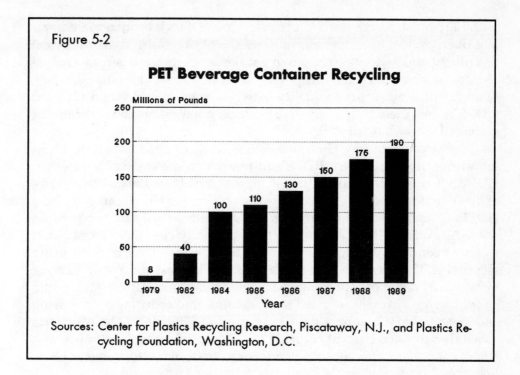

Figure 5-2

PET Beverage Container Recycling

Millions of Pounds

Sources: Center for Plastics Recycling Research, Piscataway, N.J., and Plastics Recycling Foundation, Washington, D.C.

petroleum, natural gas and, on rare occasions, coal. The resins are produced by linking small groups of molecules into long chains, called polymers. Through polymerization, propylene, a flammable gaseous hydrocarbon, is made into polypropylene; styrene into polystyrene; and vinyl chloride into polyvinyl chloride. Chemical additives are used to modify or enhance plastic resins, creating a wide range of plastic products that can be flexible or rigid, clear or opaque, quite strong or easy to tear.[32]

Commercial plastics fall under two major headings: thermoplastics, which represent about three-quarters of all plastics produced and can be recycled, and thermosets, many of which do not melt when heated (an integral step in plastics recycling) and cannot be recycled.[33] Almost all plastics used in food and beverage containers are thermoplastic, including polyethylene, the world's largest selling thermoplastic. Although thermoplastics can be recycled, they face constraints when strength or appearance is integral to the end use. Most plastic resins degrade each time they are heated.

The fact that plastics degrade during reprocessing brings into question how many times plastics can be recycled into useful products. Infinite recycling is technically impossible, but there is debate as to when quality begins to suffer.[34] The Plastics Recycling Foundation's Pearson maintains that "degradation is not a problem," noting that "no one hardly ever deals with 100 percent recycled resin" because "no one item is being recycled over and over." When industry reformulates the plastic resin, Pearson says, it usually "sprinkles in virgin resin to get the properties it desires," such as building strength back into PET polymers. Pearson concludes that although there can be a difference in quality between recycled and virgin PET and HDPE resins, there is "not much difference, not a difference that can't be managed by the industry."[35]

Tests conducted by Quantum Chemical Corp. of Cincinnati, Ohio, found that post-consumer HDPE did not match the standards of virgin HDPE. Quantum determined, however, that the higher the quality control of the recycling process, the closer the post-consumer HDPE came to virgin HDPE. Quantum is one of the largest U.S. suppliers of virgin polyolifin resins, including HDPE and low-density polyethylene (LDPE). Quantum plans to conduct additional tests to address a major obstacle to using recycled HDPE plastic in new bottles—HDPE bottles' absorption of trace materials from the products they package. These contaminants, including odors, can remain in the recycled resin, causing smoke during reprocessing and potentially contaminating a new product. For now, Quantum has concluded that 100 percent recycled HDPE should be limited to use as a blend component with virgin material or as a layer in multilayered applications.[36]

Arriving at similar conclusions, Procter & Gamble Co., in conjunction with Plastipak Packaging Inc. and Owens-Brockway Plastic Products, a division of Owens-Illinois Inc., developed a three-layered bottle for its products that sandwiches recycled HDPE in between two layers of virgin HDPE. The inner virgin layer prevents contamination, while the outer virgin layer ensures color and surface fidelity. P&G is selling its Tide laundry detergent and Downy fabric softener in these bottles. The company and the Continental Plastic Containers Division of Continental Can Co. developed a two-layered bottle that has a mix of recycled HDPE and trim scrap as its outer layer. P&G has packaged its Cheer laundry detergent in this bottle and is closely watching the outer layer's ability to hold color.[37] Drug Plastics and Glass Co. of Boyertown, Pa., also developed a plastic bottle, "Recyclepak," that sandwiches a layer of post-consumer HDPE between layers of virgin plastic. The company says many of its customers, brand-name pharmaceutical and personal care product firms, have committed to using the Recyclepak for their products, even though the bottle will cost more than a bottle made from virgin materials.[38]

In contrast to the layered approach, Soltex Polymer Corp., a subsidiary of Solvay & Cie Societe Anonyme, has come out with a compound HDPE resin. Using 25 percent recycled plastic, Soltex's compound plastic has uniform properties, which it says makes it as easy for molders to work with as with virgin HDPE.[39]

Recycling polystyrene also appears to be technically feasible. David Sheon of the National Polystyrene Recycling Co. told IRRC that recycled polystyrene, assuming it is not mixed with other plastic resins, is as good as virgin polystyrene in "99 percent of applications," and that no limits have been discovered in the number of times polystyrene can be recycled. Sheon added that the major limitations of recycled polystyrene are that the FDA has not yet allowed recycled polystyrene to be used in food packaging and that color cannot be removed from the recycled resin, whereas virgin polystyrene can be produced in a clear form.[40]

Plastics preparation: Once the plastic resins are separated, preparing them for sale to end-use manufacturers is a relatively simple process. In the case of PET and HDPE resins, the plastics processors need only separate any components (aluminum from the cap, paper and adhesive from the label and sometimes the HDPE base cup on a PET bottle) wash, dry and grind the plastic material into flakes.[41] The order of these steps varies according to the process used, but the large-scale plastics recycling facilities have automated systems to perform these tasks. Wellman Inc., for example, the country's largest PET recycler, designed its equipment to remove labels, caps and HDPE base cups from PET bottles, while Eaglebrook Plastics Inc., a major HDPE recycler, developed a process that removes milk residues and paper labels from HDPE bottles. In some cases, such as at Day Products' PET recycling plant, electrostatic separators are used to separate the aluminum. Lastly, the flakes are sometimes compressed into pellets to raise the resin's value to industry. To produce pelletized resin, the flakes are processed through an extruder, which melts the plastic into long spaghetti-like strands that are then cut into uniform pellets about the size of birdshot.[42]

The residential recyclers' tasks to recycle plastics are small; few buyers require removal of labels or base cups, although they usually ask that the containers be rinsed. As with all reclaimed waste stream components, contamination can significantly degrade the value of the recycled product. And given the fact that the bulk of plastic products are used as containers and packaging, plastics are often contaminated with food waste.

As with PET and HDPE, preparing separated, used polystyrene for industry is straightforward, although the amount of food contamination, particularly from fast food restaurants, is a hindrance. When McDonald's Corp. was recycling polystyrene, it reported that recycling plastics separated from its restaurants and schools involved the following seven steps: 1) shredding waste from schools and restaurants; 2) screening out small items such as utensils and straws; 3) air sorting light plastic foam from heavier objects; 4) pulping polystyrene and paper with water; 5) screen washing the pulp to wash away the paper fiber from the polystyrene; 6) drying the resulting polystyrene pieces; and 7) collecting the dried resin for shipment to plastics plants for re-use in new products.[43]

Box 5-1

Recycled Plastics in Food Packaging

To maintain health standards, U.S. Food and Drug Administration regulations require food packaging to be free of contamination. The high cost of achieving the required purity levels, and a costly and lengthy process involved in obtaining FDA clearance, have deterred nearly all food packaging from being recycled into the original product. Companies have taken steps, however, to crack open the lucrative food packaging market to recycled plastic resins.

In late 1989, Dolco Packaging Corp. of Sherman Oaks, Calif., the nation's largest producer of polystyrene egg cartons, obtained the first federal approval to use recycled plastics in food packaging, namely post-consumer polystyrene scrap in egg cartons. The FDA also gave the company "direction as to how to proceed to get approval for additional applications," including meat trays, fast food containers, school lunch trays and foam beverage cups, according to Richard Olson of Dolco Packaging. The company is not presently pursuing these additional applications, however, explaining to IRRC that there is a "perception problem with consumers" who view recycled material as inferior or unclean. Dolco uses between 10 to 25 percent post-consumer polystyrene in its egg cartons, and tests have demonstrated it can use up to 50 percent recycled plastic.[44]

In January 1991, Hoechst AG's Hoechst Celanese Corp. obtained FDA approval for a methanolysis process that allows it to make new PET soft drink bottles from used ones. Methanolysis uses methanol to break down, or depolymerize, PET into its components—dimethyl terephthalate and ethylene glycol. The FDA has emphasized that it does not consider Hoechst's process to be "recycling" because the scrap PET bottles are not physically

Sorting by resin type: In order to prepare used plastics as a substitute for virgin resin in the manufacturing process, the plastics must first be separated by resin type. This step is perhaps the most difficult in the recycling process and holds the key to a successful resin reclamation program. The ability to isolate resins by type is as important to the plastics industry as separating paper by grade is to the paper industry or separating glass by color is to the glass industry. Because plastic resins have different physical and chemical characteristics, they have varying melting points and react differently to reheating.[51] Recycling the different resins together is infeasible in some instances. When doing so is feasible, the value of the end product is reduced significantly and its applications are limited. Plastic lumber is the most common end product of mixed plastics, often referred to as commingled plastics.

One major obstacle to complete resin separation is that even if different

being reused. Working with Coca-Cola Co., Hoechst has FDA approval to manufacture 100 percent of its new bottles from used ones, although its first batch of bottles being sold in Charlotte, N.C., still contain 75 percent virgin plastic. Pepsi-Cola Co., which together with Coca-Cola controls about 70 percent of the U.S. soft drink market, has teamed up with Goodyear Tire & Rubber Co. to introduce its own recycled bottles. Goodyear is awaiting FDA approval for its glycolysis process, which also breaks PET down into its components. Sewell Plastics Inc. plans to produce Pepsi's soft drink bottles using Goodyear's resin.[45]

Both Eastman Chemical Co. and E.I. du Pont de Nemours & Co. also have developed methanolysis processes to depolymerize PET. Eastman Chemical's planned $2 million facility in Kingsport, Tenn., is scheduled to produce recycled resins by 1993 for Twinpak Inc., Canada's largest PET bottle manufacturer.[46] And a few weeks after Hoechst received FDA approval for its methanolysis process, Du Pont announced a new $5 million pilot methanolysis plant in Nashville, Tenn., that will supply recycled PET for food packaging applications. Du Pont plans to start up the pilot plant by mid-1991 and to begin operation of a commercial facility by the end of 1993.[47]

Many question whether soft drink bottles will ever contain large amounts of resin from used PET bottles, pointing out that depolymerization is an expensive process and that demand for used PET bottles currently outstrips supply. Thomas Duff, chief executive officer of Wellman, the country's leading PET recycler that will be competing to purchase PET bottles, is one such skeptic, remarking that the soft drink companies' announcements "must be a public relations exercise. They've lost track of the economics."[48] Coca-Cola has conceded that if using recycled resin proves to be too expensive, it will abandon its plans.[49] Pepsi has committed only to producing 135 million bottles with resin from Sewell's process.[50]

plastic products can be separated from one another, many plastic products themselves are comprised of several different resins. As a result, recycling proponents are encouraging manufacturers to redesign mixed or multi-layer plastics and produce single resin products. H.J. Heinz Co., the world's largest ketchup maker, responded in April 1990 by announcing plans to redesign its multi-layer ketchup bottle into a PET bottle in 1991. Working with Continental PET Technologies, a division of Continental Can Co., Heinz spent three years and $8 million dollars developing the new bottle, called Enviropet.[52]

Somewhat ironically, also in the spring of 1990, the Plastic Bottle Institute, a division of SPI, released competing tests indicating that multi-material ketchup bottles could be recycled with existing technology. Using ketchup bottles manufactured by American National Can, Continental Can and Owens-Brockway that contained polypropylene and an ethylene vinyl alcohol inner oxygen barrier, researchers recycled the bottles using PET bottle processing equipment.[53] A study released in early 1991 by the Society of the Plastics Industry also shows promise for polypropylene recycling. The study concluded that polypropylene can be combined with used HDPE milk jugs to make new multi-layer HDPE bottles containing up to 6 percent polypropylene. The study projects that industry can use existing reclamation methods to recycle nearly all of the post-consumer multi-layer polypropylene.[54]

Separating by color within resin type also can be important. Recycling different colored bottles together generally produces a drab olive or black resin, which has limited uses. Even though recycled HDPE resin is often the middle layer of three layers, for instance, dark resins can still show through. Gerald J. Claes, director of environmental programs for Graham Packaging Co., which recycles and produces HDPE containers, says some of its customers are particular about bottle color, explaining that "after all, Pennzoil yellow is Pennzoil yellow."[55] In order to meet customer demands, Graham Packaging has employees hand sort bales of plastic containers by color. Thomas Duff, the chief executive officer of Wellman, which turns PET soda bottles into fiberfill for carpets, also points out the limitations imposed by colored bottles even when separated, noting "You can only sell so many green carpets. It's not one of the more popular colors."[56] Some plastics processors are experimenting with dying colored plastics black, which has more applications than green.

The difficulty in separating plastics by resin type and by color is the primary reason that most recycling has been limited to single resin containers that can be easily recognized and separated from the waste stream, namely PET soft drink bottles and HDPE milk jugs.[57] Some recycling centers require that these two containers arrive separated, and many small centers that allow the containers to be delivered intermixed hand-sort them from one another. The HDPE base cup and the main PET soda bottle also can be relatively easily separated. To handle larger volumes, the CPRR at Rutgers University and some large-scale plastics recycling facilities have developed automated sorting lines. The CPRR is working on computerization of its optical detectors, which can detect clear PET from green PET and natural HDPE beverage bottles, such as milk jugs. Separating whole containers in this manner is referred to as macro separation.[58]

Micro separation involves more sophisticated automated separation techniques. Plastic processors grind whole PET and HDPE bottles, including caps, labels and base cups, and remove pieces of the paper labels through air filtration. The resulting plastic flakes are run through systems that take advantage of the plastic's different densities, often a water-based flotation system in which HDPE will float while the heavier PET sinks. A newer technology developed by the CPRR utilizes the differences in PET's and HDPE's gravity and electrical charges, separating them in an air cyclone and then electrostatically eliminating the aluminum rings from the beverage bottles' necks.[59] CPRR's technology has been licensed for $3,000 each to 18 businesses worldwide. Two of these licensees, Day Products and Hancor Inc. (a plastic drain pipe manufacturer whose subsidiary, United Resource Recovery Inc., processes 7 million pounds per year of HDPE containers) started up recycling plants in late 1989.[60] CPRR also is exploring supercritical fluid and froth flotation separation technologies.[61]

Beyond PET and HDPE: To increase the recycling rate for all plastics in the waste stream significantly, recyclers must recycle more than the well-known soda bottles and milk jugs. To assist recyclers in identifying additional plastics, the Society of the Plastics Industry Inc. has developed a coding system for most plastic containers to identify resin type. (See Box 5-2.) While the system is aiding recyclers on the conveyor lines at today's small-scale recycling centers or at the residence, the system will be difficult to implement at newer, large-scale materials recycling facilities where workers could easily become bogged down trying to read the codes, particularly if the containers are crushed.

To aid separation at large-scale facilities, Quantum Chemical is advocating the addition of fluorescent dye "tags" to plastics so that workers could identify resin content under ultraviolet light.[62] Other efforts to expand the types of resin separated and recycled include research on vinyl containers, which contain polyvinylchloride, or PVC. These efforts are described in the PVC sorting and recycling section of this chapter.

Bruce Nauman, a chemical engineer at Rensselaer Polytechnic Institute in Troy, N.Y., is attempting to reclaim different polymers by chemical means. Working under the auspices of the Plastics Recycling Foundation, Nauman has developed a process that can separate plastics that have been mixed together in the waste stream and, unlike other technologies, can separate different generic polymers that have been physically bonded together in one product. Nauman coarsely grinds the plastic waste containing as many as six different polymers and then dumps it into a vessel containing a solvent, such as xylene.[63] Nauman says that "it is a process that can get the polymers essentially in the form they left the factory."[64] Dissolution has only been carried out at a low polymer concentration, however. Following additional research on the project's economics and environmental impact, plans call for the project to be scaled up.[65]

Battelle Memorial Institute of Columbus, Ohio, also is developing a reverse polymerization process. The system reduces mixed plastics placed into a thermal reactor into molecular gases that consist of base monomers, which can then be separated and recycled. Battelle is operating a small-scale 20 pound per hour pilot plant; a commercial plant is still years away.[66]

Commingled plastics: A second course of action for recycling a variety of plastics is to develop and market products made of mixed plastic. Darrell Morrow, the CPRR's former director, foresees a need for commingled plastics recycling systems, estimating that bottle recyclers will discover that nearly 30 percent of the material they process will be commingled plastic waste.[67]

The CPRR also points out that plastic containers used in households "are of different package designs, materials and types, and may be manufactured from a variety of polymers; their colors, shapes, and materials are often specified by manufacturers for specific applications." The CPRR concludes that it "would be difficult and expensive to separate them by resin type; the value of the resulting plastic would be less than that of generic resin materials, because of the varied pigmentations and additives that are used in manufacturing."[68]

As a result, Rutgers has aggressively pursued development of commingled plastics recycling systems. In 1987, it installed the "Extruder Technology 1," or ET/1. Developed by Advanced Recycling Technology Inc. of Brakel, Belgium, the extrusion/molding machine produces a range of lumberlike products by heating ground, mixed, unsorted and uncleaned plastics, primarily HDPE, in a barrel until the material flows. The plastic is then forced into a mold and cooled in a water tank. Advantages of the process are that it can take a mix of plastics and heavily contaminated plastics. The drawbacks to using unsorted, uncleaned plastic is that the end product's properties are not always consistent and may contain voids in the center of the plank. The economics of the process also are poor unless the lumber is turned into a finished product. In addition, paper residue causes charring and gives off smells at high temperatures.[69]

Based on its experience with ET/1, Rutgers is studying refined commingled processes, which include washing and filtration steps that remove contaminants, thereby eliminating the voids and improving control over the processing of the material. The lumber, which is predominantly HDPE, has higher impact strength than virgin HDPE. Rutgers is experimenting to achieve different properties; when polystyrene is added, for example, the lumber becomes stiffer.[70] A number of companies producing plastic lumber are described in this chapter's plastic lumber section.

Researchers at Dow Chemical Co. and Du Pont are trying another approach in recycling mixed plastics, using compatibilizers, agents that can bind different forms of polymers into one homogeneous resin. Their work is based on the fact that many new resins are created by manipulating the chemical structures of existing ones. They are developing molecules that are attracted at one end to the molecule of one resin and at the other end to the molecule of another resin, thereby binding two imcompatible resins into a plastic that may have useful properties for new applications.[71]

General Electric is attempting to develop a "universal compatibilizer"

Box 5-2

Voluntary Coding System for
Plastic Containers

Efforts to recycle more than soda bottles and milk jugs have been stymied by the difficulty and expense of attempting to distinguish different types of plastic. In response to this problem, The Society of the Plastics Industry Inc. (SPI) has developed a voluntary national container material code system that identifies plastic bottles and other plastic containers by resin composition. The one-half to one-inch code, which is imprinted on or near the bottom of a plastic container, is a three-sided triangular arrow with a number in the center and letters underneath, indicating one of the six primary resin types. (See PET code at beginning of chapter.) Codes are recommended for all plastic bottles and jars that hold 16 or more ounces, and other plastic containers, such as tubs and trays, that hold eight or more ounces. Non-coded containers can still be recycled through mixed plastics recycling processes.[72]

Johnson Controls Inc., Amway Corp. and Procter & Gamble were among the first companies to adopt SPI's coding system.[73] The SPI, which introduced the system in 1988 in cooperation with the Plastic Bottle Institute, the Rigid Plastic Container Division and the Plastic Drum Institute, is projecting full industry cooperation by 1992. By early 1991, 27 states had passed legislation specifying or allowing the coding system or a variation of the system.[74]

Industry critics of the coding system contend that the labels need to be more specific. HDPE, for instance, is labeled number 2 under the system, but the number does not distinguish between blow-mold grades, which include oil bottles, milk jugs and detergent bottles, and injection-mold grades, which include cheese and butter tubs and yogurt containers. HDPE piping, which is made from a remelted blow-molding HDPE, is wrought with stress fractures if injection-mold grade is mixed in, and more is getting mixed in as recycling rates climb.[75]

Critics outside the industry oppose the SPI codes for two major reasons. They say the logo too closely resembles the traditional recycling symbol, erroneously leading consumers to believe there is a workable recycling infrastructure for all plastics. Secondly, they criticize SPI's directive that manufacturers label the primary resin in the package, thus allowing a package that is only 40 percent HDPE to be labeled HDPE. They say this directive defeats the coding system's purpose. Some states that have adopted the SPI codes have altered or eliminated the triangular arrows and some are considering raising the resin percentage requirements.[76] Critics also fear the coding could appear on degradable plastic containers that could wreak havoc with recycling systems.

that can fit four or five different polymers into its chemical structure. Du Pont, however, is skeptical that a "universal compatibilizer" is feasible, and the company is concentrating instead on developing additives that make specific groups of polymers more recyclable.[77] (GE's subsidiary, Polymerland Inc., announced a new line of recycled resins in June 1990. The recycled resins include post-consumer products, although the products, such as computer or phone systems, are normally not found in curbside recycling programs.[78])

Economics of Plastics Recycling

The economics of plastics recycling is more controversial than the economics associated with recycling any other waste stream material. Environmental groups, skeptical about the profitability of some plastic recycling ventures, accuse the industry of public relations scams designed to appease consumers' consciences. Some industry spokesmen have acknowledged that some projects are not yet economically viable but dismiss charges that the projects are mere public relations gimmicks. As Roger W. Friskey, a spokesman for Amoco Chemical Co. remarked, a firm might become involved in "experimental projects that may not be justified strictly as a business proposition but will be important politically to show that the [company] has a lot of interest and good will."[79]

For the most part, skepticism about profitability is targeted at high-profile polystyrene recycling projects. Companies such as Wellman and Eaglebrook Plastics are proof that recycling the easily recognized PET and HDPE containers can be a profitable business. Wayne E. Pearson, executive director of the Plastics Recycling Foundation, maintains that "the economics [of PET and HDPE recycling] are very favorable. The PET and HDPE can be cleaned up and positioned in the market at approximately half the price of virgin resin, in low investment, neighborhood friendly plants, and the quality of the PET recovered in flake form, can exceed 99.9 percent."[80] James Agnello of Union Carbide Corp., which plans to open a plant that will process PET, HDPE and plastic film, also told IRRC, "We're treating it [the recycling facility] strictly as a business. We think we can make money with it, or else we would not have gone this far."[81]

In some instances, however, end-users are paying more for reclaimed resin than for virgin resin. Dr. Charles Lancelot of Rubbermaid Commercial Products Inc. told IRRC that to meet its quality control specifications, Rubbermaid purchases "higher-end reclaim" for products containing recycled HDPE. Lancelot says the cost of this reclaim is 5 to 10 percent above the cost of virgin resin but that Rubbermaid is willing to pay the price because its customer base is demanding recycled content.[82]

Using recycled resins in place of virgin materials can produce considerable savings in both capital costs and energy requirements. The investment in equipment required to process PET and HDPE into flakes or pellets is significantly less than the capital required to produce virgin resins from oil and natural gas. In addition, primarily because used plastic need only be remelted in order to be reused in the manufacturing process, recycling can save 92 to 98 percent of the energy required to produce the major commodity thermoplastics—LDPE, HDPE, PS, PET and PVC—from virgin materials (not including the energy used to collect and transport recycled resins).[83] Plastics recycling facilities also emit far fewer pollutants, some of which are highly toxic, carcinogenic and flammable, than plants producing plastics from virgin materials. Volatile air emissions can be generated during the heating of plastics, however, and residues can be contained in water used to clean the plastics and cool the remelted resins.[84]

Large-scale recycling facilities that capitalize on economies of scale are key to economically successful PET recycling. The Plastics Recycling Foundation, for instance, estimates that the minimum economical capacity for a PET reclamation plant, based on its automated technology, is 20 million pounds per year in a facility that would cost $2.5 million.[85] In 1989, Howard Kibbel, a consultant with ChemSystems Inc. of Tarrytown, N.Y., calculated that if a company sold 20 million pounds annually at 25 cents per pound, yearly profits could reach $1 million on revenues of $5 million.[86] While the industry had no plants operating on that scale when he made his calculations, today several plants are that size or larger and exceeding his price quotes. In October 1990, for instance, Day Products was selling clear PET flakes produced at its $5 million, 40 million pound per year plant at 42 cents per pound and clear PET pellets at 52 cents per pound, primarily to the textile and packaging industries.[87]

Polystyrene: The economics of polystyrene recycling are not so clear cut as with PET and HDPE. Jeanne Wirka of the Environmental Action Foundation says she is skeptical of the viability of the polystyrene recycling projects and the companies' motives. Wirka and many other environmentalists claim that without the artificial support of plastics industry subsidies, polystyrene recycling projects would never get off the ground. Many environmentalists also say that instead of recycling, they would prefer to see companies focus on reducing polystyrene in packaging, which often has a useful life of less than one minute in fast-food applications.[88]

But E. James Schneiders, president and chief executive officer of the National Polystyrene Recycling Co. (NPRC), a consortium of companies pursuing polystyrene recycling, said of his organization: "The NPRC, through its objective to build a post-consumer polystyrene infrastructure for recycling, is an example of a market-driven business dedicated to improving the environment."[89] Another representative of the NPRC, David

Box 5-3

Degradable Plastics

Responding to pressure to keep used plastics out of landfills, both plastics companies and legislators began pursuing two options: recycling plastics and making plastics degradable. While recycling still enjoys support from many sectors, degradable plastics have lost many early backers.

In a rare consensus, EPA, environmentalists and most plastic industry trade groups favor source reduction and recycling over degradability as the best ways to manage plastic wastes. In late 1989, six environmental groups took their opposition to the streets and launched a national boycott against degradable plastic products. The tide also appears to be turning in state legislatures. In contrast to a spate of legislation adopted in the last few years requiring biodegradable plastics, in the fall of 1990 Rhode Island passed a bill that prohibits the sale or use of any degradable plastic container if it will interfere with the state's recycling program.[90]

Degradable plastics still have a core of supporters, however, namely manufacturers of degradable additives, corn-growing states that benefit from the production of starch additives and small-to-medium sized companies attempting to gain market share by offering new products. In addition, some large companies, such as Warner-Lambert Co., a health care and consumer products company; Imperial Chemical Industries PLC, a British chemical manufacturer; Air Products and Chemicals Inc.; and Battelle Memorial Institute, an Ohio-based research corporation, are developing a new wave of plastics made entirely from natural resources, such as starch and bacteria found in soil.[91] They argue that a truly biodegradable plastic has tremendous market potential. Despite the controversy, the U.S. market for degradable plastics is already quite large—in 1990 it was valued at $200 million.[92]

Biodegradable plastics already are in use in specialized applications, including degradable six-pack rings and surgical sutures. Costs for the polymers in surgical sutures, though, run at least $15 a pound, compared with well under a dollar a pound for conventional plastic.[93] While working to bring these costs down, some companies predict that consumers will be willing to pay a higher price for biodegradable plastics in additional niche markets where recycling seems inappropriate or impractical, such as disposable diapers and tampon applicators. EPA also predicts that other potentially useful applications may be found in areas such as composting or agriculture.[94]

Although welcomed at first, the concept of reducing waste by marketing a wide range of degradable plastic products did not pass muster under careful scrutiny. Many believe that producing degradable plastics would effectively eliminate plastic's best quality—its longevity—and inject uncertainty as to a product's reliability and strength.

The lack of consistent guidelines or government regulations governing what can be labeled or advertised as degradable is another problem. Environmentalists assert that unlike the true degradable plastics that cost $15 a pound or higher, degradable plastics found on supermarket shelves are more appropriately called "biodisintegratables," which are much cheaper but leave tiny bits of plastic after the produce degrades.[95] Ten state attorneys general who investigated plastic bag makers' environmental claims of "degradable" and "recyclable" called for the federal government to "enact a comprehensive regulatory scheme." And in response to a growing number of state packaging laws, many large consumer companies also are calling for national standards. Most manufacturers stopped printing these claims on product packaging after seven states sued Mobil Chemical Co. for claiming that its Hefty trash bags were degradable. In August 1990, Mobil agreed to withdraw all environmental claims, but is contesting fines.[96] Although Mobil is an outspoken critic of the belief that degradable plastics can solve the nation's trash problems, the company says it introduced the bags to protect its market shares.[97]

In addition to concerns about misleading advertising, environmentalists fear that plastic dust from "biodisintegratables" may carry toxic additives or leave toxic or unwanted residues in package contents or landfills.[98] Decomposing plastics in landfills may release toxics, such as lead, cadmium and stabilizers used in their production, and increase the overall amount of toxic runoff and gas emissions, including methane.[99] EPA acknowledges that the environmental products or residues of degradable plastics and their environmental impacts have not been fully identified or evaluated.

Furthermore, there is considerable controversy as to whether degradable plastics will actually break down in modern, sanitary landfills. The two most common methods of making petroleum-based plastics degradable today are biodegradation, which involves the incorporation of starch and oxidizing additives (which allow microorganisms to digest a product), and photodegradation, which involves the incorporation of photosensitive additives that break down under ultraviolet light.[100] Because landfills are designed to be void of light, air, water and microorganisms, it is questionable whether "degradable" plastics would actually degrade under these same conditions. Recent landfill excavations undertaken by Professor William Rathje of the University of Arizona have identified "a mound of guacamole thrown out in 1967, leaves raked up in 1964, lumber from 1952."[101]

Environmentalists also assert that it is more sensible to recover the plastic's petroleum rather than allow it to dissipate in a landfill, and they contend that degradables divert attention from source reduction and recycling.

In addition, EPA says the impact of degradables on plastic recycling is unclear.[102] Critics have charged that contamination of nondegradable materials with degradables could shorten the lifetime of products made from recycled resins. The structural integrity of a plastic fence post made with degradable plastics, for example, may be compromised when the fence post is continually exposed to sunlight, water and other natural elements. If degradable plastics are developed for niche markets only, however, the amount winding its way to a recycling facility would most likely be at levels too low to contaminate the end product.

Sheon, told IRRC that there is "no question that down the road it [polystyrene recycling] will be economical." Sheon added that establishing a polystyrene recycling infrastructure "takes a good amount of start-up money but it will be recovered." Sheon also said that the aluminum industry, which now has a profitable and comprehensive recycling infrastructure in place, took a loss for five years while it built up its infrastructure. Sheon says the plastics industry is increasing the collection rate of plastics faster than the aluminum industry increased its collection rate in its early years.[103] Wayne Pearson, president of the Plastics Recycling Foundation, although referring to PET and HDPE, also emphasized to IRRC that "the curve [representing the rate of plastic recycling] is steeper than the curve for aluminum in its first decade."[104]

The two major constraints to economical polystyrene recycling are transportation costs and end markets. Despite a concentrated supply of polystyrene typically found at fast-food restaurants and institutions, polystyrene's light weight, usually one of its desirable characteristics, results in trucks virtually transporting air when they ship used polystyrene to a central recycling plant. Fitchburg, Wis., the first town in the country to recycle polystyrene, believes the economics of its recycling program would be enhanced if the material could be processed and marketed close to where the material is collected. Sherrir Gruder-Adams, the town's recycling coordinator, speculated that until the infrastructure for polystyrene recycling is more fully developed, the polystyrene industry will probably need to support post-consumer prices.[105] Hardee's restaurant chain, which has begun using a clamshell container containing recycled polystyrene, collects polystyrene and old corrugated cardboard together and uses revenues from the cardboard to support the cost of the polystyrene recycling. John Merritt of Hardee's commented that "You cannot recycle polystyrene, in my opinion, without something else leveraging it."[106]

Many also question whether there is a viable market for the recycled polystyrene. Because it is too costly to process the polystyrene to meet stringent Food and Drug regulations for food packaging, the recycled plastic is remanufactured into other products, such as flower pots and video cassettes. Many wonder how long it will take the supply of recycled polystyrene to overwhelm demand for these types of products. As Donnella Meadows, an adjunct professor of environmental studies at Dartmouth College, phrased the question: "How long will it take for the relentless stream of fast-foodware to glut the market for flowerpots, yo-yos and thumbtacks?"[107]

Mixed plastics: Mixed plastics can be processed only into relatively low value items, such as plastic lumber, and some analysts question whether the markets for these products will economically support major recycling efforts.[108] Skeptics also question whether there will be a sufficient market down the road for a product whose main selling point is its indestructibility.[109] Analysts predict, however, that plastics recycling will not reach a 10 percent recycling rate in the early 1990s unless mixed plastics are included.[110]

Used PET and HDPE container prices: Used PET and HDPE plastic containers are the second-most valuable recyclable material, after aluminum, commonly collected from the post-consumer waste stream. (See Figure I-3 on p. 7 for a comparison of prices.) The average price processors and dealers paid in 1990 ranged from $132 to $170 per ton for used clear PET bottles, $106 to $172 per ton for used natural HDPE bottles, and $86 to $108 for mixed bales of PET and HDPE bottles.[111] Many end-users reported to IRRC in the fall of 1990 that they were paying up to $200 per ton for sorted clear PET and natural HDPE, with others reporting even higher prices paid.

The price of PET bottles doubled from the middle of 1989 to the middle of 1990, largely because a number of new PET processing facilities were competing to purchase a relatively steady supply of containers.[112] Similarly, Texaco Inc. and Shell Oil Co.'s demand for Graham Packaging Co.'s recycled HDPE bottles, including mixed color HDPE, inflated HDPE prices in the summer of 1990.[113]

As for PVC, Occidental Chemical Corp., the primary purchaser of PVC bottles, was offering prices ranging from $120 to $200 per ton in the first quarter of 1991.[114] A large-scale polystyrene recycling facility in California is paying $80 per ton, while an East Coast facility is paying $100 per ton.[115]

Haulers, brokers and processors vary in their requirements and the prices they pay. Payment is influenced by color, the level of contamination, the way the containers are packaged and regional markets. Once the plastic is processed, payment by end-users is further influenced by the form the plastic is in—flake or the generally more valuable pellet.

Because of variations from lot to lot resulting from dirt contamination or color variations, "most buyers feel the recycled material should sell at a discount of about 10 cents per pound below virgin material," William C. Kuhlke, with DeWitt & Co. told *Chemicalweek*. "But as long as polymer prices stay in the 40 cent per pound [$800 per ton] range or higher," Kuhlke added, "recycling projects seem viable."[116]

Given that the small amount of plastic recycled today is only a drop in the bucket compared with the total amount of virgin plastic resin produced annually, the recovery of used resins will have a negligible effect on the total market for plastic resins for the foreseeable future. In fact, Kuhlke estimates the impact of recycled polystyrene will be so small that it probably will be lost in statistical error.[117]

Transportation—As mentioned before in reference to polystyrene recycling, the bulkiness yet light weight of plastic products translates into high transportation costs. In the near term, the low number of reclamation facilities for some types of plastics, particularly polystyrene, make transportation a significant factor. Many small-scale PET and HDPE processors are located throughout the country, however, and transportation costs are not deterring these recycling programs. In fact, United Resource Recovery, an Ohio-based HDPE recycler, told IRRC that up to 10 percent of the 7 million pounds per year of HPDE containers it processes come from as far away as Texas, Denver and Florida.[118]

The bulkiness of plastics also complicates curbside collection programs. Plastics may account for just 5 percent of the weight on a curbside collection truck but up to 30 to 50 percent of the space.[119] In source-separated municipal curbside recycling programs, collecting plastic may create inefficiencies if special drop-off trips have to be made because of high volumes of plastic. As a result, densifying plastic by baling or granulating products before shipping has become a more routine, yet also costly, procedure. Shredding on-route also may result in the mixing of colors, which significantly decreases the value of the product.

Exports—The market for post-consumer plastic is primarily domestic, although some post-consumer plastics are being exported to Asia and Europe. Data are not available on the size of these export markets,[120] although they are believed to be relatively small. U.S. export of all types of scrap plastics, including post-industrial, is a $92 million per year industry, led by buyers in Hong Kong and served by ports on the West Coast.[121] As with paper, plastics are labor-intensive to recycle, providing incentives to recycle plastic materials where wages are low, such as overseas. As a result, there is potential for recycling plastics in the Far East and then selling the material back to the United States.

U.S. Plastics Industries' Recycling Initiatives

Plastics manufacturing involves two distinct processes and two separate industries. The plastic resin-production industry, composed mostly of large chemical companies that include Dow Chemical, Du Pont, Goodyear, Gulf Oil Corp., Hoeschst-Celanese, Mobil Oil, Monsanto Co., Occidental Petroleum Corp., Reichhold Chemicals Inc. and Union Carbide, converts industrial organic chemicals into plastic resins. The plastics-processing industry, made up of thousands of smaller companies, extrudes, injects, blow-molds and forms those resins into end products. The 1982 Census of Manufacturers lists 264 resin producers with 441 plants and 10,000 processors with 11,653 plants. More than half of the processing firms employed fewer than 20 people.[122]

Because recycled plastics are not usually made back into the original products, a review of company initiatives to recycle post-consumer plastics encompasses companies outside the traditional plastics industry. In addition, because preparing PET and HDPE containers for re-use by industry is relatively simple, a large number of plastic processors handling small volumes of separated plastic containers have sprung up around the country. Only the developers of large-scale recycling facilities, generally processing more than 10 million pounds per year, are discussed in this chapter.

Company initiatives: The following sections of this chapter review the potential markets, end-users and large-scale (more than 10 million pounds per year) processors that prepare the following plastics for reuse by industry: PET, HDPE, LDPE, PVC, PS and PP. Plastic lumber manufacturers that process unsorted mixed plastics also are reviewed.

Polyethylene Terephthalate (PET) Recycling

Percentage of plastic bottles: 20-30%
Percentage of plastics in the waste stream: 5%
Virgin product examples: soft drink bottles, medicine containers
Recycled product examples: fiberfill for products, including carpets and clothing; geotextile fabrics for road building or erosion control applications; nonfood containers; industrial strapping; distributor caps; bath tubs; appliances; skis and soft drink bottles.

Nine two-liter PET bottles can stuff an average decorator pillow; five bottles can fill a man's ski jacket; and 36 are sufficient for a standard-sized sleeping bag.[123] Because PET bottles have to pass federal requirements for food packaging, Thomas M. Duff, president of **Wellman**—the nation's largest PET bottle recycler—says they are purer than clothing fibers made from raw chemicals. "It's about the best polymer you can make," declared Duff.[124]

The U.S. fiberfill industry consumes a large portion of the recycled PET resin, primarily because Wellman uses the PET bottles to produce fiberfill for internal use. The 300 million pound a year U.S. fiberfill market cannot alone absorb all of the potentially recoverable PET, however. Fortunately, other large markets are plentiful. The CPRR estimates that capturing 10 percent of the PET textile market would represent approximately 350 million pound per year—an amount nearly double the amount of PET bottles collected for recycling in 1989.[125] Another potentially huge market for used PET bottles is the production of soft drink bottles. PET resin sales to the soft drink industry total about 750 million pounds,[126] and Coca-Cola has begun selling its product in bottles containing recycled PET resins. (See Box 5-1.)

Most nonfiber markets, including bottles, strapping, sheet and compounding, are more selective than the fibers markets, requiring a higher quality recycled resin and favoring clear PET. In addition, most equipment

Box 5-4

Trade Associations

Companies within the plastics industry have banded together to form a myriad of national trade organizations focusing on the role of plastics in the municipal solid waste stream. These organizations are driven by the recognition that if the plastics industry does not voluntary address plastics waste disposal, government will address it for them through product bans or procurement restrictions.

Most trade groups involved with plastic wastes are concentrating on one or more of three key elements that will keep plastic products in the supermarket, department stores and fast-food restaurants. The first element is establishment of a recycling infrastructure, which is considered essential to both consumer acceptance of plastics and economical plastics recycling. The second is combatting misinformation about the volume, characteristics and impact of plastic in the waste stream through public information campaigns. Polls consistently show that Americans believe plastics comprise a much higher portion of the nation's garbage than they actually do. Lastly, companies are jointly funding plastics recycling research through trade associations. Because plastics recycling is a relatively new field, the ability to prepare plastics for reuse by industry and to expand the types of plastic that can be recycled is highly dependent on research and experimentation. Research underway also is attempting to identify products that can be made from recycled resins and to determine if potential markets exist for these products.

The Society of the Plastics Industry (SPI), a trade organization with more than 2,000 members, including resin and machinery manufacturers, distributors, plastics products manufacturers, moldmakers and representatives of all other segments of the U.S. plastics industry, has established a number of groups to address plastic waste issues.[127] In 1986, it helped establish the **Council on Plastics and Packaging in the Environment (COPPE)**, an informal coalition of plastic resin producers, packaging manufacturers and users and trade associations. Two years later, SPI formed an affiliate, the **Council for Solid Waste Solutions (CSWS)**, which has earmarked 80 percent of its technical resources for recycling efforts. The council's "goal is to make plastics the most recycled material by the year 2000," Frank Aronhalt, Du Pont's director of environmental affairs and CSWS committee member, told conference attendees in the fall of 1989.[128] The council recently expanded its efforts to include the recycling of durable plastic products in addition to plastics packaging.[129]

In early 1991, the council unveiled a blueprint for plastics recycling designed to boost the plastic bottle recycling rate from 9 to 25 percent by 1995. The action plan calls on local governments to establish recycling programs and on industry to build more recycling plants and to use more recycled material in their products.[130]

SPI also established a division named the **Plastic Bottle Institute** to represent bottle manufacturers, and the Plastic Bottle Information Bureau, which serves as a clearinghouse for a number of plastics recycling organizations. Another division of SPI, the **Vinyl Institute,** has funded and supported a number of programs designed to integrate vinyl products into all phases of municipal solid waste management. Established in 1982, the Institute is discussed in the following section on PVC recycling for its efforts to separate PVC from other plastics.

An independent nonprofit organization, the **Plastics Recycling Foundation,** was formed in 1985 to research post-consumer plastics recycling, operate demonstration pilot plant programs and transfer the technology to the public at low cost. In March of that year, the Foundation signed a contract with Rutgers, the state university of New Jersey, to establish a recycling center— the **Center for Plastics Recycling Research (CPRR)**—which the National Science Foundation and the New Jersey Commission on Science and Technology also now support. In addition to funding the CPRR, the foundation supports research at other universities in states that provide matching funds. For the 1990-91 season, funding by 60 members representing the plastics industry, food and beverage packagers and federal and state governments totaled about $4 million.[131]

A few additional organizations focus on particular types of plastic. The **Polystyrene Packaging Council,** for instance, is comprised of manufacturers of polystyrene foam products, raw materials suppliers, equipment manufacturers and trade associations. The council says it "is dedicated to the effective use and recycling of polystyrene and to providing accurate, reliable information about environmentally sound solid waste disposal practices."[132] The organization also offers technical assistance on recycling to public officials, consumers and local businesses.

The **National Association for Plastic Container Recovery (NAPCOR)** is a not-for-profit trade association formed in 1987 to facilitate the economical recovery of plastic containers. NAPCOR is focusing on PET soft drink bottles, working with communities to develop comprehensive recycling, primarily curbside, programs that include PET bottles. The organization's members are 16 PET resin and bottle manufacturers, including Du Pont, Eastman Kodak Co.'s Eastman Chemicals Division, The Goodyear Tire & Rubber Co.'s polyester division, Gulf States Canners Inc., Hoechst Celanese Corp., ICI Americas Inc., Johnson Controls Inc., Sewell Plastics Inc. and Union Carbide Chemical & Plastics Co. NAPCOR's goal is to increase the PET soft drink bottles recycling rate—at 28 percent in 1989—to 50 percent by 1993.[133]

in these nonfiber markets is designed to use pelletized, rather than flake, PET.[134] **Procter & Gamble** has taken the lead in using bottles made out of recycled PET, selling its Spic and Span in bottles made from 100 percent post-consumer PET. Other companies, including **S.C. Johnson & Sons Inc.**, are following suit.[135]

Recycled product innovations: Additional uses for reclaimed PET are surfacing every day. **Embrace Systems Corp.** of Buffalo, N.Y., purchases clean PET flake to produce a proprietary plastic spun insulation material, called Puffibre. Established in 1983, the company bills its product as a superior alternative to fiberglass insulation, touting it as nontoxic, non-combustible, nonirritating, cost-competitive and better at heat retention. The company operates a prototype plant in Buffalo, N.Y., and plans to open additional plants in Connecticut, Massachusetts, California, Chicago and Vancouver. The plants will be designed to process 1 ton per hour of PET bottles of any color—an advantage this end use has over other applications. The company eventually hopes to recycle PVC and to manufacture auto parts with recycled plastics.[136]

MRC Polymers Inc. of Chicago is using post-consumer PET bottles and water jugs made of polycarbonate to supply a plastic blend, known as Stanuloy, to the automotive industry. Stanuloy is reportedly 25 to 30 percent cheaper than its competition. MRC recently signed a three-year contract with a major automotive supplier for 3 million pounds of Stanuloy formed into body panels, trim and spoilers for cars.[137]

PET recycling plants: There are four major (defined for this report as more than 10 million pounds per day) dedicated PET recycling plants, with an aggregate design capacity of 92 million pounds per year. Another 11 plants process both PET and HDPE containers, and four more plants plan to process PET in the future. The four dedicated PET recycling plants (which also process a small amount of HDPE comprising the base cups of PET soft drink bottles) are owned by Day Products, a subsidiary of a Philadelphia engineering firm, Day & Zimmerman; Johnson Controls, the first of the major PET soft drink container suppliers to enter the recycling field; St. Jude Polymer Corp. of Frackville, Pa.; and Star Plastics Inc., a subsidiary of wTe Corp., a solid waste processing and recycling company in Bedford, Mass.

Day Products Inc.: Day Products operates the largest dedicated PET recycling plant in the country—a 40 million pound per year facility in Bridgeport, N.J. To lend some perspective, all of the soft drink bottles consumed in a year in the state of New Jersey total 30 million pounds.[138] Day Products opened its plant in October 1989 at a cost of more than $5 million. It became the first to use commercially a PET bottle recycling system developed by the Center for Plastics Recycling Research—an air-and-water process that separates the components of plastic bottles. While polyethylene is now just a side stream at the plant, Ed Carreras of Day Products told IRRC that the company intends to increase the volume of polyethylene in the future. Day Products also plans to boost its overall production substantially, reaching 60 million annual pounds at the Bridgeport plant within the next year or so, and 300 million annual pounds companywide within the next two years.[139]

Johnson Controls Inc.: About one year after Day Products opened its plant, Johnson Controls opened a 20 million pound per year facility in Novi, Mich., adjacent to one of the company's 18 bottle producing plants. The $4 million plant uses the Re-tech PET recycling technology developed by Reko BV, a subsidiary of the large Dutch petrochemical company, DSM. The plant produces PET flake, and will eventually produce PET pellets, for use internally for automotive and other nonfood containers and for sale to outside markets. Susan Davis, director of marketing, told IRRC that the company would like to use all the recycled plastics internally but that there is "more talk than action in terms of demand for recycled content."[140]

Johnson Controls, the country's largest user of PET resin, is more cautious about expansion plans than Day Products. It says its plant will expand to 30 million pounds per year "as the need arises." Davis added that Johnson Controls is "committed to recycling" and would build additional plants if the capacity is needed, but cautioned that existing plant capacity, in combination with expansion plans, are more than sufficient for present collection rates of PET. To boost collection rates, Johnson Controls is sponsoring a statewide recycling effort in Washington state and a buy-back and park collection program in the Chicago area.[141]

St. Jude Polymer Corp.: St. Jude Polymer is one of the pioneers of PET soda bottle recycling, starting up its recycling operations back in 1978. The company is capable of processing 12 million pounds per year and plans to expand another eight million pounds per year in 1991. St. Jude sells recycled PET pellets to major resins producers who use it in engineering resin applications.[142]

wTe Recycling/Star: Formerly Star Plastics, wTe Recycling/Star processes a minimum of 20 million pounds per year of post-consumer PET and is likely to expand its operations in 1991. Parent company wTe Corp. acquired Star Plastics in 1990, upgrading its operations and introducing technologies developed at its plastics research and development facility in Benicia, Calif. Founded in 1981 as Waste Energy Technology Corp., wTe Corp. has experience separating and reclaiming a variety of plastics, as well as a broad range of solid wastes. The company's involvement in Amoco Corp.'s polystyrene recycling plant and its work with PVC recycling in Akron, Ohio, are discussed in later sections of this chapter. In addition, wTe Corp. owns ferrous scrap recovery operations at Columbus and Akron, Ohio, waste-to-energy facilities, and it acquired a scrap metals company, Kramer Scrap Inc., in Greenfield, Mass, in the fall of 1990. In the fall of 1988,

Table 5-2

Major Post-Consumer U.S. Plastics Recycling Plants Sorting and Processing PET, HDPE and Mixed Plastics

Company	Location	Plastics Recycled Now/Future	Design Capacity[a] (in million lbs./yr.)	On-Line Date
Amdak Corp.	Yonkers, N.Y.	/Mixed	12	NA
Clean Tech Inc.	Dundee, Mich.	PET & HDPE	24	Nov. 1989
Day Products Inc.	Bridgeport, N.J.	PET/HDPE	40[b]	Oct. 1989
Du Pont Co./Waste Management Inc.	Philadelphia, Pa.	PET & HDPE/Mixed	40	Mar. 1990
	Chicago, Ill.	PET & HDPE/Mixed	40	Mar. 1990
Eaglebrook Plastics Inc.	Chicago, Ill.	PET & HDPE	NA	NA
Envirothene Inc.	Chino, Calif.	PET & HDPE/Film	15[c]	Feb. 1991
Graham Packaging Co.	York, Pa.	HDPE/Mixed & Film	10[d]	Sept. 1990
Johnson Controls Inc.	Novi, Mich.	PET	20[e]	Oct. 1990
M.A. Industries Inc.	Peachtree, Ga.	PET & HDPE	60	NA
North American Plastics Recycling Corp.	Fort Edward, N.Y.	Mixed/Film	6.5[f]	NA
Orion Pacific Inc.	Odessa, Tex.	PET & HDPE/Film	24	Late 1990
Partek Corp.	Vancouver, Wash.	HDPE	10	NA

Company	Location	Plastics	Capacity (million lbs./yr.)	Start-up
Phillips Petroleum Co./Partek Corp.	Tulsa, Okla.	HDPE	15	November 1991
Polymer Resource Group Inc.	Rosedale, Md.	PET & HDPE	25-50	April 1990
Quantum Chemical Corp.	Heath, Ohio	/Mixed & Film	40	1991
St. Jude Polymer Corp.	Frackville, Pa.	PET	12[g]	1978
Secondary Polymers	Detroit, Mich.	PET & HDPE	13	July 1990
Union Carbide Corp.	Piscataway, N.J.	/PET, HDPE & Film	40	1992
wTe Recycling/Star	Albany, N.Y.	PET	20	NA
Wellman Inc.	Johnsonville, S.C.	PET & HDPE/Mixed	210/275	1978[h]

General Note: All PET recycling plants process a small amount of HDPE found in the base cups.

[a] Full capacity may not be realized in start-up year.
[b] Plans to process 60 million lbs./yr. in the next year or so at the Bridgeport plant and 300 million lbs./yr. company-wide within two years.
[c] Expanding to 50 million lbs. by 1993, including 15 million lbs./yr. plastic film line.
[d] Expanding to 20 million lbs./yr. in the summer of 1991.
[e] Expanding to 30 million lbs./yr. as the need arises.
[f] Expanding to include a 6 million lb./yr. plastic film line.
[g] Expanding to 20 million lbs./yr. during 1991.
[h] Wellman began recycling PET bottles in 1978; HDPE milk jugs in 1989; and mixed plastics in 1991.

Source: Investor Responsibility Research Center Inc.

wTe became involved in commercial recycling, joining forces with J. Sax & Co., a Boston industrial recycling firm. Named America's 52nd fastest growing private company by *Inc.* Magazine in 1988, wTe had sales totaling just over $20 million in 1990 and forecasts sales of $35 to $40 million for 1991.[143]

Pure Tech International Inc.: A publicly traded company in Paterson, N.J., Pure Tech International has developed the proprietary Pure Tech process for cleaning, sorting and preparing whole crushed bottles into flake for use by industry. The company also developed a semi-automatic de-capping technology that removes bottle caps from plastic bottles. Although Pure Tech operates a pilot plant in the United States for testing and evaluation, its goal is to sell its process to other entities rather than developing recycling facilities itself. In early 1989, for instance, the company granted an exclusive license to a company in Taiwan, Taiwan Recycling Corp., to build a post-consumer PET recycling facility using Pure Tech's process. TRC is a joint venture of the Far Eastern Textile Ltd. and Shin Kong Group. The 16 million pound per year plant began operations in September 1990.[144]

Established in 1986, Pure Tech obtained $4.5 million through an initial public stock offering in March 1989. Also in 1989, the company established a trading division to procure post-consumer plastic containers and sell plastics that the company does not use. The company is in the process of merging with REI Distributors Inc., a recycling company in Newark, N.J., with revenues of $10 million in 1990.[145]

High Density Polyethylene (HDPE) Recycling

Percentage of plastic bottles: 50-60%
Percentage of plastics in the waste stream: 21%
Virgin product examples: milk jugs, detergent bottles, toys
Recycled product examples: base cups on PET bottles (130 million pound annual market[146]), non-food bottles, trash cans and other containers, building products and toys.

Post-industrial HDPE from bottle manufacturing operations is recycled into a number of products that constitute some fairly large markets, including irrigation drainage tile, HDPE sheet, nursery pots, truck bed liners and industrial trash containers. The ability of post-consumer HDPE to make inroads in these markets is questionable, however, because as one plastics recycling company explained, most companies "view post-consumer recycled HDPE as an inferior product to industrial scrap." In the recycling company's view, "the markets that need to develop in order to make recycling of HDPE milk and detergent bottles viable long-term are non-food bottles, sheet markets, filled products, and other valued applications."[147]

As with recycled PET bottles, **Procter & Gamble** has taken the lead in selling its products in recycled HDPE containers. The company is marketing some of its detergents and cleaners, including Tide, Cheer, Era and Dash liquid detergents, in containers made with more than 25 percent recycled HDPE.[148] P&G, which reportedly uses more than 100 million pounds of HDPE annually to make containers,[149] estimates that it uses 40 million pounds per year of reclaimed plastics and that its total potential capacity for recycled material is 75 million pounds annually.[150] The company says its main constraint is finding clean supplies of post-consumer HDPE.

Other companies jumping on the bandwagon include **Lever Brothers**, which produces Wisk laundry detergent and Snuggle fabric softener; **Jennico Inc.**, a major producer of private label detergents whose customers include Walgreen's, K mart and Target stores; and **Colgate-Palmolive Co.** Lever Brothers, a unit of Unilever Group, an Anglo-Dutch consumer products company, began using bottles made with recycled HDPE in July 1990 and says that by mid-1991, 50 percent of its bottles will contain 25 percent to 35 percent recycled resins. The company's bottle suppliers are Continental Plastic Containers, Owens-Brockway and Graham Packaging, which is supplying Lever Brothers with half of its recycling plant's output.[151]

Rubbermaid's Commercial Products Division plans to use between 1 and 2 million pounds of reclaimed plastic resins during 1991, with HDPE representing three-quarters of the plastic. The Commercial Products Division produces sanitary maintenance and refuse containers with up to 25 percent recycled HDPE. Dr. Charles Lancelot of Rubbermaid estimates that the potential amount of recycled plastic resin that the entire company could use is 10 million pounds.[152]

Poly-Anna Plastic Products of Milwaukee, Wis., a recycler of the full line of post-consumer plastics, retains about 15 percent of the plastics it processes to produce storage bins made completely from recycled detergent bottles.[153]

Recycled product innovations: Du Pont says it is attempting to create a new market for HDPE products through a joint venture with the state of Illinois—the Plastics Recycling Development Partnership. Created in March 1989, the venture's goal is to "test the viability of reprocessing plastics into usable highway construction and maintenance products." The state is using highway barricades made from 100 percent recycled HDPE, and both parties hope the project will serve as a model for other state governments.[154]

Eaglebrook Plastics, Duratech Industries Inc. and **Recycled Plastics Industries Inc.** produce plastic lumber from recycled milk jugs. All three are discussed in more detail in the plastic lumber section of this chapter.

HDPE Recycling Plants: There are two large-scale dedicated HDPE recycling plants in operation, a third scheduled for operation in November 1991, another 11 that recycle HDPE containers along with PET, and four more that plan to process HDPE in the future. The operators of the three large-scale dedicated HDPE recycling plants are Graham Packaging Co., the country's largest maker of HDPE plastic bottles; Partek Corp., a plastics recycling firm in Vancouver, Wash.; and a joint venture between Partek and Phillips Petroleum Co., a major polyethylene producer.

Graham Packaging Co.: Formerly Sonoco Graham, Graham Packaging opened its $5 million "bottle-to-bottle" plastics recycling plant in York, Pa., in September 1990. The plant can recycle 10 million pounds annually of HDPE and is slated to double its capacity in the summer of 1991. The company anticipates that by 1993 the majority of the 2 billion HDPE bottles manufactured annually at its 27 bottle plants will contain recycled content, and within the next three to five years, the company plans to be recycling 100 million pounds of HDPE annually. Graham Packaging Vice President Philip Yates says the company's ultimate goal "is to be the largest consumer of recycled plastic." The company is experimenting with various percentages of recycled resin content, producing bottles with between 5 and 50 percent post-consumer HDPE. Some of its bottles for automotive products, for instance, have been produced with up to 50 percent post-consumer HDPE. In the future, the company plans to accept additional types of plastic containers and plastic film.[155]

Phillips Petroleum Co./Partek Corp.: In the same month Graham Packaging opened its recycling plant, Phillips Petroleum Co. and Partek Corp. formed a joint venture—Phillips Plastics Recycling Partnership—to recycle used HDPE containers. Phillips invested nearly $1.8 million and holds a 51 percent interest in the venture, while Partek holds the remaining 49 percent in return for its $1.7 million investment. By November 1991, the venture plans to build a facility in Tulsa, Okla., to recycle 15 million pounds annually of post-consumer and post-industrial HDPE. The venture also is considering additional plants across the country. Phillips plans to market the recycled resin along with its own virgin resin to fabricators for non-food grade applications. Robert Gaundet of Partek told IRRC that a new company will most likely be formed to serve as a source of feedstock for the joint venture and that the new company is likely to go public.[156]

Gaundet told IRRC that Partek already operates a 10 million pound per year HDPE recycling plant at its headquarters in Vancouver and has been operating a second plant in Anderson, Ill., that processes between 5 and 7 million pounds per year since August 1988. A pioneer in HDPE recycling, Partek developed a "kinetic scrub" process, which removes paper and adhesives from shredded plastic bottles without the use of solvents or hazardous chemicals. In addition, Partek's sister company, Mobile Recovery Systems, has engineered curbside collection technology that granulates plastic on-route, increasing the amount of plastic that can be collected by 95 percent. The company plans to make the system available by early 1991.[157]

Combined Polyethylene Terephthalate (PET) and High Density Polyethylene (HDPE) Recycling

PET and HDPE recycling plants: Because PET soft drink bottles and HDPE milk jugs are the most commonly collected curbside plastics, most plastics recycling companies have designed plants that can process both types of plastic simultaneously. The major challenge for these facilities is to sort efficiently the two types of containers, which often arrive in mixed bales. Eleven large-scale recycling plants currently process PET and HDPE, and Union Carbide, Quantum Chemical and Amdak Corp. plan to open PET and HDPE processing plants. In addition, Graham Packaging plans to add PET and other plastic containers to its HDPE recycling plant, and Day Products plans to upgrade its PET recycling plant to process larger volumes of HDPE.

Wellman Inc.: Wellman is the nation's largest recycler of post-consumer PET soft drink bottles. A publicly traded company, in 1990 the company recycled around 100 million pounds of PET soft drink bottles—more than half of all the PET containers recycled—and approximately 20 million pounds of HDPE milk jugs and base cups of soft drink bottles. A fiber producing company, Wellman uses the PET internally to produce fiber and sells the reclaimed HDPE to the non-food packaging industry. Wellman uses much of the reclaimed PET resin to make fiberfill for furniture and home furnishings, but the company also makes use of green PET bottles by manufacturing geotextile fabrics used in landfill and pond linings, erosion control and other civil engineering applications.[158]

Wellman was one of the first to capitalize on the collection system for post-consumer plastic containers created by bottle deposit legislation in the late 1970s and early 1980s. The company began recycling PET bottles in 1978 and expanded to HDPE containers in 1989. Wellman plans to retain its leadership role in plastics recycling by accepting all types of rigid, post-consumer containers. In the second quarter of 1991, Wellman began testing a new technology designed to sort the plastic containers at its Johnsonville, S.C., facility. This new technology will mark the company's first use of an automated separation system; to date, the company has hand-sorted all mixed bales of PET and HDPE it has received. Wellman says that its new system will be capable of processing 80 million pounds per year of mixed plastics and that its goal is to develop value-added products for the HDPE and other plastics it will soon process.[159]

Wellman's recycling facility is currently capable of processing 160 million pounds of PET bottles and 40 million pounds of PET fiber, and the company says it could use more than 400 million pounds of PET annually.[160] The company says obtaining the used containers is its main constraint to boosting capacity. Foreseeing increasing competition for plastic bottles, Wellman took two aggressive steps during the last two years to secure a steady supply. In a highly publicized joint venture announced in the spring of 1989, Wellman teamed up with waste industry giant Browning Ferris Industries Inc. to process all of the PET soda bottles and HDPE milk jugs that BFI collects through its curbside recycling programs. The venture has made great strides in establishing a sorely needed plastics recycling infrastructure. Wellman's second move was to build on its relationship with New England CRInc., a privately owned builder and operator of material recovery facilities, by acquiring it in August 1990. Previously, Wellman purchased PET bottles processed by NE CRInc.'s subsidiary, Materials Recovery, and in September 1989, Wellman signed a partnership agreement with Materials Recovery to design, build and operate material recovery facilities.[161] (For more information on NE CRInc., see Chapter 6.)

Until its November 1989 purchase of Fiber Industries, Wellman was the only mainstream fiber producer that made all of its fiber from recycled material. Post-consumer and post-industrial PET represents one-quarter of the total; photographic and x-ray film waste, about 20 percent; and fiber waste, the remainder. Through its acquisition of Fiber Industries, Wellman positioned itself as one of the largest manufacturers and distributors of polyester textile fibers, and now produces worldwide just under 900 million pounds of polyester. Wellman believes that it can replace about 20 to 25 percent of Fiber Industries' more than 700 million pounds per year raw material mix with recycled PET and that it could begin implementing this program in 1992.[162]

To capitalize on a growing international market for recycled plastics, Wellman is developing overseas operations. In June 1989, Wellman and Constar International Inc., the country's largest plastic container manufacturer, purchased an 80 percent interest in Desmacon Holding B.V., a European PET bottle manufacturer and recycler with operations in The Netherlands and France. Renamed Wellstar, and combined with the acquisition of three similar operations in The Netherlands and the United Kingdom, the joint venture is the largest PET bottle manufacturer in Europe and the only European bottle manufacturer to buy bottles back. Wellman also constructed a 25 million pound per year bottle recycling facility in The Netherlands through Wellman International Ltd., Wellman's Man-made Fibres subsidiary in Ireland. The plant primarily processes PET bottles collected in The Netherlands and Germany for use by Wellman International as a raw material.[163]

Du Pont Co./Waste Management Inc.: Another post-consumer PET and HDPE recycling plant is a high-profile joint venture uniting a plastics recycler with a leading waste management company. In the spring of 1989, Du Pont and Waste Management formed the **Plastics Recycling Alliance, L.P. (PRA)**, to recycle plastic in what they say will become the nation's largest plastics recycling and reprocessing operation. Waste Management provides plastics collected from its curbside recycling programs, while Du Pont modifies and upgrades the recycled plastics for a broad range of applications in the automotive, consumer and building industries.[164]

The joint venture began operation of two plants, one in Philadelphia, Pa., and one in Chicago, Ill., in March 1990. Each is capable of processing 40 million pounds of PET and HDPE per year. Pat Getter, senior public affairs specialist for Du Pont, told IRRC that the joint venture expects to announce a third facility on the West Coast in 1991, and plans to have a total of five plants in operation, with a combined capacity of 200 million pounds per year, by 1995.[165]

To expand the types of plastics it can accept at both operating plants, PRA is developing two partnerships. An agreement between Du Pont and American National Can Co. (ANC), a multinational manufacturer and marketer of a broad line of metal, glass and plastic packaging products, expanded the types of plastic processed at the Chicago plant in early 1991. Acceptable plastic containers include PVC, low-density polyethylene, polypropylene, polystyrene and even mixed multilayer plastic bottles. ANC says it has successfully used multilayered bottles to manufacture such items as pocket combs, pallets and office trays.[166] In January 1991, PRA also signed an agreement with Occidental Chemical Corp. to implement automated sorting of PVC containers at the Philadelphia plant. The two companies are joining forces to "invent and adapt sortation techniques," which PRA says will "result in improved product quality and sorting economics for the PRA."[167]

Polymer Resource Group Inc.: One month after PRA opened its two plants, the Polymer Resource Group, a subsidiary of **ITC**, a Baltimore minerals exporter, opened the first phase of its post-consumer PET and HDPE bottle recycling plant in Rosedale, Md. Named **PolySource Mid-Atlantic**, the plant uses a proprietary nonchemical, mechanical cleansing and sortation process that was primarily developed in-house. Procter & Gamble is the only disclosed customer of the plant. Although capacity figures for Phase 1 were not available from the company, ITC's Collingwood Harris told IRRC that Phase 2 called for a plant that would process between 25 and 50 million tons per year. Harris added that the second plant's opening hinged on the availability of feedstock.[168]

Originally planned as a joint venture with AKW Apparate & Verfahren of Hirschau, Germany, PolySource Mid-Atlantic became fully owned by ITC in the summer of 1990. Harris told IRRC that the German plastics recycling technology originally slated for use in the project was too expensive and could not meet the project's timetable. ITC first became involved in plastics recycling in May 1984, after it discovered that the technology used to refine one of its exported minerals, kaolin, also can be used to refine plastic. (Kaolin is a white clay that can be used as a filler and finisher, particularly in the production of glossy paper.) ITC plans to build additional plants in the United States and around the world and is exploring a venture in Japan.[169]

Clean Tech Inc.: A division of bottle manufacturer **Plastipak Packaging**, Clean Tech opened a post-consumer PET and HDPE recycling facility in November 1989. The Dundee, Mich., plant is designed to process 24 million pounds per year, and George Castaneda, Clean Tech's head of community relations, expects the plant to be operating at full capacity in 1991. Clean Tech purchases separated PET and HDPE bottles and produces pellets for use by Plastipak Packaging. Procter & Gamble, the bottle manufacturer's largest account, is the sole customer for the recycled bottles manufactured by Plastipak.[170]

Orion Pacific Inc.: Another company selling pellets to Plastipak Packaging, as well as other bottle manufacturers, is Orion Pacific, a division of Madison Minerals of Houston, Tex., a privately held oil and natural gas exploration firm. Orion Pacific's Jeffrey Smith told IRRC that the company planned to boost its production capacity of PET and HDPE containers to 2 million pounds per month in early 1991, which would yield 24 million pounds on an annual basis. The company began processing baled plastic containers in Odessa, Tex., at the end of 1990 and hopes to process post-consumer film by the end of 1991.[171]

Secondary Polymers: Secondary Polymers of Detroit, Mich., the plastics recycling affiliate of **Louis Kay Enterprises**, a glass recycling company that has been in business for 30 years, began producing clean flake at its post-consumer PET & HDPE recycling plant in July 1990. Gregory Boguski, a company representative, told IRRC in January 1991 that the plant was able to process around five million pounds per year and that he expected the plant to be operating at its design capacity of 13 million pounds per year by spring 1991. Boguski added that he foresaw no difficulty in obtaining additional bottles, noting that the plant had been turning them away. The plant sells its flakes to other recyclers or companies that have idle capacity and are able to extrude the flake into pellets but plans to add its own extrusion and pelletizing operations in the future.[172]

North American Plastics Recycling Corp.: North American Plastics Recycling Corp. collects and processes roughly 6.5 million pounds per year of commingled rigid containers in South Glenn Falls, N.Y. In the summer of 1991, the company plans to add a 6 million pound per year post-consumer HDPE and LDPE film processing line and consolidate all of its operations in a Fort Edwards, N.Y., processing plant, about five miles from

South Glenn Falls. Tom Tomaszek, company president, told IRRC that the company plans to add a second film processing line by the end of the year. North American plans to process the films into pellets for sale to a number of industries, including film, sheet, drainage tile and trash bag manufacturers.[173]

Envirothene Inc.: In February 1991, Envirothene opened a 15 million pound per year recycling facility in Chino, Calif. The $5 million price tag includes expanding to 50 million pounds per year by "1993 or sooner," including a separate line for processing plastic films, according to company president, Michael Kopulsky. The plant's automated sorting systems separates the primarily HDPE plastics and then produces both flakes and pellets for sale to bag manufacturers, bottle manufacturers and other plastic product manufacturers. Kopulsky says that the principals of Envirothene are "experienced at pioneering new technologies in the plastics arena," noting that Envirothene has "the same investment base" as Himolene, the first company to make high molecular weight, high density trash bags that resemble grocery bags. After Gladbag acquired market leader Himolene in June 1988, investors turned their attention and expertise to establishing Envirothene.[174]

Union Carbide Corp.: Union Carbide plans to open a large multi-materials plastics recycling facility in the company's Piscataway, N.J., technical and manufacturing complex in early 1992. The plant is scheduled to process plastic bags and film in addition to PET and HDPE containers for a total capacity of 40 million pounds per year. Union Carbide plans to compound the recycled plastics with resins and other additives to improve their physical properties and then sell the final product in pellet form. Originally slated to begin operation in early 1991, the plant was delayed because of an abandoned joint venture, according to Louis A. Agnello, Union Carbide's director of communications. Upon closer examination of the joint venture partner's separation process, Union Carbide decided to pursue its own chemical separation process in-house. The company foresees end-markets in non-food packaging, plastic lumber, mud flaps, flower pots, geo-grids for erosion prevention and heavy-duty film for agriculture and construction uses. Agnello told IRRC that Union Carbide plans to build additional plants around the country as long as the ventures become profitable.[175]

Quantum Chemical Corp.: Quantum Chemical, the country's largest polyethylene producer, plans to open a 40 million pound per year post-consumer plastics processing plant by the end of 1991. The Heath, Ohio, plant will use technology from John Brown Plastics Recycling Systems Inc. of Providence, R.I., to sort and process mixed rigid containers and eventually LDPE film. The plant is estimated to cost at least $5 million. Rumpke Recycling Inc., which is building a materials recovery facility in the Cincinnati area, will be a major supplier. Quantum says it intends to open similar plants around the country.[176]

Hank Gudrian, Quantum Chemical's director of communications, told IRRC that growing demand for recycled resin among the company's customers is a major factor behind the company's expansion into recycling. Noting that the company is one of the largest suppliers of polyethylene packaging, Gudrian added that the company is also anticipating the possibility of recycled content packaging legislation.[177] (For additional information on Quantum Chemical Corp.'s involvement with recycled HDPE, see the post-consumer plastics recycling process section of this chapter.)

Amdak Corp.: Amdak Corp. plans to build a plant that will sort and process 12 million pounds per year of commingled PET, HDPE and PP. The New York State Energy Research and Development Authority provided $400,000, and Amdak is contributing $360,000 to develop the Yonkers, N.Y., facility.[178]

M.A. Industries Inc.: M.A. Industries of Peachtree, Ga., also processes PET and HDPE containers into pellets at its Peachtree facility. Roger Geyer, vice president of M.A. Industries, told IRRC that the company is processing 20 million pounds of PET per year and 40 million pounds of HDPE. Company representative Gail Brown told IRRC, however, that the company's primary business is selling plastics recycling equipment and that it had no plans to develop additional plants. M.A. Industries became involved in plastics recycling in the early 1970s when it developed systems to recycle automobile battery cases made of polypropylene.[179]

Eaglebrook Plastics processes both PET and HDPE, selling the PET and producing plastic lumber with the HDPE. Eaglebrook's lumber operations are discussed in the plastic lumber section of this chapter.

Low Density Polyethylene (LDPE) Recycling

Percentage of plastic bottles: 5-10%
Percentage of plastics in the waste stream: 27%
Virgin product examples: Wrapping films, grocery bags
Recycled product examples: Trash bags, grocery bags, bottles

Plastic film is plentiful in the home, accounting for up to half of a household's plastic packaging waste in one Rhode Island survey. LDPE films and sheeting, however, are difficult to distinguish from similar items made from HDPE and PVC.[180] Plastic film is quite often contaminated with food and other debris and is difficult to handle and sort. As a result, there is minimal recycling of post-consumer LDPE, although recycling efforts are springing up. Major plastic grocery sack manufacturers recently have launched several grocery bag collection programs in conjunction with grocery store chains. In addition, several plastics recycling facilities, includ-

Table 5-3

Plastic Grocery Sack Recycling Programs
August 1990

Company	Stores on Line	% Bags Returned	Final Product Made	Bag Graphics
Sonoco Products	6,732	8-12	Bottles; edgeboard	♻ 2 HDPE
Mobil Chemical	2,321	20	Trash bags	♻ 2 HDPE
Vanguard Plastics	2,000-2,500	20-25	Grocery bags	♻ 2 HDPE
PCL Packaging	900-1,000	15-20	Grocery bags	♻ 4 LDPE
PCL & Eastern	347	15-20	Grocery bags	♻ 4 LDPE

Source: Arthur Amidon, "Plastic Grocery Sack Recycling," *Resource Recycling*, November 1990

ing those owned by **Envirothene, Graham Packaging, North American Plastics Recycling, Orion Pacific, Quantum Chemical** and **Union Carbide,** have announced their intention to add film processing lines to their operations. Others are likely to follow suit.

Polyvinyl Chloride (PVC) Sorting and Recycling

Percentage of plastic bottles: 5-10%
Percentage of plastics in the waste stream: 6.5%
Virgin product examples: Pipe, meat wrap, cooking oil, bottled water and shampoo bottles
Recycled product examples: non-food bottles, sewage pipe, siding, consumer containers, hoses, mats and refuse containers

PVC is the world's second largest selling thermoplastic. Negligible amounts of post-consumer PVC are recycled today, and roughly 40 percent of this resin ends up in the solid waste stream in a relatively short time, primarily disposed of as packaging.[181] Switzerland has banned PVC bottles after October 1991 because of their low recycling rate and concern that they contribute to dioxin production when solid waste is incinerated.[182] While a ban is not likely in the United States, companies within the vinyl industry are pursuing post-consumer PVC recycling in response to public pressure and in anticipation of U.S. legislation that may require recycled content in non-food grade bottles.

Industry demand for reclaimed PVC appears strong. A survey undertaken by the University of Toledo found that industry demand for PVC scrap is likely to exceed supply by more than two to one. While the industry produces 207 million pounds of PVC bottles annually, the survey estimated potential demand at 494 million pounds.[183] However, Occidental Chemical, the largest PVC resin producer with a 20 percent market share, noted in a company newsletter that packaging products, namely bottles with 25 percent recycled PVC content, appear to be the only PVC products whose price justifies the cost of using recycled plastics. Permanent applications for recycled post-consumer PVC, such as drain pipes, appear uneconomical to date. William Carroll Jr., Occidental Chemical's director of commercial development, also told IRRC that while the clear PVC bottles, which comprise the bulk of PVC containers, can be remanufactured into bottles, recycling colored resins poses greater technical difficulties that require further attention.[184]

Challenges for recycling PVC: Even if existing demand falls shy of the amount predicted in the University of Toledo's study, the ability to meet demand for recycled PVC solely in non-food containers requires substantially boosting supply. To increase supply, D'Lane Wisner, senior marketing manager for B.F. Goodrich Co., told IRRC the industry is "shooting for a closed-loop system within the community" and targeting the recycling of post-consumer PVC bottles.[185] As with most plastics, the greatest challenge lies in separating the PVC containers from the rest of the waste stream. Industry is depending heavily on municipal waste collection programs to funnel PVC bottles its way; but unlike PET and HDPE bottles, the smaller PVC bottles are difficult for residential recyclers to identify. In addition, manual separation of PVC containers at material recovery facilities appears to be neither economic nor sufficiently accurate. Occidental Chemical has determined that recycled PVC bottle resin must be 99.95 percent PET-free or better and that manual sorting would not achieve that level of purity.[186]

Accordingly, the industry's primary emphasis is on developing automated sorting technologies that can separate PVC containers from a stream of mixed plastics. As the Vinyl Institute said, the "development of separation technology is the last major hurdle to fully integrating vinyl products into consumer recycling programs."[187] To date, it is not yet clear whether automated sorting systems are economically feasible, but Fred Krause, director of environmental solutions for B.F. Goodrich, a major PVC bottle compound producer, anticipates "resolution of this [economic] issue this year," based on operating experiences at recycling facilities.[188]

The vinyl industry is not alone in its desire to remove PVC from mixed plastics. Recyclers of PET and HDPE containers are discovering that residential recyclers are putting PVC bottles out on their curb along with the PET and HDPE bottles, even when requested not to. Problems can develop if these PVC bottles go undetected, because even small amounts of PVC in a batch of PET can interfere with recovery and damage machinery by generating hydrochloric acid. As plastic collection programs grow, the need to remove PVC to ensure successful recycling of other plastics is as much an impetus for separating PVC as the desire to recycle PVC.

Company initiatives: Taking the lead in post-consumer PVC recycling initiatives are three of the four major producers of PVC bottle compounds—Occidental Chemical Corp., Georgia Gulf Corp. and B.F. Goodrich; the Vinyl Institute, a trade association representing makers of PVC plastics, raw materials and additives; the CPRR; and two companies developing sortation technologies—National Recovery Technologies Inc. and Asoma Instruments Inc. (Shintech Inc., the fourth major producer of PVC bottle compounds, was unavailable for comment.)

Occidental Chemical Corp.: The largest producer of PVC resins (and the second largest HDPE manufacturer), Occidental Chemical was the first in its industry to begin a used PVC bottle collection program. The company announced its intention to purchase 200,000 pounds of post-consumer PVC in the fall of 1989, and one year later, William Carroll of Occidental told IRRC it appeared the company would easily reach its goal. The company's longer-term goal is to recycle annually 20 million pounds, or 10 percent of all PVC bottles, by the end of 1992. Carroll says that the company's ability to meet that goal is highly dependent on the success of plastic curbside collection programs. Occidental plans to sell its recycled PVC to fabricators under the trade name "EcoVinyl™."[189]

In January 1991, Occidental Chemical announced that it had signed an agreement with the Plastics Recycling Alliance, a joint venture of Du Pont and Waste Management, to implement automated sortation of PVC in the PRA's Philadelphia plastics recycling plant. Technical personnel from both companies will join together to "invent and adapt sortation techniques from the PRA facility," and Occidental will recycle the separated PVC as part of its ongoing program.[190]

Georgia Gulf Corp.: Another major supplier of PVC bottle compounds, Georgia Gulf added a resource recovery arm to its PVC division in the summer of 1990. Its program differs from Occidental's in that Georgia Gulf has not become involved in the collection and processing of PVC containers. Instead, Frank Borelli of Georgia Gulf told IRRC that the company's "intent is to find markets for PVC," concentrating its activities in the laboratory to determine the quality of materials that can be produced from recycled PVC. Borelli also said that the company has not set any goals to acquire specific amounts of recycled PVC, noting that its ability to do so is dependent on the establishment of collection systems. To facilitate PVC collection, Georgia Gulf has funded projects under the auspices of the Vinyl Institute.[191]

B.F. Goodrich Co.: B.F. Goodrich is doing work internally on PVC sorting and also is participating in a plastics recycling project in Akron, Ohio (which is included in the discussion of ASOMA Industries).[192] In the spring of 1991, the company started a post-consumer PVC bottle-to-bottle recycling program in Waukesha County, Wis.; Avon Lake, Ohio, and other U.S. communities. Goodrich sells the reclaimed vinyl to Schoeneck Containers of New Berlin, Wis., to manufacture bottles with 25 percent recycled vinyl content.[193] In addition, to raise public awareness about plastics recycling, B.F. Goodrich donated a conservation garden, including benches, signs, fenceposts and a tile walkway made from recycled vinyl or commingled plastics, to the Akron Zoo.[194]

National Recovery Technologies Inc. (NRT): NRT of Nashville, Tenn., developed an electromagnetic scanner that sorts vinyl from mixed post-consumer rigid plastic containers through research sponsored by EPA and the Vinyl Institute. A privately held company and manufacturer of municipal waste processing systems, NRT installed its equipment in a Manchester, England, facility owned by Reprise Ltd., a joint venture company, in 1991. XL Recycling Corp. abandoned plans to install a 10 million pound per year commercial prototype at its Chicago area material recovery facility, citing concerns over electromagnetic radiation.[195]

The NRT separation system is estimated to cost between $100,000 and $150,000. Given the system's high costs and the relatively small amount of PVC in plastics captured through post-consumer recycling programs, analysts are speculating that the system will be more economically feasible for a dedicated plastics recycling center than a full materials recovery facility.[196] (See Chapter 7 for additional information on NRT.)

Asoma Instruments Inc.: Asoma Instruments of Austin, Tex., which is sponsored by the CPRR, also developed a sortation system that detects PVC with an x-ray fluorescence technology and uses a stream of air to blow containers from the waste stream. An Akron, Ohio, mixed plastics recycling research and demonstration project began using the ASOMA technology in late 1990. Although the technology worked well at Rutgers State University using clean, whole bottles, the system encountered difficulties at an operating materials recovery facility, where materials jammed up the feeding system and dirt and oil interfered with the detection system. The project is making modifications to address the materials handling problems and will be reevaluating the technology during 1991.[197] The technology is estimated to cost $25,000 to $30,000 to integrate into an existing sortation line.[198] The major participants in the Akron mixed plastics recycling project are **wTe Corp.**, the city of Akron, **B.F. Goodrich** and **Dow Chemical**.

The Akron project was not Dow's first involvement in a project attempting to separate mixed plastics. In April 1990, Dow and Domtar Inc., a Canadian firm, abandoned the first recycling program in North America designed to tackle mixed plastics, saying that Dow's chemically driven plastics separation technology was not successful. Dow had difficulty completely separating the PVC from the PET in mixed batches of post-consumer plastic waste. The company said its separation system, which is based on chlorinated solvents, could be made to work but that it was not worth the added expense. (The company had already invested several million dollars in the technology.) The two companies established the failed joint venture in September 1988, announcing plans to build a 40 to 80 million pound a year recycling plant in Midland, Mich. Domtar says it will continue to purchase post-consumer plastics from its contracted suppliers, although it will try to eliminate purchases of PVC. Dow says it will continue to explore new uses for recycled plastics through a new research and development arm, the Applied Plastic Materials Group, formed in the summer of 1990, but it plans to focus on plastics more relevant to its business, such as polystyrene and polyethylene, and no longer pursue PET recycling.[199]

Polystyrene (PS) Recycling

Percentage of plastic bottles: 5-10%
Percentage of plastics in the waste stream: 16%
Virgin product examples: coffee cups, "clamshells," utensils
Recycled product examples: "clamshells," office products, flower pots, serving trays, insulation board, carpet fibers, video cassettes, hangers and waste receptacles.

Roughly 26 percent of the polystyrene produced in 1989 was used in packaging.[200] Of the more than 5 billion pounds of polystyrene produced in 1989, roughly 20 million pounds of polystyrene, essentially all post-industrial, was recycled.[201] Although the polystyrene industry recycles nearly all in-plant polystyrene wastes, there has been virtually no recycling of polystyrene found in the post-consumer waste stream until the last year or so.

Rubbermaid Commercial Products has produced special order items made from recycled polystyrene and plans to introduce desk-top accessories made from low percentages of reclaimed polystyrene as a standard inventory item in 1991. Dr. Charles Lancelot of Rubbermaid says the opening of new polystyrene recycling facilities is making it possible for Rubbermaid to produce standard inventory items, stressing that the company's largest constraint has been availability of a quality supply. Donald Awbrey of Rubbermaid also told IRRC that we "use every pound [of polystyrene] that we can get." Lancelot added that as more recycled polystyrene becomes available, Rubbermaid will be able to increase the recycled content of its products, noting that it has produced black-colored items with up to 50 percent recycled polystyrene.[202]

Acme United Corp. recently began marketing "Kleen Earth" products—namely scissor handles and rulers—made of 90 percent post-consumer coffee cups, burger containers and other forms of styrofoam. The company is marketing the product to school children, and it expects school districts to be a major source of the plastic.[203]

The industry broke new ground in the spring of 1991 when the Hardee's restaurant chain announced that it would use polystyrene clamshells with a 50 percent recycled content. Manufactured by **Lin Pac Plastics** of Wilson, N.C., the new containers, called Recoup, have an inner layer of recycled post-consumer polystyrene surrounded by thin layers of impermeable virgin polystyrene. They sell for the same price as virgin polystyrene foam. Because the recycled material is not coming into direct contact with food, Lin Pac is not seeking approval from the U.S. Food and Drug Administration. Lin Pac produces Recoup at plants in Sebring, Fla., and Wilson, N.C., using a proprietary technology developed by a German sister company, Lin Tec. A U.S. subsidiary of the Lin Pac Group, a British company, Lin Pac also is making egg cartons with recycled polystyrene for sale to Publix Super Markets Inc. and Winn-Dixie Stores Inc. in the South.[204]

Challenges to recycling PS: Hardee's announcement served as a counterweight to McDonald's announcement in the fall of 1990 that it was replacing its polystyrene foam boxes with cellophane-coated paper packaging developed by James River Corp.[205] McDonald's, which had been quite active in establishing polystyrene recycling programs at its fast-food restaurants, uses about 100 million pounds per year of foam packaging, roughly 10 percent of the 1 billion pound per year U.S. foam packaging market. McDonald's decision represents a phaseout of about 75 percent of its total polystyrene packaging; the remaining 25 percent of McDonald's polystyrene packaging includes plastic utensils and the clear plastic containers commonly used at salad bars.[206]

Despite this setback, companies attempting to recycle polystyrene are optimistic about establishing a recycling infrastructure, saying the heavy concentration of polystyrene at large fast-food restaurants and institutional dining halls is a significant factor in their favor. Virtually no residential recycling programs include polystyrene, although Timothy Herman, vice president of business development for Aagard Environmental Services Inc., which is involved in a pilot project with SuperCycle Inc. that recycles polystyrene from 27 restaurants in St. Paul, says that half of the polystyrene waste at a fast food restaurant goes out through the drive-through.[207] David Sheon, a representative of the National Polystyrene Recycling Co., a consortium of companies recycling polystyrene, says concern over the lack of residential polystyrene recycling programs is "misplaced," and he maintains that very little polystyrene actually goes to the home. Sheon added that Fitchburg, Wis., and Naperville, Ill., were undertaking pilot polystyrene recycling programs and that in some communities, McDonald's had welcomed customers bringing in polystyrene from their homes to place in McDonald's polystyrene collection bins.[208]

In its nine-month pilot project funded by Amoco Corp., the town of Fitchburg concluded that the main costs associated with polystyrene recycling were processing and shipping. The project, which yielded five tons of polystyrene, also indicated that residents put polystyrene out for curbside pick-up infrequently.[209]

Polystyrene recycling facilities: Two major initiatives are underway to recycle post-consumer polystyrene around the country. (There are several smaller polystyrene recycling operations, primarily geared toward commercial wastes. Patricia Ireland, an environmental affairs representative with Dart Container Corp., says there are at least 50 polystyrene reclamation facilities throughout the United States.[210]) The National Polystyrene Recycling Co., a consortium of eight polystyrene manufacturers, is spearheading the most comprehensive initiative—a network of four recycling plants. Dart Container Corp., a company that converts polystyrene resins into the final product, also has polystyrene recycling projects underway. Amoco Corp., a polystyrene manufacturer, recently closed its two-year-old polystyrene recycling facility.

National Polystyrene Recycling Co. (NPRC): In June 1989, seven polystyrene manufacturers—**Amoco Chemical Co., ARCO Chemical Co., Dow Chemical U.S.A., Fina Oil and Chemical Co., Huntsman Chemical Co., Mobil Chemical Co.** and **Novacor Inc.**—formed the $14 million National Polystyrene Recycling Co., and announced a goal to play a major role in the recycling of more than 25 percent of all disposable polystyrene, or 250 million pounds annually, by 1995. Chevron Chemical Co. joined the Lincolnshire, Ill., venture soon after it was formed, bringing the total contribution to $16 million. Lee Thomas, former administrator of EPA, agreed to serve as the overall project engineer and manager. The venture planned to operate one existing plant and establish four new regional processing facilities by October 1990, but only the existing plant was operating at that time.[211]

The NPRC operates two plants, one of which it plans to shut down in 1991, and plans to open three additional plants in 1991. NPRC is planning to shut down operations at Plastics Again, a polystyrene recycling plant in Leominster, Mass., that it acquired at cost from Mobil and Genpak Corp. of

Table 5-4

Major U.S. Post-Consumer
Polystyrene Recycling Plants

Company	Location	Design Capacity (in million lbs./yr.)	On-Line Date
National Polystyrene Recycling Co.	Leominster, Mass.	3	1989-1991
	Corona, Calif.	13	Oct. 1990
	Hayward, Calif.	13	1991
	Chicago, Ill.	13	1991
	Bridgeport, N.J.	13	1991
Dart Container Corp.	Mason, Mich.	4	June 1989
	Leola, Pa.	2.5	July 1990
	Plant City, Fla.	1.5	August 1990
Polystyrene Recycling Inc. (Amoco Foam Products subsidiary)	Brooklyn, N.J.	2	1989-1991

Source: Investor Responsibility Research Center Inc.

Middletown, N.Y., a polystyrene container manufacturer, in October 1989. Citing a shortage of polystyrene, a lack of space for expansion at Plastic Again and its decentralized location, the NPRC says it will re-route the polystyrene collected in the Northeast to a new facility in Bridgeport, N.J. In a move to expand collection capabilities in the Northeast, NPRC opened four commercial post-consumer polystyrene consolidation sites in Walpole, Mass., Lowell, Mass., Ft. Edward, N.Y., and Providence, R.I., in July 1991. Plastics Again never reached its processing capacity of 3 million pounds per year and reportedly produced sporadic supply at sporadic quality. The plant has sold small pellets of polystyrene resin to a number of customers, including Traex, which makes trays for McDonald's, and Rubbermaid. Plastics Again also has shipped some pellets to an Amoco insulation facility in Winchester, Va. In the fall of 1990 the pellets were selling for between 40 and 50 cents per pound.[212]

The NPRC incorporated lessons learned at Plastics Again into a new plant that began operation in November 1990 in Corona, Calif. Substantially larger than the Plastics Again operation, the project is capable of processing 13 million pounds of post-consumer and post-industrial polystyrene annually. As with all of NPRC's plants, an independent company—in this case Talco Recycling—will operate the plant. E. James Schneiders, president of NPRC, told *The Wall Street Journal* in August 1990 that he expects the plant to operate at a profit by 1992. The project will pay 4 cents per pound for the polystyrene at the plant, compared with 5 cents per pound paid by Plastics Again, and is reportedly selling resin pellets for between 45 and 60 cents per pound.[213]

NPRC's three additional plants include a plant near San Francisco in Hayward, Calif., that will be operated by wTe Corp; a plant in Bridgeport, N.J., that will be operated by New England CRInc., a developer of materials recovery facilities discussed in Chapter 6; and a plant in Chicago to be operated by Eaglebrook Plastics, a plastics processor and lumber producer.[214]

Dart Container Corp.: A privately held company and the world's largest manufacturer of polystyrene-based foam cups, Dart Container also recycles post-consumer polystyrene. The company has processing plants in Mason, Mich.; Campbellford, Ontario; Leola, Pa.; and Plant City, Fla., with a combined capacity of 10 million pounds annually. The projects produce polystyrene pellets after processing separated polystyrene delivered by institutions, such as schools and grocery chains, as well as a few fast-food restaurants and industry. Until October 1990, when the Mason plant began accepting plastic contaminated with food, all of the projects accepted only clean polystyrene. Noting that "It's tougher to guarantee consistent quality" with post-consumer polystyrene, Patricia Ireland, an environmental affairs representative with Dart Container, told IRRC that the company has more difficulty finding markets for its post-consumer polystyrene pellets than its purer post-industrial pellets. Dart sells its post-consumer pellets to three customers: a New Jersey firm that manufactures hangers and office accessories, a Texas broker that sells the pellets to China, and a New York firm.[215]

The company also is becoming directly involved in collecting polystyrene for the first time, establishing polystyrene drop-off sites in a 40-county area in Michigan. Dart estimates that roughly 70 percent of the population of Michigan will have access to these sites. To further aid collection efforts, Dart is marketing two collection devices, a "respenser" or reverse cup dispenser for low volume areas, and a multi-holed collection unit for higher volume areas that is designed to nest cups, thereby saving space, as they are discarded.[216]

Amoco Corp.: Amoco began operation of the nation's first large-scale polystyrene recycling plant in Brooklyn, N.Y., in April 1989. Polystyrene Recycling Inc., a subsidiary of Amoco Foam Products of Atlanta, operated the pilot project until late June 1991, when Amoco closed the plant, saying

---

Box 5-5

The Disposable Diaper Debate

Disposable diapers have pitted parents dependent on the convenience of disposable diapers against city and county officials desperate to find ways to cut down on the amount of garbage going to landfills. Statistics on diaper production are staggering. The average two-and-one-half-year-old child has gone through 7,800 diapers. Disposable diapers comprise 85 percent of the total diaper market, and approximately 18 billion disposable diapers end up in landfills each year. In terms of the nation's total solid waste crisis, however, disposable diapers account for less than 2 percent of the nation's total garbage—although a highly visible and symbolic 2 percent that is unmatched by any other single consumer product except for newspapers and beverage and food containers.[217]

Bills attempting to ban or tax disposable diapers have sprung up in state houses across the nation. Nebraska passed a ban on nondegradable disposable diapers that will take effect in 1993, while Maine passed a law requiring day-care centers to accept children with cloth diapers. Day-care centers have become a battle ground in the disposable diaper controversy, with the majority, including the national child-care chain, Kinder-Care Learning Centers Inc., requiring disposable diapers except when a child is allergic to them. Both the American Academy of Pediatrics and the American Public Health Association recommend disposable diapers for out-of-home care child-care programs, citing the potential for infectious diseases with cloth diapers.[218]

Companies in the $3.5 billion U.S. disposable diaper market are trying to

---

it was not cost-effective. Unlike Plastics Again, which processes source-separated feedstock, the Amoco project attempted to process mixed waste from McDonald's restaurants, schools and area businesses using a system designed by wTe Corp. After only a few months of operation, however, Amoco determined this method was not economical, particularly with polystyrene comprising only 10 percent of McDonald's trash. Amoco subsequently required all new feedstock to be source-separated and had hoped eventually to eliminate mixed waste entirely.[222]

In the fall of 1990, the Amoco plant was producing 3,000 pounds per day of polystyrene flakes, which would yield 800,000 pounds on an annual basis. Lee Messer, the plant's manager, told IRRC the goal was to produce 1,000 pounds per hour, or nearly 2 million pounds per year. In the fall of 1990, the plant was neither receiving payment for the polystyrene flake nor paying for the polystyrene waste. Not licensed to produce a finished product, the plant gave the flake to Plastics Again to produce a polystyrene resin.[223]

convince legislators and the public that diapers are getting far more attention than they deserve. Kimberly-Clark Corp., which holds 32.5 percent of the market, mobilized parents in Wisconsin to defeat a proposed tax on disposables. Disposable diaper companies tout the health benefits of disposables— keeping babies dry and cutting down on diaper rash—and point out that making and washing cloth diapers also has an environmental impact. Procter & Gamble, the largest maker of disposable diapers with 50 percent of the market, funded a 1990 study by Arthur D. Little that concluded disposable diapers cause less damage to the environment than cloth ones over the lifetime of the products, because cloth diapers consume more energy and water, resulting in greater air and water pollution emissions and cost than disposables.[219]

Countering studies also have emerged, however. A 1991 study funded by the National Association of Diaper Services and supported by several environmental groups concluded that "single use diapers have a greater environmental impact than reusable diapers." The study found specifically that disposables consume 70 percent more energy than cloth diapers.[220]

While some disposable diaper manufacturers are pushing biodegradable diapers, Procter & Gamble maintains that no diaper is biodegradable in a modern landfill and instead promotes composting and recycling. In October 1990, P&G announced plans to market compostable diapers, adding that the company planned to commit $20 million to advance municipal solid waste composting worldwide. P&G also has explored the feasibility of recycling the plastic outer layer of diapers into flower pots and grocery bags and the wood-pulp padding into cardboard boxes and building insulation.[221]

James McLellan, Amoco's director of waste management, told *Chemical Week* in December 1989 that he believed the key to economical polystyrene recycling was to collect the plastic with other materials. "If it is collected with other materials, the incremental cost of separating out polystyrene foam is not significant," says McLellan.[224] Although separating polystyrene from a mixed waste stream was abandoned at the Brooklyn facility, Amoco is pursuing the collection of polystyrene with other recyclables, providing $15,000 to fund the first residential polystyrene recycling collection program in Fitchburg, Wis.[225]

Polypropylene (PP) Recycling

Percentage of plastic bottles: 5-10%
Percentage of plastics in the waste stream: 16%
Virgin product examples: bottle caps, straws, labels, liners, syrup

bottles, yogurt tubs, diapers

Recycled product examples: multi-layer HDPE bottles

Given the variety of forms PP takes in the municipal waste stream, and the low quantity of each, it is difficult to collect PP in marketable quantities.[226] Accordingly, minimal PP recycling is taking place. Technical advances in PP recycling are discussed in the post-consumer plastics recycling process section of this chapter.

Plastic Lumber Production

Producing plastic lumber entails granulating plastic scraps, melting them and processing them in an extruder. The molten plastic is then forced into a mold cavity of the shape and size of the final product.[227] Unsorted mixed plastics is the most common feedstock of these molded products, primarily in the form of lumber, for applications such as fences, park benches, picnic tables, traffic sign posts, floating docks, flooring and speed bumps. The CPRR estimates the market for mixed plastic products could grow significantly from its existing 3 million pounds per year in six potentially high-volume markets: treated lumber, a more than 3 billion pound market; landscape timbers, a 500 million pound market; horse fencing; farm pens for poultry, pigs and cattle; roadside posts; and pallets, a 30 billion pound market.[228]

Plastic lumber manufacturers have an advantage over other plastics recyclers of being able to use all types of plastics, ranging from the more commonly recycled plastic containers to toys, cassette tapes, and other products made of difficult-to-identify plastic resins. While commingled plastics arriving at plastic lumber plants can include all different types of discarded plastics packaging, generally the higher value PET and HDPE containers have been "mined" from commingled plastics, leaving primarily polyethylene in the remaining material. (PET also has a higher flow temperature than the other plastics, making it unpopular with lumber producers.) As a result, commingled plastics represent a more uniform feedstock than might be expected. Studies also have shown that polystyrene, in both its foamed and non-foamed form, has a beneficial effect on the properties of recycled plastic molded products by increasing the strength of the product.[229]

Plastic lumber manufacturers also have the advantage of being able to tolerate higher levels of contaminants in their feedstock than other plastic recyclers, making them less likely to reject loads of plastic. National Waste Technologies, for instance, says its feedstock can have 15 to 25 percent impurities, while ARW Polywood says it can accept loads with 12 to 15 percent non-plastic contaminants, such as paper labels and aluminum neck rings.

Manufacturers of aseptic packages, a common example of which are single serving juice boxes made from 70 percent paper, 23 percent polyethylene and 7 percent aluminum, have been quick to take advantage of these high tolerance levels. Eager to demonstrate that their packages can be recycled in order to counter mounting opposition to their multi-material composition, aseptic packaging manufacturers have struck agreements with two plastic lumber producers—National Waste Technologies and Superwood International Ltd.—to recycle their products.[230]

Plastic lumber has some characteristics that are superior to wood lumber, and others that are not. On the plus side, plastic lumber is less subject to weather damage, insect infestation and water absorption, and as a result, has a considerably longer life then wood lumber. Conventional woodworking tools are suitable for most types of plastic lumber, which is virtually maintenance free once the product is created. In addition, National Waste Technologies touts its product as being "splinter and graffiti proof, able to hold nails or screws better than wood, able to be worked on with conventional power tools and available in assorted colors" that are permanent.[231]

To better understand the limitations of using recycled plastics in lumber applications, the CPRR conducted a series of nail and screw pull-out experiments and concluded that plastic lumber behaves quite differently than wooden lumber. The CPRR found that mixed plastics held nails approximately 40 percent better than typical wood at room temperature. This advantage, however, was rapidly lost at elevated temperatures of approximately 149 degrees Fahrenheit. As a result of its studies, the Center concluded that "utilization of lumber made from recycled plastics must be carefully evaluated regarding the environment in which it will be used in order to avoid inappropriate applications."[232]

The major disadvantage of plastic lumber is that it is substantially more costly than wood lumber—at least double the price. The primary reason for the high cost is slow production speed, but manufacturers maintain that production speeds will improve as new equipment and processes are developed.[233] In the meantime, plastic lumber manufacturers maintain that even today the full life-cycle costs of plastic lumber are much more favorable than wood lumber's, given the long life of plastic. Another disadvantage is that while the American Society for Testing and Materials and some industry trade organizations have established general standards and methods for measuring the characteristics of specific building materials, no standards or measures have been established for plastic lumber.[234]

Plastic lumber manufacturers: The fledgling plastics lumber industry is quite young. Two-thirds of the companies have been in commercial operation for less than a year, and no one has been manufacturing plastic lumber from mixed plastics for more than four years. Because plastic lumber is considerably more expensive than wood lumber, all but Polymerix Inc. and Recycled Plastics Industries Inc. have chosen to produce products, such as picnic tables, made from their plastic lumber, rather than sell the plastic lumber itself.[235]

Hammers Plastic Recycling Corp.: Hammers Plastic Recycling of Iowa Falls, Iowa, claims it is the largest plastic lumber manufacturer. In the fall of 1990, company president Floyd Hammer told *Recycling Times* that "We're going in being the leader. We intend to stay in that position. We are confident there's a market out there for finished products."[236] Hammers derived sales of $4.2 million in 1989 from its two plastic lumber plants in Iowa Falls and Mulberry, Fla.[237] Company representative Mark Nesbitt told IRRC that Hammers uses the full-range of post-consumer plastics, with the percentage of post-consumer material "varying with time and predicated on supply." The company produces a wide range of finished products for sale, with the lumber being "more expensive by a factor of at least two."[238] As part of a a three-year contract with the Chicago Park District, Hammers sold $1.2 million of landscaping timbers to the district in 1990.[239]

Established in 1987, Hammers acquired Polymer Products, also of Iowa Falls, which used mixed plastics to produce car stops, fence posts and bleacher seats. In early 1990, Hammers formed a joint venture with Air & Water Technologies Corp. of Branchburg, N.J., that included the sale of 10 percent of Hammers to Air & Water Technologies.[240] The joint venture plans to build half of Hammer Plastics Recycling's ambitious construction plans, which call for 16 mixed plastics recycling facilities operating throughout the country by 1992. Designed to process between 8 and 10 million pounds annually, the plants will accept both mixed post-consumer and post-industrial plastic waste, including HDPE, film, PP trim from diaper factories, and some non-foam PS. Because some of the company's products are used in marine applications, such as docks and pilings, Hammers would like to locate several plants near seaports.[241]

Advanced Environmental Recycling Technologies Inc. (AERT): Publicly traded AERT of Springdale, Ark., produces "Moistureshield," a composite building material made of post-consumer HDPE containers, wood fiber waste and post-industrial polyethylene. The company plans to market Moistureshield as a substitute for wood and plastic subsurface supports for standard door frames and window sills, highlighting its waterproof characteristics. In spring 1991, Peachtree Windows & Doors, a national manufacturer of residential doors and windows, accepted its first shipment of Moistureshield. AERT says the component piece part of the $5 billion door and window market is $2.3 billion. Douglas Brooks of AERT says that Moistureshield has timed its entrance into the market quite well, maintaining that competing wood lumber for these applications, such as Ponderosa pine, redwood cedar and pressure treated lumber, is a finite resource and that concern over environmental issues, most notably the spotted owl, is forcing industry to find substitutes for these types of wood. While the company says its product is priced competitively with these types of wood, it also cautions that Moistureshield is not as strong as conventional wood and plastic building materials, cannot be easily painted or laminated, and "cannot be sawed, milled, or otherwise worked as easily as wood." In late 1990 the company signed a confidentiality agreement to work with Dow Chemical on recycling post-consumer plastic film and to address the weaknesses in Moistureshield.[242]

AERT undertook an initial public offering in November 1989 that yielded net proceeds of $5.4 million. Today, the company operates a plastics reclamation plant in Rogers, Ark., that supplies waste plastic to its Moistureshield production plant in Junction City, Tex. Brooks estimates that the Arkansas plant will consume about 15 million pounds of plastic in 1991 and between 25 and 30 million in 1992. HDPE containers will represent 3 million pounds of the 15 million pounds in 1991, and the remainder will be split between hydropulp waste and plastic film. In addition to the reclaimed plastics, the Texas production plant will use waste wood from an adjacent mill that extracts cedar oil for perfumes and industrial detergents. The company expects to search for new plant sites in the next 24 months as production at its existing facilities reaches full capacity.[243]

Polymerix Inc.: TriMax of Long Island, a subsidiary of publicly traded Polymerix, estimates that its Ronkonkoma, N.Y., facility will process about 30 million pounds of plastic in 1991.[244] In contrast to the other plastic lumber companies, Polymerix produces TriMax lumber for sale in lieu of producing value added products. The company says that its goal is to be a high volume producer and that its process is geared toward larger production runs. The company says it uses a "high percentage" of post-consumer plastics to produce its lumber.[245]

In early 1990, the company decided to pursue technology licensing opportunities instead of forming joint manufacturing ventures. In early 1991, Polymerix licensed its technology to a joint venture partnership between Energy Answers Corp., a waste-to-energy developer, and On Line Management Associates Inc., a consulting firm in Hauppauge, N.Y. The joint venture is reportedly pursuing a plant in Florida.[246] Jeffrey Bachrach, Polymerix's chief financial officer, told IRRC that Polymerix is pursuing licensing because although it would prefer to develop its own plants, high capital costs are deterring it from doing so. Polymerix made an initial public stock offering in August 1987 and in December 1989 began devoting its resources exclusively to the development of recycled plastic lumber products, discontinuing its engineering plastics product line made from recycled scrap and waste plastics.[247]

National Waste Technologies Inc.: Ronkonkoma also is the site of

Table 5-5

U.S. Plastic Lumber Manufacturers

Company	Plant Location	Plastics Con- sumed	Start of Commercial Operation
ARW Polywood	Hamilton, Ohio	Mixed	NA
Advanced Environmen- tal Recycling Tech- nologies Inc.	Junction City, Tex.	Mixed	NA
BTW Industries Inc.	Pembroke Park, Fla.	Mixed	1991
Duratech Industries Inc.	Lake Odessa, Mich.	HDPE	1987
Eaglebrook Plastics Inc.	Chicago, Ill.	HDPE	NA
Hammers Plastic Recycling Corp.	Iowa Falls, Iowa Mulberry, Fla.	Mixed	1987
Innovative Plastic Products Inc.	Greensboro, Ga.	Mixed	1990
National Waste Tech- nologies Inc.	Ronkonkoma, N.Y.	Mixed	1990
The Plastic Lumber Co.	Akron, Ohio	Mixed	1989
Plastic Pilings	Rancho Cucamonga, Calif.	Mixed	1987
Polymerix Inc. (TriMax of LI)	Ronkonkoma, N.Y.	Mixed	1989
Recycled Plastics Industries Inc.	Green Bay, Wis.	HDPE	1990
Superwood of Alabama	Selma, Ala.	Mixed	1990

Sources: Investor Responsibility Research Center Inc., except for "Start of Commercial Operation," which was provided by *Resource Recycling*, July 1990, for
all but Duratech Industries, BTW and Recycled Plastics.

another plastic lumber production facility opened in November 1989 by National Waste Technologies. The $2 million plant processes 4 million pounds per year of mixed post-consumer plastics into $1 million worth of plastic lumber called Syntal. The price of Syntal is "generally comparable to treated lumber and about twice the cost of regular wood," according to Carl Lanza of NWT. Like Hammers, NWT produces finished products for sale, including decking, sidewalks and docks, speed bumps and retaining walls. NWT uses a patented process called Extruder Technology 1, or ET/1, to produce the lumber from mixed plastics, which are dominated by HDPE and LDPE. (See section on the post-consumer plastics recycling process for additional information on the ET/1 process.) National Waste Technologies obtained rights to the technology from Advanced Recycling Technology of Belgium, signing a $10 million U.S. licensing agreement in late summer 1989. NWT plans to build a second plastic lumber plant in Florida and was proceeding with site selection in early 1991.[248]

Superwood of Alabama: Superwood of Alabama began operation in the spring of 1990 under license to Superwood International Ltd. of Ireland. Superwood International was incorporated in 1984 by the original promoters of Superwood Ltd., which began operation in 1981 after acquiring the exclusive Irish rights to the Klobbie process patented by Lankhorst Touwfabrieken B.V. Both companies are subsidiaries of Superwood Holdings plc, which was floated on the Irish Stock Exchange in November 1987. The Irish manufacturer produces basic solid plastic elongated products such as posts, poles, stakes and boards. The Selma, Ala., plant produces fence posts for sale, and Superwood Ontario Ltd. of Mississauga, another independent company that also is using the Superwood technology, produces products for the agricultural market.[249]

Eaglebrook Plastics Inc.: Eaglebrook Plastics of Chicago is another plastic lumber producer, although it produces lumber from 100 percent post-consumer HDPE bottles, as opposed to mixed plastics. Eaglebrook accepts HDPE and PET containers, processing them for resale to industry and for use by Eaglebrook Products, its plastic lumber affiliate. Eaglebrook Products makes Durawood for sale primarily to manufacturers and state and local governments. Durawood can be installed with standard woodworking tools, although because it has greater flexibility than wood lumber, it is not recommended for use in a support structure. The lumber costs up to three and a half times as much as wood.[250]

Duratech Industries Inc.: In Lake Odessa, Mich., Duratech Industries also produces products made from plastic lumber produced primarily from milk jugs. The company produced 80,000 pounds of plastic lumber in 1990 and estimates that it will process roughly double that amount in 1991. The four-year-old company produces a variety of plastic products, including picnic tables, benches, bird feeders and waste receptacles. Marketing primarily to municipalities and state parks, the company estimates that the price of its picnic table is roughly equal to the price of a picnic table for the municipal market and roughly three times more than a picnic table for the residential market. Noting that its tables eliminate maintenance costs because they do not have to be moved during the winter, Mark Rogers, the company's vice president and general manager, maintains that when amortized over the life of the product, the cost of its table is cheaper.[251]

Recycled Plastics Industries Inc.: Recycled Plastics Industries of Green Bay, Wis., is a third company making plastic lumber from HDPE. Using 100 percent post-consumer material, the company produces lumber only, no finished products. The company supplies lumber, which costs about two to two and a half times as much as wood, to parks and recreation departments as well as pallet and dock pier markets.[252]

ARW Polywood: ARW Polywood of Hamilton, Ohio, produced about 4.8 million pounds of plastic lumber in 1990, with post-consumer polyethylene and polypropylene representing about 80 percent of its feedstock. Roger Many, the company's chief executive officer, says the company has eliminated a processing step by purchasing preground plastics in place of whole plastic bottles. Many also told IRRC that ARW will be able to produce 5 million pounds of lumber on its existing machine in 1991 and that it is considering starting up a second machine. The company's plastic lumber is roughly two to two and a half times the cost of conventional lumber.[253]

BTW Industries Inc.: BTW also uses the ET/1 technology to produce plastic lumber that it sells in the form of park benches and picnic tables. BTW acquired the equipment from Plastic Recyclers of Wyandanch, N.Y., which closed down its operations. Having launched its pilot project in March 1991 in Pembroke Pines, Fla., BTW is processing around 200,000 pounds per month and plans to increase production to 3 million pounds per year.[254]

According to the Council for Solid Waste Solutions and the Plastics Recycling Foundation, **Innovative Plastic Products Inc**. of Greensboro, Ga.; **Plastic Lumber Co.** of Akron, Ohio; **Plastics Pilings Inc**. of Rancho Cucamonga, Calif.; and **Unicorn** of Angola, N.Y., also manufacture products made from recycled mixed plastics.[255]

Future Market for Post-Consumer Plastics

Largely because the plastics industry is reclaiming such a small percentage of plastics from the waste stream today, it has tremendous potential to increase recycling rates multifold. Moreover, a significant increase in plastics recycling rates and the subsequent surge in availability of recycled resins could substantially alter traditional business practices. To meet the 25 percent plastics recycling goal by 1995, the Council for Solid Waste Solutions estimates that industry will have to consume one and one-half to two billion pounds per year of recycled resin in place of virgin plastics. "As a result," said Edward Woolard, chairman of Du Pont, "it will definitely change the way the plastics industry does business."[256] Put another way, post-consumer plastics "will be a multi-billion industry," says Darrell R. Murrow of the Center for Plastics Recycling.[257]

The plastics industry says that it is ready to reorient its industrial processes to use recycled resins and that it is willing to make the necessary capital investments. The Council for Solid Waste Solutions estimated in the spring of 1991 that the plastics industry has invested around $200 million in plastics recycling and that it will need to invest a similar amount to meet its 25 percent recycling goal. The council estimates another 15 to 20 major recycling plants will need to be built to process the expected increase in supply of plastics from the waste stream.[258] The plastics industry has an advantage over the paper industry in that its recycling plants can be built relatively quickly. Citing Day Products Inc.'s PET recycling facility as an example, Wayne Pearson, executive director of the Plastics Recycling Foundation, said that plastic recycling plants can be up and operating in 10 months, compared with up to three years for a recycled paper mill.[259]

Today, the industry says demand for plastic reclaimed from the waste stream outweighs supply substantially, estimating that plastics reclaimers are working at only two-thirds of capacity.[260] A major impediment to plastics recycling facilities working at full capacity is the immature infrastructure for reclaiming plastics discarded in the waste stream. There are only two main avenues of collection: states with container deposit legislation and curbside recycling programs. Only recently have traditional scrap dealers begun expanding their operations to include plastics. Substantially boosting collection rates is essential to successful plastics recycling. Bruce Bond of wTe Corp. told recycling conference attendees in May 1990 that in order for plastics companies to convert their processes to utilize recycled resins, they want steady supplies of 100 million pounds per year, not 1 or 2 million pounds per year.[261]

The industry plans to make significant inroads in the collection area primarily through curbside recycling programs. The Council for Solid Waste Solutions reported in the spring of 1991 that about one-third of more than 1,500 municipalities with curbside recycling programs include plastics in their programs. To achieve the 25 percent plastics recycling goal, however, the council is planning on the number of plastics recycling programs doubling every year until 1995, when the number of programs would total 4,000.[262] Convincing municipalities to include plastics in their programs is not always easy. Because municipalities and haulers pay tipping, or disposal, fees based on weight, there is less incentive to remove light-weight plastics from the waste stream than some other heavier materials. The bulkiness of plastics also can pose some logistical problems in curbside collection programs. Citizens often voice great support for plastics recycling programs, though, because plastics comprise a large and highly visible volume of a household's trash.

A second major impediment to plastics recycling is the difficulty of separating different types of plastic resins commingled in the waste stream— a requirement if the recycled resins are to replace virgin resins in industrial processes. There is a trend toward expanding the types of plastics accepted at recycling facilities across the country, but additional research is needed for automated separation technologies to become commercially available. The industry is tackling this challenge aggressively, however, for two major reasons. The industry is under increasing public pressure to recycle more than the well-known PET soda bottles and HDPE milk jugs. In addition, the Center for Plastics Recycling Research has discovered that residential recyclers tend to put materials out for collection that they think should be recycled, regardless of whether the local recycler is capable of processing the material.[263] In the case of plastics, residential recyclers often include several types of plastic containers, and even toys, among the requested PET and HDPE bottles. Because plastics recycling facilities are receiving a mixture of plastics, they essentially are being forced to upgrade their facilities to distinguish between the various types of plastics in order to supply industry with uncontaminated supplies of plastic resins.

Another technical challenge to plastics recycling is that plastics degrade each time they are reheated and recycled. Because of the low rate of plastics recycling and the small amount of recycled content in most plastic products, the potential degradation of recycled plastic has minimal near-term impact. As higher recycling rates are achieved, however, degradation will become an issue that industry will have to address.

The establishment of industry standards and specifications for recycled resins would assist in the integration of recycled plastic resins into the plastics industry. Roger Geyer, vice president and technical director for M.A. Industries Inc., told recycling conference attendees in May 1990 that there is a prejudice against recycled post-consumer plastics within the plastics industry. Geyer said that although his company is convinced its recycled plastic resins meet design specifications, the industry overtests the recycled plastics to ensure they can compete with steel and other materials. Industry standards and specifications could assuage concerns of industry members with minimal experience with recycled plastics resins and could also avoid costly testing procedures.[264]

The plastics industry is quite bullish about the future of plastics recycling. "In my judgment," Geoffrey Place of Procter & Gamble told recycling conference attendees in March 1990, "the opportunity to recycle plastic is even greater than was true for aluminum—and I believe we can achieve a comparable level of success for plastics recycling in the next five years as opposed to the 20 years it has taken for aluminum."[265] Many environmentalists and competing industries contend, however, that the driving force behind the growth in aluminum recycling has been the underlying economics of doing so. They are skeptical that the economics of plastics recycling is as compelling and question the profitability of some plastics recycling projects. The next few years should provide some clues as to the actual profitability of plastics recycling plants, and by the middle of the decade, the cost-effectiveness of these efforts should become apparent.

Chapter VI
SOURCE-SEPARATED
MATERIALS PROCESSING

The face of the solid waste industry is changing rapidly as it comes to terms with its evolving mission. Once limited to hauling solid waste to landfills, the industry has expanded to include waste-to-energy development and is now incorporating recycling services. In part because of these new aspects to solid waste management, the industry has seen dramatic growth. "When total waste industry revenue grows from an estimated $1 billion in 1970 to $25 billion today, surely there's been a major change in the business of dealing with discards," Eugene Wingerter, executive director and chief executive officer of the National Solid Wastes Management Association, told industry members in September 1990. "Our industry is becoming in fact a materials handling industry where we segregate, transport, process and dispose of a vast array of consumer and industrial byproducts."[1]

A booming sector of this materials handling industry is curbside collection of recyclables and the subsequent processing of recyclables at materials recovery facilities, better known as MRFs (pronounced murfs). Recovering recyclables at curbside puts the onus on the residential recycler to prevent recyclable materials from mixing in with the rest of the waste stream, thereby keeping recyclable materials clean and more marketable. Once residential recyclers have done their part, however, a host of companies are stepping in to ensure that the recyclables then make the transformation from used product to industrial feedstock. While some companies are playing a role in the transformation by either hauling or processing the recyclables, others, namely the large solid waste management firms, are overseeing the process from start to finish, encompassing collection, processing, marketing, packaging and shipping responsibilities. The seven largest solid waste management companies have all jumped on the recycling bandwagon, highlighting their curbside recycling programs in their annual reports to shareholders.

Curbside recycling programs now reach an estimated 15 percent of the nation's population, and growing demand by municipalities for these services ensures that they will continue to draw increasing numbers of residents into the recycling loop. To keep pace with the burgeoning number of curbside recycling programs, MRFs have been springing up across the country over the last decade, and experts predict that by the mid-1990s all major U.S. communities will employ some type of MRF to process recyclables.[2] This explosion in MRFs has led Peter Grogan, director of materials recovery for R.W. Beck and Associates, a consulting firm in Denver, Colo., to predict that MRFs "will become a community institution, similar to the local firehouse, and 'MRF' will become a household word" across the country.[3]

Recycling Activities At the Nation's Leading Solid Waste Management Companies

Collection and disposal of the nation's municipal solid waste is primarily in the hands of private companies. Private firms own approximately 15 percent of the country's landfills and half of its landfill capacity.[4] Excluding the developing markets for waste-to-energy and recycling plants and services, private companies represent 70 percent of the nation's municipal solid waste market.[5] The solid waste management industry is dominated by six publicly traded industry giants and one employee-owned firm that together represent nearly 30 percent of the municipal solid waste market. Small private operators represent another 40 percent of the market, and municipalities hold the remaining 30 percent.[6] The solid waste industry is consolidating rapidly, replacing the fragmented waste industry of old. Escalating costs of doing business and the degree of sophistication required to meet increasingly stringent environmental regulations are pushing many smaller companies out of the industry or leading to their acquisition by industry leaders.

In addition to sorting through the quagmire of environmental regulations, small hauling companies are having difficulty taking on the added role of commodities broker—a role forced onto them as a result of the recycling frenzy sweeping the country. Individual haulers and their trade associations have concluded that the nation has embraced the idea of an integrated solid waste management strategy and that, as a result, collecting and marketing recyclables has become a component of the hauling business. While many haulers are reluctant to move into this new territory, Wayne

Trewhitt, chairman of the National Solid Wastes Management Association (NSWMA), warned association members, "Recycling is here to stay. Haulers that don't get into recycling today won't be around 10 years from now....Our business is dramatically changing. It is becoming more sophisticated. We can no longer just process refuse; we are now in the commodities business."[7]

Most waste management companies, both large and small, agree with this interpretation. Pointing to the strong public demand for recycling, Richard Widrig of Western Waste Industries, one of the nation's seven largest solid waste disposal companies, told IRRC that if Western Waste were "not involved in recycling programs, we would not be in business."[8] Larry Knutson, president of a local waste company in Minneapolis, also views expansion into recycling as a key to his business's survival, saying that "if haulers don't get into the recycling business, recyclers will get into the hauling business."[9]

The pressing question for haulers is now "Can we make any money recycling?" Given current market conditions, profitability stems not from the revenues derived from marketing recyclables but from the savings from avoided disposal fees and service fees paid for processing recyclables. As Knutson pointed out, haulers have an advantage in this situation because "haulers have the incentive of avoided tip fees [waste disposal fees], and recyclers don't."[10] The key to profitability for haulers lies in the terms of the operating contract negotiated with the municipality or other entity contracting to dispose of its wastes. In turn, whether it makes economic sense for a municipality to seek curbside recycling services is largely dependent on the municipality's current waste disposal costs. (See Box 6-1 for further information on the economics of curbside recycling programs.)

The profitability of recycling programs among the nation's leading solid waste management firms is mixed. Many solid waste company representatives acknowledged to IRRC that their companies view many existing recycling programs as loss leaders. Cautioning about the difficulty in tracing dollars spent on recycling given that companies offer it as part of an array of services, Widrig of Western Waste Industries told IRRC that Western Waste has concluded that its recycling programs are not yet profitable "if you just look at that part of the business."[11] Richard Riley, recycling director of Laidlaw Inc., says, however, that Laidlaw's recycling programs are "at least as profitable as its other residential work."[12] And Joseph Ruiz, vice president of Attwoods Inc., reported that Attwoods's recycling programs have been "very profitable," attributing the company's success to Attwoods's involvement in its recycling programs from "cradle to grave."[13]

Regardless of whether companies consider their recycling programs profitable today, nearly all contend that recycling has the potential to be a

Box 6-1

Curbside Recycling Programs

Curbside recycling programs are the fastest growing collection method for source-separated recyclables. These programs enjoy strong support from the glass, steel and plastics industries, which lack a highly developed recycling infrastructure and look to curbside collection as the primary means of reclaiming their materials from the waste stream. The glass and steel industries in particular favor curbside collection over container deposit legislation. (See Box 6-2 for information on container deposit legislation.) Some companies in the aluminum industry, however, which has the most comprehensive recycling infrastructure, have expressed concern that curbside collection may have an adverse impact on the industry's existing collection efforts. The aluminum industry also is opposed to aluminum subsidizing the cost of recycling other containers and is concerned about aluminum becoming contaminated with other recyclables collected in curbside recycling programs.

The key to determining whether curbside recycling can be economical for a municipality is the avoided disposal cost. At least with current markets, revenues from most recycled materials are not sufficient to cover the costs of a recycling program. According to one study commissioned by the Glass Packaging Institute in 1988, revenues from the sale of recyclables cover less than half of a recycling program's operating costs.[14] Aluminum is the only material where the price paid by end-users continually covers the expense of collection and processing.

But as Charles Papke, president of Resource Management Associates, a San Francisco consulting firm, points out, "Curbside collection programs

profit center within the next few years. As Jane Witheridge, a staff vice president for Waste Management Inc., the nation's largest curbside recycler, told IRRC, "While some areas are not as profitable as we would like, these should become profitable in the very near future." Witheridge added that a number of factors determine profitability, including whether the company or municipality takes the risk that prices for recyclables may plummet and whether a MRF is available to sort recyclables. Stressing the importance of being able to handle and process recyclables in a cost-effective manner, Witheridge says WMI has gained a better understanding of the costs involved in offering recycling services and is better prepared to negotiate its new contracts.[19]

Residential recycling programs at the leading solid waste management firms: The six largest publicly held waste industry companies operating in the United States, in order of their 1990 solid waste

always cost more money to operate than the revenues you can get from selling the materials, but if you look at recycling as a waste management tool, then it's often the cheapest way to handle the trash."[15] Tim Goss, an environmental analyst for Seattle's Solid Waste Utility, says Seattle's recycling program (which has one of the highest participation rates in the nation) is only marginally cost effective but that, "even at a break-even point, the program is worth the effort....[Disposal cost will] continue to skyrocket, pushing the avoided cost—and the savings—higher in the future."[16]

While low avoided disposal costs may deter recycling programs in some parts of the country, Rutgers State University's Center for Plastics Recycling Research (CPRR) estimates that recycling is generally economical if landfill costs exceed $40 to $50 per ton.[17] The factors determining the economic viability of a recycling program, however, will vary from community to community. Whether a municipality owns or has to purchase land on which it can build a MRF, whether existing municipal workers can work on the recycling program or whether new personnel must be hired, and the cost and structure of its existing collection system are just some of the factors determining the economics of a particular community's recycling program.

Curbside recycling programs appear to be the most effective of three options for collecting source-separated materials. The other two methods are buy-back centers, which pay residential recyclers for the materials they recycle, or drop-off centers, which merely provide a central collection point for recyclables. Curbside collection programs, which require the least effort on the part of residential recyclers, capture the greatest amount of recyclables from the waste stream. According to the CPRR, curbside collection recovers about 70 to 90 percent of beverage cans in the waste stream, while the recovery rate for buy-back centers is only about 15 to 20 percent and just 10 percent for drop-off centers.[18]

operations revenues, are: Waste Management Inc., Browning-Ferris Industries Inc., Laidlaw Inc., Attwoods Inc., Chambers Development Co. and Western Waste Industries.[20] A summary of their residential recycling activities is shown in Table 6-1. Any composting projects these companies have underway are described in Chapter 7.

Waste Management Inc. (WMI): WMI is the nation's largest waste services firm, largest curbside recycler and largest provider of recycling services for North America's commercial and industrial facilities. WMI's recycling subsidiary, Recycle America[R], provides recycling services to more than 3 million households, a 150 percent increase from the 1.2 million households serviced in 1989. WMI has more than 70 facilities processing recyclables, including MRFs, transfer stations and commercial balers.[21] In 1990, Recycle America[R] handled more than 1 million tons of recyclables from residential and commercial solid waste streams.[22]

The key to economical recycling, maintains WMI's Jane Witheridge, is to get away from having the truck driver sort the recyclables, sorting them at a central facility instead.[23] WMI took a major step toward this goal in 1989, acquiring the Brini system—a waste classification method reported to recover 80 percent of incoming municipal solid waste for recycling or for the production of refuse-derived fuel. Developed by Sellbergs Engineering of Stockholm, Sweden, 24 Brini-equipped systems have been sold in 12 European countries and Japan.[24] WMI has been using the Brini technology at its Pinellas Park, Fla., MRF since 1990 to process commercial, light industrial and commingled recyclables from curbside and since early 1991 at a plant in Etobicoke, Ontario, to process commercial and industrial waste.[25] The Brini system separates paper from heavier recyclables, allowing WMI to collect fully commingled loads and eliminate the dual processing lines for paper and containers typical at most MRFs.[26] The Swedish system sorts incoming materials into three portions: a light portion composed of different types of paper and plastic film that is then manually sorted; a heavy portion containing rigid containers that also is then manually sorted, and a screened portion of residue, mainly grit, sand, glass shards and other small nonrecyclables.[27]

WMI estimates that the Brini technology increases a MRF's processing capacity by 30 to 50 percent. While processing costs are higher, William Moore, WMI's director of waste reduction, says that collection costs, which normally account for 70 percent of a recycling program's total costs, drop considerably.[28] Moore also is confident that WMI's Brini system will remove one of the major obstacles to a fully commingled collection system—separation of the glass shards from the paper portion. Moore estimates that WMI will have 80 percent of its anticipated 8,000 curbside recycling collection programs requiring only one or two sorts by 1993.[29]

WMI believes the Brini system also will enable it one day to pursue a wet/dry recycling program, whereby residential recyclers place two bags of garbage at their curb: one with wet trash, such as food scraps and soil paper, and one with dry trash, such as glass and aluminum containers. The Brini system would automatically separate the dry materials. A wet/dry pilot program in Guelph, Ontario, sent materials down to the Pinellas facility for testing, and the community reportedly plans to proceed with a full-scale program.[30]

In 1990, WMI inaugurated another program designed to get the truck driver away from sorting, or even handling, garbage—an automated garbage collection system to recycle, collect and transfer wastes. The new system places transferable containers on lightweight, maneuverable vehicles, allowing drivers rapidly to exchange their full containers for empty ones and finish their routes before hauling the collected material to recycling centers or treatment and disposal sites.[31]

Table 6-1

U.S. Residential Recycling Activities
of Six Major Waste Disposal Companies

Company	# of Households Served	# of Households Provided Curbside Recycling	# of Drop-Off or Buy-Back Centers	# of MRFs Operating/ Planned	# of Mixed Waste Facilities
Attwoods	625,000	475,000	15	2/3	0
BFI	5,800,000	2,200,000	70+[a]	b	b
Chambers	NA	NA	15[c]	2/NA	0
Laidlaw	1,000,000	500,000	0	0/1	0
WMI	9,300,000+	3,000,000+	NA	53[d]/NA	0
Western Waste	500,000	170,000	3[e]	4[f]/NA	1

a BFI operates 70 drop-off centers and another 11 centers that offer a variety of services, including some buy-back facilities.
b BFI operates 20 Recycleries™, some of which process commingled recyclables and some of which process mixed waste; a breakdown of specific activities at each Recyclery™ was not available.
c Chambers operates 15 drop-off facilities.
d WMI has more than 70 facilities that process recyclables; 53 process commingled recyclables collected at curbside.
e Western Waste has three permanent buy-back centers and additional mobile units.
f Western Waste wholly owns and operates three of the MRFs; the fourth is a joint venture.

Source: Investor Responsibility Research Center Inc.

In 1990, WMI increased its ownership in Wheelabrator Technologies Inc., a waste-to-energy developer highlighted in Chapter 8, to 55 percent.[32]

Browning-Ferris Industries Inc. (BFI): BFI is the second largest publicly held solid waste company, serving 5.8 million households. BFI's RecycleNOW™ programs provide curbside collection for 2.2 million households in 300 cities, up significantly from only 47,000 homes in 10 cities in April 1988. The company also operates 70 drop-off centers and an additional 11 locations that offer a variety of services, including buy-back centers and composting facilities.[33]

BFI operates 20 Recycleries™ around the country. The Recycleries vary in how they process recyclables; some process sorted recyclables, while others sort and process commingled recyclables. Still others separate recyclables from mixed waste streams.[34] Although details were not available on the activities at each Recyclery, BFI is more geared to curbside sorting than sorting recyclables at a centralized facility. In the fall of 1990, about 90 percent of its recycling programs did curbside sorting.[35]

BFI opened its largest Recyclery in San Jose, Calif., in the spring of 1991. The $11 million facility has the ability to process up to 1,600 tons per day of both residential and commercial recyclables, but concentrates on the commercial side. The project includes a buy-back center, wood fuel processing and a $1 million education center.[36]

BFI is pursuing the Eagle Mountain Project, a waste-by-rail system in the Los Angeles area that would haul waste to a landfill site at a dormant iron ore mine 200 miles east of Los Angeles. Still in the planning stages, the project plans to separate recyclables at transfer stations before the remaining waste is transported to the landfill. One option under consideration is to store items that are recyclable but not currently marketable at the mine until market conditions improve.[37]

BFI also develops waste-to-energy facilities through a joint venture— American Ref-Fuel Co.—with Air Products and Chemicals Inc. American Ref-Fuel is discussed in Chapter 8.

Laidlaw Inc.: Laidlaw Waste Systems, a division of Laidlaw Inc., is Canada's largest recycler and North America's third largest waste management company. The company also owns 34.2 percent of Attwoods plc. Laidlaw prides itself on having pioneered North America's first residential curbside recycling program in Kitchener, Ontario.[38] Today, the company serves roughly 1 million U.S. residences and collects recyclables from approximately 500,000 U.S. homes. Laidlaw does not operate buy-back or drop-off centers and plans to open its first MRF to sort commingled recyclables in 1991—a 100 ton per day MRF outside Chicago in Schaumberg, Ill. For most of its recycling programs, Laidlaw has required either the residential recyclers or the truck operators to sort the recyclables.[39]

Attwoods Inc.: Attwoods plc is a British waste management and quarrying industries firm traded on the London Stock Exchange and in the United States on the NASDAQ exchange. Attwoods Inc. of Miami, Fla., oversees the company's U.S. waste operations and has been providing recycling services under the trade name Community Recycling since October 1988. The company told IRRC it now serves 625,000 residential units and provides curbside recycling to all but 150,000 of them. Most of the company's programs use a truck-side sort. In March 1990, however, Dade County, Fla., awarded Attwoods a contract for the largest single curbside recycling contract in the country that includes a MRF to separate commingled recyclables. Attwoods owns and operates the MRF, which serves an estimated 225,000 single-family households as well as some business and industrial accounts. In 1991, collection is expanding to include Dade County's 150,000 multi-family units. Attwoods operates a second Florida MRF in Fort Walton Beach, which has contracted with Waste Management to process residential recyclables from 35,000 households, and has three more MRFs under development in the mid-Atlantic states. Despite this current emphasis, Attwoods Vice President Joseph Ruiz told IRRC that processing mixed waste, rather than commingled recyclables, was "most likely the way of the future." Altogether, the company has more than 20 facilities involved in recycling activities, including the two MRFs, 14 buy-back facilities, one drop-off site, a ferrous shredding operation and an aluminum smelting facility.[40]

Attwoods acquired Laidlaw's Florida operations following Laidlaw's purchase of 34.2 percent of Attwoods in 1989.[41] Also in 1989, Attwoods acquired Mindis International Corp. of Atlanta, Ga., a metals recycling business and one of the Southeast's largest recycling companies, for up to $65 million in cash and shares.[42] Since acquiring a scrap yard in 1987, Mindis has expanded its services to process and market a wide range of recyclables and has increased revenues from $240,000 per year to more than $100 million in 1990.[43]

Chambers Development Co.: One of the fastest growing solid waste companies in the nation, Chambers Development of Pittsburgh, Pa., has grown from a small trash hauler in southwestern Pennsylvania to a leading waste management firm. Chambers is a proponent of mandatory recycling, saying it "actively supports strict regulations mandating community participation in recycling programs." The company has curbside recycling programs in Georgia, Indiana, New Jersey, Rhode Island and South Carolina. In 1989, Chambers Development Co. established western Pennsylvania's largest residential curbside recycling program.[44]

Chambers operates two MRFS: a 150 ton per day facility in Pittsburgh that began operation in the fall of 1990 and a plant in Pleasantville, N.J. The company also operates 15 drop off sites. In 1989, Chambers acquired exclusive U.S. rights to the proprietary recycling, composting and wastewater treatment technologies of Voest-Alpine, one of the largest companies in Austria, but has not utilized the technology in the United States.[45]

Western Waste Industries: Western Waste Industries of Gardena, Calif., serves 500,000 households in seven Sunbelt states, providing commingled curbside recycling services to approximately 170,000 of them. The company has four MRFs, one of which is owned through a joint venture, to sort and process the commingled recyclables. Western Waste also has one facility in Carson, Calif., that separates recyclables from a mixed residential and commercial waste stream. Richard Widrig of Western Waste told IRRC that the company is studying the advantages and disadvantages of processing commingled recyclables versus processing mixed waste and that it plans

Box 6-2

The Bottle Bill Battle

Nine states—Oregon, Vermont, Maine, Michigan, Connecticut, Iowa, Massachusetts, Delaware and New York—have mandatory deposit systems designed to reclaim beverage containers, and California has a modified law. (See Box 6-3 for information on California's law.) Originally conceived to combat litter, these "bottle bills" require the consumer to pay a per-container deposit that can be redeemed only if they return the used container to retailers. Despite the fact that 1982 was the most recent year in which a state passed deposit legislation, and despite the fact that in nearly two decades Congress has only once even considered a national bottle bill, and even then—in 1976—it was defeated overwhelmingly,[46] bottle bills continue to be a source of heated debate between environmentalists and the bottling/packaging industry. Moreover, the push to recycle has added a new urgency to the debate along with a new focus—the compatibility of bottle deposit legislation with curbside recycling.

Proponents of deposit legislation argue that bottle bills are a simple, consistent and proven method of recycling that have helped establish the recycling infrastructure. Studies indicate the nine bottle bill states have supplied up to two-thirds of the glass bottles, nearly half of the aluminum cans and 98 percent of the plastic soft drink containers recycled in the country.[47] In addition, deposit laws appear to reduce the nation's municipal solid waste by between 3 and 4 percent. Beer and soft drink containers represent around 4 percent of the municipal solid waste stream by weight,[48] and officials from deposit states estimate that between 72 and 98 percent of these beverage containers are redeemed for deposit.[49] Another 1.1 percent of the waste stream is in the form of wine and liquor bottles,[50] and Maine and Iowa require deposits on wine and liquor containers, while Vermont requires deposits on liquor containers.[51]

The subject of fierce debate today is whether bottle bills are continuing to contribute to the nation's recycling effort or whether they are undermining it. Proponents of bottle bills, officials in bottle bill states, and a report released by the U.S. Government Accounting Office in November 1990 all say that curbside and deposit systems are compatible.[52] Maintaining that a combination of the two produces the highest possible recycling rates, proponents point to successful programs in Connecticut, New York, Oregon and Michigan, which have both bottle bills and comprehensive recycling.[53] Proponents also cite a study funded by Anheuser-Busch Inc. that determined that between 17 and 35 percent more materials would be removed with a combined curbside and deposit system than from a curbside program alone.[54] Those in favor of bottle bills tout them as a means of getting 100 percent of the population involved in recycling at no cost to government, adding that the high recovery rates achieved under deposit legislation are not being reached through curbside collection.[55] Saying that curbside programs serve only about 15 percent of the nation's population, they also argue that these programs may never become commonplace in rural areas and that many do not include plastic beverage containers.

Another advantage, say proponents, is that unclaimed container deposits could help fund comprehensive recycling programs. A new provision in the most recently proposed national bottle bill would allow the federal government to collect deposits consumers fail to reclaim. Rep. Paul Henry (R-Mich.), sponsor of the bill, estimates the recycling trust fund could accumulate more than $1.2 billion each year and finance the reauthorization of the Resource Conservation and Recovery Act as well as provide grants for state and local recycling initiatives.[56]

Opponents of deposit legislation deride its effectiveness as a solid waste management strategy and reject the idea that it is compatible with curbside programs. They argue that curbside programs address a much larger percentage of the waste stream than narrowly focused deposit systems and that non-deposit states with comprehensive recycling programs have the highest recycling rates. James Finkelstein, vice president for communications with the National Soft Drink Association, notes that comprehensive recycling not only keeps beverage containers out of the waste stream "but also keeps out the mayonnaise jars and the pickle jars."[57] Lewis Andrews, president of the Glass Packaging Institute, also argues that bottle deposit legislation reduces participation in curbside recycling because "people think they are doing all the recycling that is necessary when they return their beverage containers."[58] An economic concern for municipal recyclers is that revenues from beverage containers, particularly aluminum cans, account for a large percentage of the total revenues of curbside programs, as much as 65 percent according to the National Soft Drink Association.[59] "[Bottle bills] are a contradiction as far as recycling is concerned," argues Finkelstein, "because it takes the most valuable part of the municipal waste stream."[60] The Pennsylvania Glass Recycling Corp. also argues that proposals for combined bottle bill and curbside collection programs "ignore the fragile economics of recycling and the adverse impact of siphoning off even a portion of the most salable curbside recyclables."[61] Proponents of bottle bills counter that a combined bottle bill and deposit system could lower a community's overall disposal costs, noting that communities pay the bulk of the costs of recycling programs because their costs are not covered by revenues from recyclables. They concede, however, that the "economics can still be a problem" from the perspective of a private sector MRF operator.[62]

Table 6-2

States with Beverage Container
Deposit Legislation

State	Year Signed	Year Implemented
Oregon	1971	1972
Vermont	1972	1973
Maine	1976	1978
Michigan	1976	1978
Connecticut	1978	1980
Iowa	1978	1979
Massachusetts	1981	1983
Delaware	1982	1982[a]
New York	1982	1983

[a]For wholesalers; implemented in 1983 for retailers

Source: National Container Recycling Coalition, Washington, D.C.

to continue pursuing both avenues in the near-term. Western Waste also operates two permanent buy-back centers in southern California and one in Florida, along with a number of mobile buy-back units.[63] The company reports that it was a pioneer in curbside recycling programs in the early 1970s and that it began operating its first recycling center in Redondo Beach, Calif., in 1983.[64]

Alliances with product manufacturers—To guarantee markets for the growing amount of recyclables collected in curbside recycling programs, most of the leading solid waste disposal companies have begun teaming up with companies that will produce new products with the recyclables. WMI and BFI have most aggressively pursued this strategy, finding long-term end-users for several items collected at curbside.

WMI has established long-term markets for plastic, aluminum, steel and glass containers and waste paper. In the fall of 1990, WMI formed a partnership with American National Can Co., a multinational manufacturer and marketer of a broad line of metal, glass and plastic packaging products. The partnership—Container Recycling Alliance—is marketing the metal and glass containers WMI collects at curbside.[65] To secure a market for its paper, WMI formed a paper recycling joint venture—Paper Recycling International—with Stone Container Corp., the world's largest recycler of brown waste paper grades and a major consumer of other paper grades.

WMI formed the alliance in July 1990, a few months after it canceled a joint venture with Jefferson Smurfit Corp., the world's largest paper recycler, to own and operate waste paper processing plants.[66] To find a stable outlet for the plastics collected at curbside, WMI established a joint venture in the spring of 1989 with E.I. du Pont de Nemours & Co. The two companies say the venture, named the Plastics Recycling Alliance, will become the nation's largest plastics recycling and reprocessing operation.[67]

BFI's first long-term pact was with Wellman Inc., the country's largest post-consumer plastics recycler, in May 1989. Wellman agreed to purchase all of the post-consumer plastic bottles that BFI collects through its Recycle-NOW™ curbside recycling programs.[68] About one year later, BFI entered into an agreement with Alcoa Recycling Co., a subsidiary of the Aluminum Co. of America, to sell all of the aluminum beverage and food cans that BFI collects in the United States and Canada, wherever practical.[69] Weyerhaeuser Paper Co. of Tacoma, Wash., became BFI's third long-term market in the spring of 1990. Weyerhaeuser has agreed to purchase 10,000 tons per month of recycled paper from BFI's West Coast recycling programs, including newspapers, corrugated cardboard and high grade office paper.[70] BFI's most recent contract is an eight-year agreement with Augusta Newsprint Co. of Atlanta, Ga., reached in the spring of 1991. The paper company has agreed to take all of the old newspapers and magazines collected by BFI in Jacksonville, Fla.[71] BFI says it plans to form additional regional partnerships in all of its collection regions.[72]

Laidlaw also has secured an end market for old newsprint. Laidlaw is the exclusive supplier of recycled newsprint and magazines to Canadian Pacific Forest Products Ltd.[73] The other leading waste disposal companies have not established long-term markets. **Chambers** told IRRC it was examining some long-term options,[74] while **Attwoods** said it believes it can "do better in the open market place" and that by selling to the highest bidder it is "probably outperforming the contract prices."[75] **Western Waste Industries** says it "has not found the need" to establish formal contracts with brokers or end-users, adding that the company is one of the few, if not the only, that can claim it has never landfilled a load of recyclables.[76]

In addition to establishing long-term markets with product manufacturers, **BFI** and **WMI** are acquiring paper recycling companies. In the summer of 1990, BFI signed an agreement to acquire ACCO Waste Paper Companies, the Southwest's largest waste paper processing operation, with plants in Houston, San Antonio and Austin. ACCO also has a 100,000-plus residential curbside program in Austin.[77] To boost its paper handling capabilities further, WMI acquired U.S. Recycling Industries of Denver, Colo., the nation's largest independent secondary paper fiber handler, in July 1990, and Durbin Paper Stock Co. Inc., a waste paper processor and broker in Miami, in the fall of 1990.[78]

Box 6-3

California's Mandatory Recycling and Redemption Legislation

California leads the country in solid waste production, disposing of roughly 40 million tons per year. The Golden State buries more than 90 percent of that waste in landfills and will run out of landfill space by the year 2000 unless it changes its waste disposal methods.[79] Repeated attempts to control beverage cans in the solid waste stream through conventional container deposit legislation have been struck down. (See Box 6-2 for information on container deposit legislation in nine states.) In 1986, however, the state passed a compromise bill, Assembly Bill 2020—the California Beverage Container Recycling and Litter Reduction Act, which went into effect in the fall of 1987.

Described by the California Department of Conservation (DOC) as new "checks and balances and carrot and stick incentives" that "motivate industry to support recycling,"[80] California's unique law requires wholesalers to pay the DOC a redemption value for each container and major supermarkets to provide recycling centers. The recycling centers pay consumers 5 cents for returning two small containers, plus the used cans' scrap value, and recover their 5-cent payments from the state.[81]

The California redemption value per container is less than in most bottle bills states, which pay a nickel or more for each container. The law initially required the distributor to pay the state 1 cent per container but included provisions for increasing the redemption value if recycling goals were not met. Because no type of containers had achieved a 65 percent recycling rate by the end of 1989, the redemption value rose to 5 cents for two in 1990. Big containers are redeemed for a nickel each. As Table 6-3 shows, aluminum cans exceeded the 65 percent target in 1990. If the recycling rates for glass and plastic containers do not reach 65 percent in 1992, their redemption rates will rise to 5 or 10 cents per container, depending on size, in 1993.[82]

AB 2020 also attempted to ease the burden on retailers by requiring only that recycling collection centers be within a half mile of major supermarkets, defined as those that do more than $2 million in business annually. As a result, the law required the establishment of at least 1,700 new collection centers to service the more than 2,700 major supermarkets in the state. Many supermarkets, facing penalties of having to take back the containers themselves or paying a $100 daily fine, signed contracts with recycling companies to set up recycling centers.[83]

The California law is unusual in that it requires a manufacturer to pay an extra processing fee to the state if the DOC determines that the scrap value of a container is less than the costs of recycling and processing, plus a reasonable financial return. "That is a radical notion, a revolutionary departure, not just from traditional beverage marketing practices, but from the entire structure of our throw-away economy," said William Shireman, executive director of

Californians Against Waste, which sponsored unsuccessful bottle bill initiatives.[84] The DOC reported the following 1989 collecting and processing costs, as well as scrap value, for the following containers: aluminum cans—$439 per ton to recycle, $1,114 in scrap value; glass—$98 per ton to recycle, $72 in scrap value; and plastics—$1,107 per ton to recycle, $681 in scrap value.[85]

Because the cost to recycle all containers but the aluminum cans is less than their scrap value, the state imposed a processing fee of about six-and-a-half-tenths of 1 cent on each glass container, eight-tenths of 1 cent on each plastic beverage container, and nearly 4 cents on each nonaluminum metal beverage container.[86] The state estimates the glass processing fee will generate about $20 million, half of which will be spent on glass recycling incentive payments. The glass fund will pay glass container manufacturers, or processors that find alternative markets such as asphalt or fiberglass manufacturers, $22 for each ton of cullet they purchase. The other half of the glass fund will reimburse recyclers and certified glass processors for their costs.[87]

The legislation appears to be effective in reclaiming beverage cans from the waste stream. The DOC reports that the overall recovery rate for beverage containers through the redemption program is nearly 70 percent. The return rate for nonredemption containers is less than 10 percent, according to Californians Against Waste, which is lobbying to expand the redemption program to include the state's more than 600 million wine and liquor bottles.[88]

The bill is not without its detractors, however. The Plastic Recycling Coalition of California (PRCC) filed suit against the state to challenge its methods for calculating recycling costs.[89] The PRCC and others also question the costs of AB 2020, which has more administrative expenses than other bottle bills because of its complexity. Labeling AB 2020 a "bureaucratic nightmare," Floyd Flexon, chairman of PRCC, said the law "is ineffective, inadequate and inefficient." Flexon added that "the state receives more than $260 million each year for a recycling program that addresses less than 5 percent of the municipal solid waste stream and takes $19 million for the division of recycling to administer. In addition the program supports a surplus of supermarket recycling locations."[90]

Reynolds Aluminum Recycling Co. appears to have prompted the PRCC's calls for overhauling the bill by refusing to accept glass and plastic containers at three of its 145 locations. Taking this action to express its own displeasure with AB 2020, Reynolds's Andrew McCutcheon said, "We want to send a message, not ruin the law." Reynolds contends that aluminum used beverage cans are subsidizing the costs of processing glass and plastic, adding that it wants to return to the original intent of the law and have every beverage container pay its own way through the recycling process.[91]

California glass container manufacturers have their own gripe with AB 2020, contending that the law has placed them at a competitive disadvantage with other U.S. and Mexican glass container manufacturers. They say the price they must pay for used glass in California is significantly higher than the cost of raw materials which averaged between $50 and $55 per ton in 1990.[92]

Table 6-3

**California Beverage Container
Recovery Rates**

Material	Pre-AB 2020	1988	1989	1990
Aluminum	50	61	64	75
Glass	14	35	40	55
Plastic (PET)	0	4	7	30
Overall	39	52	56	69

Source: "Rigid Containers," *Bottle/Can Recycling Update*, March 1991

Materials Recovery Facilities

Materials recovery facilities, or MRFs, lack a standard definition. Waste industry members use the term MRF to describe anything from a mobile trailer that prepares sorted recyclables for market to facilities that separate recyclables from the mixed municipal waste stream. For the purposes of this report, MRFs will be defined as facilities that centrally process commingled recyclables that have been source separated from the municipal waste stream. As such, processes undertaken at MRFs include sorting, removing contaminants, densifying and/or baling, marketing and shipping to end-users. MRFs typically process less than 400 tons per day of the materials highlighted in this report: glass containers; aluminum, steel and bi-metal cans; mixed paper, primarily newspaper but also office paper and corrugated cardboard; and most recently, plastic. (See Table 6-4 for processing capacity of MRFs.) Facilities that are not involved in sorting, but clean and process sorted recyclables for market, will be referred to as intermediate processing centers (IPCs).

Recyclables processed at large-scale MRFs and IPCs have an advantage in the marketplace because they produce large volumes of recyclables with consistent quality—increasingly important characteristics to industries that are beginning to rely on recyclables as an industrial feedstock. "We manufacture commodities. [That is] our strength and forte," Peter Karter, president of Resource Recovery Systems Inc., a leading MRF developer, told IRRC.[93] Karter also said that "we're supplying commodities to other manufacturers, based on their specifications, not to our level of capabilities." To maintain quality control, shift supervisors at Resource Recovery Systems inspect every truckload of outgoing material. If two loads are rejected, the supervisor is fired. "It sounds tough," said Karter, "but in this new business, it is important to build and maintain buyers' confidence in your products."[94]

Because commercial waste loads tend to be more homogeneous, usually paper-rich, and often contain cleaner, drier and easier-to-process wastes than loads from residential sources, most existing processing centers draw their materials from commercial sources.[95] As the number of curbside recycling programs grow, however, so will the number of MRFs processing residential recyclables. Today, there are nearly 100 MRFs that are either operating or scheduled to begin operation by the end of 1991, according to *Waste Age* magazine. *Waste Age* defines MRFs more liberally than IRRC, including facilities that separate and process both commingled and sorted recyclables and help market the recyclables to brokers or end-users.[96] Governmental Advisory Associates (GAA), which publishes a directory of MRFs, predicted in early 1990 that there would be 120 MRFs in operation by 1993 if all the planned MRFs began operation. These facilities would prepare roughly 3.8 million tons of recyclables annually, serve 22 million people or 9 percent of the population, and represent a $500 million capital investment. GAA also reported that New York is leading the way with 20 operating or planned facilities, followed closely by New Jersey with 15, California with 14 and Pennsylvania with 13. For its purposes, GAA defined MRFs quite broadly, including all installations that separate at least some portion of commingled municipal solid waste into marketable recyclables and partici-pate in the sale of recyclables.[97]

Technologies: MRFs traditionally have depended on manual sorting, or handpicking, and today many are still extremely labor-intensive. In many instances, including sorting paper by grade, glass containers by color, or plastics by color and resin type, no existing technology is as efficient as the human eye and hand. "With the machinery we've seen, everyone starts talking in the 90 percent range for quality," said Simon Sinnreich, president of Distributors Recycling Inc., a Newark, N.J., recycler, "but our customers want better than 90 percent quality. We're looking to supply them with 99.9 percent quality. You can't do that with machinery right now." Sinnreich added, "If you can't deliver quality, all you're doing is creating separate mountains of garbage."[98]

A predominantly manual sorting operation consists of conveyors that carry commingled materials from the tipping floor, where garbage is delivered, to rooms where workers sort the materials into bins. Workers then use machinery to bail, compact, crush, densify or granulate the materials in preparation for shipment to end-users.[99]

Although the mechanical sorting and processing technologies em-ployed at MRFs are in their infancy, MRFs are becoming increasingly mechanized in order to lower labor and other costs and increase processing rates—a must if MRFs are to keep up with the growing volumes of recyclables. The increase in mechanization also reduces demands on residential recyclers. Unlike in the 1970s, residential recyclers do not have to peel labels off cans or bottles, for instance, or remove both ends from steel cans. Today, either machines handle these functions or else innovations within the industries make these steps unnecessary.

Separation technologies include screens, conveyors, magnets and other devices. Almost every MRF employs a magnetic belt or drum to remove steel cans and other ferrous materials. Some MRFs also use eddy current separators to separate aluminum. Additional mechanical processes, such as air classification (blowers), screening devices and proprietary methods, can separate heavy materials, such as glass containers, from lighter materials, including plastics and aluminum.[100] Isolated HDPE and PET plastic containers also can be separated from one another by capitalizing on their density differences, and new technology is being used to separate PVC plastic, such as meat wrap and cooking oil bottles. (A fuller description of the sorting processes for aluminum, glass, steel, plastic and paper and a discussion of the degree of sorting required by end-users can be found in Chapters 1 through 5.)

Several MRF developers are offering proprietary sorting and processing systems, many of which are European. The Rhode Island MRF operated by New England CRInc., for instance, uses a patented, automated German technology. A conveyor belt carrying a stream of commingled recyclables—steel, aluminum, glass and plastic containers—passes by an electromagnet that removes the ferrous materials. The other recyclables continue to a rolling curtain of chains that hold back the lighter aluminum and plastic but allow the heavier glass containers to pass through. The glass is then manually sorted by color. Electrodes on either side of a conveyor belt carrying the diverted plastic and aluminum induce a positive charge in the aluminum cans. The belt pulls the cans a few inches farther into a second positively charged electric field that repels them off of the belt. Plastic items move on to be manually sorted by resin type.[101]

Not all of the material delivered to MRFs can be shipped to end-users. Most MRFs produce residues, which often must be landfilled, of 5 to 20 percent (by weight) of the materials delivered for processing. Paper sorting and baling systems generally produce less than 5 percent residue, while systems for sorting and densifying commingled containers may create as much as 25 percent residue. Glass breakage and the method of sorting broken, multi-colored glass are the primary determinants of residue amount.[102]

The Center for Plastics Recycling Research at Rutgers State University has determined that a population of 300,000 to 500,000 is desirable to support a MRF.[103] To meet the needs of smaller communities, companies recently began offering small-scale and mobile handling and sorting equipment. Count Recycling Systems Inc., a subsidiary of Resource Recycling

Technologies Inc., has sold five "McMRFs"—each consisting of $99,500 in equipment that processes up to 20 tons per eight-hour shift. In addition, New England CRInc. markets a 20-ton-per-shift MRF that is available on wheels or can be skid-mounted. Built by Ptarmigan Equipment Corp. of Santa Rosa, Calif., six motor vehicle-equipped MRFs are used by NE CRInc., and about 40 are in operation around the country, some of which are shared in regional cooperatives.[104]

Operating conditions—MRFs do pose some potentially negative health effects for workers, but these can be avoided with proper planning. In addition to hazards typically associated with the use of heavy equipment, three additional health concerns are particular to MRFs: contact with hazardous materials that are inadvertently mixed in with recyclables; the inhalation of airborne particles, particularly around glass crushers, paper balers and air classification equipment; and physical injuries caused by repetitive motion. In 1990, a propane tank from a backyard grill appeared empty but contained enough gas to blow up at a Rhode Island recycling center.[105] Although no one was injured, the incident highlighted the importance of public education as well as the need to design a system where operators have a clear view of what they are handling. To combat the second health hazard, the newer MRFs are installing ventilation systems and air purifiers, or cyclones, that take dust out of the air. Eugene Wingerter of the National Solid Wastes Management Association pointed out that MRF designers also need to give consideration to ergonomics (the movement of the body in doing work) and potential long-term cumulative trauma injuries and repetitive motion injuries.[106] Designs requiring workers to stoop constantly or stretch may invite stress-related injuries.[107] And as Wingerter noted, excessive health claims can be "very costly and can be disastrous to a firm's insurance plan—and thus to its very existence."[108]

Siting—Although MRFs and other recycling centers are essential components of recycling, which enjoys wide public support, they are not immune to the NIMBY (Not In My Backyard) syndrome. The Aluminum Association reports that zoning restrictions "have caused delays and, in some markets, posed insurmountable barriers to the expansion of recycling."[109] Although MRFS and other recycling centers are such a new phenomenon that they are seldom directly referred to in most zoning ordinances, many communities are confining MRFs to heavy industrial zones, which are not usually conveniently located for the public. MRF operations, however, are more typical of light industrial facilities, which can be located much closer to population centers. The main negative impacts of MRFs are increased traffic, aesthetics and noise.[110]

Financing: Most MRF financings are relatively small compared with landfill or waste-to-energy financings. In 1990, Governmental Advisory Associates (GAA) surveyed 40 operating and 60 planned MRFs and found

---

Box 6-4

Collecting at Curbside for MRFs

The degree of sophistication required of a MRF is inversely proportional to the degree of sophistication of the collection system funneling recyclables its way. The most sophisticated MRFs enable municipalities to implement collection systems that make minimal demands on their residents; conversely, elaborate collection systems dramatically reduce the need for sorting at a central processing plant, whose use becomes limited to inspecting and packaging recyclables for shipment.

There are four basic options for curbside collection of recyclables being shipped to a MRF: allowing residential recyclers and truck operators to commingle all recyclables; allowing residential recyclers to commingle recyclables but requiring the truck operator to sort the recyclables into compartmentalized trucks; requiring residential recyclers to separate all recyclables from one another; and requiring residential recyclers to separate recyclables into a few groupings. Commingling the recyclables is easiest for the residents, and studies have shown that convenience is a key to high participation rates. In addition, trucks that carry commingled recyclables can serve a longer route before unloading.

Browning-Ferris Industries Inc. and Chambers Development Co. are experimenting with a variation on the typical commingled recyclables curbside pickup by collecting commingled recyclables and garbage simultaneously. Residents put recyclable items in special blue bags that are collected with the rest of the garbage. BFI, however, does not collect glass under this system because of the high amount of breakage. Both companies believe this system

---

that the average capital cost was $4.7 million, with a range of $11,000 to $48 million. The planned facilities, mostly larger than existing ones, reported higher capital costs.[114] Capital costs of MRFs vary widely, however, depending on the end product produced and the existing infrastructure. Some MRFs, for instance, are set up in existing buildings, which reduces costs. In addition, some MRFs enhance the value of their end product to the end-user through additional processing. For example, while some MRFs may simply crush color-sorted glass and ship it out, other MRFs further process the glass to remove contaminants, such as plastic and metal, so it can be used directly in a glass furnace.

More than 42 percent of the GAA-surveyed projects reported private sources of capital financing; the remainder employed public sector methods such as grants, bonds and general revenues. Three-fifths of existing MRFs reported private investment participation, compared with only 31 percent of planned plants. GAA attributes these trends to the fact that many more

is more cost effective and requires far less capital investment. Greater public education efforts are required, however, to remind residents to purchase the blue bags and to place them out with their garbage.[111]

Commingling, however, often leads to cross contamination among recyclables, with glass fragments being the primary culprit. The Center for Plastic Recycling Research at Rutgers maintains, however, that compacting commingled recyclables on-truck prevents breakage because the plastics and metal cushion the glass containers. The center also found that on-truck compaction decreased the volume of recyclables in a single truck by 35 percent, allowing a truck to make up to 50 percent more stops before returning to empty its load.[112]

To maintain both convenience for the residential recycler and quality control, some communities have the truck operator sort commingled recyclables. This method produces a cleaner product than residentially separated recyclables and provides immediate feedback to residential recyclers by leaving unacceptable objects at the curb. Truck-side separation, however, slows down the collection process considerably. Although actual costs vary widely depending on the community, studies show it can take up to 10 percent more time to have the truck operator sort recyclables at the curb.[113]

Some communities ask the residential recyclers to separate the recyclables. While this approach may lower the participation rate, it also lowers costs by making use of essentially unpaid labor. If the municipality is providing recycling bins, however, the costs of providing many bins could become expensive. In addition, as the number of collected recyclables increases, it is unlikely collection trucks will have sufficient compartments to keep all recyclables separate. One compromise is to separate recyclables into two categories, such as mixed containers and mixed papers.

planned MRFS will be owned by government entities. GAA determined there was almost an even split between public and private ownership of the surveyed MRFs, but that many more planned projects will be publicly owned. GAA also reported that the private sector operates approximately four-fifths of the surveyed MRFs.[115]

Procuring MRFs through competitive bidding is becoming more common among municipalities, which can finance the projects through general obligation bonds or tax-exempt bonds.[116] Largely because existing MRFs are relatively small projects, most MRF financings have been backed by a community's general obligation pledge to repay the bonds. This mode of financing is a departure from the general trend in solid waste finance toward less municipal obligation and more risk sharing and is unlikely to continue as MRFs grow in size and cost.[117] Instead, MRF developers are beginning to follow the example of the waste-to-energy industry and use project financing methods. A Springfield, Mass., MRF that began operation in 1990 led the way, with State Street Bank underwriting a $2.5 million tax-exempt bond issue for the plant.

While tax-exempt bonds are the most economical means of financing a MRF, particularly for projects larger than $3 to $5 million, a disadvantage is that privately owned MRFs must compete with other public works projects for the bonds. Under the 1986 Tax Reform Act, privately owned facilities seeking tax-exempt financing must compete for a private purpose bond cap allocation from the state. Government-owned MRFs, however, avoid this competition.[118]

Although paying a tipping, or disposal, fee has not been a common feature of recycling projects, tipping fees may become more common in order for MRFs to obtain project financing. Lenders looking only to the project for repayment may require a "put or pay" contract by a municipality. Common in contracts for waste-to-energy facilities, a "put or pay" contract requires a municipality to pay a minimum tipping fee whether or not it delivers the tonnage.[119] Although MRFs can generate revenues both through tipping fees and the sale of recyclables, investors believe that their primary source of revenues should be tipping fees or an operating contract and that sales of the end product should be counted on only as supplemental income given the instability of most markets.[120] Lenders also may require MRFs to demonstrate alternatives in case the recyclables cannot be marketed. One solution is for local governments to commit to reserved landfill space at determinable prices.[121]

In 1991, Resource Recycling Technologies Inc. (RRT) pioneered a new financing vehicle for MRFs in the form of tax-exempt leasing and says it plans to use similar financing techniques in the future. When Monroe County, N.Y., awarded RRT a contract to design, build and operate a MRF but could not find funds for the project, RRT pursued tax-exempt leasing with investment bankers and New York state officials. RRT's investment banker successfully sold certificates of participation totaling $11.4 million for the tax-exempt project, marking the first time tax exempt leasing was used to finance a solid waste facility in New York state.[122]

Waste industry giants, such as Waste Management and Browning-Ferris Industries, which typically retain ownership of their MRFs, appear to have financed their recycling programs as normal balance sheet corporate assets.[123]

The most recent trend in solid waste financing is system financing, whereby a municipality finances a MRF and an incinerator or landfill, or all three, as one system. As more communities embrace an integrated solid waste management strategy, this type of financing is likely to increase. System financings are attractive to lenders because of the diversity of both the facilities and their revenues. Because MRFs represent a small fraction of the total capital needs of the system, system financings can be structured to encourage recycling. MRFs, for example, could charge a reduced tipping fee, or no tipping fee at all, as long as the system as a whole still has sufficient revenues to pay costs and expenses. Because MRFs do not provide ultimate disposal for waste, even lenders that are not requiring system financing often like to be assured that a landfill or waste-to-energy project is at least in the planning stages.[124]

Developers: The nation's leading solid waste management companies are all developing MRFs, and their activities are discussed in a previous section of this chapter. In addition, a number of other companies are competing to build MRFs for municipalities, and some are building merchant facilities to process the ever growing amount of recyclables being collected at curbside. These MRF developers are discussed below, and the three leading independent MRF developers—New England CRInc., Resource Recovery Systems Inc. and Resource Recycling Technologies Inc.— and their projects are listed in Table 6-4.

New England CRInc.: A subsidiary of publicly traded **Wellman Inc.**, the nation's largest plastics recycler, New England CRInc. has participated in the development of nine U.S. MRFs scheduled to be operating by 1992 and is developing a tenth MRF slated to begin operation in Toronto, Canada, in 1992.[125] In addition, in partnership with Anchor Glass Container Corp., NE CRInc. operates two 150 ton per shift glass processing plants in California,[126] and the company plans to open a 13 million pound per year polystyrene processing plant in 1991 that will be owned by the National Polystyrene Recycling Co.[127] NE CRInc. also designs and operates recycling programs, such as intermediate processing facilities, and mobile recycling vehicles for smaller communities.[128]

Massachusetts beer distributors established New England CRInc. in 1982 in response to the Massachusetts bottle bill. At first the company collected only empty beverage containers, but it eventually expanded its operations to include additional recyclables.[129] In 1987, it formed Materials Recovery Inc. to design, construct and operate MRFs. Before Wellman acquired NE CRInc. in August 1990, Wellman was purchasing PET bottles processed by Materials Recovery Inc.'s MRFs, and in September 1989, Wellman had signed a partnership agreement with Materials Recovery Inc. to design, build and operate MRFs. When Wellman acquired NE CRInc., NE CRInc.'s former shareholders formed a new limited partnership to continue the company's deposit container and curbside pick-ups in Massachusetts, New Hampshire and Vermont.[130]

NE CRInc. holds the exclusive North American rights to the patented German Bezner automated materials sortation technology, which is used in approximately 30 MRF-type facilities in Europe.[131] (A description of this system is included in a previous section of this chapter on MRF technologies.) Opening in 1989 and employing the Bezner system, NE CRInc.'s

Johnston, R.I., facility is the longest-operating, automated MRF in the country.[132] NE CRInc.'s Quonset Point MRF, which is scheduled to begin operation in 1992, will serve the remainder of the state and also will be owned by the Rhode Island Solid Waste Management Corp. The Quonset Point MRF will employ a third-generation Bezner sorting system to sort HDPE, PET and mixed rigid plastics as well as traditional materials.[133]

NE CRInc. usually designs and operates MRFs, but in the case of the DuPage County, Ill., plant, it has a separate equipment supply contract. In addition, the company designed and constructed but is not operating the Cumberland County, N.J., MRF. A labor-intensive facility, it does not employ the Bezner system.[134]

Resource Recovery Systems (RRS): RRS has been developing MRFs for nearly 20 years, opening its first MRF in 1975—a research and development facility in Branford, Conn. Since then, the company has developed four additional MRFs and has another four under development, all but one of which are in the Northeast. RRS forged a relationship with Foster Wheeler Corp., a waste-to-energy developer discussed in Chapter 8, to offer jointly recycling and waste-to-energy technologies. The duo won a contract to build a combined recycling, leaf and yard waste composting and waste-to-energy complex in Montreal, Quebec, that will include a 500 ton per day MRF.[135]

Following the R&D project in Branford, RRS developed three additional projects that came on-line in the 1980s, all of which were financed by the public entities that owned them. In 1990, RRS began operation of the first MRF to be financed through project financing. The 240 ton per day, Springfield, Mass., plant is a public/private partnership. RRS has a five-year operating contract and owns the equipment; the state owns the building and land. The plant has two processing lines: one dedicated to paper and the other to glass and aluminum containers. RRS has three additional U.S. MRFs under development, including a 600 ton per day MRF on the Fresh Kills landfill in Staten Island that will serve New York City.[136]

Resource Recycling Technologies Inc. (RRT): Publicly traded RRT of Binghamton, N.Y., is a vertically integrated recycling company whose strategy is to "efficiently and profitably recover, recycle, add value to and market the maximum quantity of raw materials reclaimable from solid waste." The company operates through four business units: design and construction, material recycling operations, deposit legislation operations and plastics operations, and has four wholly-owned subsidiaries: RRT Design & Construction Corp., which designs and builds MRFs; RRT Equipment Corp.; RRT Empire Returns Corp., which operates MRFs and markets their output, and RRT Plastics Corp., also known as the Ricard Group.[137]

RRT has seven planned and operating MRFs. In 1990, its material recycling division processed and marketed 156,200 tons of recyclables. RRT

Table 6-4

U.S. Materials Recovery Facilities
of Leading Independent MRF Developers

Company	Location	Year	Tons/ Day	Capital Cost (in millions)	Owner
New England CRInc.	Johnston, R.I.	1989	200	$5	RI SWM Corp.[a]
	Cumberland Cty., N.J.	1990	80	$2.9	Cumberland Cty.[b]
	Montgomery Cty., Md.	1991	480	$8	NA
	Dutchess Cty., N.Y.	1991	75	$1.9	Dutchess Cty. RRA[c]
	Brookhaven, N.Y.	1991	400	$7.94	Brookhaven, N.Y.
	DuPage Cty., Ill.	1991	150	$2.787[d]	DuPage Cty. DEC[e]
	Waukesha Cty., Wis.	1991	40	NA	NA
	Quonset Point, R.I.	1992	160	$6.7	RI SWM Corp.[a]
	Prince George's Cty., Md.	1992	400	$8	Prince George's Cty.
Resource Recovery Systems Inc.	Groton, Conn.	1982	40	NA	NA
	Camden, N.J.	1986	70	NA	NA
	East Harlem, N.Y.	1988	100	NA	NA
	Springfield, Mass.	1990	240	NA	NA
	Berlin, Conn.	1991	70-80	NA	NA
	Elmira, N.Y.	1991	100	NA	Chemung Cty.
	New York, N.Y.	1993	600	NA	New York City
Resource Recycling Technologies Inc.	Doylestown, Pa.	1989	100	$0.5[f]	Bucks County
	Syracuse, N.Y.	1989[g]	300	$4	RRT
	Woodbine, N.J.	1990	225	$5	Cape May Muni. Authority
	Lakewood, N.J.	1991	300	$6.75	Ocean County
	Palm Beach, Fla.	1991	250	$6.25	Palm Beach Cty. SWM[g]
	Hartford, Conn.	1991	200	$2.1	Connecticut RRA[h]
	Rochester, N.Y.	1992[i]	300	$8.5	Monroe County

Note: The leading solid waste management firms also develop MRFs. See Table 6-1 and previous section for more details.

[a] Rhode Island Solid Waste Management Corp.
[b] Cumberland County Improvement Authority
[c] Dutchess County Resource Recovery Agency
[d] plus building
[e] DuPage County Department of Environmental Conservation
[f] The project was a renovation of an existing facility.
[g] Palm Beach County Solid Waste Management Authority
[h] Connecticut Resource Recovery Authority
[i] Also has processed bottles redeemed under container deposit legislation since 1983.

Source: Investor Responsibility Research Center Inc.

says its Cape May, N.J., facility is the first municipally owned and vendor designed, built and operated MRF in the country. The plant also is the first MRF in the country to receive totally mixed residential and commercial waste paper, according to the company. RRT's Ocean County, N.J., MRF is the first plant to accommodate a dual mixed-container recycling system developed by Count Recycling Systems, a manufacturer of recycling equipment and systems in which RRT became a 50 percent owner in May 1989. As noted earlier, in 1990 Count Recycling introduced a small-scale "off-the-shelf" processing system for less than $100,000 known as the McMRF.[138]

In addition to the plants that RRT designs, builds and operates, RRT Design and Construction Corp. designed and built a $500,000 MRF in Woodbridge, N.J., operated by the town. In addition, in areas where market conditions and the waste hauling infrastructure will not support municipally owned turnkey MRFs, RRT markets its municipal recycling project development expertise to private waste haulers and scrap processors. RRT has negotiated contracts for a small commercial MRF in Brooklyn, N.Y., for Waste Management Recycling Inc. and a more than $1 million MRF in Danbury, Conn., that a local waste hauler will operate.[139]

As part of its strategy to add value to recyclables, in May 1990 RRT purchased the Ricard Group, which became its plastic recycling division but still operates under the name Ricard Group. The division trades and compounds industrial plastic resins and operates industrial plastics recycling plants in Roosevelt, N.Y., and Trenton, N.J. In late 1991, RRT plans to enter the post-consumer scrap plastics industry by opening a 15 million pound per year separating and cleaning line in its Trenton facility that will produce clean flake from post-consumer containers and contaminated industrial scrap. Lawrence J. Schorr, RRT's president, told IRRC that he envisions developing similar plants throughout the country.[140] RRT also owns a small percentage of Polymerix Inc., which owns the TriMax process for producing plastic lumber from mixed plastic scrap.[141] (See Chapter 5 for more details on Polymerix.)

Created in 1983 in response to New York State's bottle bill, RRT's deposit legislation division provides scrap processing, data collection and accounting services to more than 125 beverage bottlers and distributors and more than 2,000 food retailers. This division accounted for 38 percent of RRT's revenues in 1990.[142]

Other companies developing MRFs: Omni Technical Services Inc. has played a key role in two New York MRFs but is focusing its future efforts on processing mixed waste streams. In August 1988, Omni began operation of a merchant MRF in Westbury, N.Y., on Long Island. Having lost a bid to build another Long Island materials recovery facility, Omni decided to proceed without any firm contracts and is currently processing 75 to 80 tons per day. In the fall of 1989, Islip, N.Y., selected Omni to design and renovate one of the nation's first MRFs. By January 1991, the $9 million plant had a single stream system capable of processing 400 tons per day of mixed recyclables. The company recently acquired an exclusive U.S. license for a German composting technology and is developing a 500 ton per day composting facility, which is described in Chapter 7.[143]

In early 1991, publicly traded **Integrated Waste Services Inc. (IWSI)** of Amherst, N.Y., began operation of a 300 ton per day MRF in Buffalo, N.Y., that processes recyclables collected through a voluntary program. Charging a tipping fee of $36 per ton under a five-year contract, the $2 million plant is "highly mechanical," employing only seven people. Edward J. Rutkowski, a company vice president, told IRRC that IWSI intends to pursue additional opportunities to build MRFs as they arise. IWSI is a nonhazardous waste management firm founded in 1986 that provides collection, transfer and disposal of solid waste, tire shredding, industrial cleaning, demolition and materials recovery. In May 1991, *Business Week* ranked the company at the top of its list of the "100 Best Small Corporations."[144]

Rabanco Inc. operates a $10 million, 500 ton per day MRF in Seattle, Wash., that serves 80,000 homes. Because of the high degree of glass breakage, Rabanco ordered custom-designed trucks that have special compartments for three-color separation of glass bottles. The remaining recyclables are commingled.[145]

Automated Recycling Technology (ART) operates a 175 ton per day MRF in Long Branch, N.J., that began operation in 1990. A privately financed facility owned by ART, the $1 million plant processes mixed containers. Robert Blenden of ART told IRRC that the company is aggressively pursuing additional projects.[146]

Commercial Metals Co. (CMC), a publicly traded company that manufactures, recycles and markets steel and metal products, is expanding into the municipal recycling business. In Jacksonville, Fla., the company built and operated a facility to process source-separated recyclables for a pilot program serving 44,000 households. (When the project went full-scale, Browning-Ferris Industries won the contract.) Since December 1990, CMC has been operating another pilot program under a one-year contract with the city of Dallas, Tex. CMC is responsible for pick-up, processing and marketing of recyclables from 14,000 homes. CMC sorts the glass by color and paper at truck-side and separates the cans and plastic at a processing facility. CMC also recently won recycling contracts to serve two outlying Dallas neighborhoods.[147]

Waste-to-energy developers—**Foster Wheeler**, a waste-to-energy developer, has joined forces with MRF developer Resource Recovery Systems and is discussed earlier in this section. In addition, **Wheelabrator Technologies Inc.** is building its first MRF in Bucks County, Pa. The town required Wheelabrator to open a drop-off center before building a waste-to-energy plant, but Wheelabrator decided to build "a full blown MRF." Scheduled to begin operation in mid-1992, the plant is designed to process between 150 and 200 tons per day of newspapers and glass, metal and plastic containers. The plant plans eventually to process corrugated cardboard and office paper. Otter Recycling, a local recycler, will operate the plant. Wheelabrator says that it will pursue MRF development in other areas where it has waste-to-energy projects and that Waste Management, which owns 55 percent of Wheelabrator, will pursue MRF development elsewhere.[148] **Westinghouse Corp.** is developing facilities to recover recyclables at the front-end of two of its facilities,[149] and **American Ref-Fuel Co.**, which is partially owned by BFI, offers to build Recycleries. **Ogden Projects Inc.** also is bidding on contracts with municipalities to build MRFs. To date, however, the company has not been awarded any MRF contracts.[150] (See Chapter 8 for additional information on these waste-to-energy developers.)

Future of Materials Processing

The days of the conventional transfer station—the purpose of which is limited to serving as a drop-off point for smaller collection trucks and a loading station for larger, long-haul vehicles—are nearly over. As rising disposal costs make diverting materials from the waste stream a financially attractive (and in some cases, necessary) option, waste processing is becoming the norm. The jury is still out, however, as to the best way to collect and process recyclables from the waste stream. As Richard Widrig of Western Waste Industries told IRRC, the waste processing industry "is in its infancy and hasn't found the best way of doing things."[151] Haulers and MRF developers are pursuing a variety of options, ranging from curbside recycling to mixed waste processing. (Mixed waste processing is discussed in detail in Chapter 8.)

The advantage to curbside recycling is that it produces a cleaner product than mixed waste processing. But it also is inefficient as currently practiced. Curbside recycling typically requires additional pick-up routes and makes additional demands on workers and equipment. Costs of $100 per ton for a curbside recycling program are not uncommon. Several waste haulers told IRRC that making better use of people and equipment and reducing the number of pick-up routes is the key to future profitability. Continued experimentation in a growing number of communities will provide haulers with the necessary experience to determine the optimum curbside program. Flexibility is a must in these programs as the definition of optimum will evolve over time. Market price swings for recyclables picked up at curbside are inevitable, and programs will need to accommodate the collection of additional recyclables as new markets develop for other items currently discarded.

Existing equipment used to sort recyclables at MRFS will be continually upgraded to meet the quality standards of increasingly selective end-users who will be able to purchase materials from a growing number of recycling programs. MRF developers have a number of research programs underway designed to improve the separation process; they run the gamut from improved sorting techniques based on time-motion studies to processing improvements.

MRF developers also are moving beyond simply processing recyclables to producing value-added products. Resource Recycling Technologies, for example, is expanding into plastics processing in order to produce clean flake for sale to industry, as opposed to selling used plastic containers. At its Springfield, Mass., MRF, Resource Recovery Systems says it is producing an aggregate of ceramics and glass that can be used as a direct substitute for sand. This aggregate will allow the company to make use not only of mixed-color glass but also the myriad of ceramic items that are currently thrown out in trash. Additional R&D programs in this area are designed to increase the scope of materials that can be transformed into commodities for industry while keeping the recycling process convenient for the residential recycler.

High participation rates in a curbside recycling program can be achieved only if the recycling program is convenient and easy to use. With this goal in mind, many experts in the field told IRRC they foresee the day when residents will be able to set their garbage at the curb in just two bags: one with wet trash and one with dry trash. They envision that processing equipment will be developed to sort the dry trash into feedstock for industry and to process the wet trash into a feedstock suitable for composting. While no facilities of this type are operating in the United States, several reportedly are in operation in Europe.

Chapter VII
MIXED MUNICIPAL SOLID
WASTE PROCESSING

Mixed waste processing facilities that process unsorted garbage are an alternative to material recovery facilities, which process commingled recyclables that residential and commercial recyclers have kept separate from the municipal waste stream. Because automated mixed waste processing is a more sophisticated, and thus more costly, option, fewer such facilities are operating in the United States. Using a combination of manual and mechanical systems, often European in origin, these facilities generally emphasize producing an end product other than recyclables, usually either compost or densified refuse derived fuel.[1]

Skeptics of mixed waste processing systems abound. Doubts stem from three main concerns: the missed opportunity to educate the public about source reduction and recycling; whether materials are being put to their best use; and lack of appropriate markets for the end product. At the core of the controversy over mixed waste processing is a philosophical difference over waste generation in the United States. The beauty—or disadvantage, according to some—of mixed waste processing plants is that they require no participation by those producing the waste. Haulers merely transport the garbage bags to a mixed waste processing facility rather than the landfill or a waste-to-energy facility. Claiming 100 percent participation rates while relieving residents of all recycling responsibilities, mixed waste processors herald the concept because it does not require people to change their ways. XL Disposal Corp., a mixed waste processor, says its processing system "makes obsolete the need for curbside recycling."[2] Those opposed to mixed waste processing on philosophical grounds argue that people should be changing their ways. They prefer curbside recycling precisely because it is effective at educating residents about the need for waste reduction and the need to change "wasteful habits."[3]

Critics of mixed waste processing plants also argue that the system does not put materials to their best use. They would prefer to see more materials recycled, and point to the low level of recycling and the lower quality of recyclables that have been mixed in with the waste stream. Raising similar arguments to those over whether commingled recyclables collected at curbside are more contaminated, and therefore less valuable, than recyclables sorted at curbside, opponents of mixed waste processing plants say recyclables pulled from the mixed waste stream are likely to be even more contaminated. Charles F. Oyler, recycling manager at a Philadelphia materials recovery facility operated by Browning-Ferris Industries Inc., maintains "There is no practical way to process completely mixed materials. Once something is mixed with trash, it becomes trash."[4] Opponents of mixed waste processing are further concerned that as more recycling programs and mixed waste processing facilities begin operation, end-users will become more particular about the materials they purchase.

Others are concerned about the cost of reclaiming recyclables in this manner. David Buckner, vice president for new business opportunities for BFI, is skeptical that any mixed waste sorting systems should be considered a substitute for curbside recycling. Buckner believes that "the sooner you separate recyclables from the waste stream, the less expensive it will be."[5] James Eckar of Resource Conservation Services Inc., which operates a composting facility in Maine, also is convinced that "source separation is the key to compost quality," adding that processing a mixed waste stream adds "tremendous layers of problems and dollars" that can be avoided.[6] Mixed waste processing vendors counter that the quality of their products has not prevented them from finding markets for them. But more importantly, they say, the goal of these plants is not simply to process recyclables; they are designed to produce an end product—a goal as worthy as recycling. They also note that in some areas, local officials have accepted mixed waste processing as a method of recycling.[7]

The third area of controversy is whether there are sufficient markets for the end products produced at mixed waste processing facilities. Both Orfa Corp. and Reuter Inc. serve as painful reminders of the pitfalls associated with mixed waste processing plants if markets for end products fail to materialize. Publicly traded Orfa Corp., which filed for Chapter 11 bankruptcy in the spring of 1990, operated a $30 million, 300 ton per day processing plant in Philadelphia. The plant processed the municipal waste stream to produce cellulose Orfa fiber, its primary product, as well as ferrous metal and a granulate, which consisted of glass, plastics, mixed sand, dust, grit, nonferrous metals and other heavy substances. Orfa believed that its fiber would have applications in the pulp and paper, agriculture, energy and building materials industries. At the time of the bankruptcy, however, more than 1,000 tons of Orfa fiber were stored at the plant. Ranging in price from $0 to $40 per ton, the Orfa fiber has been used in the manufacture of paperboard, a component of the waste paper market. This market, however, became depressed because of the abundance of secondary paper. In addition, some pulp and paper mills complained about the high dust and grit content in the fiber. Despite its troubles, Orfa continues to explore additional uses for the fiber, including bedding for chickens, an additive to mushroom soil and insulation behind car dashboards and seating.[8]

Markets for densified refuse derived fuel also have proven difficult to develop, as Reuter has discovered. "Reuter did not develop markets for [its densified refuse derived fuel] pellets; it developed the engineering. You can produce pellets until you're blue in the face, but it doesn't do any good if you can't sell them," commented Vern Genzlinger, the associate administrator of Hennepin County, Minn., where Reuter has its densified refuse derived fuel production facility.[9] Having lost more than $9 million at its plant through 1989, Reuter acknowledged in its 1990 annual report that its inability to find end-users for its pellets was still preventing the plant from operating profitably. In late 1990, following a fire at one of its warehouses storing unsold fuel pellets and the imposition of stringent operating conditions by the local waste authority, Reuter chose not to warehouse any more processed fuel material. As a result, the company has had to accept less waste for processing until it can ship more fuel to end-users.

Reuter remains optimistic about future sales, however, saying that it recently has improved the quality of its densified refuse derived fuel pellets and that it has completed successful test burns with potential large users. Reuter also believes that passage of the Clean Air Act amendments will prompt coal-burning utilities to supplement their fuel with its pellets as a low-cost means of reducing air emissions. Nonetheless, the company concluded in its 1990 annual report that "we will not build a fuel production plant again until we have a contract with a buyer for the product."[10] Reuter may be hesitant to build another densified refuse derived fuel plant, but it has not given up on the idea of mixed waste processing. The company is building a large-scale municipal solid waste composting facility in Pembroke Pines, Fla., and says the plant "will be the flagship operation of Reuter Inc."[11]

Municipal solid waste composting companies are confident that composting markets hold more promise than densified refuse derived fuel markets ever have, allowing them to avoid the plights of Reuter and Orfa. With only a small number of operating composting plants and numerous composting facilities under development, it remains to be seen whether markets can be developed to absorb the compost. Composting the full potential of two-thirds of the country's 180 million annual tons of municipal garbage would annually generate 36 million tons of compost.

Composting

Composting—the controlled biological decomposition of organic materials—is emerging as one of the most important solid waste disposal options in the country. Composting alternatives range from extremely low-tech backyard compost piles for yard and food wastes to more sophisticated facilities that tackle the entire solid waste stream. While composting yard waste in the backyard or at larger municipal sites is universally applauded as a solid waste management tool, composting the entire municipal waste stream is much more controversial.

Historically thwarted by its inability to compete with inexpensive landfills, municipal solid waste composting is enticing because the two largest components of America's municipal garbage—paper and yard waste—are organic materials well-suited to the composting process. In addition, municipal solid waste composting facilities are less complex than waste-to-energy plants and have substantially lower capital costs. Composting also complements other forms of waste disposal and enjoys public support as a natural process. Although odor can be a problem at some improperly operated facilities, composting does not face the problems of air emissions and ash disposal that have stymied waste-to-energy development.

The content of the compost and the definition of suitable applications lie at the heart of the controversy over composting municipal solid waste. A major concern of environmentalists is that heavy metals, such as cadmium and mercury, toxic wastes, and shards of plastic and glass that are common in household trash could enter the food chain if compost is used in agricultural settings. Environmentalists would prefer to see only the organic portions of the waste stream composted, such as yard waste and paper, and most maintain that separating these materials at the source is the only means of achieving this goal. John Ruston, an economist at the Environmental Defense Fund (which believes that composting should be limited to types of paper for which recycling is not technically or economically feasible), comments, "If you try to compost an undifferentiated waste stream you will mix batteries with old spaghetti and you will wind up with contaminants."[12]

"There is good composting and bad composting," adds Jeanne Wirka, a solid waste analyst with the Environmental Action Foundation. "Some in industry are pushing for one-stop shopping. But why not do it right by separating leaves, yard waste and food waste to produce a high-quality compost?" asks Wirka. Environmentalists are not alone in questioning the suitability of mixed refuse for composting. Dan Kemna, composting manager for solid waste giant Waste Management Inc., acknowledges that his company is "not convinced it makes sense to compost the whole mixed waste stream. The cleaner the material that goes in, the better it is when it comes out."[13]

Some composting companies, however, say they are capable of composting the entire solid waste stream (except for bulky items and hazardous wastes that are removed when the waste is delivered to the plant); they tout minimal preprocessing of mixed waste as an advantage to their systems. Other composting companies agree with environmentalists that inorganic material should be separated from compostable material before the composting process begins, but they argue that their manual and mechanical separation systems effectively separate the wastes. In addition, the Solid Waste Composting Council, a trade organization formed in early 1990 to represent consumer products companies and composting vendors, counters that compost products vary with the amount of processing and that it is simply a matter of matching a particular quality of compost with an appropriate end use. While high quality separation and processing may be necessary for agricultural markets, for instance, the council maintains that even an imperfect separation system can produce compost that would have many nonagricultural applications, such as serving as a substitute for dirt in covering landfills and in the repair of damaged roadsides.[14]

Environmentalists remain unpersuaded by these arguments, however, fearing that some of the low-quality compost would still wind up in the wrong place. The Environmental Defense Fund believes that some composts have such high levels of contaminants that anywhere other than a lined landfill is the "wrong" place for these materials. Moreover, environmentalists question the size of markets for low-grade compost products.[15]

While arguments rage on as to what materials should be composted and what type of preprocessing is appropriate to ensure that only selected materials end up in the compost product, most agree that composting in one form or another will play a large role in reducing the volume of materials going to landfills. In describing major changes he foresaw in the waste industry, Wayne Trewhitt, the National Solid Waste Management Association's chairman of the board, predicted that "composting will become an essential part of waste management, whether using only yard waste or all organic waste."[16] Don Clay, the Environmental Protection Agency's assistant administrator for the Office of Solid Waste, also has predicted that recycling and composting will become the major disposal options in the later portion of this decade.[17] In its January 1991 draft of *The Municipal Solid Waste Dilemma: Challenges for the 90's*, EPA classifies composting as a form of recycling—the second-tier of EPA's four-tier solid waste management hierarchy. (EPA's preferred waste disposal option is source reduction, followed by recycling, waste combustion and landfilling.) In addition, the Solid Waste Composting Council is lobbying Congress to have composting recognized as a recycling technology under the Resource Conservation and

Recovery Act, which is expected to be reauthorized in 1992.

While municipal solid waste composting in the United States is in its infancy, composting sewage sludge has become increasingly popular in the United States over the last decade. An estimated 150 operating plants[18] compost approximately 10 percent of all sewage sludge.[19] Composting remains the fastest growing sludge management technique,[20] and many proposed municipal solid waste composting plants plan to co-compost sewage sludge.

Compostable Products in the Municipal Waste Stream

Analysts estimate that from one-third to two-thirds of the U.S. municipal solid waste stream consists of organic material—waste paper, yard wastes and food wastes—that is appropriate for composting. As Figure 7-1 shows, EPA estimates that yard wastes, including grass, leaves and bush trimmings, represented 18 percent of municipal solid waste by weight in 1988. Food wastes, such as vegetable peelings, corn cobs and uneaten food, represented 7.4 percent, and waste paper, another 40 percent. In terms of volume, EPA estimates yard waste represented 10.3 percent of municipal solid waste discards in 1988, food wastes, 3.3 percent, and paper, 34.1 percent.[21] The amount and composition of yard wastes, however, vary significantly by season and by region. In some months, yard wastes may account for as much as 25 to 50 percent of a community's municipal solid waste stream.[22]

EPA estimates that while the amount of yard and food wastes in the municipal waste stream has increased, their percentage of the waste stream has declined. Yard wastes have increased from 20 million tons in 1960 to 31.6 million tons in 1988, and food wastes have increased over the same period from 12.2 million tons to 13.2 million tons. Yard wastes, however, fell from 23 percent of the total waste stream by weight in 1960 to 18 percent in 1988, and food wastes fell from 13.9 percent to 7.4 percent. EPA attributes the decline in food wastes to increased use of garbage disposals, which send food wastes to sewer systems, and the increased use of prepared foods; wastes from food packaging plants are classified as industrial wastes rather than municipal solid wastes. EPA analysts expect the trend to continue, with food wastes declining as a percentage of the waste stream to 5.5 percent in 2010 and yard wastes declining to around 14 percent, at 36 million tons.[23]

EPA reports that minimal yard or food wastes are being recovered. The EPA estimates that only half a million tons of yard wastes, or less than 2 percent, were composted in 1988 and that no significant amount of food wastes were recovered. It should be noted that these estimates do not account for any backyard composting; the yard waste estimates are based

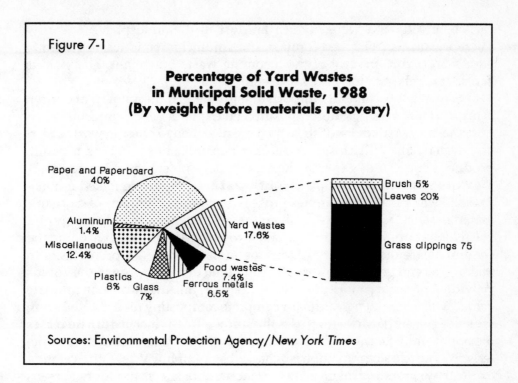

Figure 7-1

**Percentage of Yard Wastes
in Municipal Solid Waste, 1988
(By weight before materials recovery)**

Paper and Paperboard
40%

Aluminum
1.4%

Miscellaneous
12.4%

Plastics
8%

Glass
7%

Ferrous metals
6.5%

Food wastes
7.4%

Yard Wastes
17.6%

Brush 5%

Leaves 20%

Grass clippings 75

Sources: Environmental Protection Agency/*New York Times*

on sampling studies at landfills or transfer stations. EPA projects that a new emphasis on composting programs will enable composting projects to remove 20 to 33 percent of yard wastes from the waste stream by 1995 and that new food waste composting programs will remove up to 8 percent of food wastes from the waste stream by 1995.[24] More detailed information on paper in the waste stream can be found in Chapter 4.

The Composting Process

Farmers have composted vegetable wastes with animal and human manures for at least 4,000 years.[25] Using the natural composting process as the basis of their operations, modern composting facilities speed up the process and handle hundreds of tons of material daily by controlling environmental conditions—primarily oxygen levels, moisture content, temperature and the amount of microorganisms, such as bacteria, fungi and actinomycetes. The composting process generates energy and heat, which at temperatures higher than 132 degrees Fahrenheit destroys human and plant pathogens and weed seeds. In approximately one to three months, the carbon in the compostable material is converted to compost, or humus;

carbon dioxide and water, which are lost to the atmosphere; and new microorganisms.[26] Finished compost from municipal solid waste generally equals around 30 percent of the incoming waste by weight. The yield is considerably higher for yard waste composting.[27]

Oxygen is a particularly important ingredient. If the amount of oxygen is insufficient, anaerobic decomposition takes place, which emits malodorous smells.[28] (Modern landfills, which are designed to entomb waste in air- and water-tight cells, foster anaerobic decomposition and, as a result, produce a number of gases, such as methane, a potent greenhouse gas.[29])

Composting municipal solid waste: Composting mixed municipal solid waste is a more complex process than composting singular organic materials, such as yard waste. Given the heterogeneity of municipal solid waste, additional steps must be taken to ensure that the environmental conditions are uniform throughout the mass of waste—a prerequisite to making the end product uniform. The material to be composted, the liquids providing necessary moisture and the microorganisms must be in intimate contact with each other in order for complete composting to occur. Reducing the size of waste particles increases the surface area, which in turn increases the opportunity for microbial contact and improves waste handling characteristics. Particle size reduction is achieved by tumbling wastes in a rotating drum or by shredding them using hammermills or shear shredders. Screens are often then used to separate particles larger than a desired size. Water, or sometimes sewage sludge or wastes from food processing industries, are used to boost the moisture content of municipal solid waste, generally at between 20 to 30 percent, to the more optimum level of 50 to 60 percent.[30]

Almost every municipal solid waste composting vendor offers some form of preprocessing to remove bulky items and hazardous material. Removing hazardous material at this point, while it is still in a recognizable form and before it mixes further with the waste, is important to producing a safe, quality end product. After this step, the amount of additional preprocessing varies widely. Most companies utilize magnetic separators to extract ferrous metals, and many manually pick off a select group of recyclables, such as corrugated cardboard, depending on market conditions. Several composting companies offer mechanical separation systems at the front-end of the composting process to separate inorganics from the material to be composted. Noncompostable material is either recycled, landfilled, or in a few cases, made into densified refuse derived fuel for incineration.[31]

After initial composting, the compost is screened to remove noncomposted material, usually stone, glass, plastic and other inorganics. The extent of the screening is dependent on both the amount of preprocessing and end uses. Some compost also is ground in preparation for markets. As a final step, the compost is often cured for 30 to 180 days, which allows the

Box 7-1

Composting Technologies

Composting technologies vary in the way they supply air, control temperature, mix and turn the material to be composted and in the amount of time required to produce a finished product. Composting technologies, which also vary in capital and operating costs, can be classified into three general categories: windrows, aerated static piles and in-vessels.[32]

Windrow—A windrow is an elongated pile or row, which typically measures seven feet high and 14 to 16 feet wide at the base. Turning the pile provides the primary means of active aeration, and piles may be turned as much as once per week using machines equipped with augers, paddles or tines, or even a front-end loader or bulldozer equipped with a blade. Temperature control is more difficult to achieve in a windrow in comparison with other technologies, and the time required for composting is generally longer. Windrow composting can be used in combination with an in-vessel technology and generally is the method used to cure compost.[33]

Aerated static piles—Using a nonproprietary composting technology, piles of composting materials are placed over a network of pipes connected to an air blower. Forced aeration is the only method of aerating the pile; it is not turned or agitated through any other method. This design decreases the need for large land areas by allowing the construction of large-sized piles. The piles are broken up for the first time when the composting process is nearly complete, generally between six and 12 weeks. Aerated static piles have lower capital costs than either in-vessel systems or windrow systems, although they do continually require electricity to supply air to the compost piles. Aerated static piles have been used extensively for sewage sludge.[34]

In-vessel composting—Using mostly proprietary technologies, in-vessel systems place the materials to be composted in a chamber or vessel that provides mixing, aeration and moisture control. Common in-vessel systems include drums, silos, digester bins and tunnels where the environmental conditions are carefully controlled. The extent of preprocessing varies widely among in-vessel systems, yet all require additional processing after the material has been discharged from the vessel. Most systems are continuous-feed systems. In-vessel composting produces an end product quite rapidly—from one to two weeks—reducing land needs considerably.[35]

Table 7-1

Comparison of Three Municipal Solid Waste Technologies

Technology	Time to Produce End Product	Odors	Leachate	Amt. of Land Required
Windrow	2-6 months	Some	Yes	Largest
Static pile	6-12 weeks	Some to none	Yes	Smaller
In-vessel	1-2 weeks	None	No	Smallest

Source: Aga S. Razvi, Philip R. O'Leary and Patrick Walsh, "Composting Municipal Solid
     Wastes," *Waste Age*, August 1989

compost to attain a biologically stable condition and complete its transformation into a soil-like substance.[36]

Compost characteristics: Compost offers many benefits as a soil conditioner and soil additive, including moisture and nutrient retention, decreased soil erosion, improved drainage and aeration, and plant disease suppression. Although the nutrient concentration of compost is small compared with chemical fertilizers, compost has a nutrient-holding capacity that releases plant nutrients over an extended period. This characteristic reduces dependence on chemical fertilizers and aids water quality by decreasing chemical run-off and leachates. In addition, compost applied to disturbed or damaged lands can help restore both the soil and its organic content—the single most important measure of a soil's fertility. Compost also can have a buffering effect on the pH level of soil and aid in regulating soil temperature. Some composting companies also tout compost as providing trace elements that plants require.[37]

Disadvantages of compost can include potentially high concentrations of salts, heavy metals, plant and human pathogens, weed seeds and bits of inorganic material, such as plastic. The maturity of the compost, pH level or plant nutrient imbalances may also pose some risk to plants. While altering the composting process can eliminate some risks, such as plant or human pathogens, it cannot remove heavy metals or soluble salts. These factors are determined by the type of material being made into compost.[38]

Both Bruce Fulford of the Tellus Institute, a nonprofit consulting firm in Boston, and Urs Maire, sales manager for Buhler Inc., a composting vendor that has many facilities in Europe, report a trend away from municipal solid waste composting in Europe because of concern over heavy metals and physical contaminants. Maire says European standards for heavy metals are much stricter than in the United States, and Fulford told IRRC that while there is a debate in the scientific community as to what are acceptable levels of contaminants from a health standpoint, public opposition and the regulatory environment have led to the abandonment of a number of solid waste composting facilities in Europe.[39]

Sources of heavy metal in municipal solid waste include household pottery, cleaners, paints, oils and pesticides.[40] Co-composting with sewage sludge, particularly industrial sludge, often creates even higher levels of metals and other contaminants. Some analysts estimate that as much as one-third of 1 percent of municipal solid waste is hazardous.[41] That calculation results in an 800 ton per day municipal solid waste composting facility having to identify and dispose of close to three tons of hazardous waste per day.

Economics of Composting

A potential oversupply of municipal solid waste compost in the 1990s is the principal concern for those financing composting facilities. Although composting facilities normally will derive their revenue primarily from tipping fees and use the sale of the compost only as a supplemental revenue source, there is still the potential of being unable to move huge inventories of compost products and having to reduce prices or even pay to dispose of the compost in landfills.

Not only is there a surging number of municipal composting projects planning to market compost in the next several years, but an amendment to the 1990 farm bill passed by Congress also encourages agricultural composting. The bill requires the Department of Agriculture to "identify and compile" appropriate methods of composting agricultural wastes and the potential uses for such compost, and to make the information available to government agencies, private authorities and the general public.[42] In addition, food processors and other commercial and industrial users are beginning to embrace composting as a means of decreasing their disposal costs. Although farm and food compost could be viewed as competition for municipal solid waste compost, proponents of municipal solid waste composting view an increase in farm and food composting as complementary to municipal solid waste composting. Because farm, and often food, wastes contain high levels of nitrogen, mixing them with municipal solid wastes would produce a compost product with a superior carbon-nitrogen ratio.[43]

Box 7-2

Composting Yard Wastes

Grappling with burgeoning landfills, the federal and state governments have begun targeting yard wastes as one of the simpler and more economical means of diverting material from landfills. "For the biggest bang for your buck, yard waste recovery is the way to go," said James Darling, director of public works for Urbana, Ill., and a participant in a national study on controlling recycling costs.[44] Given the growing popularity of yard waste programs, analysts estimate that at least 2,000 new yard waste composting facilities will be established nationwide within the next five years.[45]

EPA made yard wastes a linchpin of its proposed plan to divert and recycle 25 percent of the material delivered to waste-to-energy plants. Although EPA abandoned its goal in December 1990 under pressure from the Presidential Council on Competitiveness, it had projected that yard wastes could fulfill 10 percent of the 25 percent diversion goal from waste-to-energy plants. EPA is still counting on yard wastes to help reach its nationwide recycling goal of 25 percent by 1992 and is urging local governments to establish programs to divert yard wastes from landfills. EPA recommends that nurseries and lawn care services use yard waste programs to establish their own compost and mulch programs.[46]

Many states are also eyeing yard wastes as a way to reduce the strain on their landfills significantly. A dozen states have passed legislation banning yard wastes from landfills and incinerators, and many other states are proposing bans. Some states, such as Iowa, Massachusetts, Minnesota and Florida, have established financial assistance programs to get composting programs off the ground.[47]

Most experts involved with yard waste composting programs agree that yard waste disposal is more of a management challenge than a technical one.[48] Many states and municipalities are encouraging backyard composting, which is actually a form of source reduction because the waste never gets into the garbage stream. Seattle, for example, provided 9,000 residents with free composting bins and an hour consultation as part of an expanded backyard composting program.[49] In addition, several communities and university extension specialists recommend that grass clippings be left on lawns to return valuable nutrients to the soil.

From a community's perspective, backyard composting is the most cost effective means of yard waste disposal because it eliminates collection, transportation and processing costs for the community. Given the simplicity of yard waste composting, the collection and transportation costs often are much greater than the costs of the compost process itself—one to 11 times greater, a ccording to one study.[50] The study of eight municipal yard waste composting programs across the country reported that while collection and transportation costs ranged from $0 to $80 per ton, processing costs ranged from $4 to $23 per ton.[51] Yard waste collection programs include less expensive drop-off programs as well as more costly, yet more convenient, curbside collection programs.

Management and operation of municipal yard waste composting facilities vary widely. For the most part, municipalities manage their own programs. Some, however, contract with companies offering yard waste composting services that are usually small, local operations. The number of times the piles of yard wastes need to be turned and the need to supplement the yard wastes with moisture depends on the climate, the desired rate of decomposition and the composition of the yard wastes. If left alone, yard wastes will generally break down over five years or more.[52] Some communities with no land or space constraints simply stack the yard wastes in piles as high as 10 to 20 feet. Because no processing is involved, many argue that these are not true composting operations. Others oppose operations of this type for health reasons. In early 1989, neighbors of a Hillsdale, N.J., compost site claimed they became ill when the municipality began turning five-year-old leaves.[53] Many blamed a fungus, asperillus fumigatus, that is known to grow on composting leaves as the culprit. Low-effort yard waste composting, which takes about three years to make compost, includes turning windrows once a year. The odors emitted during the annual turning, however, are quite strong. More regular turning can produce compost in about 18 months. Although in-vessel composting is generally too costly for yard wastes, large cities that need to process large volumes of yard wastes quickly may utilize this technique in the future.[54]

Yard waste composition: Yard wastes have three main components: grass clippings, leaves and brush. Analysts estimate that grass clippings account for about 75 percent of yard wastes (largely because the grass season is several months longer than the leaf season), leaves about 20 percent and brush about 5 percent.[55] These three components decompose at different rates, with the woody materials in brush taking the longest. Some communities, rather than composting these materials, separate and chip them to produce mulch.[56]

Grass, which has the greatest amount of nitrogen and moisture, decomposes the fastest. Without sufficient oxygen, however, grass clippings produce pungent gases and becomes extremely malodorous. (Grass clippings are often combined with leaves for composting to raise the carbon-nitrogen ratio.) Leaching nitrates could become a public health concern if they entered a community's water supply, and grass clippings also carry the possibility of heavy metals and residual herbicides and pesticides.[57] Studies suggest that pesticides break down during composting,[58] however, and testing done in communities so far has not shown them to be a problem.

Table 7-2

States Banning Yard Wastes

State	Effective Date	Leaves	Grass, Prunings and Tree Trimmings
Connecticut	1991	X	
District of Columbia	1989	X	X
Florida	1992	X	X
Illinois	1990	X	X
Iowa	1991	X	X
Minnesota	1992[a]	X	X
Missouri	1992	X	X
New Jersey	1988	X	
North Carolina	1993	X	X
Ohio	1993	X	X
Pennsylvania	1990	X	
Wisconsin	1993	X	X

[a] Yard wastes were banned in 1990 from the metropolitan region of Minneapolis and St. Paul.

Source: *Resource Recycling,* 1990

Potential composting markets are quite large and include public works projects, land reclamation, landscaping, parks, golf courses, forestry, landfill cover, nurseries, potting soil and agriculture.[59] Some 955,000 short tons of peat moss were produced in this country in 1987, and another 515,000 short tons were imported, to meet the demand of nurseries and landscapers.[60] In addition, farmland around the world loses up to one inch of topsoil each year,[61] and 65 tons of compost are needed to add one inch of compost to an acre of land. Of the 413 million acres of cropland in this country, an estimated 25 million acres of American cropland have severe erosion problems (losing more than 15 tons of soil per acre per year).[62]

The various markets have different standards for compost. Home gardeners, for instance, usually want small pieces of glass, plastic and stones screened out, while lower-grade compost may be suitable for landfill cover or revegetating construction sites.[63] Accordingly, the ability to offer more than one type of compost product and to tailor compost to different markets can help to ensure compost sales. While the end product differs depending on what portion of the waste stream is being composted, compost also can be supplemented with plant nutrients, minerals or organic materials, or offered in a variety of particle sizes or pH levels.[64]

Because compost is a relatively low-value, bulky material that can be costly to handle and transport, compost markets generally are regional, as opposed to national. Some composting facilities ensure sales by gearing their operations to local demand. Davis, Calif., for instance, composts only the amount of leaves that can be absorbed by existing residential demand for its compost material.[65]

Regulations: Many experts in the composting field emphasize that standardized regulations and testing are essential to market development. At present, however, no national and few state regulations for solid waste composting exist. Minnesota, Florida and New York are the only states that have established standards for municipal solid waste compost processing and quality, and Minnesota and Florida are the only states with both guidelines and actual experience with operating plants.[66] Other states, including California, Connecticut, Maine, Maryland, New Hampshire, Ohio, Rhode Island, South Carolina, Vermont, Washington and Wisconsin, are reportedly developing standards.[67] California's Integrated Waste Management Act of 1989 is attempting to spur compost use by requiring buyers of commercial fertilizers to document reasons why they do not purchase compost products.[68] Minnesota also has reportedly ordered state agencies to give solid waste compost preference when buying soil enhancing material for landscaping highways and parks.[69]

At the federal level, EPA and the Department of Agriculture have extensive standards regulating sewage sludge composting and application, but neither has developed standards for the municipal solid waste composting process.[70] EPA says it will first develop guidelines for compost from yard wastes. The agency also is completing a technical guide on the operation of compost facilities, has drafted "Market Development Study for Compost," and is considering developing procurement guidelines for compost.[71]

On behalf of the composting industry, the Solid Waste Composting Council is seeking standardized national compost guidelines from EPA and endorses standardized testing of compost.[72] Chemical tests proposed include pH, soluble salts, organic matter content, carbon to nitrogen ratio, micronutrient content and heavy metal concentration. Physical tests proposed include particle size, moisture content and presence of physical contaminants such as plastics, glass or gravel fragments. Biological tests could include stability, presence of pathogens and the response of various plants to different application rates of the compost.[73]

Financing municipal solid waste composting projects: Invest-

Box 7-3

Municipal Solid Waste Compost Sales

Prices for municipal solid waste compost range from $0 to $20 per ton, according to the Solid Waste Composting Council.[74] Revenues for yard waste compost reportedly range from $0 (or even a negative price) to $25 per ton.[75] The market is evolving, however, and prices are generally subject to local outlets because the weight and bulkiness of compost can make transportation costs a prohibitive factor.

Municipal solid waste composting facilities in Delaware, Florida and Minnesota have produced and successfully marketed compost. The nation's oldest co-composting facility—the Delaware Reclamation Project—began operation in 1984 near Wilmington, Del., and began marketing "Fairgrow" for sale in June 1990 after product liability issues and state permits were resolved. Distributed under a state marketing permit to landscaping professionals, the compost has sold for $4.50 per yard, compared with topsoil which costs $9 per yard. **Raytheon Service Co.**, a division of **Raytheon Corp.** that took over operation of the facility in 1989 from Fairfield Service Co., says it sold 2,100 tons of compost from June through September 1990. The presence of nickel in sludge used for co-composting, attributed primarily to an industrial source, has limited its distribution.[76]

Sumter County, Fla., owns a municipal solid waste composting plant that has been operating since 1988. Processing around 60 tons per day, the plant has produced compost for use in county landscaping projects and for experiments at the state university. Gary Breedon, the county's director of public works, told IRRC that the county is awaiting approval from the state department of environmental regulation but that it has commitments from compost customers for $30 per ton. Breedon added that he believes the price will eventually settle down to around $10 per ton.[77]

Agripost Inc. says that Agrisoil, the end product of its Fort Lauderdale plant, qualifies as a "Class A" compost under the state of Florida's compost regulations, allowing it unrestricted usage. Although the plant has suspended operations, Diane D'Angelo, Agripost's controller and assistant secretary, told IRRC that all compost produced by the plant that has undergone the final shredding stage has left the premises and that some of the compost was sold for $8 per yard. D'Angelo added that many of the company's customers have written the county commissioners in support of the plant.[78]

Recomp Inc. sells compost produced at its St. Cloud, Minn., plant to parks, highway projects and Christmas tree farms for $6 per ton. Karen Hyndman, Recomp's marketing coordinator, told IRRC that because there are no regulations for agricultural use at present, the company is steering clear of this market.[79]

ments in the municipal solid waste composting plants listed in Table 7-4 ranged from $22,500 to $71,000 per daily ton of installed capacity. E&A Environmental Consultants of Stoughton, Mass., estimates that operating costs of municipal solid waste composting plants range from $30 to $40 per ton.[80]

Most composting projects are either sponsored by a municipality or secured by a long-term waste supply contract with a municipality. As with materials recovery facilities and waste-to-energy facilities, the tipping fee serves as the primary source of revenue for a municipal solid waste composting project. Revenues from the sale of compost supplement the tipping fee and often are structured like electricity revenues in a waste-to-energy transaction; they primarily serve as a credit to the service fee paid by the municipality.[81]

As noted previously, the biggest concern to lenders is that the compost cannot be sold or even given away to end-users, producing unexpected disposal fees. Another major concern is whether the facility and other waste disposal methods used by the municipality have been properly sized, not only to absorb peak waste generation periods but also to operate at reasonably full capacities during off-peak periods. In addition, because many composting technologies are not proven in this country, and because the number of experienced operators is limited, many municipalities are requiring a suitable guarantee of technological performance from the project sponsor or its parent to ensure that the project debt is repaid.[82]

Most large municipal composting projects have been project financed, with debt issued in the form of tax-exempt municipal bonds, and analysts anticipate that municipal bond financings will continue to dominate the field.[83] A number of European financial institutions have been involved in the project financings, a factor that may be explained by their familiarity with European composting technologies. **Reidel Environmental Technologies Inc.**'s Portland, Ore., plant was the first U.S. municipal solid waste composting facility to be financed by revenue bonds and was also the first to obtain a "AAA" letter of credit.[84] Paine Webber handled the underwriting, arranging the $30 million financial package with the sale of $26.6 million of bonds and a $3.2 million equity contribution from Reidel. Credit Suisse served as guarantor of the plant, issuing the primary credit support for bondholders.[85]

To finance **Daneco Inc.**'s plant in Mora, Minn., the East Central Solid Waste Commission authorized the sale of $14 million in resource recovery bonds and accepted a $2 million grant from the Minnesota Office of Waste Management.[86] In addition, the Massachusetts Industrial Finance Agency has given preliminary approval for revenue bond financings for the two Massachusetts plants under development by **Environmental Recovery Systems Inc.**[87]

In contrast to these public financings, **Agripost Inc.**'s $25 million project in Fort Lauderdale was privately financed through an equity partnership and bank-provided debt capital.[88] National Westminster Bank USA and Dresdner Bank AG supplied $19 million, and Agripost and a limited partnership contributed equity to the project.[89]

U.S. Municipal Solid Waste Composting Projects and Players

Composting projects: There are 14 operating municipal solid waste composting projects in the United States, 13 full-scale and one research project. Table 7-3 provides a listing of these plants. (Another plant in Skamania County, Wash., ceased operating because the land on which it was located was slated for development as a conference center. The project, however, is expected to reopen within the next year at a new location.[90]) As of November 1990, an additional 10 municipal solid waste composting plants were under construction, and another 65 were in various phases of development. These figures compare with a total of 75 plants under development or operating in 1989, up from 42 in 1988.[91]

The U.S. municipal solid waste composting industry is an immature industry, and most of the operating plants are considered first generation facilities. Many facilities are constantly undergoing refinements to improve efficiency and the quality of the finished compost and are making investments in new equipment and process controls.[92] In addition, many plants in the planning, development and construction phases are considerably larger than existing U.S. plants and are incorporating equipment and processes that existing facilities do not employ.[93] Nearly all of the proprietary materials handling and composting systems being incorporated into large-scale municipal solid waste composting projects are European systems.

Tipping fees—Tipping fees at municipal composting facilities vary widely throughout the country. A plant in New Castle, Del., charges $42.30 per ton, while plants in Sumter and Dade County, Fla., charge in the mid-20s.[94] Cape May, N.J., which has a plant scheduled to begin operation in late 1993 or 1994, will be charging $130 per ton.[95] Portland, Ore., will pay $42 per ton to have its municipal solid waste composted.[96] Minnesota's Office of Waste Management reports the following tipping fees paid per ton at its five operating projects: Fillmore County—$30 for sorted municipal solid waste, $70 for unsorted; Lake of the Woods County—no charge (service fee is $40 per household per year); Pennington County—$45; St. Cloud—$76 plus tax; and Swift County—$75. Tipping fees for four Minnesota facilities under development will be as follows: Martin and Faribault counties—$72; Wright County—$65; Mora—$61 per ton; and Scott and Carver counties—$72.75 per ton.[97]

Space requirements—Municipal solid waste composting facilities require a larger site than waste-to-energy plants. Generally speaking, small facilities processing less than 100 tons per day require from five to 10 acres, 100 to 400 ton per day facilities require 10 to 20 acres,[98] 500 ton per day plants require 20 acres, and 1,000 ton per day facilities require 25 acres.[99]

Composting companies: While several small communities have designed municipal solid waste composting systems with the help of a consultant,[100] a municipal solid waste composting industry is emerging to compete for the business of a growing number of municipalities that are looking to private industry for composting services. Composting companies offer a variety of composting strategies. The major differences between the systems offered by these companies include the amount of preprocessing and recycling of materials before composting; the incorporation of sewage sludge and septage (co-compost); and the use of shredding and grinding equipment versus in-vessel systems to reduce particle size.[101] While Agripost and Bedminster Bioconversion Corp., for instance, tout minimal preprocessing as a benefit of their systems, Environmental Recovery Systems and Daneco stress the importance of preprocessing. In a marketing brochure that describes its front-end material separation system, Daneco says that "to produce a marketable compost from mixed solid waste, the process must include equipment to separate out the noncompostable materials such as metals and plastics."[102] Developers that use drums or in-vessel systems, such as Recomp and Reidel, argue that because their method does not shred materials with hammermills and shredders, it is easier to identify and remove inorganic materials.

More than a dozen companies are pursuing municipal solid waste composting development. The leading municipal solid waste composting developers are discussed below, and companies with firm projects are listed in Table 7-4. A number of companies also offer yard waste composting services to communities. Companies offering yard waste composting services are not covered in this report as they are generally smaller, local companies providing projects with low capital investments. International Process Systems Inc., which was recently acquired by Wheelabrator Technologies Inc., is an exception and is discussed along with Wheelabrator.

Companies with firm projects—**Agripost Inc.:** Agripost is a small publicly traded company that built the country's first large-scale composting facility, which has currently suspended operation. The 800 ton per day, $30 million plant began operation in November 1989 in Ft. Lauderdale, Fla., and by late 1990 was processing between 200 and 300 tons per day. The plant has since stopped receiving municipal solid waste, however, maintaining that it was losing money operating the plant without modifications to its contract with Dade County. The modifications requested included increasing the tipping fee of $22 per ton as well as increasing the percentage

Table 7-3

Operational U.S. Municipal Solid Waste Composting Facilities

Location	Plant Operator	System	Tons of MSW Processed/Day	Year On-Line
New Castle, Del.	Raytheon Service Co.	In-vessel	250-350 [a]	1984
Dade County, Fla.	Agripost Inc.	Enclosed windrow	250-300 [b]	1989
Escambia County, Fla.	NA	Windrow	400	1990
Sumter County, Fla.	American Recycling Co.	Windrow	60 [c]	1988
Des Moines, Iowa	TRS Industries Inc.	Windrow	200 [d]	1991
Fillmore County, Minn.	County	Aerated windrow	18	1987
Lake of the Woods County, Minn.	County	Aerated windrow	10	1990
Thief River Falls, Minn. (Pennington County)	County	Lundell with windrow composting	10 [e]	1985
St. Cloud, Minn.	Recomp Inc.	Digester [f]	100 [g]	1988
Swift County, Minn.	County	Aerated windrow	25	[h]
Portland, Ore.	Reidel Env. Technologies Inc.	Drum	600	1991
Hidalgo County, Tex.	NA	Windrow	300	1990
Big Sandy, Tex	Vital Earth Resources	Digester with windrow	30 [i]	1982
Portage, Wis.	Casey Brothers Construction	Drum with windrow	16	1986

a Plant accepts 1,000 tons per day; after processing, Fairfield system composts 250 to 300 tons per day with 230 wet tons of sludge; 600 tons per day of refuse derived fuel also is produced.

b Plant operation is suspended; design capacity is 800 tons per day.

c Design capacity is 200 tons per day.

d With 100 wet tons per day of sludge and 50 to 60 tons per day of yard waste.

e Composts 10 tons per day of refuse derived fuel residuals.

f With enclosed agitated bed curing.

g Plant accepts 250 tons per day; 100 tons per day is composted and 150 tons per day is shipped off to become refuse derived fuel.

h 1989 or 1990.

i With 15 to 20 wet tons of sludge. A Eweson/Bedminster Bioconversion Corp. research facility, the plant uses municipal solid waste as feedstock only half a dozen times per year for demonstration purposes.

Sources: Nora Goldstein and Robert Spencer,"Solid Waste Composting in the United States," *BioCycle*, November 1990, and various sources

Box 7-4

Procter & Gamble Promotes Composting

Procter & Gamble Co. (P&G) spearheaded the creation of the Solid Waste Composting Council in Washington, D.C., which has a diverse membership including not only compost producers, marketers and users, but also consumer products companies, academic institutions, consultants, public officials, nonprofit organizations and waste management firms. The establishment of the council in early 1990 was somewhat unusual in that the driving force came not from composting vendors but from consumer products companies, many of which have been under fire from environmentalists for marketing disposable products. P&G found support from other corporate giants such as Archer Daniels Midland Co., E.I. du Pont de Nemours & Co., Grand Metropolitan PLC (which owns Burger King and Pillsbury), International Paper Co., Kraft General Foods Corp., Warner-Lambert Co., and Weyerhaeuser Corp.

The council is involved in research, public education, development of compost standards, expansion of markets and the enlistment of government officials' support for composting as a solid waste solution. The council told IRRC it firmly believes that separating compostable materials from the remainder of the waste stream before composting is necessary for quality composting and for public confidence in the end product.[103]

In addition to its work with the Solid Waste Composting Council, Procter & Gamble is mounting its own aggressive $20 million initiative to promote composting nationwide. Saying that it is "putting our money where our mouth is and promoting a solution,"[104] Procter & Gamble plans to fund what it views as three key project areas: 1) large-scale municipal solid waste composting projects, as large as 800 tons per day, that demonstrate how composting could be integrated into a community's total solid waste system; 2) projects that show how composted solid waste humus can improve the quality of topsoil; and 3) projects to advance composting technology for high population areas, such as New York City, Boston and San Francisco.

To meet its second objective, P&G has initiated a five-year study with the U.S. Bureau of Mines to reclaim open-pit ore mines with solid waste compost. P&G also is funding research at the University of Minnesota to test compost for growing crops such as corn, alfalfa and barley, as well as research at the University of Giessen, Germany, to investigate plant growth in compost enriched agricultural soils.[105]

of reject material the county disposes of from 5 percent to 25 percent. Agripost says it needs to increase the tipping fee in order to secure another $7 to $8 million of financing for planned capital improvements that would allow the plant to operate at full capacity, including additional processing at the front-end and an air collection and odor treatment system. The Dade County Commissioners rejected any modifications to the contract but voted for discussions with Agripost about relocating the plant, a move that Agripost opposes.[106]

The Agripost plant has been controversial since its inception because Agripost's process uses minimal preprocessing—a characteristic opposed by many environmentalists. Although its proposed modifications would significantly alter its preprocessing capabilities, to date the company has removed only bulky items and potentially hazardous or toxic items, which represent about 2 to 3 percent of the waste stream by weight, according to the company. Agripost shreds the remaining waste twice before composting, physically breaking it down through the use of large-scale, high-powered shredding equipment. Because the solid waste is pulverized a number of times in Agripost's process, practically everything comes out as compost. At the end of the composting process, the compost goes through a tertiary shredder. Touting its process as "an ideal complement to community source separation programs," Agripost says that it can incorporate systems to recover recyclable materials but that it "supports separation of recyclable materials at the source because centralized systems of separating mixed waste can be costly and relatively ineffective." Agripost adds that "virtually all remaining unseparated materials, or separated materials for which there is no existing secondary market, can be processed by Agripost." Agripost says the benefit of its system is that material that would otherwise be landfilled can be retained in the end product.[107]

Agripost's process is based on a system first developed in 1955 by Howard Burr, a Pittsburgh engineer. Burr built an experimental plant in Miami in the early 1950s and then used his own funds to build a 400 ton per day plant in McKeesport, Pa., in the late 1950s. The plant sold compost to New York and Pennsylvania but closed down when McKeesport refused to pay a tipping fee. Burr transferred the composting operations to Kingston, Jamaica, which had a high demand for fertilizers. Burr operated a 400 ton per day plant in Jamaica for 12 years until leaving for political reasons. The plant sold its compost in Jamaica, the Bahamas, Trinidad and the United States, where the Department of Agriculture approved its importation without agricultural restrictions. Disney World in Orlando, Fla., was a major customer.[108]

Diane D'Angelo, Agripost's controller and assistant secretary, told IRRC that although the company is talking with a number of communities, no contracts have been signed for additional plants. In addition, a proposed

Table 7-4

U.S. Facilities of Leading MSW Composting Developers

Company	Location	System	Tons of MSW Processed/Day	Year on-Line	Cost (in millions)
Agripost Inc.	Dade County, Fla.	Windrows	800	1989	30
Approved Waste Recycling Corp.	Hooksett, N.H.	Windrows	800	1992	24-32
Bedminster Bioconversion Corp.	Big Sandy, Tex.[a]	Digester	30	1982	NA
	Southwest	Digester	10	1991	NA
Daneco Inc.	Mora, Minn.	ASP	250	1991	11.2
	Cape May, N.J.	ASP	400[b]	1993-94	36
	Petersburg, N.Y.	ASP	NA	NA	NA
	Rensselaer Cty., N.Y.	ASP	100-150	NA	NA
Environmental Recovery Systems Inc.	Somerset, Mass.	Windrows	700	1992	45-50
	Leominster, Mass.	Windrows	700	1992	45-50
	Wrentham, Mass.	Windrows	700	1992	45-50
	New Milford, Conn.	Windrows	700	1992	45-50
F&E Resource Systems Technology Inc.	Baltimore, Md.	In-vessel	700[c]	1992	40
	P.G. County, Md.	ASP	350	1992	12-15
Omni Technical Services Inc.	Riverhead, N.Y.	In-vessel agitated bin	500	1992-93	NA
OTVD/Seres Systems Inc.	Truman, Minn.	In-vessel	100	1991	6.9

Recomp. Inc. (subsidiary of Bonneville Pacific Corp.)	St. Cloud, Minn.	Digester	100 [d]	1988	NA
	Bellingham, Wash.	Digester	120 [e]	1991	6 [f]
	Freeport, Ill.	Digester	60	NA	NA
Reidel Environmental Technologies Inc.	Portland, Ore.	Drum	600	1991	30
Reuter Inc.	Pembroke Pines, Fla.	Drum	660	1992	48
TRS Industries Inc.	Des Moines, Iowa	Windrows	200 [g]	1991	4.5
Tyson Environmental Systems & Services Inc.	Scott County, Minn.	Drum	250	1993	15.3

[a] Research facility that processes only 30 tons per day of MSW plus 15 to 200 wet tons per day of sewage sludge a half dozen times per year.

[b] 400 ton per day average; the plant is designed to process up to 1,000 tons per day because it services a seasonal resort town.

[c] Multi-family and commercial waste.

[d] The plant accepts 250 tons per day of MSW; 100 tons per day is composted and 150 tons per day is made into refuse derived fuel.

[e] The plant accepts 250 tons per day; 120 tons per day is composted, 100 tons per day is incinerated, and the remainder is landfilled.

[f] For composting facility and MRF.

[g] Also processes 100 wet tons per day of sewage sludge and 50 to 60 tons per day of yard waste.

Source: Investor Responsibility Research Center Inc.

merger with F&E Resources Systems Technology Inc., another composting company, has been postponed until the situation in Dade County is resolved.[109]

Approved Waste Recycling Corp.: Approved Waste Recycling Corp. is developing an 800 ton per day facility in Hooksett, N.H., slated to begin operation in the fall of 1992. Approved Waste has a license in 10 northeastern states to use the composting process of Geophile International Inc. of Siloam Springs, Ark. The Geophile International process was the basis for a municipal waste composting project in Sumter County, Fla. (Designed to process 200 tons per day, the Sumter County project began operation in 1988 and is currently processing 60 tons per day.) Estimated to cost between $24 and $32 million, the Hooksett plant plans to separate a wide range of recyclable material, primarily through manual sorting, before composting. The compostable material will be placed in enclosed windrows for four to six weeks and will then be screened. The compost may then be stockpiled for an additional 15 to 20 days, depending on the end use. Don Rondeau of Approved Waste told IRRC the company has a contract in place with an out-of-state entity for nearly all of the compost that the facility will produce. A small amount also will be used on New Hampshire roadways.[110]

Bedminster Bioconversion Corp.: Bedminster Bioconversion Corp. of Cherry Hill, N.J., was incorporated in 1981 to hold the patents and rights to the Eweson digester, which is the basis for two municipal solid waste composting systems operating in the United States. The Eweson digester is a compartmented rotary kiln that co-composts municipal solid waste and sewage sludge. Offering to finance, design, build, own and operate municipal solid waste composting plants, Bedminster says its system will achieve a volume reduction of about 85 percent and a weight reduction of about 80 percent.[111]

Each "third generation" Eweson digester processes approximately 50 tons per day of municipal solid waste, plus about 25 wet tons per day of sewage sludge. Like Agripost, Bedminster composts unsegregated residential, commercial and institutional waste in unopened residential-sized garbage bags. The company told IRRC that it prefers not to install pre-processing in its plants but that it will sub-contract out pre-processing and recycling services if a municipality "insists." Bedminster adds that a picking line would increase volume reduction by about 5 to 8 percent only. Unlike Agripost, the company does not grind or shred solid waste. As a result, says Bedminster, nondegradable objects, including potentially toxic materials such as batteries, are not broken open during the composting process and can be removed by magnets when the solid waste is discharged after three days in the digester. The material is then turned on a daily basis for two weeks. After curing, the compost is stored in piles from two to four weeks.[112]

A Eweson digester in Big Sandy, Tex., operated from 1972 to 1976, manufacturing compost from municipal solid waste and sewage sludge to rehabilitate a large piece of land that had been given to Ambassador College. In 1982, Eweson purchased the plant and converted it to a commercial operation under the name of Vital Earth Resources. Citing low tipping fees and the costs of screening and landfilling nondegradable residues, Vital Earth Resources chose to process agricultural waste, sawdust, brewery sludge and other materials in place of municipal solid waste. Half a dozen times a year, however, the company processes municipal solid waste and sewage sludge for demonstration purposes.[113]

In addition to the Big Sandy plant, the Eweson digester was the basis for another municipal solid waste composting facility in St. Paul, Minn. Recomp, the company that operates the plant, says it has upgraded the system and now considers the system its own.[114] Bedminster owns 16 percent of Recomp, acquiring the stock in exchange for a license to its system. Bedminster told IRRC that a contract for a plant in Okeechobee County, Fla., was canceled for failure to meet deadlines, but that the company was renegotiating the contract in March 1991. Hugh Ettinger, a company vice president, also told IRRC that a small resort town in the Southwest planned to begin operation of a "mini-plant" by mid-year. Driven by the need to dispose of sewage sludge, the digester will process 10 tons per day of municipal solid waste and three wet tons per day of sewage sludge.[115]

Daneco Inc.: Daneco, which is developing four municipal solid waste composting plants in the United States, is a member of The Daneco Group, which employs more than 100 people that design, construct and service the fields of solid waste resource recovery and air and noise pollution control for the steelmaking industry. The Daneco Group says that its composting technology has been used in 14 projects worldwide and that it has successfully marketed solid waste compost since 1975. Daneco Danieli Ecologia S.p.A. has its headquarters in northeastern Italy and is the parent company of the Daneco Group, which also includes another subsidiary—Daneco Gestione Impianti S.p.A.—that operates plants designed and constructed by Daneco outside of the United States.[116]

Established in 1988, Daneco employs two types of processing systems at its U.S. composting plants. The company has its own aerated static pile composting system that produces compost in four to seven weeks and includes a proprietary wet separation process that separates glass, stones and sand from compostable materials. Daneco also is the exclusive licensee for an automated separation technology developed by **Horstmann** of Germany, which has been involved in more than 50 materials recovery projects in Europe, that separates recyclables at the front end of the composting system. Daneco will use its own mechanical and manual separation technology at its Mora, Minn., plant but will use the Horstmann technology at its Cape May, N.J., facility.[117]

Daneco is pursuing plants in Rensselaer County and Petersburg, N.Y., and has been involved with a composting project in Southold, N.Y. The Southold project, which is designed to co-compost sewage sludge with between 100 and 200 tons per day of municipal solid waste, was put on hold after the town rejected a $9 million general obligation bond referendum. In April 1991, Daneco told IRRC that the company also was a finalist for another four or five municipal waste composting projects.[118]

Daneco also has proprietary technology to produce refuse derived fuel, but Ted Gentile, the company's national sales manager, told IRRC that weak markets have deterred the company from pursuing this option. Daneco also is the U.S. licensee for the Finnish solid waste gasification system, Bioneer. Gentile says that although the company installed one system near its headquarters in Italy that is performing well, the company "is still evaluating applications in the United States. [Bioneer] is not the primary system that Daneco is trying to market."[119]

Environmental Recovery Systems Inc. (ERS): ERS of Denver, Colo., has four municipal solid waste composting plants in the permitting stage in Connecticut and Massachusetts and has another three plants under development in Connecticut and the mid-Atlantic. "We selected Connecticut as the site of our first plants because it has one of the most pressing waste problems in the country," said Lauren Lehman, an ERS representative.[120] The cost of each fully enclosed plant will range from $45 to $50 million, and each will process approximately 700 tons per day. A Leominster, Mass., plant will also process up to 180 wet tons per day of pre-treated sewage sludge.[121]

Timothy Weins, senior vice president of ERS, told IRRC that the company was created in 1986 "to take the most environmentally safe [composting] technology available to market." Describing its facilities as "reverse manufacturing plants," the company says it spent several years and approximately $7 million[122] developing an "extensive front-end separation" system. The patented system includes the mechanical and manual separation of recyclable materials, which the company estimates comprise approximately 50 percent of the waste stream. ERS estimates that another 40 percent is organic and inert material suitable for composting and that the remaining 10 percent is nonprocessable. ERS's processing system combines "existing off-the-shelf technology" from several industries, such as a pneumatic air classification system used by the paper industry to capture paper. Once the compostable material is separated at the front-end, it is placed in windrows and periodically aerated for four weeks.[123]

F&E Resource Systems Technology Inc.: F&E Resource Systems Technology of Laurel, Md., is developing two private recycling and composting facilities in Maryland. Chrysler Capital Corp. is a limited partner in F&E's Baltimore project, which is designed to process up to 700 tons per day of waste from multifamily and commercial establishments. (Most residential waste in the area is already contracted to go to Wheelabrator Technologies Inc.'s Baltimore waste-to-energy facility.) Slated to begin operation in the fall of 1992, the $40 million plant will mechanically separate ferrous and manually separate cardboard, paper, plastic and aluminum, leaving an estimated 365 tons per day of compostable material. Ashbrook-Simon-Hartley, a member of the Simon Group, is supplying the in-vessel composting technology—a concrete tunnel that composts the material for 18 days. Additional curing of up to 30 days may be needed. The project will be the first U.S. application of the German technology in a solid waste facility.[124]

F&E Resource Systems' second project is a 350 ton per day facility in Prince George's County, Md., that will use an aerated static pile to compost residential waste. Also scheduled to begin operation in the fall of 1992, the plant is estimated to cost $12 to $15 million. F&E told IRRC that it was pursuing a number of additional private facilities but that it was not bidding for municipal work. Plans to merge with Agripost, another developer of municipal solid waste composting facilities, were suspended in the fall of 1990.[125]

Omni Technical Services Inc.: Rated by *Inc.* magazine as the 74th fastest growing operation[126], Omni Technical Services of Uniondale, N.Y., builds and operates materials recycling facilities and is expanding its services to include processing the entire waste stream. Omni has an exclusive U.S. license with Koch, a German materials handling firm that has more than 100 installations in Germany and Portugal, including three municipal solid waste composting facilities. Omni is seeking permitting for its first project to use the Koch technology—a 500 tons per day recycling and composting facility in Riverhead, N.Y. Slated to begin operation in 1992 or 1993, the plant will utilize an agitated bin composting process. Omni told IRRC it has signed contracts for its compost product.[127] (Additional information on Omni's materials recovery facilities is included in Chapter 6.)

OTVD/Seres Systems Inc.: OTVD Inc., a U.S. subsidiary of Omnium de Traitements et de Valorisation des Dechets, and Seres Systems of Minneapolis, a subsidiary of Ryan Construction Co., plan to begin operation of a 100 ton per day composting facility in Truman, Minn., by the end of 1991. Serving Martin and Faribault counties, the plant will be the first U.S. application of the French composting system, which has operated in more than 30 composting facilities in Europe, Africa and the Middle East. OTVD has a patented SILODA process, which composts waste in 10 concrete silos using a forced aeration paddle. Because the Minnesota counties have effective curbside recycling programs, recovering recyclables for market is not a major goal of the plant. Preprocessing is still designed, however, to separate ferrous materials, as well as aluminum and plastic from the compostable material. After 30 days in the silo system, the compost is cured in an enclosed area for another 60 days. The counties plan to use the compost for farms and public works projects. Norm Schenck of OTVD told IRRC that the company is negotiating with communities in the Northeast, including upstate New York, for additional U.S. projects.[128]

Recomp Inc.: Owned by publicly traded **Bonneville Pacific Corp.**, a diversified alternative energy company, Recomp calls itself "the original United States recycling and composting company."[129] Recomp owns a facility in St. Cloud, Minn., that accepts 250 tons per day of municipal solid waste. Recomp processes 100 tons per day for composting and ships off the remaining 150 tons per day to Northern States Power, a Minnesota utility, to produce and burn refuse derived fuel at its generating facility. Of the 100 tons of solid waste that Recomp processes, roughly 60 to 70 percent is made into compost; the remainder is noncompostable and goes to a landfill.[130]

Recomp says Eweson technology was the basis of its St. Cloud operations but that the technology has been modified so extensively that "it no longer qualifies as Eweson technology." The only pre-processing at the plant is removal of hazardous waste and magnetic separation of ferrous materials. Karen Lyndman, marketing coordinator for Recomp, told IRRC that the company "only pulls out what we can economically recycle," adding that it discontinued separating more materials because they "just ended up being landfilled." Recomp says it deliberately avoids shredding or hammermilling in order to screen out inorganic materials after composting. The waste material is sent to a drum for three days where it is mixed with urea, a soluble, weakly basic nitrogenous compound, to add moisture. Recomp uses urea in place of sewage sludge because Minnesota compost regulations prevent compost made from sewage sludge from qualifying as a "Class I" compost—the highest quality compost. While the compost is now mechanically aerated after discharging from the drum and cured in windrows outside for anywhere from 30 to 120 days, Recomp is constructing an aerated trough system that will allow the compost to be ready for market within one to two months. Recomp sells the compost to parks, highway projects and Christmas tree farms. Lyndman says that because there are no regulations for agricultural use at present, the company is steering clear of this market.[131]

Recomp planned to begin composting municipal solid waste at a second plant in Bellingham, Wash., at the beginning of June 1991. In January 1990, Recomp acquired Thermal Reduction Co., which opened Washington state's first municipal waste incineration facility in 1974. The plant is being upgraded to accept 250 tons per day of municipal solid waste, composting 120 tons per day and incinerating 100 tons per day. The plant also plans to recover cardboard, aluminum and ferrous. The 2.5 megawatt plant sells power to Puget Sound Power & Light Co. Excess heat will be sold to a mushroom growing facility that will be built, owned and operated by

Bonneville Foods, another Bonneville Pacific Corp. subsidiary.[132] Recomp also plans to use a technology developed by the Pacific Northwest Laboratory to convert ash residue into "environmentally safe glass."[133]

Recomp told IRRC that the company is negotiating contracts for a 60 ton per day composting plant in Freeport, Ill., and that it is pursuing municipal solid waste composting opportunities in Vermont with Vermont Integrated Waste Solutions, which owns two incinerators in Vermont. The joint venture hopes to reactivate an existing waste-to-energy plant in Rutland, composting between 100 to 250 tons per day and incinerating the remainder.[134]

In 1989, Recomp paid $1.5 million to acquire Super Cycle Inc., which has provided curbside recycling services to communities in Minneapolis and St. Paul since 1986 and now collects, processes and markets 80 tons per day.[135] Recomp also undertook a pilot project with Procter & Gamble at its St. Cloud facility that determined that Procter & Gamble's Pampers and Luvs diapers were 80 percent compostable.[136]

Reidel Waste Disposal Systems Inc.: A subsidiary of Reidel Environmental Technologies, a provider of solid and hazardous waste disposal services, Reidel Waste Disposal Systems is a co-licensee along with **Resource Systems Corp.** of Portland, Ore., to the **Dano** composting system (in all 50 states except for Minnesota). A Swiss firm, Dano AG says it is the world's oldest and largest recycler and composter of municipal solid waste. Developed in 1939, the Dano system is used in more than 100 plants around the world[137] that recycle and compost more than 5 million tons of urban waste each year.[138]

In the spring of 1991, Reidel began operation of the first composting facility to be procured with a full service contract (whereby the vendor provides guarantees for construction and operation) between a vendor and municipality. In the fall of 1989, the Metropolitan Service District of Portland, Ore., signed a 20-year contract with Reidel to design, construct and operate a 600 ton per day plant.[139] Because Portland has a high participation rate in its curbside recycling program, a good portion of the recyclables already have been removed from the residential waste coming into the plant. Further manual sorting of recyclables and hazardous wastes takes place at the plant. (The hazardous waste will be trucked to a permitted hazardous waste transfer station in Portland that Reidel owns.)[140]

The waste material is then fed into slowly rotating drums that are 12 feet in diameter and 80 feet long. After six to eight hours, the organic material reaches the discharge end of the drums and is in a pulverized state. Following screening, the compostable material is distributed into aerated static piles on an outdoor aeration slab. After three weeks on the aeration slab, the material is 90 percent composted and is transported to static maturation beds for an additional three weeks.[141] End-users, including tree farmers and landscapers, have reportedly agreed to take the plant's first year production of compost free-of-charge.[142]

Reuter Inc.: Reuter is developing a 660 ton per day municipal solid waste composting facility in Pembroke Pines, Fla., which has the capability of expanding to 1,000 tons per day. Slated for operation in 1992, the Broward County plant is designed to reduce the amount of waste going to landfill by approximately 85 percent, recovering 12 to 15 percent of the waste stream in the form of recyclables. Another 55 to 65 percent will be composted. Reuter says it has entered into an agreement with a sales organization to purchase all of the compost produced by the Pembroke Pines facility.[143]

As with its Eden Prairie, Minn., densified refuse derived fuel plant, Reuter will use the Buhler processing system. (Further details on Reuter's refuse derived fuel plant are included in the refuse derived fuel section of this chapter.) **Buhler**, with U.S. headquarters in Minneapolis, has installed more than 100 waste processing plants in Europe, the Middle East, Asia, Africa, Central America and the United States, ranging in size from 50 to 700 tons per day. More than 80 of these plants produce compost. The Swiss system feeds waste into a large screening drum where oversize pieces are separated from finer material. The finer material leaving the large screening drum goes through a magnetic separator to remove ferrous metals and is then mixed in a drum with a liquid for composting. After six weeks in windrows, the compost is mature and metered into a hammermill and then a fine screening drum, where reject materials such as plastic, paper and wood are removed. The compost then goes to a ballistic separator where glass particles and stones are removed. The oversize pieces, after being shredded in a hammermill, can be processed into refuse derived fuel. To do so, these coarse materials are fed into an air classifier, which separates the heavy portion from the light portion. The heavy portion is discharged and the light portion, mostly paper and cardboard, passes through a cyclone, a shredder and a conditioner before being made into densified refuse derived fuel pellets.[144]

Buhler, which is a system designer and equipment manufacturer that manufactures 90 percent of its equipment, told IRRC it would prefer to work with developers rather than own and operate its own facilities. Buhler terminated an agreement making Reuter its exclusive U.S. agent in December 1988 and more recently terminated a marketing agreement with Wheelabrator Technologies in January 1991. In addition to Reuter's Eden Prairie and Broward County, Fla., facilities, a Buhler system is scheduled to begin operation in the fall of 1992 in Wright County, Minn. M.A. Mortenson Co. of Minneapolis is the general contractor for the 165 ton per day composting facility, which has an estimated capital cost of $14 million.[145]

TRS Industries Inc.: TRS Industries is supplying the equipment and operating a facility in Des Moines, Iowa, designed to process 200 tons per day of municipal solid waste, 100 wet tons per day of sludge and 50 to 60 tons per day of yard waste. Scheduled to begin operation in the spring of 1991, the $4.5 million project is an upgraded version of a pilot project that has been processing 60 tons per day of municipal solid waste and 30 wet tons per day of sewage sludge. The pilot plant has been composting between 75 and 80 percent of the incoming waste, although the amount going to the landfill will most likely increase in the scaled-up version because of additional screening. The material is composted in outdoor windrows in roughly eight weeks. Des Moines has a commingled curbside recycling program underway, reducing demands for pre-processing on the plant.[146]

William Chiles of TRS Industries told IRRC that future systems marketed by his company will include a materials recovery facility. TRS also is exploring a trough-type composting system that is more capital intensive than windrows yet would speed up the composting process. TRS makes all of its own equipment and plans to sell its systems to municipalities. Two years ago TRS sold a 30 to 60 ton per day processing system to Eagle River, Wis. The company's primary objective, however, is to own and operate its facilities.[147]

Tyson Environmental Systems & Services Inc.: Tyson Environmental Systems & Services plans to design, construct and operate a 250 ton per day facility that will use the Dano composting system. Scheduled to begin operation in 1993, the project is in Scott County, Minn. Part of the Tyson Cos., a material handling, transportation and distribution company founded in 1930, Tyson Environmental Systems & Services told IRRC it has rights to the sale of Dano technology in 13 states.[148]

Additional companies offering composting services—Ameri- **can Recovery Corp. (ARC)** has exclusive U.S. and Canadian rights to the Sorain solid waste recovery system, which has processed more than 15 million tons of refuse in 12 plants in Europe, South America and Canada since 1964. ARC is a joint venture formed in January 1988 by Sorain Cecchini, S.p.A. of Rome, and Potomac Capital Investment Corp., a wholly owned subsidiary of the Potomac Electric Power Co. (The company's affiliate, American Energy Corp., offers a modular mass burn waste-to-energy technology.) Sorain's waste separation technology includes a patented bag breaker and a unique characteristic—the ability to recover film plastic mechanically and reprocess it into plastic bags, pipe and conduit. Sorain also offers composting and refuse derived fuel systems. Three of Sorain's operating plants produce compost in approximately one month, but none produces refuse derived fuel. Although the company does not have any full-scale municipal solid waste facilities operating in the United States, it has operated a small project in Santa Barbara, Calif., for testing purposes. Since October 1989, the company has tested batches of between one and two tons of the organic portion of municipal solid waste, yard waste and sewage sludge in varying compositions.[149]

Another company that is marketing the composting system developed by Howard Burr and employed at Agripost's Fort Lauderdale project is **Burr Universal Resource Recovery Inc.** Formed in 1989, the company has no planned plants to date but says it is negotiating with a number of communities for plants in the 800 to 1,000 ton per day range. Burr Universal says it will provide all financing and that it will be "completely responsible for the plant operation and disposal of the end product"—Burrtilizer, which can be produced in three to four weeks. Burr Universal, of which Edwin Burr, Howard Burr's brother, is an officer, acquired the assets of Conservational International of Florida Inc., which designed and engineered the layout of the Miami, McKeesport and Kingston plant described earlier, but had not conducted active operations for more than eight years. Burr Universal undertook a private placement offering of its common stock in March 1991.[150]

Waste-to-energy firms—**Foster Wheeler Corp.**, a waste-to-energy developer that is discussed in Chapter 8, and **Resource Recovery Systems Inc.**, a materials recovery facility developer that is described in Chapter 6, are jointly building a combined recycling and waste-to-energy complex in Montreal, Quebec, that will have a composting component.[151] In addition, Resource Recovery Systems is planning a composting pilot project in conjunction with its Springfield, Mass., material recovery facility for items such as soiled paper and pizza boxes.[152]

Harbert/Triga, a waste-to-energy developer, also offers composting services. While the company has not developed any U.S. composting projects, Triga, a subsidiary of S.I.T.A., S.A., the waste management arm of the Lyonnaise des Eaux Group and one of the largest municipal service contractors in Europe, has designed and built more than 40 composting plants since 1962.[153]

In the spring of 1991, **Wheelabrator Technologies**, a leading waste-to-energy developer described in Chapter 8, acquired **International Process Systems** of Glastonbury, Conn., a company with a proprietary agitated multi-bay system that composts sewage sludge along with shredded papers, magazines, leaves and yard wastes. IPS operates four composting facilities, has another seven under construction on the East Coast and an additional dozen in the design phase.[154] In early 1991, Wheelabrator discontinued its marketing agreement with Buhler, a composting vendor.

Waste management firms—None of the country's six largest publicly traded solid waste management firms—Attwoods Inc., Browning-Ferris Industries Inc., Chambers Development Co., Laidlaw Inc., Waste Management Inc. and Western Waste Industries Inc.—have a municipal solid waste composting project under development. All but Western Waste Industries, however, have at least one large-scale yard waste composting facility. (Additional details on the residential recycling operations of these companies are included in Chapter 6.)

In the fall of 1990, employee-owned **Norcal Solid Waste Systems Inc.** of San Francisco acquired Del Norte Disposal Co., which is planning to build a 70 ton per day combined materials recovery and composting plant. Scheduled to begin operation in the fall of 1991, the plant will use an aerated static pile composting system.[155] In addition, the city of San Jose awarded a contract to a Norcal subsidiary to compost up to 50,000 tons per year of residential and civic yard wastes beginning in the spring of 1991.[156]

Browning-Ferris Industries Inc. told IRRC that it has 11 centers that offer a variety of services and that some of these include yard waste composting.[157] In addition, in May 1991, BFI acquired **Resource Conservation Services Inc.** of Yarmouth, Maine, which operates a unique composting facility in Unity, Maine. Rated as the 136th fastest growing small business by *Inc.* magazine in 1990, RCS operates a 100 ton per day plant for six municipal wastewater treatment districts that composts sewage sludge and sawdust, wood ash, potato and fish wastes, pre-consumer waste paper and paper mill sludge in windrows. The company foresees a tremendous market for composting mixed paper and sewage sludge once concerns about inks and dyes have been resolved. The Unity plant also serves as a research facility, conducting trials for manufacturers of different paper products, as well as for Kentucky Fried Chicken and McDonald's. The plant sells its compost for highway construction, landfill and gravel pit closures, and landscaping. As long as the paper mill sludge has been excluded, the state has given the compost unrestricted usage. RCS says it is pursuing three additional composting facilities in New England.[158]

In 1989 **Chambers Development Co.** became the exclusive North American vendor of the Voest-Alpine compost system—a proprietary Austrian recycling, composting and wastewater treatment technology. No U.S. plants have yet been developed using this technology, however. As for yard wastes, Chambers has set aside an area for leaf composting at three landfills.[159]

Recycle America[R], a service of **Waste Management Inc.**, has more than 20 yard waste composting facilities in operation or under development in the United States.[160] **Attwoods** has one compost site for construction and demolition waste; the site is for the company's own use as a volume reduction measure.[161] **Laidlaw** operates a 100 ton per day yard waste composting system in Rockford, Ill.[162]

Food composting: While there are no large-scale food composting projects operating in the United States, a number of companies are testing the waters in this area. **Ebara Environmental Corp.** of Greensburg, Pa., has a pilot project with the capacity of composting two tons per day of food waste from the Seven Springs Mountain Resort near Pittsburgh, Pa. The facility began processing food waste, along with sawdust or recycled compost as a bulking agent, in February 1990. Ebara Environmental Corp. has two U.S. sewage sludge composting facilities in the permitting stage, and its parent company, Ebara Corp., which has its headquarters in Tokyo, operates 30 systems in Japan, including municipal solid waste composting facilities.[163]

As mentioned earlier, **Resource Conservation Services**, which was acquired by **Browning-Ferris Industries** in May 1991, composts potato and fish wastes and is conducting trials for Kentucky Fried Chicken and McDonald's food and paper wastes. Other commercial establishments, such as Ocean Spray and North Atlantic Products, are pursuing composting of food wastes as well.[164]

Some 3,500 households in Brooklyn are planning to sort food wastes, tissue paper, tea bags and coffee filters into compostable bags for composting with leaves at the Fresh Kills landfill on Staten Island. The New York City Department of Sanitation says it decided to pursue the pilot project after determining that research "turned up next to nothing in the U.S. on which to model their program."[165] **Woods End Laboratory** of Mount Vernon, Maine, which has experience composting potato culls and fishery wastes, and **Organic Recycling** of Valley Cottage, N.Y., are collaborating on the project.[166] The pilot project is in question, however, because of New York City's budget constraints.[167] **E&A Environmental Consultants** is developing a food waste and composting facility for East Hampton, N.Y., on Long Island.[168]

Densified Refuse Derived Fuel Production

For the purposes of this report, densified refuse derived fuel is defined as a fuel derived from the waste stream that is designed to be burned off-site in existing boilers, primarily coal burners. Reuter Inc.'s densified refuse derived fuel pellets, for example, are designed to burn in a one to three ratio with coal to replace any type of solid fuel.[169] Fuel derived from the waste stream that is processed to be burned on-site in new, specially designed waste-to-energy plants, such as at Asea Brown Boveri Resource Recovery Systems' Hartford, Conn., plant, is defined as refuse derived fuel and is discussed in Chapter 8.

The track record of densified refuse derived fuel plants has been spotty. Of 11 large-scale (200 ton per day or more) densified refuse derived fuel facilities built or financed prior to 1982, seven have ceased operation. Moreover, two of the remaining four operate only intermittently. Experts in the field attribute the failure of many of the early densified refuse derived fuel plants to their inability to reliably produce a uniform fuel product to specification. Since 1982, only one large-scale densified refuse derived fuel plant has been built—Reuter Inc.'s Eden Prairie, Minn., plant—and it has had difficulty producing a quality fuel pellet.[170]

Despite the difficulties of the past, several companies are pursuing densified refuse derived fuel production, and several more plan to in the near future. Many believe that passage of the Clean Air Act amendments will create a market for densified refuse derived fuel as a low-cost means of reducing air emissions. They are banking on coal-burning companies, including utilities, replacing a portion of their fuel with fuel produced from garbage. Refuse derived fuel pellets reportedly produce the same amount of Btu per ton as low-level coal, yet sell at less than half the price, at around $12/ton.[171] In addition, if incinerators use municipal solid waste for only a portion of the fuel stream (30 percent or less), they are exempt from EPA's emission standards for municipal waste incineration.

Reuter Inc. opened its 400 ton per day Eden Prairie, Minn., densified refuse derived fuel production facility in 1987. The $19 million plant separates recyclables from the waste stream and produces densified refuse derived fuel pellets using the Buhler processing system. (For more details on the Buhler system, see discussion of Reuter's composting facility in a previous section of this chapter.) Reuter has operated the plant under a cloud of controversy and primarily has been plagued by a lack of markets for its densified refuse derived fuel pellets. By the spring of 1991, Reuter had sold only about 35 percent of the pellets it had produced.[172] The plant saw its first profit in the last quarter of 1989—$7,000—after losing more than $9 million since start-up.[173]

In early 1990, an increase in both waste disposal fees and the volume of waste delivered to the plant raised its prospects further, but the project received a number of blows beginning in the spring of 1990. Unable to sell its pellets, Reuter stored them in area warehouses. In April 1990, a fire swept through one of its warehouses, and 5,000 tons of its pellets were destroyed by water damage. The fire raised serious safety questions about Reuter's operations and highlighted the fact that Reuter had no market for its pellets. Reuter also faced accusations that it was landfilling more waste than it was recycling or converting to densified refuse derived fuel, taking advantage of a more than $50 disparity between what it charged to accept waste and what it paid to landfill waste. In July 1990, the Metropolitan Council, a multi-governing body for the Minneapolis-St. Paul area, imposed a number of conditions on the Eden Prairie facility in order for the plant to continue accepting municipal solid waste. The key conditions included abating 60 percent of the plant's incoming waste by mid-1991 and 70 percent by 1993, and initiating significant construction activities on a composting facility by the end of June 1991. By mid-1991, Reuter had abated about 70 percent of its incoming waste but had yet to find a site for a compost facility.[174]

Because Reuter is no longer warehousing pellets, it has had to accept less waste until it can ship more pellets to end-users. As a result, the plant is unable to operate profitably. Reuter attributes the difficulty in developing markets for its pellets to the plant's inability to consistently manufacture good quality pellets. Maintaining that it has resolved quality problems in recent months, primarily through the addition of lime, Reuter says it is negotiating with several large users and that it expects its marketing problems to be resolved in 1991.[175]

Although Reuter has developed the only large-scale densified refuse derived fuel plant since 1982, there are several small scale plants in operation. **Lundell Manufacturing Co.** of Cherokee, Iowa, has manufactured the equipment for about a dozen small-scale systems, ranging in size from 50 to 200 tons per day. Primarily in the Midwest, the plants are designed to produce densified refuse derived fuel and separate material for composting.[176]

National Recovery Technologies Inc. (NRT) also markets automated recycling equipment that is capable of producing densified refuse derived fuel and compostable material. Founded in 1981 by a group of physicists from Vanderbilt University in Nashville, Tenn., privately owned NRT has four proprietary separation systems: a rotary material separator, which opens bags of waste and removes the ferrous metals, glass and compost components; an electropneumatic aluminum concentrator, which uses air nozzles, activated by detectors, to eject aluminum cans along with adjacent materials into what the firm calls an aluminum-rich concentrate; a pulsed eddy current aluminum separator, which then removes the aluminum from the concentrate; and a vinyl separator, which combines the air ejection system with a microprocessor scanning process that ejects plastic containers containing polyvinyl chloride. (See the polyvinyl chloride sorting and recycling section of chapter 5 for additional information.)[177]

NRT has various combinations of its systems operating at 20 locations worldwide.[178] NRT equipment is in use at a Crestwood, Ill., facility operated by XL Recycling Corp. and a planned Louisville, Ky., facility, discussed below. NRT also recently completed an installation of its equipment in Ashland, Ky., with Addington Environmental Inc. and is developing a project in Cleveland, Ohio, with Mid-American Waste Systems Inc., and a project in Toronto, Canada. The city of Nashville plans to add NRT equipment to an existing incinerator that burns unprocessed garbage and to modify the incinerator's boilers to burn a refuse derived fuel. After the expansion, the project is slated to process a total of 1,700 tons per day of municipal solid waste. Expanding overseas, NRT formed a partnership with the Marubeni America Corp., Japan's third largest trading corporation, to market NRT's system in the Far East.[179]

In September 1989, **XL Recycling Corp.**, an affiliate of XL Disposal

Corp., dedicated a 400 ton per day mixed waste processing facility in Crestwood, Ill., that uses NRT equipment. Peter Brown of XL Recycling Corp. estimates that the plant recycles about 25 percent of its incoming waste. At the front end of the processing system, employees manually recover concrete, lumber, automobile batteries, glass and paper. NRT's automated waste separation system then processes the remainder of the mixed waste. The Crestwood facility recently began producing a densified refuse derived fuel and plans to begin composting organic materials separated from the mixed waste stream in the near future. (The Crestwood facility is not considered a large-scale densified refuse derived fuel plant, however. In contrast to Reuter's plant, whose primary purpose is to produce a densified refuse derived fuel, densified refuse derived fuel is one of many methods employed by the Crestwood facility to divert solid waste from landfills.) Brown also told IRRC that XL Recycling plans to expand its operations in Crestwood and to begin operation of a slightly larger mixed waste processing facility in Champagne County, Ill., in 1992. The facility will most likely use NRT equipment.[180]

JWP Energy and Environment Inc., a subsidiary of **JWP Inc.**, and **Ventech Energy & Development Corp.**, a subsidiary of **Ventech Inc.** of Pasadena, Tex., a privately owned engineering and construction firm, are developing a 600 ton per day facility in Louisville, Ky., that will use NRT separation equipment to recover recyclables from the mixed waste stream and burn densified refuse derived fuel. Another JWP subsidiary, Energy Products Inc., will supply a fluidized bed combustor to burn the fuel. The plant will produce steam for sale to a local plant owned by E.I. du Pont de Nemours & Co. and its combustion ash will be used in the production of Portland cement.[181]

Other Mixed Waste Processing Facilities

Neutralysis Industries Inc., a wholly owned subsidiary of **Neutralysis Industries Ltd. Pty.**, is pursuing development of plants that produce lightweight aggregate from municipal solid waste. The aggregate can be added to concrete to form a block one-third lighter than normal cement blocks that still retains its strength. Lightweight structural concrete has many building applications, including skyscrapers, and Neutralysis estimates the lightweight aggregate market to be 8 to 10 million tons per year. Robert Merdes of Neutralysis Industries told IRRC that unlike most waste disposal systems, the Brisbane system was spurred on by a need for inexpensive lightweight aggregate, not the garbage crisis. Neutralysis's patented system, which has been in operation at a small demonstration plant in Brisbane, Australia, since 1988, combines municipal solid waste with clay and some form of moisture, most likely sewage sludge. The garbage serves as both a fuel source and bloating agent for the mix, which is fired at 2,100 degrees Fahrenheit yet produces no bottom ash. The company envisions receiving revenues from solid waste and sewage sludge disposal fees and from sales of the aggregate. Because the waste must be processed to remove metals before it is made into aggregate, Neutralysis plants also will have the capability to recover and sell recyclables from the waste stream.[182]

Neutralysis Industries is pursuing plants outside Chicago and in Michigan, New England and the Southeast. Merdes says the company is considering vertically integrating to produce the lightweight blocks itself, adding that it also is investigating the production of plastic lumber. Neutralysis is planning a private placement offering in 1991.[183]

In contrast to the mixed waste processing plants discussed thus far that include a heavily automated component, some companies use primarily manual labor to process mixed waste. The waste often is commercial waste, which is generally rich with paper. Unless properly managed, however, manually picking recyclables out of the mixed waste stream poses hazards: dangers include cuts from sharp objects hidden in the waste stream, such as glass, metals and needles, and the spread of infectious diseases.

Allied Sanitation, a Brooklyn firm hauling commercial waste, recycles more than 300 of the 1,500 tons per day of mixed waste it hauls. Allied Sanitation dumps the commercial waste into one of three areas at its processing facility: recyclables-rich, recyclables-light, or average. The waste is then fed onto elevated conveyors from which workers manually pick off cardboard, metal, wood and computer print-outs.[184]

Rabanco Inc. of Seattle, Wash., which processes source-separated recyclables at its materials recovery facility, also accepts selected mixed commercial loads that have less than 10 percent unrecoverable material. Its employees pull out some recyclables and garbage as the mixed waste moves down a conveyor belt. Corrugated containers and mixed waste paper continue down the conveyor to a baler. In a joint venture with Browning-Ferris Industries Inc., called Trans Industries, Rabanco is designing a new $18.3 million transfer station that will recover as much as 25 percent of incoming wastes. Most of the recovery will be from commercial wastes and construction and demolition debris; only 6 percent of household wastes are expected to be retrieved for recycling.[185]

Wastech Inc. of Portland, Ore., accepts loads with as much as 60 to 70 percent unrecoverable material. To process the material, it uses conveyors to spread out the waste, a trommel to separate waste into large and small sizes, and workers to pull out the desired items for baling. Wastech is planning an expansion at its plant and plans to produce densified refuse derived fuel from contaminated paper.[186]

Delta Waste Services Inc. of Roswell, Ga., designed and constructed a 500 ton per day plant in High Point, N.C., that processes primarily commercial, but also residential, wastes. R. Vance Howard of Delta Waste Services told IRRC that about 25 percent of the incoming waste is separated, primarily through manual means. The plant also uses some magnetic separation for ferrous metals. The company plans to build a 250 ton per day facility in Onslow County, N.C., that will process a mixture of residential and commercial waste, also primarily through manual separation.[187]

Future of Mixed Waste Processing

Of the companies offering mixed waste processing—primarily composting companies, densified refuse derived fuel producers and companies focusing on retrieving recyclables—the composting vendors are making the most headway today. Many municipalities have become wary of densified refuse derived fuel facilities after watching the difficulties their operators have encountered in establishing markets and producing a quality fuel product. Passage of the Clean Air Act amendments may spur renewed industrial interest in refuse derived fuel, though, providing densified refuse derived fuel developers with an opportunity to restore confidence in their systems.

The future of mixed waste processors focusing on retrieving recyclables from the waste stream is, in large part, dependent on the success of curbside recycling programs. When implementing a recycling program, most municipalities have opted for a program involving source separation, generally curbside recycling programs that sometimes include a materials recovery facility. Vendors of mixed waste processing have had limited success thus far in persuading municipalities that mixed waste processing is a superior method of retrieving recyclables from the waste stream. Given the relatively short life of most municipal recycling programs, good cost data are limited. If curbside programs prove to be substantially more expensive than expected or if citizens balk at participating in these programs, mixed waste processors may be able to make more inroads as a recycling alternative. Mixed waste vendors tout their technology as the most economical means of meeting state or locally mandated recycling requirements. National Recovery Technologies Inc. says its system sorts for about $12 a ton what it would cost a materials recovery facility more than $100 a ton or more to sort.[188] Guaranteeing 100 percent participation rates each time garbage is collected, some vendors report diversion rates of around 25 percent—a common goal of state and local entities and EPA's goal for the nation by 1992. Critics of mixed waste processing, though, say the poor quality of materials pulled from an unsorted waste stream will render them of little value to industry. They add that a good portion of the material mixed waste processors say they are diverting is simply an aggregate of glass and grit that is used as a landfill cover and is of no use to industry.

Composting, though, has attracted the interest of municipalities around the country. A recent survey of 165 solid waste managers found that the number of communities including some type of composting as an element of their solid waste management plans will increase from approximately 20 percent to nearly 40 percent within the next five years.[189] Although more than 100 MSW composting facilities have been built around the world (primarily in Europe, South America and the Middle East),[190] composting facilities have a limited operating history in the United States. The two most pressing issues determining the future of the U.S. composting industry center on which materials are suitable for composting and market development. These two issues are integrally tied together, as the source of the compost has a direct effect on the end product and its potential market.

The nation lacks a consensus as to what materials are suitable for composting. Nearly all agree that yard wastes should be diverted from landfills and that composting is a logical means of handling them. Experts within the composting field disagree, though, whether waste that is not source separated should be composted. Many argue that composting mixed municipal solid waste without careful screening of recyclables and hazardous household wastes will virtually guarantee high levels of heavy metals in the finished product. Opponents also argue that "hot spots" of contaminants in the compost could go undetected even if the compost were tested several times. Other U.S. and European studies suggest, however, that if recyclables are pulled out, heavy metals are not a problem. Analysts also question the impact of compost made from municipal solid waste in the event that land use is changed. They question the consequences, for instance, if a golf course that used mixed waste compost is turned into an agricultural field 20 years down the road.

While wary of mixed waste composting, environmentalists approve of source-separated composting, where residents separate organic materials for recycling. Source-separated composting projects are on the rise, though the number is still quite small. It is questionable whether this strategy will be able to address components of the waste stream beyond yard wastes and some food wastes, though. Many question whether the costs of having residents separate organics from the waste stream—in combination with further processing at a centralized facility and a necessary public education program to eliminate contaminants—will price this option out of the waste disposal market. Others question whether Americans will be sufficiently educated and conscientious when sorting the waste stream to ensure a noncontaminated supply of organic materials. Industrial organic waste, such as waste from food processors, may be a more economical source of source-separated organic wastes.

Composting may not be the best option for all organic materials, however. Recycling some grades of paper for use by industry as a replacement for virgin materials, for instance, may be a more valuable use of waste paper than compost. But once paper has been repeatedly recycled or soiled, composting may be the most effective means of handling it.

Because it is an emerging industry, composting faces the added obstacle that it is a relatively unknown solid waste disposal option. "Even though interest in composting has increased, most local government officials—waste management staff and politicians alike—lack knowledge about composting technologies, environmental impacts and markets," says a report by the Gildea Resource Center's Community Environmental Council of Santa Barbara, Calif. "As a result, few composting projects move forward, even though composting will unquestionably play a vital role in achieving [state-mandated] goals."[191] (Several states, including New York, Florida, Louisiana, Maine and North Carolina, have determined that composting will qualify a municipality for having met state-mandated recycling guidelines.[192])

Procter & Gamble Co., a strong supporter of composting, estimates that when garbage disposal costs pass $50 per ton, a municipality or private operation will save money by installing a composting facility.[193] Environmental groups, counter, however, that regulators have been cautioning municipalities that some vendors may be understating the operation and maintenance costs of proposed facilities in order to close a deal.[194] Analysts also question the size of the market for compost derived from the mixed municipal solid waste stream, cautioning that it could become swamped if the country aggressively pursued a nationwide municipal solid waste composting strategy. Some analysts also question whether plants can count on a market for compost 20 years from now, given that most plants have an expected life of 20 to 30 years.

Procter & Gamble estimates that composting can reduce the country's solid waste burden by 49 percent, which is far greater than its 32 percent reduction estimate for recycling.[195] It is too soon to tell, however, if composting is a viable means of disposing of a sizable portion of the nation's municipal solid waste. The 1990s will serve as a proving ground for municipal solid waste composting systems in the United States, as a number of plants are scheduled to begin operation over the next few years. Moreover, composting developers told IRRC they see a steady stream of requests for proposals by communities seeking companies to build composting systems, which could translate into a steady stream of composting facilities beginning operation throughout the decade.

Chapter VIII
RECOVERING ENERGY FROM MUNICIPAL SOLID WASTE

Waste-to-energy facilities burn municipal solid waste—a heterogeneous, low-energy value, combustible fuel—and convert it into salable energy. Initiated in the 1970s by a handful of corporations and a government funded research and development program, the U.S. waste-to-energy industry burns more than 15 percent of the nation's municipal solid waste.[1] The Environmental Protection Agency formally has recognized waste-to-energy as the third tier in its four-tier solid waste management hierarchy of reduction, recycling, incineration and landfilling.[2]

Following a burst of orders for waste-to-energy plants in the mid-1980s, the waste-to-energy industry's momentum has slowed considerably. Kidder, Peabody & Co. Inc.'s annual survey of waste-to-energy project awards reveals that awards between 1986 and 1990 remained flat, totaling close to 13,000 tons per day each year. In 1989, it appeared that awards had risen 24 percent, but about one-third of those awards have since fallen by the wayside. The title of Kidder, Peabody's 1990 annual survey described the situation aptly: "Business Remains Sluggish."[3] Richard Sweetnam Jr., vice president of Kidder, Peabody, commented in early 1991 that "It will be tough for the waste-to-energy industry to get any slower than it has been in the last two years. Also, many plants that have been awarded have been subsequently canceled. That trend is clearly continuing."[4] Despite Sweetnam's prediction, however, preliminary information suggests that 1991 has been an even slower year for the industry, with awards down from 1990 levels.[5]

The cancellations and downturn in orders can be attributed to a number of factors, including an emphasis (sometimes mandated) on municipal recycling programs, insufficient data on the amount of waste a community can recycle and a resulting uncertainty regarding how large to size a waste-to-energy plant, continuing public acceptance and siting problems, uncertainty over air pollution control requirements (that largely were resolved in late 1990 with passage of the Clean Air Act amendments), uncertainty over ash disposal requirements, and tax law changes that eliminated tax credits and made it more difficult to obtain tax-exempt financing.

Waste-to-energy plants release air emissions and produce an ash that must be disposed of in landfills. The extent of the air pollution and toxicity of the ash are highly controversial topics debated at length between supporters and opponents of these plants. In addition, some opponents of the plants, who would prefer to see a reduction in the amount of waste generated and more emphasis given to recycling, contend that building waste-to-energy plants provides incentives to generate garbage in order to make projects profitable. Few of the first communities that chose the waste-to-energy option placed significant weight on the potential impact of recycling. They sized plants to dispose of virtually the entire waste stream and signed "put or pay clauses"—a traditional component of waste-to-energy contracts to assure financing, whereby municipalities pay for the disposal of a minimum tonnage of waste, regardless of whether they deliver it to the plant. Some communities that later decided to pursue recycling programs discovered that they would compete for waste needed to meet tonnage requirements.

In recent years, waste-to-energy projects have deflected criticisms that incineration is incompatible with recycling by structuring projects to provide recycling incentives, such as service fee reductions, adjustments to the "put or pay" guarantees, and system financing to construct and operate recycling facilities along with waste-to-energy facilities. As for plants in the planning and procurement stage, municipalities and the industry have become more cognizant of factoring in the impact of a recycling program on the waste stream when sizing waste-to-energy plants. Moreover, the surge in recycling programs in recent years has provided municipalities with better data to help them make that assessment.

Despite the downturn in awards for new waste-to-energy facilities, Figure 8-1 shows that plant completions have been steady in the latter part of the 1980s and into the 1990s. These projects generally were begun in the boom years of the mid-1980s. Because the market has remained flat since then, and given the long lead time needed to build these facilities, there will be a fall-off in plant completions beginning in the mid-1990s.

In the fall of 1990, 128 waste-to-energy facilities and another 40 municipal solid waste incinerators were operating in the United States. Altogether, these plants have the capacity to process 28.6 million tons of municipal solid waste annually. Another 19 waste-to-energy plants, with the capacity to process 6 million tons of waste, were under construction, and another 75

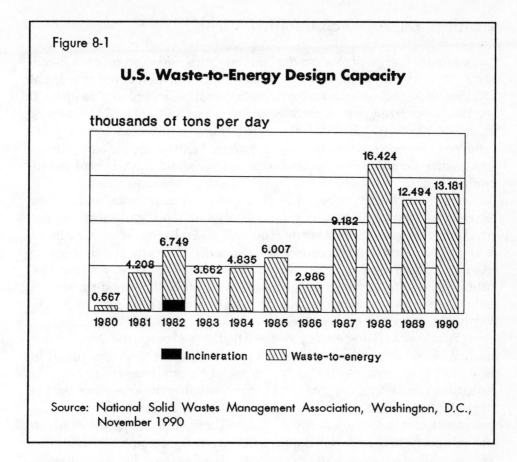

Figure 8-1

U.S. Waste-to-Energy Design Capacity

thousands of tons per day

16.424

13.181

12.494

9.182

6.749

6.007

4.835

4.208

3.662

2.986

0.567

1980 1981 1982 1983 1984 1985 1986 1987 1988 1989 1990

■ Incineration   ▨ Waste-to-energy

Source: National Solid Wastes Management Association, Washington, D.C., November 1990

(including inactive projects) were in the planning stages.[6] (Some of these projects in the planning stage are unlikely to be completed.)

A major reason for the growth of these plants during the 1980s has been greater access to the electricity market created by The Public Utility Regulatory Policies Act. In the past, the high capital costs associated with incineration made most projects financially or politically infeasible. Selling recovered energy could have provided the additional revenue to make projects economically or politically palatable, but reliable energy buyers were not in abundance during the 1970s. Steam customers, who historically have composed the bulk of the energy buyers' market, often will not sign long-term purchase contracts, which can contribute to a project's financial viability. Passage of PURPA in 1978, however, created a more stable market for energy production in the form of electricity sales to utilities. Accordingly, financing proposals for new waste-to-energy facilities rely on energy revenues to offset from 35 to 70 percent of the capital and operating costs of waste-to-energy plants.

Waste-to-Energy Technologies

Waste-to-energy plants are designed to burn waste around the clock, seven days a week, at high temperatures. Nearly 80 percent of municipal solid waste is combustible, and incineration reduces its volume by up to 90 percent. The average ton of garbage will produce 4,000 to 6,000 pounds of steam or 400 to 600 kWh of electricity, the amount used by a typical residential electric customer over one month. With noncombustible items removed, it takes about two pounds of municipal solid waste to replace one pound of coal.

Garbage incineration began in 1885 in the United States, and energy recovery started in 1898. The primary focus of these early incineration efforts was the reduction of waste. The 1973 oil embargo, however, placed new emphasis on energy sources at the same time the public became concerned about the potentially adverse environmental impact of landfills. Public demand for environmentally sound landfills, the founding of EPA and its subsequent regulations, and the enactment of the Clean Air Act all began adding to landfill expenses.

In response to rising energy and waste disposal costs, the government began funding the research and development of waste-to-energy plants in the early 1970s, primarily through EPA and the Department of Energy. At the same time, several corporations began pursuing the emerging market for privatization of full service design, engineering, construction and operation of modern waste-to-energy facilities. These firms acquired rights to incineration technologies developed primarily by Europeans, who had been burning municipal solid waste since the 1950s using mass-burn technology, which is designed to incinerate unprocessed solid waste.

Spurred by both the energy crisis and the burgeoning environmental movement, EPA chose to experiment with new incineration technologies, such as refuse derived fuel systems and pyrolysis, which chemically decomposes organic wastes in a high-temperature, oxygen-deficient chamber. Refuse derived fuel plants built during the 1970s were designed to recover ferrous metals, glass and other noncombustibles and process the remaining solid waste into a transportable fuel. As these plants experienced machinery jams, explosions and other problems, however, the majority were closed down. Their failure has been attributed to unproven and complex resource recovery technologies, overly technical and elaborate concepts, the unsuccessful scale-up of demonstration models and underestimated capital and operating costs. In addition, markets for the recovered material failed to materialize. *Fortune* reported that write-offs on these plants between 1980 and the end of 1984 alone totaled an estimated $300 million.

Today's U.S. waste-to-energy industry is developing second, third and fourth generations of resource recovery facilities, producing from 1 mega-watt of power to nearly 80 megawatts. The nation's 128 waste-to-energy plants, including both electricity and steam producers, have the capacity to generate more than 2,000 megawatts of electricity.[7]

The first major wave of new mass burn plants that produce electricity began operating in 1987. The bulk of these plants are waterwall mass-burn facilities. Other mass burn waste-to-energy plants are controlled-air or refractory-lined incinerators, and some plants rely on refuse derived fuel technology. Each is described below.

Mass burn: Mass burn technology is the technology of choice for most modern waste-to-energy facilities. A mass burn system incinerates munici-pal waste with little pre-processing, and its simpler operating system translates into lower capital costs. In most instances, collection trucks dump refuse into a receiving pit and the refuse is then transferred by overhead cranes to a furnace feed chute, where moving grates carry the waste through a furnace. Any materials to be recovered, usually only ferrous metals, are retrieved from the ash after combustion has taken place.

Technology specifically designed for mass burning municipal solid waste dates back to the end of the 19th century, and the technologies deriving energy from it were developed in Germany after World War II. Most of the U.S. mass burn facilities employ European technologies that have a proven track record in Europe and Southeast Asia. The more recently developed waterwall incinerators are constructed with walls of welded tubes through which water is circulated to absorb the heat of combustion. The steam produced often is used to generate electricity for sale to a utility. Refractory furnaces, which are seldom ordered today, have a temperature resistant coating that decreases the transfer of heat produced during the combustion process; energy is recovered by a boiler that is downstream from the combustion chamber.

The modular controlled-air incineration systems, with a design capacity of less than 50 tons per day for each modular unit, generally are pre-fabricated and shipped to the site. Also called starved-air incineration systems, they feed waste into a primary chamber where incomplete com-bustion results in the generation of combustible gas, which is burned in a second chamber, often in conjunction with natural gas or oil. This technol-ogy greatly reduces particulate emissions and generally produces low pressure steam for sale or in-house use rather than high pressure steam, which is used to generate electricity for sale to utilities.

Refuse derived fuel: Vendors of refuse derived fuel facilities have chosen to pursue the basic concept of preprocessing municipal solid waste before it is burned. These vendors, however, are employing new, simpler and more rugged technology than was found in the first generation of refuse derived fuel plants. Most will use dry processing to shred waste mechani-

Table 8-1

Waste-To-Energy Technologies

Technology	Number of Operating Plants	Annual Capacity (Million Tons)[a]	Number of Plants Under Construction	Annual Capacity (millions tons)[a]
Mass burn	53	15.2	15	5.4
RDF (burned on-site)	17	8.1	1	0.2
RDF (burned off-site)	8	1.0	1	N/A
Modular	50	1.8	1	<0.1

[a] Annual total assumes that plants operate at 85 percent of design capacity.

Source: National Solid Wastes Management Association, Washington, D.C., November 1990

cally, recover ferrous and other noncombustible materials, and produce fuel particles ranging up to six inches in size. Refuse derived fuel has a higher heat value than unprocessed waste, and the potentially higher energy revenues could help to offset the capital and operating costs of processing equipment. The removal of ferrous and other metals before combustion also results in fewer potential air pollutants.

Because of the failures associated with first generation plants of this technology, however, many municipalities have been deterred from selecting a second generation refuse derived fuel facility. In addition, many consider preprocessing itself a major disadvantage when waste can be burned with no preparation in a mass burn system. The high front end costs of refuse derived fuel technology make it uneconomic for most modular resource recovery systems.

A variation of the refuse derived fuel technology is the production of densified refuse derived fuel, which is designed to be burned off-site and often in conjunction with coal or other fuels. This technology and densified refuse derived fuel project developers are discussed in Chapter 7.

Efforts to commercialize pyrolysis have dwindled. Pyrolysis plants in Baltimore, Orlando and San Diego all have been closed down.

Economics of Waste-to-Energy Development

Waste-to-energy plants are capital-intensive, ranging in cost up to $300 million, and often constitute the largest public works project undertaken by a municipality. Some $7.5 billion has been spent on the 128 operating waste-to-energy plants and another 12 processing plants that produce densified refuse derived fuel, according to Governmental Advisory Associates Inc., a research firm in New York City that conducts an annual survey of resource recovery projects.[8]

Table 8-2 lists the construction costs, which range from $38 million to $276 million, of projects developed by the country's leading waste-to-energy developers. On a daily tonnage basis, the costs of projects in Table 8-2 range from $40,000 to $150,000 per daily ton of installed capacity. Tipping fees at modern waste-to-energy facilities range from less than $20 per ton to more than $80 per ton (including ash management).[9]

Most modern waste-to-energy projects have been developed through an alliance between a developer/vendor and the governmental body responsible for waste disposal—a municipality, county, district or regional waste authority. A public entity typically contracts with a full service vendor to build and operate a waste-to-energy facility for 20 to 30 years. Municipalities have commonly issued tax-exempt industrial development bonds and lent the proceeds to the developer/vendor to construct the plant. The developer/vendor generally has contributed from 20 to 30 percent of the estimated project cost in equity, making the investment through a limited or special purpose company or a limited or general partnership. In a few instances, project developers have used third-party leases to finance waste-to-energy facilities.

The bulk of electricity producing waste-to-energy facilities financed after 1980 are privately owned. William Montrone of Dillon, Read & Co. told IRRC that between 1980 and 1987 approximately 60 of the 65 major resource recovery financings of $25 million and more were privately owned. Municipalities have preferred private ownership for several reasons. Because of the failures of the 1970s, many municipalities have chosen to shift risks to an outside party, including construction cost and schedule, operating costs and technical performance. In addition, through 1985, private ownership allowed developers to invest up to 25 percent equity to take advantage of tax benefits, which resulted in lower bond issues, and therefore lower disposal costs, than if the project were publicly owned. Tax advantages applicable to waste-to-energy facilities through 1985 included relatively rapid depreciation, a 10 percent investment tax credit, and a deduction for interest expenses.

The 1986 Tax Reform Act, however, eliminated the investment tax credit for new projects, although it did include a transition rule that grandfathered projects that had a binding municipal agreement or had commitments of $200,000 by March 1986. Developers who anticipated that tax changes would be effective at the beginning of 1986 rushed to arrange financing in 1985, resulting in a surge of bond issues that closed in the last quarter of that year. (It should be noted, though, that some escrow financings completed at the end of 1984 and 1985 to capture tax benefits did not result in completed projects.) The elimination of tax credits has produced a more even split between public and private ownership for planned projects. The National Solid Wastes Management Association reports that public and private project ownership is roughly equal for plants under construction, in the planning stage and inactive. The private sector, though, is slated to operate nearly 95 percent of these planned plants.[10]

The 1986 Tax Reform Act also required states to lower their caps on private activity tax-exempt bonds—bonds commonly used by waste-to-energy developers. The bill reduced state allocations by one-third to $50 per capita in 1988, down from $75 per capita in 1986. Resource recovery bond activity surged again in the last quarter of 1987 as developers rushed to obtain an allocation of a state's cap on private activity tax-exempt bonds. As Figure 8-2 shows, tax-exempt bonds have dominated waste-to-energy financings. As a result of the 1986 tax bill, however, the number of taxable bonds is likely to grow as public works projects compete for money allocated under the state caps.

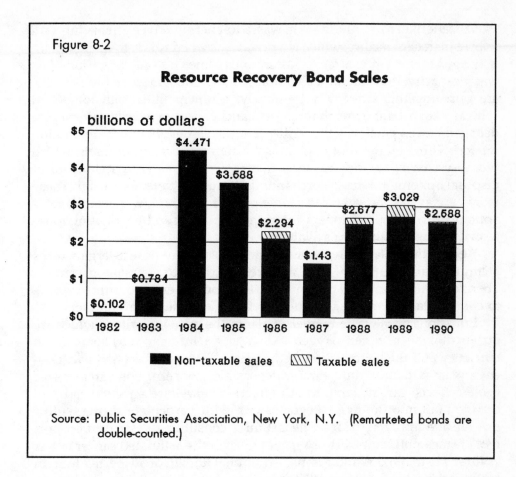

Figure 8-2

Resource Recovery Bond Sales

billions of dollars

1982: $0.102
1983: $0.784
1984: $4.471
1985: $3.588
1986: $2.294
1987: $1.43
1988: $2.677
1989: $3.029
1990: $2.588

■ Non-taxable sales   ▨ Taxable sales

Source: Public Securities Association, New York, N.Y. (Remarketed bonds are double-counted.)

Waste-to-energy projects are typically financed through a project financing approach, with limited recourse to the private sponsor and the municipality. Disposal (or tipping) fees, energy revenues and recovered materials compose the revenue stream of a waste-to-energy facility, with the first two generally under long-term contract. Recovered materials, primarily ferrous materials, generally account for less than 5 percent of total revenues. Energy revenues can contribute from 35 to 70 percent of the plant's revenues, and disposal fees provide the balance. In some states, the local government has the power to raise additional revenues for a project through property taxes, assessments and service charges levied against property owners. The most recent trend in solid waste financing is system financing, whereby a municipality finances a waste-to-energy facility or landfill and a materials recovery facility. As more communities pursue an integrated waste management plan, this type of financing is likely to increase.

An alternative to traditional waste-to-energy project financing is a hybrid merchant facility, which is a privately owned waste-to-energy plant that signs long-term contracts with municipalities for only a portion of its waste capacity. Wheelabrator Technologies Inc. and American Ref-Fuel Co. are pursuing this strategy aggressively. Municipalities with long-term contracts serve as the merchant plant's anchor and may issue tax-exempt debt to finance a portion of the facility. The developer obtains the remaining capacity either on the spot market or through short-term contracts, which typically pay higher tipping fees. If sited in an area with a shortage of disposal options, a hybrid merchant plant could be very successful. These plants are at risk, however, to municipalities finding lower cost disposal options or to other developers entering the market and negotiating long-term contracts for the area's available waste.

Regulation: Generally, waste-to-energy plants are close to large sources of municipal solid waste and, as a result, close to population centers. Therefore, environmental concerns raised about air emissions from waste-to-energy plants are a major issue affecting their rate of development.

Emissions from waste-to-energy plants, the great majority of which are carbon dioxide, nitrogen, oxygen and water, are influenced by combustion efficiency and the composition of the waste. EPA has classified waste-to-energy air pollutants into three categories of concern: non-carcinogenic health effects, carcinogenic health effects and welfare effects. Lead and mercury fall into the first category along with particulate matter, sulfur dioxide and nitrogen oxides. The last three constitute the greatest proportion of stack pollutants. EPA says that most of the estimated cancer risk is attributable to dioxins and furans. Additional known or suspected human carcinogens are arsenic, beryllium, cadmium and chromium, which are heavy metals. Also included in the second category are organic carcinogens, such as chlorobenzenes, chlorophenols, formaldehyde, polycyclic aromatic hydrocarbons and polychlorinated biphenyls. As for the third category—welfare effects—acid gas hydrogen chloride is of top concern.

In early 1991, EPA issued its long-awaited New Source Performance Standards (NSPS) for municipal waste combustors with capacities of more than 250 tons per day. William Rosenberg, EPA's assistant administrator for air and radiation, estimated that the new rule will eliminate "more than 200,000 tons of pollutants a year by 1994," the date by which the NSPS are to be fully implemented. New plants, defined as plants that began construction after December 1989, must limit emissions of heavy metals and organics, such as dioxins and furans, by more than 99 percent, sulfur dioxide and hydrogen chloride by 90 to 95 percent and nitrogen oxide by about 40 percent. The NSPS also sets operating standards for optimum combustion as a means of reducing pollutants. For operating plants, the NSPS calls for scrubbers and for plants to take steps to "insure optimum combustion."

They also must reduce heavy metal emissions by 97 percent, organic emissions by 95 percent and acid gases by about 75 percent.[11]

The Clean Air Act amendments signed into law by President Bush in November 1990 require EPA to bring the NSPS into compliance with the Clean Air Act by November 1991 (for plants larger than 250 tons per day). EPA, however, is not likely to promulgate the standards for at least another year. The Clean Air Act amendments stipulate that the standards reflect maximum achievable control technology (MACT), which is a step up from the Best Demonstrated Technology (BDT) that EPA uses as a basis for establishing performance standards. For new plants, MACT can be no less stringent than the best performing similar unit. For existing plants, MACT can be no less stringent than the best performing 12 percent of existing units.[12] Under the Clean Air Act amendments, EPA also is required to issue specific limitations for lead, cadmium and mercury.[13]

The most common form of air pollution control device at operating waste-to-energy facilities is electrostatic precipitators, which remove particulate matter. As Figure 8-3 shows, nearly 50 percent of 52 operating mass burn plants surveyed by the National Solid Wastes Management Association have electrostatic precipitators. A combination of a scrubber and fabric filter is used at nearly 40 percent of these plants, and 50 percent have continuous emissions monitoring. Electrostatic precipitators are losing ground in the waste-to-energy field, though. Stricter state permitting standards have virtually dictated that air pollution control devices at planned waste-to-energy plants be a combination of scrubbers and fabric filters. In addition, continuous emissions monitoring, with the results sometimes going directly to an overseeing state agency, is becoming the standard for waste-to-energy facilities. John Phillips of Ogden Martin Systems Inc. credits the waste-to-energy industry with having pioneered continuous emissions monitoring in response to permit requirements, adding that the industry is one of the country's most regulated.[14] Nearly 65 percent of 46 planned mass burn facilities surveyed by the NSWMA will have continuous monitoring systems.[15] Measurements often required include levels of oxygen, carbon monoxide, carbon dioxide, nitrogen oxide, hydrochloric acid, total hydrocarbons, temperature and opacity.[16]

Under a proposed version of NSPS, EPA called for waste-to-energy plants to separate 25 percent of their incoming waste for recycling. EPA abandoned this measure in December 1990, though, under pressure from the Presidential Council on Competitiveness, whose chairman is Vice President Dan Quayle.[17] Both industry and some municipalities had argued that the requirement was an impractical attempt to make industry an enforcer of public policy, adding that the requirement could jeopardize badly needed disposal capacity. In the spring of 1991, though, the Natural Resources Defense Council and the state attorneys general for New York and Florida sued EPA to reinstate a recycling requirement for waste-to-energy facilities. NRDC's David Doniger asserted that "the council's decision reneged on President Bush's campaign promise to support recycling."[18]

The Clean Air Act amendments also require operator training and certification for waste-to-energy plant operators. The waste-to-energy industry already has begun addressing this issue, working with the American Society of Mechanical Engineers to develop and implement the "Standard for the Qualification and Certification of Resource Recovery Facility Operators." Released in March 1990, the standard sets forth the qualifications for the two principal operators at combustion facilities but does not involve any training.[19]

Ash disposal—Another pressing environmental issue is ash disposal. Although waste-to-energy plants can reduce the volume of waste by up to 90 percent, the ash resulting from combustion typically goes to a landfill. Generally, ash from waste-to-energy plants goes to local sanitary landfills. At issue is whether incinerator ash should be sent to a dedicated ash landfill (monofill) or be classified as a hazardous waste and be sent to more costly hazardous waste landfills that have more stringent standards for design and operation.

Ash from waste-to-energy plants may contain concentrated heavy metals, polyaromatic hydrocarbons and dioxins. Fly ash—the ash captured from stack gases—normally contains higher heavy metal concentrations than bottom ash, which is the ash remaining on the combustion grates or in the furnace after the refuse is burned. Bottom ash accounts for roughly 90 percent of a plant's ash, and most facilities have been mixing the fly and bottom ash regularly before disposal.

In 1987, EPA announced that waste-to-energy facility operators had a legal obligation to determine whether their ash has hazardous characteristics or the potential to become toxic. EPA developed a toxicity test to make this determination, and at the direction of Congress, replaced it with a new test in the fall of 1990. The new test—the Toxic Characteristic Leaching Procedure (TCLP)—identifies levels of 25 organic chemicals in addition to the eight metals and six pesticides and herbicides included in the old test. Results from the two tests on metals have been similar, with the exception of lead, which has tested higher under the new one.[20]

EPA has lobbied Congress to modify the Resource Conservation and Recovery Act to create a special category for municipal incinerator ash and says it is looking to Congress to clarify the issue before it publishes final guidelines on waste-to-energy ash disposal. When it passed the Clean Air Act amendments n the fall of 1990, Congress exempted ash from regulation as a hazardous waste for two years, with the intent of allowing itself time to deal with ash disposal under RCRA.

Figure 8-3

Air Pollution Control Equipment
Percentage in Existing Waste-to-Energy Plants

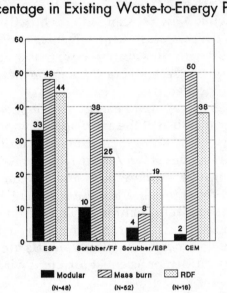

Modular (N=48) **Mass burn** (N=52) **RDF** (N=16)

Percentage in Planned Waste-to-Energy Plants

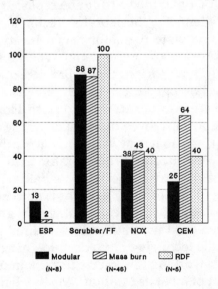

Modular (N=8) **Mass burn** (N=46) **RDF** (N=5)

Source: National Solid Wastes Management Association, Washington, D.C., November 1990

EPA's position has left a vacuum at the federal level on the issue of ash disposal. Moreover, reauthorization of RCRA is not expected until 1992. Not waiting for federal action, several states have taken the lead on ash disposal and have come up with various strategies. Michigan, for example, has legislated incinerator ash as a "special" waste that must be disposed of in dedicated landfills, while New York and Massachusetts regulate waste-to-energy ash as a "special" waste. In Pennsylvania, New Jersey and Rhode Island, ash is tested to determine appropriate disposal, and still other states are requiring testing of ash to establish a database on the effects of recycling, rather than to determine disposal.[21]

Looking to the future, waste-to-energy developers envision the day when they will eliminate much of the ash disposal by producing products with ash. This strategy would allow them to avoid landfill disposal fees and potentially generate revenues simultaneously. Potential uses for ash, primarily bottom ash, include offshore reefs and erosion control, roadbase material, asphalt and cover for landfills. Environmentalists, however, are opposed to mixing ash with asphalt or concrete, citing the potential for contamination. "If you do that, it's out of a controlled environment and into the general stream of commerce. The heavy metals are still there," commented Richard Denison, senior scientist for the Environmental Defense Fund."[22]

The New York State Energy Research and Development Authority released a study in the spring of 1991 determining that up to 30 percent of aggregate from asphalt paving mixes could be replaced by processed ash from waste-to-energy plants.[23] Wheelabrator Technologies also has been working with federal and state regulatory agencies to demonstrate that bottom ash can be used as an aggregate material. Wheelabrator worked with the State University of New York at Stony Brook, Long Island, and the Florida Institute of Technology in the development of ocean reefs and construction material made partially from bottom ash. Florida's department of environmental regulation approved the company's use of "McKaynite"— a material made from ash that can substitute for other aggregates in roadbase and asphalt construction. Wheelabrator used bottom ash in an 800-foot section of an asphalt road leading to its Baltimore, Md., facility.[24] Asea Brown Boveri Resource Recovery Systems is marketing the Aardelite process, a Dutch technology that creates a light weight gravel from fly ash. The technology has been used with ash from coal-fired plants since 1988, and ABB is marketing the technology for waste-to-energy facilities.[25]

Wheelabrator also is working to stabilize its remaining ash, namely fly ash, and has built a pilot plant at its Millbury, Mass., plant to test technologies. In 1990, Wheelabrator's patented PureFill™ technology was licensed for use by one of its competitors at a New York facility.[26]

The Waste-to-Energy Industry

Waste-to-energy is a maturing industry, with most vendors serving as developers. A few companies in the industry have a background in waste services and access to landfills—American Ref-Fuel, which is partially owned by Browning-Ferris Industries Inc., and Wheelabrator Technologies, which is partially owned by Waste Management Inc., are prime examples. The majority of companies in this field have engineering and construction experience, primarily in the power and process industries. As their traditional markets waned in the early 1980s, these companies began targeting the waste-to-energy market for future growth. Many adopted the strategy of designing, building, operating and often owning waste-to-energy plants. Many have created resource recovery subsidiaries or divisions within their companies, and, in several cases, also have obtained rights to a proprietary European incineration technology. The leading companies in the power and process industry also have an advantage in the waste-to-energy industry because the investment community and municipalities often prefer to work with "brand-name" companies.

The waste-to-energy field is very competitive. Although many companies have been interested in entering the industry, a much smaller number have successfully penetrated the market and negotiated contracts with municipalities. High market entry costs deter most small companies from entering the business, although a few have been successful by initiating a project and then teaming up with a major developer. In addition, the long lead-time associated with waste-to-energy plant development means that it takes years until projects begin producing revenues to replenish the developers' coffers. Claims have surfaced in the industry that vendors are abandoning sound pricing and underbidding to win contracts. In any event, increasing competition in bidding has driven some players from the market and has prevented many others from entering. One of the most publicized exits was made by Dravo Corp., which left the waste-to-energy field after posting major losses that were attributed, in part, to cost overruns for waste-to-energy projects.

The new emphasis on integrated solid waste management has led many waste-to-energy vendors to incorporate some form of support for recycling into their corporate policies. While some companies simply state their support for recycling efforts, others are becoming actively involved in offering a variety of waste disposal services. Sweetnam of Kidder, Peabody maintains that success in the resource recovery business will require "a well thought-out business strategy, not just dealing with the waste-to-energy industry per se, but the solid waste collection and disposal market as a whole. It's becoming a more complicated game."[27] Ogden Projects Inc. is offering collection services for recyclables and to build and operate materials recovery facilities either as stand-alone operations or in combination with waste-to-energy plants, and Wheelabrator Technologies can draw upon the expertise of Waste Management Inc., its majority owner, to provide recycling services. Wheelabrator also recently acquired a company that composts yard wastes.

Waste-to-energy developers maintain that recycling and waste incineration are compatible, and complementary, solid waste disposal options. Acknowledging that "recycling is the major trend for the 1990s," ABB Resource Recovery Systems President James H. Miller says his company is supportive of recycling programs, adding that recycling "is important from a pollution prevention standpoint for combustion, and can play an important economic role, too."[28] Recycling removes or reduces several types of materials that yield no benefit to the combustion process but that can damage boilers in waste-to-energy plants. Glass cans and bottles, for instance, have no heating value yet melt in boilers at 2,000 degrees Fahrenheit to form slag. (Waste-to-energy plants typically run at maximum temperatures ranging from 1,800 to 2,200 degrees Fahrenheit.) Slag builds up on the tube surface and reduces heat transfer and, therefore, a plant's energy efficiency. Aluminum melts at 1,200 degrees Fahrenheit and clogs air circulation holes in some plants' boilers, also reducing energy efficiency.[29] Economics also play a role because all the glass and metal entering an incinerator ends us in the incinerator ash, which is sometimes costly to landfill.[30] ABB also points out that removing metal improves the potential for developing other uses for ash.[31]

Yard wastes, which compose nearly 20 percent of the municipal solid waste stream, can lead to inefficient combustion in a waste-to-energy plant. Wet leaves can actually have a net negative heating value, while dry leaves can have a heat value of up to 7,000 Btus per pound. The wide variability in the heat value requires greater operator attention and control and can increase emissions and ash generation. The seasonal nature of yard waste also creates problems, with the influx of leaves in autumn in some communities straining the capacity of facilities.[32]

Paper and plastics are the primary combustible elements in trash. Paper and plastics together contribute 80 to 90 percent of the chlorine, which corrodes metal tubes in the boilers, in municipal solid waste. Reducing these materials could reduce maintenance over the life of a waste-to-energy unit.[33] Plastic products, which are made from petrochemicals, have the highest fuel energy value for modern waste-to-energy incinerators. Polystyrene, for example, has an energy content of 17,800 Btu a pound, roughly four times that of average municipal solid waste.[34] While at first glance, it would seem illogical for waste-to-energy developers to welcome giving up this tremendous heat source, Wheelabrator argues that removal of a portion of the plastics is beneficial. Wheelabrator says that because waste-to-energy facilities are Btu-input restricted, less trash moves through the furnace when the heat value increases. Therefore, removing some plastics controls the potentially excessive heat value of trash, allows more trash to be processed, and increases revenues.[35]

Miller of ABB says that "recycling does reduce the total Btu level by reducing the quantity of waste available from existing supply sources, but over the long haul, the effect will not be of a major impact. The waste we see today is increasing in Btu content, and a great deal of paper is not recoverable."[36] Foster Wheeler also has determined that energy output and revenues do not decline as much as might be expected when a recycling program removes materials going to a waste-to-energy facility. Foster Wheeler compared two facilities, each designed to process 1,000 tons of waste daily. One burned all 1,000 tons; the other burned 650 tons a day and recycled and composted the remainder. Foster Wheeler determined that although the fuel for the second plant declined by 35 percent, energy output and earnings declined by only 26 percent. Foster attributed the results to a higher energy content of a more uniform fuel following recycling.[37] Producing a more uniform fuel also is a plus; the heterogeneous nature of solid waste creates many operational challenges.

Waste-to-energy developers: Kidder, Peabody & Co. has identified 20 vendors that have been awarded two or more contracts to build waste-to-energy facilities. The vendors are dominated by a handful of companies that held 5 percent or more of the capacity of projects awarded through the fall of 1990. Wheelabrator Technologies led the pack with 18 percent of the market, followed closely by Ogden Projects, which represented 17 percent of the market. American Ref-Fuel, a joint venture of Air Products and Chemicals Inc. and Browning-Ferris Industries, held 8 percent of the market; Westinghouse Corp., 7 percent; Asea Brown Boveri Resource Recovery Systems, 7 percent; and Foster Wheeler Corp., 5 percent.[38] Each of these companies is discussed in more detail below. Table 8-2 lists their waste-to-energy projects, including location, year of operation, municipal solid waste processing capacity, construction cost and plant owners.

Wheelabrator Environmental Systems Inc.: Wheelabrator Environmental Systems is an operating group of Wheelabrator Technologies Inc., which develops facilities and provides services to the energy, environmental and general industries markets. The first major player in the industry, Wheelabrator began processing municipal solid waste in 1975, and its facilities have cumulatively processed more than 25 million tons of municipal solid waste.[39] Wheelabrator has exclusive rights in the United States and Mexico to build waste-to-energy plants utilizing the Swiss Von Roll mass-burning technology, which has been in use since 1954. Wheelabrator operates 12 waste-to-energy plants and has two plants under construction that range in size from 200 to 3,000 tons per day. (Wheelabrator declined to provide information on projects under development.) All but four of the projects recover ferrous material from incinerator ash. Although Wheelabrator Environmental Systems' contract awards of 27,625 tons per day led the industry in the fall of 1990, the company received no awards in 1990 and only one in 1989.[40]

Wheelabrator Technologies became a separate public company in December 1988 as part of a corporate reorganization of The Henley Group Inc. Also in 1988, Wheelabrator acquired certain assets of waste industry giant Waste Management Inc. in exchange for 22 percent of its common stock. In addition to three waste-to-energy projects, Waste Management contributed options on parcels of land at more than 100 waste disposal sites that it operates across the country—sites that could host future waste-to-energy facilities. In 1990, Waste Management increased its equity ownership of Wheelabrator Technologies' common stock from 22 percent to 55 percent.[41]

Wheelabrator's merger with Waste Management, the country's largest curbside recycler, strengthened its ability to offer recycling services. (See Chapter 6 for additional information on Waste Management's residential recycling programs.) Through Recycle First™, Wheelabrator offers its client communities front-end processing, materials recovery and yard waste recovery. Wheelabrator plans to build its first materials recovery facility in 1991 in Bucks County, Pa., and says it will be the nation's first project combining recycling and waste-to-energy to be built by the same developer. (See chapter 6 for additional information on the facility.) Wheelabrator says that it will pursue development of materials recovery facilities in other areas where it has waste-to-energy projects and that Waste Management will pursue materials recovery facilities elsewhere.[42] Wheelabrator also strengthened its ability to offer yard waste composting through a recent acquisition of International Process Systems Inc. of Glastonbury, Conn., which has a proprietary system that composts sewage sludge along with shredded papers, magazines, leaves and yard wastes.[43]

Ogden Martin Systems Inc.: Ogden Martin, which is a subsidiary of Ogden Projects Inc. along with Ogden Environmental Services Inc. and Ogden Recycling Systems Inc., is a full service waste-to-energy vendor, providing financing, design, engineering, construction, operation, maintenance and management services. Ogden Martin has exclusive rights to the Martin mass burning technology in the United States, Mexico, certain Caribbean countries and Canada.

In August 1989, Ogden Corp. had an initial public stock offering of 2.5 million shares, or a 7 percent stake, in its Ogden Projects subsidiary that yielded the company $35 million.[44] Ogden Corp. retains an 85 percent interest in Ogden Martin.[45]

By the fall of 1990, Ogden Projects had passed Wheelabrator Technologies in terms of the number of waste-to-energy contracts it had been awarded, but ranked second in terms of the amount of capacity awarded.[46] Ogden has 17 operating plants and 12 under development. The aggregate capacity of these plants is more than 28,000 tons per day. Ogden Projects recently acquired three projects through the purchase of Blount Energy Resource Corp. in May 1991. Blount had developed waste-to-energy projects in Warren County, N.J., and Minneapolis, Minn., and had been awarded a contract to develop a third in N. Kingston, R.I.

In the fall of 1987, Ogden Martin developed a corporate policy endorsing an integrated approach to resource recovery and recycling, saying that both are "integral to a sensible, comprehensive, and lasting policy" on solid waste disposal. Ogden says that it will work with communities in which it is building waste-to-energy plants to promote and coordinate recycling programs and that it will advise client communities on how to size waste-to-energy facilities that incorporate recycling programs. Ogden Projects also created a subsidiary, Ogden Recycling Systems Inc., to build recycling materials recovery facilities either as stand-alone facilities or in combination with waste-to-energy plants. To date, the company has not been awarded any projects.

American Ref-Fuel Co.: In 1984, Air Products and Chemicals Inc., an international supplier of industrial gases, chemicals, process equipment and related technology, and waste industry leader Browning-Ferris Industries (BFI) formed American Ref-Fuel to design, build, own and operate waste-to-energy plants. The joint venture is involved in six projects that cost between $88 million and $260 million and range in size from 600 to 2,250 tons per day. Its first project began operation in 1989 in Hempstead, N.Y.

American Ref-Fuel generally owns the projects it develops, often providing about 25 percent of the plant's equity. American Ref-Fuel also assists communities in analyzing recycling and landfilling opportunities and offers to develop Recycleries™—BFI systems that mechanically or manually sort recyclable materials. (See Chapter 6 for more information on BFI's residential recycling programs.) The terms of the Hempstead, N.Y., contract, for instance, called for BFI to assist the town in developing a recycling program. American Ref-Fuel is recovering ferrous metals from incinerator ash at its Hempstead, N.Y., facility and plans to do the same at its Oyster Bay, N.Y., and Newark, N.J., facilities.

American Ref-Fuel draws upon Air Products' experience in building and operating large industrial gas and chemical plants and in overseeing power purchase contracts with utilities. BFI contributes its knowledge of the municipal solid waste market and its exclusive North American licensing arrangement to market a German mass burning technology. In 1980, BFI acquired rights to Deutsche Babcock Anlagen's proprietary "Duesseldorf

Roller Grate," composed of a series of downward sloping, slowly rotating cylinders. The technology was developed more than 20 years ago and is used worldwide in 60 waste-to-energy plants, ranging in size from 250 to 3,000 tons per day. Deutsche Babcock Anlagen (DBA), a member of the multinational Deutsche Babcock Group, also designs and constructs codisposal waste-to-energy facilities that burn municipal solid waste and sewage sludge, and manufactures air quality control equipment. In some instances, BFI also may be able to provide private landfill capacity for ash or overflow from American Ref-Fuel's waste-to-energy plants.

Westinghouse Corp.: Westinghouse constructs and operates its waste-to-energy plants through its resource energy systems division. In 1990, Westinghouse represented 10 percent of waste-to-energy contracts awards, and in 1989 it represented 27 percent of the total awards.[47] Westinghouse operates three plants and has another five under development. The plants range in size from 400 to 2,688 tons per day and in cost from $38 million to $276 million.

Westinghouse's preferred role in the waste-to-energy market is an overall project manager, furnishing, maintaining and operating an engineered, procured and constructed facility. Westinghouse has provided, though, the combustor and boiler systems for waste-to-energy plants developed by other waste-to-energy companies. Westinghouse has patent rights to the water-cooled rotary O'Connor Combustor—the only mass burn technology developed in the United States. The technology involves feeding refuse into a slightly inclined barrel, which slowly turns the burning materials. Dry wastes are incinerated first, and moister wastes are burned as they tumble down to an afterburning grate. The O'Connor Combustor technology was licensed in Japan by Ishikawajime-Harima Heavy Industries in the mid-1970s, and more than 13 combustor units are operating in seven facilities in the United States and Japan.

Westinghouse offers an integrated approach that includes front-end recycling of noncombustible material, waste-to-energy and waste management. Monmouth County, N.J., selected Westinghouse to design, build and operate a waste-to-energy facility and a processing facility to separate recyclables from the waste stream.[48] Gaston County, N.C., also selected Westinghouse as the preferred vendor for an $8 million recycling facility that will be integrated with a waste-to-energy plant. The facility will process 3,500 tons of unsorted waste a week for recycling. Waste that cannot be recycled will be burned in the adjacent combustor.[49]

Asea Brown Boveri Resource Recovery Systems (ABB): ABB is a subsidiary of Asea Brown Boveri Group Ltd., a Swedish-Swiss company that has 1,150 fully or partly owned companies around the world.[50] Nearly 75 percent of the equipment, systems and services used in a typical refuse derived fuel plant are available through ABB operating subsidiaries. In early

Table 8-2

U.S. Projects of Leading Waste-To-Energy Developers

Company	Location	Year	Tons/Day	Construction Cost ($000)	Plant Owner
American Ref-Fuel Co.	Hempstead, N.Y.	1989	2,250	252,000	ARF
	Newark, N.J.	1991	2,250	260,000	ARF
	Preston, Conn.	1992	600	88,000	ARF
	Oyster Bay, N.Y.	1993	1,080	144,500	ARF
	Albany, N.Y.	1994	1,500	NA	ARF
	E. Bridgewater, Mass.	1994	1,500	NA	ARF
Asea Brown Boveri	Hartford, Conn.	1988	2,000	154,000	CRRA[a]
	Detroit, Mich.	1989	4,000	230,000	Detroit RRA[b]
	Honolulu, Hawaii	1990	2,160	193,500	Ford Motor[c]
	Rosemont, Minn.	1993	800	104,000	Dakota Cty.
Foster Wheeler Corp.	Norfolk, Va.	1967	360	NA	U.S. Navy
	Niagara Falls, N.Y.	1980	2,000	NA	Occidental[d]
	Commerce, Calif.	1986	400	NA	LA Sanitation[e]
	Charleston, S.C.	1989	600	65,000	AT&T
	Camden Cty., N.J.	1991	1,050	130,000	NA
	Hudson Falls, N.Y.	NA	400	60,000	FW[f]
	Broome Cty., N.Y.	NA	600	69,000	FW
	Morris Cty., N.J.	NA	1,340	142,000	Morris Cty.[g]

Ogden Projects Inc.

Location	Year			Operator
Lawrence, Mass.	1984[h]	900	NA	OPI[i]
Tulsa, Okla.	1986	1,125	76,000	CIT Group[j]
Marion Cty., Ore.	1986	550	47,500	OPI
Hillsborough Cty., Fla.	1987	1,200	80,100	Hillsborough Cty.
Bristol, Conn.	1987	650	58,500	OPI
Alexandria, Va.	1987	975	75,900	OPI
Indianapolis, Ind.	1988	2,250	89,000	OPI
Stanislaus Cty., Calif.	1989	800	82,200	OPI
Babylon, N.Y.	1989	750	83,900	OPI
Haverhill, Mass.	1989	1,650	120,000	OPI
Wallingford, Conn.	1989	420	40,000	OPI
Kent Cty., Mich.	1989	625	62,200	Kent Cty.
Warren Cty., N.J.[k]	1989	400	50,000	OPI
Fairfax Cty., Va.	1990	3,000	195,500	OPI
Minneapolis, Minn.[k]	1990	1,200	80,000	GE Credit Corp.
Huntsville, Ala.	1990	690	71,500	Huntsville, Ala.
Lancaster Cty., Pa.	1991	1,200	98,000	Lancaster SWM[l]
Lake Cty., Fla.	1991	528	66,000	OPI
Pasco Cty., Fla.	1991	1,050	90,300	Pasco Cty., Fla.
Huntington, N.Y.	1991	750	NA	OPI
Hudson Cty., N.J.	NA	1,500	148,000	OPI
Union Cty., N.J.	NA	1,440	107,000	Union Cty.[m]
Johnston, R.I.	NA	750	80,000	RI SW Corp.[n]
Connecticut	NA	550	78,000	NA
N. Kingston, R.I.[k]	NA	710	72,000	NA
Onondaga Cty., N.Y.	NA	990	132,000	OPI
Montgomery Cty., Md.	NA	NA	NA	NA

Westinghouse Corp.				
Lee Cty., Fla.	NA	1,800	147,000	Lee County
Mercer Cty., N.Y.	NA	NA	NA	NA
Bay Cty., Fla.	1987	510	38,000	Ford Motor[c]
York Cty., Pa.	1990	1,344	87,500	York Cty.[o]
Poughkeepsie, N.Y.	1989	400	53,000	Dutchess Cty.[p]
Chester, Pa.	1991	2,688	276,000	Delaware SWA[q]
San Juan, Puerto Rico	1993	1,040	85,000	NA
Gaston Cty., N.C.	1993	400	42,000	NA
Oakland Cty., Mich.	1994	2,000	NA	NA
Monmouth Cty., N.J.	1996	1,700	214,000	NA
Wheelabrator Technologies Inc.				
Saugus, Mass.	1975	1,500	NA	WTI
Pinellas Cty., Fla.	1983	3,000	NA	Pinellas Cty.
Peekskill, N.Y.	1984	2,250	NA	WTI[r]
Baltimore, Md.	1985	2,250	NA	Ford Motor[c]
North Andover, Mass.	1985	1,500	NA	WTI
Tampa, Fla.	1985	1,000	NA	Tampa, Fla.
Claremont, N.H.	1987	200	NA	WTI
Millbury, Mass.	1987	1,500	NA	Ford Motor[c]
Bridgeport, Conn.	1988	2,250	NA	Ford Motor[c]
Concord, N.H.	1989	575	NA	WTI
Gloucester Cty., N.J.	1989	575	NA	WTI
S. Broward Cty., Fla.	1990	2,250	NA	WTI
N. Broward Cty., Fla.	1991	2,250	NA	WTI
Spokane, Wash.	1991	800	NA	Spokane, Wash.

a Connecticut Resource Recovery Agency
b Greater Detroit Resource Recovery Authority
c Ford Motor Credit Corp.
d Occidental Chemical Corp.
e Los Angeles Sanitation District
f Foster Wheeler Corp. and Adirondack Resource Recovery Associates
g Morris County Municipal Utilities Authority
h Ogden acquired the plant in 1986.
i Ogden owns 65.3 percent; SBR owns the remainder.
j CIT Group/Capital Financing Inc.
k Ogden acquired the plant from Blount Energy Resources Corp. in May 1991.
l Lancaster Solid Waste Management Authority
m Union County Utilities Authority
n Rhode Island Solid Waste Management Corp.
o York County Solid Waste Authority
p Dutchess County Resource Recovery Agency
q Delaware Solid Waste Authority
r Wheelabrator owns 75 percent; John Hancock Mutual Life Insurance Co. owns 25 percent

Source: Investor Responsibility Research Center Inc.

1990, ABB acquired Combustion Engineering, a major U.S. waste-to-energy developer and worldwide supplier to the process, power and public sector markets, for $1.6 billion.[51] ABB also purchased European rights to the Widmer & Ernst technology from Blount.[52]

ABB Resource Recovery Systems offers both a refuse derived fuel and a mass burn incineration technology. ABB's mass burn system is premised on its steam generating and burning capabilities, which incorporate the DeBartolomeis SpA grate system, for which ABB has an exclusive North American license. ABB also has a license for the technology and experience of Energie- und Verfahrenstechnik GmbH (EVT), a West German boiler supplier.

ABB has three operating waste-to-energy plants, all refuse derived fuel plants, and one mass burn facility under development. ABB operates the country's largest waste-to-energy facility, a 4,000 ton per day plant in Detroit, Mich. Project costs range from $104 million for its planned facility to $230 million for the Detroit plant. ABB's three operating plants recover ferrous metals during front-end processing.[53]

Foster Wheeler Power Systems Inc.: Established in 1983 by Foster Wheeler Corp. to penetrate the waste-to-energy market, Foster Wheeler Power Systems is a single source vendor, utilizing several wholly owned subsidiaries that also market their products and services to other power plant developers. In addition to providing combustion systems, Foster Wheeler designs and manufactures fuel handling and control systems, pollution control equipment and other parts of waste-to-energy plants.

Although Foster Wheeler represents only 5 percent of the capacity of waste-to-energy projects awarded through the fall of 1990, it represented 12 percent of the awards for waste-to-energy projects in 1990 and 21 percent of the awards in 1989.[54] The company credits its increasing market share to its integrated approach. Foster Wheeler says it is the first company in the waste-to-energy industry to bid recycling and composting on a stand-alone basis. In 1988, it aligned with Resource Recovery Systems Inc., a materials recovery facility developer described in more detail in Chapter 6, to offer recycling and waste-to-energy technologies. Foster Wheeler won a contract to build the first recycling, composting and waste-to-energy facility in North America to be run under the auspices of one company.[55] The plant is designed to process 2,200 tons per day in Montreal.[56] In the United States, Foster Wheeler built four waste-to-energy plants and has another four under development. The plants range in size from 360 to 2,000 tons per day.

Foster Wheeler can provide both mass burn and refuse derived fuel boilers, although all of its resource recovery plants under development utilize mass burn technology. Foster Wheeler designed and built the first waterwall mass burn refuse plant in North America, which began commercial operation in 1967 and continues to process 360 tons per day of solid waste and produce steam for the Norfolk Naval Shipyard in Virginia. With more than 80 years in the boiler island business, Foster Wheeler has experience burning a wide variety of fuels, including municipal solid waste, waste woods, bagasse, sugar cane and coke, using both the fluidized bed design and the more conventional grate-fired systems. The company also has developed methods to burn municipal solid waste along with conventional fuels in utility steam generators.

Future of Waste-to-Energy Development

Although recent activity in the waste-to-energy industry has not matched the explosive growth of the early to mid-1980s, waste-to-energy continues to make inroads as a solid waste disposal option. In fact, analysts within and outside the waste-to-energy industry are quite bullish about its future. Ultimately, waste-to-energy vendors are confident that business will pick up in the years ahead as communities begin to recognize that recycling and other disposal options cannot address the entire waste stream. At that point, say waste-to-energy vendors, waste-to-energy projects often will appear more attractive than landfills—a chief alternative to waste-to-energy plants. Scott Mackin, president of Ogden Projects, said in the spring of 1991 that in the near term, there would not be the steady flow of requests for proposals by municipalities for waste-to-energy projects that there was in the late 1980s "because communities will be grappling with size and recycling issues. That will just the delay the projects, however. It will not stop them, because ultimately waste-to-energy is an appropriate element of an integrated waste management plan." Mackin foresees more requests for proposals coming out "in the '93 and '94 time frame."[57]

The U.S. government also expects waste-to-energy plants to dispose of increasing amounts of the nation's waste. The Bush administration's *National Energy Strategy* is quite supportive of combusting municipal solid waste and estimates that waste-to-energy plants will provide up to 2.1 quads of energy for electricity generation by the year 2010—seven times the amount of energy generated by waste-to-energy plants today.[58] EPA estimates that the nation will burn nearly 23 percent, or 45.5 million tons, of its garbage in 1995 and more than 25 percent, or 55 million tons, in the year 2000.[59] The National Solid Wastes Management Association reports that the waste-to-energy plants operating and under construction will process 17 percent of the 200 million tons of waste EPA has forecasted for 1995.[60] Planned plants in the pipeline not yet under construction will boost that amount still higher.

Private research firms also foresee tremendous growth in the industry. Leading Edge Reports, a market research company in Cleveland Heights, Ohio, estimated that the number of waste-to-energy plants in North America will rise from 160 to 350 plants, with a total capacity of 250,000 tons per day by the year 2000. The report estimated that the industry's ton per day capacity will grow at an annual rate of 12 percent and that the number of plants will increase roughly 6.7 percent a year.[61] The Freedonia Group, a market research firm in Cleveland, estimated that $19.4 billion will be spent on waste-to-energy plants, including plants that burn wood and agricultural wastes and landfill gas, in the United States in the 1990s. The firm projected that the number of municipal solid waste-to-energy plants would increase to 230 in 1994 and to 300 in the year 2000.[62]

The forces behind the retrenchment in waste-to-energy development still exist, though, and have to be reckoned with if the industry is to meet its growth potential. Waste-to-energy plants are capital intensive, and the 1986 Tax Reform Act eliminated tax incentives for them, thus forcing them to compete with other public works projects for tax-exempt bonds. Although the Clean Air Act amendments and the EPA's New Source Performance Standards go a long way toward reducing uncertainty in the area of air emissions, the ash issue remains unresolved at the federal level. If Congress determines that ash from waste-to-energy plants should be treated as a hazardous waste under RCRA, the necessary increase in tipping fees needed to cover the additional costs may deter many municipalities from selecting this disposal option. It is more likely, however, that Congress will support a separate classification for ash from waste-to-energy plants that will not be so costly.

Local opponents of these plants have proven to be an effective political force, successfully canceling or delaying some projects, primarily on environmental grounds. The future of waste-to-energy development will depend in large part on the ability of developers and community leaders to overcome the NIMBY ("Not In My Backyard") syndrome and site waste-to-energy facilities. On the other hand, the NIMBY syndrome also plays a large role in siting landfills. If Congress passes legislation calling for dedicated landfills for ash from waste-to-energy facilities, many communities will be faced with the choice of a waste-to-energy facility and ash landfill or a traditional sanitary landfill that accepts municipal solid waste.

The future of waste-to-energy plants also will depend on the success of industry in integrating waste-to-energy with community emphasis on recycling and source reduction. ABB Resource Recovery Systems President Miller says "The types of plants that are being bid now and into the 1990s will be refuse derived fuel or hybrid mass burn technologies."[63] (Hybrid mass burn technologies refer to projects that preprocess waste to recover materials before it is delivered to a mass burn facility and combusted.) Given the emphasis on recycling and the resulting downsizing of many planned plants, there is likely to be a growing market niche for companies offering smaller, modular plants. While large-scale mass burn plants have dominated the industry in the 1980s and into the 1990s, William Darcy, president of the Connecticut Resource Recovery Authority, points out that plants also are limited at the upper size range "because the major metropolitan areas that want waste-to-energy are already served by large plants."[64] Pending NSPS standards to be issued by the EPA under the Clean Air Act within the next two years call into question the economics of small plants, however. The cost of air pollution control devices may make small plants too expensive. Communities also have the option of banding together to form regional compacts that would generate sufficient waste for mid-size (between 400 and 1,000 tons per day) plants.

Waste-to-energy companies are expanding their services to include recycling to capture a larger share of the waste market. To date, even though communities may be employing an integrated waste management strategy, they appear to be bidding out components of such an approach separately. For instance, a community may issue a request for proposal for a materials recovery plant and then issue a separate request for proposal for a waste-to-energy facility. The number of communities seeking one company to pursue an integrated approach is growing, however, and waste-to-energy companies are positioning themselves to be able to serve this growing market.

CONCLUSIONS

Landfills are clearly on the decline as a means of disposing of U.S. municipal solid waste. What is not clear, though, is which solid waste disposal alternative will fill the void created by their closure. If the nation adopts the Environmental Protection Agency's strategy of integrated waste management (See Box I-1 on p. 4), no single method will dominate waste disposal as landfills have in the past. Under EPA's strategy, each of the four major disposal options—recycling, composting, incineration and landfilling—will be utilized to deal with some portion of the waste stream that remains after source reduction, EPA's preferred method of handling the nation's waste.

The looming questions for the municipal solid waste disposal industry are: What percentage of the waste stream will each solid waste disposal alternative take care of? What percentage of the waste stream can the nation realistically recycle? What portion of the waste stream is suitable for composting? How much waste will be left to burn following source reduction, recycling and composting? Could disenchantment with the three major solid waste disposal alternatives result in a resurgence of modern sanitary landfills?

The nation has not yet had sufficient experience with the emerging solid waste disposal alternatives to answer these questions authoritatively. The most recent round of modern waste-to-energy plants did not begin operation until the late 1980s, and the United States is just beginning to test the recycling waters. Composting is in an even earlier stage. Moreover, each of these solid waste disposal options has promises and pitfalls.

Recycling has tremendous popular and political support, although the public can be fickle. It remains to be seen whether the majority of Americans are willing to make the extra effort required to separate recyclables from the waste stream. (At present, around 15 percent of the population has access to curbside recycling programs, and participation rates vary widely.) Many are optimistic that the nation will make recycling a way of life and that what at first seems like an inconvenience quickly becomes a matter of routine. Others, however, are skeptical that Americans have the temperament to recycle.

Recycling programs also have to battle the misconception that they do not cost money. Even if recycling is a less expensive alternative than landfilling, citizens often become disgruntled when they discover that recycling has a price. Moreover, the costs of some curbside recycling programs have been higher than municipalities expected, and budgetary constraints cities are facing may trigger a review of costly ventures. Recycling companies are confident, though, that experience will increase efficiencies and bring costs down. In addition, in instances where programs are mandated by the state, costs may not determine a program's fate.

Recycling has momentum on its side. If the momentum can be sustained, its prospects are quite good. "If the infrastructure gets put into place, with collection systems, processing centers and end-user markets, then it will not matter if the current 'feel good' attitude subsides," commented William D. Ruckelshaus, chairman of Browning-Ferris Industries Inc. "Economics will take over and the system will be self-sustaining."[1] Still, such preconditions represent formidable obstacles to sustainable recycling. Developing such a system will no doubt take time and is not likely to go smoothly. Moreover, progress on this front also will be left open to interpretation. Some will think recycling programs, particularly mandated ones, "flood" markets, depress prices for recycled materials and disillusion program participants. Others will view such developments as inevitable growing pains in an evolving market. "Gluts and scarcities will be signals not that there's no market but that the market is working the way it always works—in fits and starts," contends Donella Meadows, an adjunct professor of environmental studies at Dartmouth College. "The only way the market can sense a large potential supply of something new is to let that something accumulate somewhere. The only way the market can stimulate demand is to bring the price down low enough, and be sufficiently assuring about future supply, to stimulate new users."[2]

Regardless of how one views the collection process, there is no doubt that the recycling frenzy sweeping the nation has launched the five industries discussed in *Trash to Cash* into the midst of an industrial transformation. Companies are gearing up to use an increasing amount of recycled materials in their feedstock and are constantly pursuing innovative ways to use more. The steel industry, for instance, began experimenting with steel cans in its feedstock directly in response to the nation's "garbage crisis" and consequently discovered that steel mills could not only use, but benefit, from incorporating much higher amounts of unprocessed steel cans in their feedstock than they previously thought possible. The glass industry is experimenting with mixed-color used glass, a common byproduct of processing facilities that the industry seldom uses, to determine if glass furnaces could increase their usage without adversely affecting glass container production.

The municipal solid waste composting industry also is banking on end-users finding ways to use its product. Developing markets for compost is perhaps more critical to the industry's success than any other factor. At present, the fledgling industry is impeded by controversy and high cost. Nearly all agree that landfills, particularly modern ones, are an overly technical and costly means of disposing of yard wastes and that yard wastes should be composted instead. The lack of a national consensus on what other portions of the waste stream are appropriate to compost, though, is a major obstacle to mixed solid waste composting. The costs and inconvenience of separating out food and other organic wastes from household or industrial waste has deterred that option, but as landfill fees continue to rise, all of the composting options will become more attractive. The new wave of municipal solid waste composting facilities scheduled to begin operation in the next few years will provide valuable data and experience to assist in evaluating this solid waste disposal option. The plants also will provide an indication of the potential markets for compost produced from municipal solid waste.

In many respects, the fate of waste incineration is dependent on the success of recycling and composting. Given the current emphasis on recycling, waste-to-energy developers are stressing the compatability of this waste disposal option and are sizing their plants to dispose of the waste stream that remains following source reduction, recycling and, in some instances, composting. In the event that recycling and composting fall out of favor, however, the waste-to-energy industry is fully prepared to burn the entire waste stream. In either case, many analysts are quite bullish on the industry's future, predicting that orders for new plants will pick up once again in the middle of the decade as the limitations of recycling and composting in disposing of the entire waste stream become apparent. The industry, however, lacks the public support that recycling enjoys and must gain public acceptance before many additional waste-to-energy plants will be sited.

Blurring the Lines

As companies attempt to carve out niches for themselves in the growing waste disposal market, the industry is becoming more difficult to define. Recycling has forced many companies to expand their traditional services across industry lines. Waste-to-energy developers have begun offering recycling and composting services. Garbage haulers are becoming secondary commodities brokers as they search for markets for post-consumer items they now pick up at curbside. Recycling companies, including scrap dealers, are expanding the types of material they process, and recycling companies and product manufacturers are getting into the collection business.

Tidewater Fibre of Chesapeake, Va., a paper recycling firm, says it was one of the first paper recycling companies to go multi-recyclable in order to remain viable in an era of low paper prices. "Companies, in order to survive, are going to be forced to handle all recyclables at their recycling centers," concluded John Benedetto, Tidewater's president.[3] A subsidiary of Southeast Paper Manufacturing Co. of Marietta, Ga., a recycled newsprint producer, also is processing glass, aluminum and plastic containers. As is the case with many companies, Southeast is expanding reluctantly, but believes it must do so to obtain enough old newsprint. "We would like to just do paper, but we'd like to protect that supply line," said Southeast's George Elder. Southeast Paper also has begun to bid on curbside collection and processing contracts to ensure a steady supply of newsprint.[4] In late 1990, Weyerhaeuser Paper Co. cited customer demand as the major reason it purchased a recycling company that recycles glass, aluminum and plastics, as well as paper. "We need to maintain our concentration on waste paper, but it is in our best interest to help our customers find markets for those other recyclables," said company spokesman Roger Higle.[5]

Container Recovery Corp. (CRC), a subsidiary of Anheuser-Busch Inc. that developed one of the nation's largest aluminum beverage can collection programs, is expanding into the collection of glass, paper and plastics. CRC also is offering communities assistance in developing and operating municipal recycling systems. Other product manufacturers are becoming involved in the collection of recyclables for the first time. In the fall of 1989, Occidental Chemical Corp. became the first in its industry to begin a collection program for used polyvinyl chloride bottles.

Though the definition of the solid waste industry is blurring and the future of each of the emerging waste disposal alternatives is still unresolved, there will, of course, be winners and losers as the dynamic waste market evolves. In fact, casualties already exist. Publicly traded Tri-R Systems Corp. of Denver, Colo., which processes and markets a wide range of recyclables, filed for Chapter 11 bankruptcy in April 1991. Tri-R was the first seller of buy-back center franchises. Its motto was "Where Recycling Really Pays," but it had no specialized processing equipment or technology. When prices for recyclables, particularly old newspapers and aluminum cans, plummeted, so did the fortunes of the company.[6] Publicly traded Orfa Corp. is another example. As discussed in Chapter 7, Orfa Corp. filed for Chapter 11 bankruptcy one year before Tri-R Systems, after encountering difficulties developing markets for a cellulose fiber produced from unsorted municipal solid waste.

A sizeable amount of capital is likely to be invested in projects and programs that will fail or be overly costly. Agripost Inc., a private composting company, shut down its privately financed composting facility—the nation's largest—just one year after it began operation. Agripost cited operating problems, additional capital requirements of addressing these problems and the county's unwillingness to raise the plant's processing fee as reasons for the closing. Proponents of source-separated recycling, primarily curbside recycling, contend that this will not be an isolated event. They maintain that most mixed waste processing plants will prove to be unprofitable or close because markets for their end products, usually compost or refuse derived fuel, will fail to develop. They also contend that recyclables retrieved from the mixed waste stream will be too contaminated with other wastes to be valuable to industry. Opponents of source-separated recycling, on the other hand, argue that an excessive amount of money already is being spent on mandatory curbside recycling programs.

All solid waste disposal options, particularly plants with a projected 30-year lifetime, will need to be flexible to accommodate the changing waste stream. Source reduction, packaging redesign, mandatory recycled content legislation, labeling standards, new products and materials, and increasingly sophisticated life-cycle analyses of competing packaging materials are all factors that will change the composition of the nation's municipal solid waste stream over time. Consumers, corporations and federal, state and local governments exercising their purchasing power also will affect the composition of the waste stream if they choose to signal a clear preference for recycled goods. McDonald's Corp. has taken the lead among large corporations in having publicly pledged to spend $100 million on recycled equipment and supplies in 1990, up from $5 to $6 million spent on similar goods in 1989.

Congress will be grappling with solid waste issues in its coming reauthorization of the Resource Conservation and Recovery Act, which could have a tremendous impact on the future of municipal solid waste management in the United States. Now that the nation is turning its attention to this issue, new and better data, particularly cost data, on these solid waste disposal alternatives is becoming available, and more professionals are joining the field and conducting analyses based on this growing body of information. Another issue that could have a dramatic influence on solid waste disposal decisions is the growing movement to have those residents and commercial entities that are not already doing so pay disposal fees based on the amount of garbage generated. Better price signals will help sort out the disposal options. Regardless of which waste disposal options gain favor in the United States, the days of inexpensive municipal solid waste disposal are over, and innovative methods of processing the nation's municipal solid waste are emerging rapidly. The 1990s will provide a myriad of business opportunities for companies that offer cost effective, innovative solid waste disposal options.

Notes to Introduction

1. "Characterization of Municipal Solid Waste in the United States: 1990 Update," EPA/ 530-SW-90-042, U.S. Environmental Protection Agency, Office of Solid Waste and Emergency Response, Washington, D.C., June 1990.
2. *"The Municipal Solid Waste Dilemma: Challenges for the 90's,"* U.S. Environmental Protection Agency, January 1991, Revised Draft.
3. See note 1, above.
4. Jonathan V.L. Kiser, "A Comprehensive Report on the Status of Municipal Waste Combustion," *Waste Age*, November 1990.
5. William P. Hulligan, Waste Management of North America Inc., "Recycling—The Waste Industry's Perspective," presentation at "Building Confidence in Recycling" conference sponsored by the U.S. Conference of Mayors, Washington, D.C., March 29, 1990.
6. Keith Schneider, "As Recycling Becomes a Growth Industry, Its Paradoxes Also Multiply," *The New York Times*, Jan. 20, 1991.
7. Jerry Powell, "How Are We Doing? the 1990 Report," Resource Recycling, April 1991.
8. "A Better Environment for Recycling Industry," *The Washington Post*, Feb. 26, 1990.
9. See note 2, above.
10. Ben Rose, "Other Viewpoints," *Solid Waste & Power*, April 1990.
11. Jackie Prince, Environmental Defense Fund, written communication, July 17, 1991.
12. See note 1, above.
13. "Americans Prefer Recyclable Containers by More Than 3 to 1; Comprehensive Curbside Collection Gains Strong Support," Glass Packaging Institute, Washington, D.C., Jan. 17, 1990, press release.
14. Austin Fiore, presentation at the World Recycling Conference & Exposition, Baltimore, Md., June 27, 1990.
15. See note 1, above.
16. "Recycling Works!: State and Local Solutions to Solid Waste Management Problems," EPA/530-SW-89-014, U.S. Environmental Protection Agency, Office of Solid Waste, Washington, D.C., January 1989.
17. See note 1, above.
18. See note 1, above.
19. Jim Glenn and David Riggle, "The State of Garbage in America," *BioCycle*, April 1991.
20. Catherine Cooney, "Wall Street Sees Gold Mine in Garbage Stocks," *Environment Week*, Sept. 13, 1990.

Notes to Chapter 1

1. Aluminum Association Inc., Report to the Coalition of Northeastern Governors on Aluminum Recycling Rates and Recycled Content, Washington, D.C., Aug. 27, 1990.
2. "State and Province Watch," *Bottle/Can Recycling Update*, August 1990.
3. "Rigid Containers," *Bottle/Can Recycling Update*, March 1991.
4. "Characterization of Municipal Solid Waste in the United States: 1990 Update," EPA/ 530-SW-90-042, U.S. Environmental Protection Agency, Office of Solid Waste and Emergency Response, Washington, D.C., June 1990.

5. U.S. Congress, Office of Technology Assessment, *Facing America's Trash: What Next for Municipal Solid Waste*, OTA-0-424, Washington, D.C.: U.S. Government Printing Office, October 1989, p. 155.

6. See note 1, above.

7. Aluminum Association Inc., personal communication, April 11, 1991.

8. "Recycling Nonferrous Scrap Metals," Institute of Scrap Recycling Industries Inc., Washington, D.C., 1990.

9. "Questions and Answers About...," Reynolds Aluminum Recycling Co., undated brochure.

10. See note 4, above.

11. See note 4, above.

12. "Aluminum Beverage Can Recycling Sets New Record During 1990," Aluminum Association Inc., Washington, D.C., March 6, 1991, press release.

13. "Aluminum Recycling: America's Environmental Success Story," Aluminum Association Inc., Washington, D.C., 1990.

14. See note 1, above.

15. See note 13, above.

16. Brian W. Sturgell, Alcan Aluminum Corp., "Statement of the Aluminum Association Inc. on Recycling and Municipal Solid Waste Management," presentation at "Building Confidence in Recycling" conference sponsored by the U.S. Conference of Mayors, Washington, D.C., March 29, 1990.

17. See note 1, above.

18. Aluminum Association Inc., personal communication, June 26, 1990.

19. Ron Kofmehl, Ravenswood Aluminum Corp., personal communication, March 8, 1991.

20. See note 16, above.

21. Michael Misner, "The Aluminum Can's Future Glistens," *Waste Age*, December 1989.

22. "Campbell's Turns to Aluminum," *Recycling Today*, March 15, 1990.

23. "UBC Recycling News," *Bottle/Can Recycling Update*, July 1990.

24. Bill Paul, "New Methods May Help U.S. Recycle More Plastics, a Scourge of Landfills," *The Wall Street Journal*, Feb. 9, 1989.

25. National Recovery Technologies Inc., undated brochure.

26. See note 9, above; Aluminum Co. of America exhibit, World Recycling Conference & Exposition, Baltimore, Md., June 27, 1990.

27. Jim Pierce, Environmental Action Foundation, personal communication, Oct. 21, 1990; William L. Kovacs, "The Coming Era of Conservation and Industrial Utilization of Recyclable Materials," *Ecology Law Quarterly*, University of California, 1988; *Resource Recovery Report*, January and November 1987; and "Plastic Soft Drink Can Expands Market," *COPPE Update*, Council on Plastics and Packaging in the Environment, Washington, D.C., November 1987.

28. See note 27, above.

29. "Packages That Won't Go Away," *Bottle/Can Recycling Update*, August 1990.

30. Jerry Powell, *Resource Recycling*, personal communication, Nov. 26, 1990.

31. See note 5, above.

32. See note 21, above.

33. See note 13, above.

34. See note 16, above.

35. See note 16, above.

36. See note 1, above; Brian Sturgell, Alcan Aluminum Corp., personal communication, Nov. 2, 1990; Gresh Sackett, Reynolds Metals Co., personal communication, Nov. 2, 1990.

37. See note 16, above.

38. See note 9, above.

39. "Americans Earn Millions Recycling Billions of Aluminum Cans," Aluminum Association Inc., Washington, D.C., March 30, 1990, press release.

40. "On March 21, 1968, Reynolds Metals Company Discovered the Richest Aluminum Mine in the World," Reynolds Metals Co., undated brochure.

41. See note 18, above.

42. Cynthia Pollock Shea, *Mining Urban Wastes: The Potential for Recycling*, Worldwatch Institute, Washington, D.C., April 1987.

43. "Recycling Waste to Save Energy," U.S. Department of Energy's Conservation and Renewable Energy Inquiry and Referral Service, FS 227, January 1989.

44. See note 5, above, p. 192.

45. See note 16, above.

46. "UBC Market Analysis," *Bottle/Can Recycling Update*, March 1991.

47. See note 16, above.

48. "UBC Market Analysis," *Bottle/Can Recycling Update*, February 1991.

49. See note 16, above.

50. See note 46, above.

51. "Recycling Record Established," *Recycling Today*, April 15, 1990.

52. See note 16, above.

53. Martha M. Hamilton, "Recycling: Can Do," *The Washington Post*, Feb. 26, 1990.

54. See note 16, above.

55. See note 1, above.

56. "How the Aluminum Beverage Can Recycling Rate is Calculated," Aluminum Association Inc., Washington, D.C., 1990.

57. See note 18, above.

58. See note 1, above.

59. Jerry Powell, "How Are We Doing? The 1990 Report," *Resource Recycling*, April 1991.

60. Aluminum Co. of America's 1990 annual report.

61. Steve Apotheker, "Alcoa's On the Move," *Resource Recycling*, September 1989.

62. Kathleen Meade, "BFI Agrees to Market All of Its Aluminum Cans to Alcoa," *Recycling Times*, July 17, 1990.

63. "Alcoa's 1990 UBC Recycling Plans," *Bottle/Can Recycling Update*, April 1990; "Some are Questioning Alcoa's Moves," *Bottle/Can Recycling Update*, January 1990.

64. "HARC!, News From Alcoa Recycling Co.," Alcoa Recycling Co., April 1989.

65. See note 63, above.

66. See note 9, above.

67. Andrew McCutcheon, Reynolds Metals Co., personal communication, Nov. 2, 1990.

68. See note 59, above.

69. "Position on Municipal Solid Waste Management," Reynolds Metals Co., undated brochure.

70. See note 67, above.

71. "UBC Recycling News," *Bottle/Can Recycling Update*, March 1991.

72. Brian Sturgell, Alcan Aluminum Corp., personal communication, Nov. 2, 1990; Steve Apotheker, "Alcan Strengthens Presence in UBC Market," *Resource Recycling*, October 1990.

73. See note 59, above.

74. "Metals/non-ferrous," *Resource Recycling*, September 1990.

75. Julie Wessels, Golden Aluminum Co., personal communication, Nov. 8, 1990; Adolph Coors Co.'s 1989 annual report.

76. See note 16, above.

77. "UBC Recycling News," *Bottle/Can Recycling Update*, September 1990.

78. Michael G. Malloy, "Waste Industry Companies," *Waste Age*, May 1991.
79. IMCO Recycling Inc.'s 1989 annual report and Form 10-K.
80. See note 79, above; "Market Update," *Resource Recycling*, January 1991; "IMCO Recycling Equity Brief," *Franklin's Insight*, Franklin Research and Development Corp., Boston, Mass., November 1990.
81. Steve Bettcher, Kaiser Aluminum and Chemical Corp., personal communication, Nov. 2, 1990; EnviroSource Inc.'s 1989 annual report and Form 10-K.
82. EnviroSource Inc.'s 1989 annual report and Form 10-K.
83. "A Pledge and a Promise: The Continuing Anheuser-Busch Commitment to a Quality Environment," Anheuser-Busch Inc. report, 1990.
84. Jerry Powell, "The Changing Aluminum Can Recycling Market," *Resource Recycling*, October 1990.
85. "Coming Up," *Bottle/Can Recycling Update*, January 1990.
86. "Machine Provides New Incentives for Recycling Cans," *Chemecology*, April 1990.
87. "Recycling Equipment News," *Bottle/Can Recycling Update*, September 1990.

Notes to Chapter 2

1. "Glass...The 'Ideal' Environmental Package," Owens-Brockway Glass Containers, undated brochure.
2. "A Right Cross to the Chin," *Bottle/Can Recycling Update*, November/December 1990; Kathleen Meade, "Container Wars 1990: The Impure Strikes Back," *Recycling Times*, Dec. 4, 1990.
3. "Glass Container Industry Grows: Outlook Bright for 1990," Glass Packaging Institute, Washington, D.C., Feb. 7, 1990, press release.
4. Austin Fiore, Owens-Brockway Glass Containers, personal communication, June 27, 1990; James Luci, Anchor Glass Container Corp., personal communication, June 18, 1990; Thomas McKnight, Ball-Incon Glass Packaging Corp., personal communication, June 21, 1990.
5. Cynthia Pollock Shea, *Mining Urban Wastes: The Potential for Recycling*, Worldwatch Institute, Washington, D.C., April 1987.
6. See note 1, above.
7. "Characterization of Municipal Solid Waste in the United States: 1990 Update," EPA/ 530-SW-90-042, U.S. Environmental Protection Agency, Office of Solid Waste and Emergency Response, Washington, D.C., June 1990.
8. See note 7, above.
9. See note 7, above.
10. See note 7, above.
11. U.S. Congress, Office of Technology Assessment, *Facing America's Trash: What Next for Municipal Solid Waste*, OTA-O-424, Washington, D.C.: U.S. Government Printing Office, October 1989, p. 150.
12. "Things You've Always Wanted To Know About Soft Drink Container Recycling," National Soft Drink Association, Washington, D.C., 1990.
13. Chaz Miller, Glass Packaging Institute, personal communication, May 22, 1990.
14. See note 13, above.
15. James Luci, Anchor Glass Container Corp., personal communication, June 18, 1990; Austin Fiore, Owens-Brockway Glass Containers, personal communication, June 27,

1990; Robert Ryder, Latchford Glass Co., personal communication, June 20, 1990.

16. James Luci, Anchor Glass Container Corp., personal communication, June 18, 1990.

17. Chaz Miller, Glass Packaging Institute, written communication, March 26, 1991.

18. See note 13, above.

19. Thomas McKnight, Ball-Incon Glass Packaging Corp., personal communication, June 21, 1990.

20. Arnie Rosenberg, "Glass Makers are Perfectly Clear on Cullet's Rise to Prominence," *Recycling Today*, December 1989.

21. Austin Fiore, Owens-Brockway Glass Containers, personal communication, June 27, 1990.

22. See note 1, above.

23. See note 21, above.

24. See notes 1 and 17, above.

25. See note 13, above.

26. "Recycling Waste to Save Energy," U.S. Department of Energy's Conservation and Renewable Energy Inquiry and Referral Service, FS 227, January 1989.

27. See note 11 above, p. 152.

28. William K. Reilly, Administrator of the U.S. Environmental Protection Agency, "The Federal Government and Recycling in the '90s," *Resource Recycling*, December 1989.

29. See note 21, above.

30. See note 11, above.

31. "Waste Reduction News," *Resource Recycling*, October 1990.

32. See note 12, above.

33. Austin Fiore, Owens-Brockway Glass Containers, personal communication, Oct. 30, 1990.

34. Michael Misner, *Recycling Times*, personal communication, Feb. 6, 1990.

35. Michael Misner, "The Markets Page," *Recycling Times*, Nov. 6, 1990.

36. "Owens Cuts Glass Prices," *Recycling Today*, June 15, 1990.

37. See note 16, above.

38. John Zabowski, "A Manufacturer's View of Glass Recycling," *Waste Age*, July 1987.

39. See note 19, above.

40. See note 16, above.

41. See note 13, above.

42. See note 17, above.

43. Kathleen Meade, "Freedonia Report Predicts Increase in Glass Recycling," *Recycling Times*, Oct. 23, 1990.

44. Michael Misner, "Pricing Trends," *Recycling Times*, March 12, 1991.

45. See note 21, above.

46. "Glass Container Recycling Review," *Bottle/Can Recycling Update*, January 1990; Wayne Trewhitt, "Recycling: Doing It Right to Make It Work," *Waste Age*, May 1990; Chaz Miller, "Glass Rejection Percentages Remained Steady in California," *Recycling Times*, July 17, 1990.

47. See note 17, above.

48. Allen Newfeld, Consumers Packaging Inc., personal communication, Oct. 30, 1990.

49. Roger D. Hecht, Allwaste Resource Recovery, personal communication, Oct. 31, 1990.

50. "Glass Recycling," Owens-Brockway Glass Containers, November 1988; John Zabowski, "A Manufacturer's View of Glass Recycling," *Waste Age*, July 1987.

51. Lewis Andrews, Glass Packaging Institute, "Glass Container Industry Overview," presentation at "Building Confidence in Recycling" conference sponsored by the U.S. Conference of Mayors, Washington, D.C., March 29, 1990.

52. See note 3, above.

53. "Recycling: The Need is Clear: A Report on the Glass Container Industry's State Recycling Program," Glass Packaging Institute, Washington, D.C., 1987.

54. Glass Packaging Institute's 1988-89 annual report; Lewis Andrews, Glass Packaging Institute, "Glass Container Industry Overview," presentation at "Building Confidence in Recycling" conference sponsored by the U.S. Conference of Mayors, Washington, D.C., March 29, 1990; "Glass," *Warmer Bulletin*, Spring 1990.

55. See note 51, above.

56. "Glass 'G' Gaining Converts," *Recycling Today*, Sept. 14, 1990.

57. See note 11, above.

58. Ball Corp.'s 1989 annual report.

59. "Glass Recycling: Why? How?," Glass Packaging Institute, Washington, D.C., undated brochure.

60. John Hoff, Owens-Brockway Glass Containers, personal communication, July 2, 1991.

61. Owens-Illinois Inc. press release, Feb. 13, 1990.

62. "Glass Container Recycling News," *Bottle/Can Recycling Update*, November/December 1990.

63. Noting that the glass container industry has "a history of market allocation and antitrust violations," the administrative law judge found that the merger concentrated too much glass industry capacity in one company, thereby reducing competition. Owens-Illinois appealed the decision to the full commission in early 1990. John Hoff of Owens-Brockway told IRRC that the issue at hand is whether to consider the glass industry or the entire rigid container industry, which would include plastics companies, as Owens-Brockway's competition. John Hoff, Owens-Brockway Glass Containers, personal communication, Oct. 30, 1990; "Glass, unclassified," *Resource Recycling*, January 1990.

64. Frank Reid, Anchor Glass Container Corp., personal communication, July 8, 1991.

65. "Vitro Completes Tender Offer," *The Wall Street Journal*, Nov. 3, 1989; "Anchor Glass Set to Be Purchased by Mexico's Vitro," *The Wall Street Journal*, Oct. 16, 1989.

66. Anchor Glass Container Corp.'s 1988 annual report.

67. See note 13, above.

68. See note 51, above.

69. Chaz Miller, "Glass Recycling: Where We've Been and Where We're Going," *Resource Recycling*, December 1989.

70. See note 16, above.

71. See note 21, above.

72. Kathleen Meade, "Fibres International Opens New Glass Recycling Plant in Washington," *Recycling Times*, Nov. 6, 1990.

73. Susan Combs, "WMI, American National Can to Market Glass and Metal," *Recycling Times*, Oct. 9, 1990.

74. Steve Apotheker, "Fiberglass Manufacturers Revisit Cullet," *Resource Recycling*, June 1990; "Glass Container Recycling News," *Bottle/Can Recycling Update*, May 1990.

75. "Ask Garbage," *Garbage*, September/October 1990.

76. Allen Karyo, Catamount Inc., personal communication, Oct. 30, 1990.

77. Steve Apotheker, "Fiberglass Manufacturers Revisit Cullet," *Resource Recycling*, June 1990.

78. See note 33, above.

79. See note 49, above.

80. See note 17, above.

81. "El Dorado," *The New Yorker*, Nov. 19, 1990.

82. See note 33, above.

83. *Resource Recovery Report*, March 1990.

84. See note 17, above.

85. See note 11, above, p. 153.
86. Susan Combs, "N.J. Broker Finds Market for Unwanted Glass Residual," *Recycling Times*, Nov. 20, 1990.
87. Susan Combs, "Broker Negotiates to Export Glass," *Recycling Times*, July 17, 1990.
88. "Glass Recycling: Why? How?," Glass Packaging Institute, Washington, D.C., April 1988.
89. "How To Curb The Solid Waste Crisis," Glass Packaging Institute, Washington, D.C., undated brochure.
90. See note 49, above.
91. "Glass Container Recycling," *Bottle/Can Recycling Update*, February 1991.
92. Allwaste Inc.'s 1989 annual report.
93. Ben Davol, Mid-Atlantic Glass Recycling Program, presentation at the World Recycling Conference & Exposition, Baltimore, Md., June 27, 1990.
94. See note 19, above.

Notes to Chapter 3

1. Kurt Smallberg, Steel Can Recycling Institute, "Steel Can Recycling: The Future is Today," presentation at "Building Confidence in Recycling" conference sponsored by the U.S. Conference of Mayors, Washington, D.C., March 29, 1990.
2. "Steel Can Recycling Hits 25%," *Recycling Times*, May 21, 1991.
3. See note 1, above.
4. "Steel. Building on a History of Recycling Leadership," Steel Can Recycling Institute, Pittsburgh, Pa., March 1990.
5. Michael Misner, "The Steel Can's Push for Recycling Respect," *Waste Age*, February 1991.
6. Deborah Barcikowski, "Industry Improvements Force Steel to Take Aim at Beverage Can Market," *Recycling Today*, June 15, 1990.
7. See note 6, above.
8. "Recycling Scrap Iron and Steel," Institute of Scrap Recycling Industries Inc., Washington, D.C., 1990.
9. William Heenan Jr., Steel Can Recycling Institute, personal communication, Feb. 13, 1991.
10. "Characterization of Municipal Solid Waste in the United States: 1990 Update," EPA/530-SW-90-042, United States Environmental Protection Agency, Office of Solid Waste and Emergency Response, Washington, D.C., June 1990.
11. U.S. Congress, Office of Technology Assessment, *Facing America's Trash: What Next for Municipal Solid Waste*, OTA-0-424, Washington, D.C.: U.S. Government Printing Office, October 1989, p. 161.
12. See note 10, above.
13. Kurt Smallberg, Steel Can Recycling Institute, personal communication, June 27, 1990.
14. See note 11, above, p. 162.
15. See note 9, above.
16. See note 9, above.
17. Discussion based on analysis in note 11, above, p. 162.
18. See note 9, above.
19. George J. McManus, "Recycling Alone Won't Scrap Need for New Steel," *Iron Age*, November 1990.
20. See note 4, above.
21. See note 10, above.

22. See note 2, above.

23. See note 1, above.

24. John Risser, USS Division of USX Corp., personal communication, Nov. 26, 1990.

25. See note 11, above, p. 163.

26. "Plants Retrieve WTE Scrap," *Recycling Today*, Sept. 14, 1990.

27. Daniel Sandoval, "Hot Source for Scrap," *Recycling Today*, Nov. 15, 1990; "Bi-Metal Sees Ferrous Ups and Downs," *Resource Recovery Report*, April 1991.

28. *Resource Recovery Report*, December 1990.

29. See note 13, above.

30. George J. McManus, "Detinners Go Down to the Dumps," *Iron Age*, November 1990.

31. Paris R. Wolfe, "Post-Consumer Market Presents Opportunity," *Recycling Today*, Sept. 14, 1990.

32. See note 24, above.

33. William Heenan Jr., Steel Can Recycling Institute, personal communication, April 5, 1991.

34. See note 24, above.

35. See note 31, above.

36. Ron Laker, David J. Joseph Co., personal communication, Nov. 29, 1990.

37. "Recyclable Steel Cans: An Integral Part of Your Curbside Recycling Program," Steel Can Recycling Institute, Pittsburgh, Pa., Summer 1990.

38. "Things You've Always Wanted to Know About Soft Drink Container Recycling," National Soft Drink Association, Washington, D.C., 1990.

39. "Steel. It's a Natural Friend of the Environment," Steel Can Recycling Institute, Pittsburgh, Pa., March 1990.

40. See note 11, above, p. 163.

41. See note 8, above.

42. "Aluminum and Bi-Metal Used Beverage Can Prices: National Averages—1990," *Recycling Times*, Dec. 31, 1990.

43. See note 33, above.

44. Michael Misner, *Recycling Times*, personal communication, Feb. 7, 1990; Clare Ansberry, "Steel Industry Gears Up to Recast Image of the Lowly Tin Can as Earth Friendly," *The Wall Street Journal*, Nov. 20, 1990.

45. John Risser, USS Division of USX Corp., personal communication, Feb. 8, 1991; Gus Perfetti, Bethlehem Steel Corp., personal communication, Nov. 26, 1990; William Heenan Jr., Steel Can Recycling Institute, personal communication, April 5, 1991.

46. See note 11, above, p. 165.

47. Clare Ansberry, "Steel Industry Gears Up to Recast Image of the Lowly Tin Can as Earth Friendly," *The Wall Street Journal*, Nov. 20, 1990.

48. See note 4, above.

49. See note 1, above.

50. See note 13, above.

51. See note 6, above.

52. "Steel Recycling—A New Era," Steel Can Recycling Institute, Pittsburgh, Pa., undated.

53. "Cans Get Boost from SMA," *Recycling Today*, April 15, 1990.

54. See note 13, above.

55. See note 52, above.

56. "Discover the True Nature of Steel," Steel Can Recycling Institute, Pittsburgh, Pa., undated advertisement; *The Recycling Magnet*, Steel Can Recycling Institute, Pittsburgh, Pa., Spring 1991.

57. See note 39, above.

58. See note 53, above.

59. See note 6, above.

60. See note 4, above.

61. David Weisman, Resource Recycling Technologies Inc., presentation at the World Recycling Conference & Exposition, Baltimore, Md., June 27, 1990.

62. See note 37, above.

63. Cynthia Pollock Shea, *Mining Urban Wastes: The Potential for Recycling*, Worldwatch Institute, Washington, D.C., April 1987.

64. See note 11, above, p. 164.

65. James Ordendorff, AMG Resources Corp., personal communication, Nov. 27, 1990.

66. "Steel Can Recycling News," *Bottle/Can Recycling Update*, April 1991; Michael Misner, "Proler Closes Houston Can Detinning Plant," *Recycling Times*, May 7, 1991.

67. William Proler, Proler International Corp., personal communication, Nov. 26, 1990; Proler International Corp., undated press release.

68. William Lambert, MacLeod Metals Corp., personal communication, Nov. 26, 1990.

69. See note 11, above, p. 162.

70. "Steel Recycling and Recycled Content," *The Recycling Magnet*, Steel Can Recycling Institute, Pittsburgh, Pa., Fall 1990.

71. See note 24, above.

72. See note 36, above.

73. Steven Wulff, David J. Joseph Co., personal communication, Dec. 6, 1990.

74. Gus Perfetti, Bethlehem Steel Corp., personal communication, Nov. 26, 1990.

75. See note 37, above.

76. See note 13, above.

77. "David J. Joseph Co. Municipal Recycling Div.," *The Recycling Magnet*, Steel Can Recycling Institute, Pittsburgh, Pa., Summer 1990.

78. See notes 6 and 47, above.

79. "Steel and Bi-Metal Can Recycling News," *Bottle/Can Recycling Update*, July 1990.

80. See note 1, above.

81. "Coinbak to Enhance Collection," *Recycling Today*, Aug. 15, 1990.

82. See note 10, above.

83. See note 11, above, p. 162.

84. See note 33, above.

85. "Steel Cans and Recycling: Today's Environmental Partnership," Steel Can Recycling Institute, Pittsburgh, Pa., undated brochure.

86. See note 33, above.

87. Elizabeth H. Olenbush, Steel Can Recycling Institute, personal communication, July 11, 1991.

88. See note 19, above.

Notes to Chapter 4

1. Michael Misner, "Pricing Trends," *Recycling Times*, Dec. 18, 1990.

2. Prall Culviner, "Paper Chase in the '90s," *Waste Age*, February 1991.

3. *PaperMatcher: A Directory of Paper Recycling Resources*, American Paper Institute Inc., New York, N.Y., December 1990.

4. See note 3, above.

5. Alan Davis and Susan Kinsella, "Recycled Paper: Exploding the Myths," *Garbage*, May/June 1990.

6. Tonda F. Rush, American Newspaper Publishers Association, personal communication, July 1, 1991.

7. See note 2, above.

8. See note 2, above.

9. Kathleen Meade, "Recycled Newsprint Roundup," *Recycling Times*, July 3, 1990.

10. John Holusha, "Old Newspapers Hit a Logjam," *The New York Times*, Sept. 10, 1989.

11. See note 10, above; G. Pierre Goad, "Recycling Siren Lures Newsprint Makers," *The Wall Street Journal*, Nov. 10, 1989; "Is Recycling Important?," *Orion*, Winter 1990.

12. "Newsprint Mills Rushing to Recycle," *The Environmental Newspaper*, American Newspaper Publishers Association, Reston, Va., Spring/Summer 1991.

13. Carl Espe, "Solid Waste Issue Creates Boom in Recycled Fiber Capacity Growth," *Resource Recycling*, November 1990.

14. Edward Sparks, Browning-Ferris Industries Inc., panel discussion at the National Solid Wastes Management Association's Waste Expo '91, Atlanta, Ga., April 9, 1991.

15. "Key Questions and Answers on Paper Recycling and its Role in Municipal Solid Waste Management," American Paper Institute Inc., New York, N.Y., undated brochure; Kathleen Meade, "API: Recycling Growth Higher Than Expected," *Recycling Times*, Feb. 12, 1991.

16. G. Pierre Goad, "Recycling Siren Lures Newsprint Makers," *The Wall Street Journal*, Nov. 10, 1989.

17. See note 16, above.

18. Catherine Cooney, "U.S. Executives Back Newsprint Recycling Efforts," *Environment Week*, May 31, 1990.

19. "Newsprint Compared," *Resource Recycling*, October 1990.

20. "Recycling Paper," Paper Stock Institute, a division of the Institute of Scrap Recycling Industries Inc., Washington, D.C., 1990.

21. "Characterization of Municipal Solid Waste in the United States: 1990 27."Key Questions and Answers on Paper Recycling and its Role in Municipal Solid Waste Management," American Paper Institute Inc., New York, N.Y., undated brochure.

22. See note 21, above.

23. Jerry Powell, "How Are We Doing? The 1990 Report," *Resource Recycling*, April 1991.

24. "89 Paper Exports Strong," *Recycling Today*, June 15, 1990; "1990 Waste Paper Data," *Recycling Times*, April 9, 1991; Kathleen Meade, "Waste Paper Recovery Closer to 1995 Goal, API Report Says," *Recycling Times*, April 9, 1991.

25. "89 Paper Exports Strong," *Recycling Today*, June 15, 1990.

26. J. Rodney Edwards, American Paper Institute Inc., personal communication, Aug. 14, 1991

27. "Key Questions and Answers on Paper Recycling and its Role in Municipal Solid Waste Management," American Paper Institute Inc., New York, N.Y., undated brochure.

28. Robert J. Brennan, "Paper Makers See Slower Growth, More Recycling," *The Wall Street Journal*, Dec. 10, 1990.

29. "Paper Recycling and its Role in Solid Waste Management," American Paper Institute Inc., New York, N.Y., undated report.

30. See note 27, above.

31. See note 27, above.

32. See note 29, above.

33. See note 3, above.

34. See note 27, above.

35. See note 27, above.

36. See note 16, above.

37. See note 10, above.
38. See note 3, above.
39. Scott Klinger and Carolyn M. Dever, "Lumbering in the Concrete Forest," *Franklin's Insight*, Franklin Research and Development Corp., Boston, Mass., September 1989.
40. See note 29, above.
41. See note 3, above.
42. See note 29, above; John Holusha, "The Tough Business of Recycling Newsprint," *The New York Times*, Jan. 6, 1991; Southeast Paper Manufacturing Co. brochure, undated.
43. John Holusha, "The Tough Business of Recycling Newsprint," *The New York Times*, Jan. 6, 1991.
44. Michael Misner, "Demand for Old Magazines to Increase with Deinking," *Recycling Times*, June 19, 1990.
45. Edward Sparks, "Dynamics Affecting Future Waste Paper Markets," *Resource Recycling*, January 1990.
46. Jamie Hill, "Old Magazines Stay Afloat," *Waste Age*, March 1991.
47. See note 43, above.
48. See note 5, above.
49. See note 5, above.
50. See note 26, above.
51. David Stipp, "Recycling Waste Paper With a Pressure Cooker," *The Wall Street Journal*, Jan. 7, 1991; Michael Misner, "Steam Explosion Will Help Consumers' Paper Recycling," *Recycling Times*, May 21, 1991; Michael Misner, "Steam Explosion Offers New Paper Recycling Opportunities," *Recycling Times*, Dec. 18., 1990; "Technology Developed To Recycled Paper," *Chemical and Engineering News*, Dec. 17, 1990.
52. See note 5, above.
53. Michael Misner, "Deinking Process Could Boost Laser Printed Paper's Value," *Recycling Times*, Feb. 26, 1991.
54. See note 5, above.
55. "Recycling Scrap Materials Contributes to a Better Environment," Institute of Scrap Recycling Industries Inc., Washington, D.C., undated fact sheet.
56. Steve Apotheker, "Mixed Reviews for Mixed Paper," *Resource Recycling*, January 1990.
57. J. Rodney Edwards, American Paper Institute Inc., personal communication, July 17, 1991.
58. See note 29, above.
59. Steve Apotheker, "The Newark Group Thrives On High Recycled Fiber Diet," *Resource Recycling*, January 1991.
60. See note 29, above.
61. See note 20, above.
62. See note 24, above.
63. See note 45, above.
64. See note 56, above.
65. See note 21, above.
66. "How Newspapers Were Recycled in 1990," *The Environmental Newspaper*, American Newspaper Publishers Association, Reston, Va., Spring/Summer 1991.
67. "Read. Then Recycle," American Newspaper Publishers Association, Washington, D.C., February 1990; Bill Paul, "Market for Recycled Newspapers in U.S. Collapses, Adding to Solid Waste Woes," *The Wall Street Journal*, Jan. 25, 1989.
68. "NSWMA Releases ONP Study," *Waste Age*, June 1990.
69. See note 2, above.
70. Susan Combs, "EPA Report Predicts Growth in Most Waste Paper Markets," *Recycling Times*, July 17, 1990.

71. "The Greenpeace Guide to Paper," Greenpeace USA, Washington, D.C., January 1990.
72. Kathleen Meade, "Newsprint Producers Positive About Recycling," *Waste Age*, September 1990.
73. "Papers Demand Recycled Newsprint," *The Environmental Newspaper*, American Newspaper Publishers Association, Reston, Va., Spring/Summer 1991.
74. *The Wall Street Journal*, May 2, 1990.
75. Edward P. Sparks, "The Outlook for Old Newspaper Recycling in North America," presentation at the National Solid Wastes Management Association's Waste Expo '91, Atlanta, Ga., April 9, 1991.
76. Dan Goldberg, "Markets Beyond the Paper Mill," *Waste Age*, December 1989.
77. "Markets for Old Newspapers," memo from the U.S. Congressional Research Service to the House Energy and Commerce Committee, Feb. 13, 1990.
78. See note 57, above.
79. See note 75, above.
80. See note 77, above.
81. Michael Misner, "Insulation Market Heats Up ONP Demand," *Recycling Times*, Feb. 26, 1991.
82. See note 77, above.
83. Steve Apotheker, "Animal Bedding—A Capital Idea," *Resource Recycling*, July 1990.
84. "Read. Then Recycle," American Newspaper Publishers Association, Washington, D.C., February 1990.
85. Matthew Witten, "The State of the State: Recycling in Vermont," *Resource Recycling*, October 1990.
86. Tom Watson, "State Recycling Officials Look to the Future," *Resource Recycling*, December 1989.
87. *Resource Recovery Report*, March 1990.
88. Dan Billin, "Newsprint Down On the Farm," *Valley News*, Feb. 26, 1990.
89. See note 77, above.
90. See note 77, above.
91. "Computer Print-out Made From Old News," *Recycling Times*, May 9, 1989.
92. "1990 Waste Paper Data," *Recycling Times*, April 9, 1991; Kathleen Meade, "Waste Paper Recovery Closer to 1995 Goal, API Report Says," *Recycling Times*, April 9, 1991.
93. See note 29, above.
94. See note 5, above.
95. Kathleen Meade, "Congressional Committee Beefs Up EPA's Paper Guidelines," *Recycling Times*, July 31, 1990; Gina Gill, "Pulling for Recycled Paper," *New England Sierran*.
96. "Suit Rejected," *Resource Recycling*, December 1989; "Court Upholds Recycled Paper Guidelines," *Resource Recovery Report*, January 1990.
97. "Recycling Primer," P.H. Glatfelter Co. brochure, undated; "Envision™: Environmentally Friendly Paper Products," Fort Howard Corp. brochure, undated.
98. "Recycled Content Standards Argued," *Resource Recycling*, January 1991.
99. "EPA Policy Undermines Paper Recycling Effort, Company Says," *Environment Week*, June 21, 1990.
100. Kathleen Meade, "Elder: Post-Consumer Push Could Displace Pre-consumer Recycling," *Recycling Times*, Aug. 28, 1990.
101. Daniel Sandoval, "Has the Paper Recycling Industry Turned the Corner On its Problems?," *Fibre Market News* in *Recycling Today*, Oct. 15, 1990.
102. Kathleen Meade, "EPA Allows Sawdust to Count as Recycled Content in Paper," *Recycling Times*, June 19, 1990.
103. Kathleen Meade, "EPA Requests Comment on Recycled Paper Procurement," *Recy-*

cling Times, Oct. 23, 1990.

104. Kathleen Meade, "RAC Passes First Paper Recycling Recommendations," *Recycling Times*, May 7, 1991.

105. Michael Misner, "ASTM Will Set the Standards for Paper Recycling in 1992," *Recycling Times*, Nov. 6, 1990.

106. Joseph T. Sedlock, "Conservatree Blasts EPA's Guidelines with Agenda," *Recycling Times*, Dec. 18, 1990.

107. See note 106, above.

108. Kathleen Meade, "Paper Industry Focuses on MWP Recycling, Content Definitions," *Recycling Times*, April 23, 1991.

109. See note 29, above.

110. See note 24, above.

111. See note 56, above.

112. See note 45, above.

113. See note 56, above.

114. See note 56, above.

115. See note 56, above.

116. *Resource Recovery Report*, December 1989.

117. See note 56, above.

118. See note 56, above; "At Press Time," *Resource Recycling*, November 1990.

119. Kathleen Meade, "Magazine Publishers Plan More Recycling in the '90s," *Recycling Times*, Dec. 4, 1990.

120. See note 44, above.

121. "Magazine Recycling Capacity Continues to Increase," *Recycling Times*, Dec. 4, 1990.

122. See note 119, above.

123. See note 119, above.

124. See note 75, above.

125. See note 45, above.

126. See note 26, above.

127. See note 20, above; William L. Kovacs, "The Coming Era of Conservation and Industrial Utilization of Recyclable Materials," *Ecology Law Quarterly*, University of California, 1988.

128. See note 23, above.

129. See note 75, above.

130. David Stipp, "Paper Recycling Is Being Trimmed By Shipping Woes," *The Wall Street Journal*, April 21, 1991; "Paper Recycling Markets," *Resource Recycling*, April 1991.

131. Marlise Simons, "U.S. Wastepaper Burdening Dutch," *The New York Times*, Dec. 11, 1990.

132. See note 45, above.

133. See note 26, above; Jonathan V.L. Kiser, "National Waste Strategies Compared," *Waste Age*, November 1989.

134. Richard Hertzberg, "The Business of Waste Paper Reuse," *BioCycle*, May/June 1987.

135. See note 23, above.

136. See note 25, above.

137. Robert W. Dellinger, Virgil Horton and Darlene Snow, "Waiting for the ONP Market to Improve," *Waste Age*, June 1990.

138. See note 75, above.

139. Ken McEntee, "The Current and Future Paper Recycling Market," *Secondary Fiber Supplement* in *Resource Recycling*, November 1990.

140. See note 45, above.

141. See note 27, above.

142. John Ruston, "Recycling: The Newsprint Industry Gets Religion," *EDF Letter*, Environmental Defense Fund, New York, N.Y., August 1990.
143. See note 67, above.
144. "Old Newspaper Prices: National Averages—1990," *Recycling Times*, Dec. 31, 1990.
145. "Old Corrugated Cardboard Prices: National Averages—1990," *Recycling Times*, Dec. 31, 1990.
146. "Laser-Free Computer Print-out Waste Paper Prices: National Averages—1990," *Recycling Times*, Dec. 31, 1990; "Sorted White Ledger Prices: National Averages—1990," *Recycling Times*, Dec. 31, 1990.
147. Michael Misner, "Pricing Trends," *Recycling Times*, April 24, 1990.
148. "Mixed Waste Paper Prices: National Averages—1990," *Recycling Times*, Jan. 15, 1991.
149. Daniel Sandoval, "Financial Aid Could Benefit Private Paper Recycling Industry," *Fibre Market News* in *Recycling Today*, Oct. 15, 1990.
150. "N.J. Gives Paper Co. $3-Million Recycling Loan," *Waste Age*, September 1990.
151. "New York Mill Sited," *Recycling Today*, Nov. 15, 1990.
152. Kathleen Meade, "W. Va. Plant Will Recycle Mixed Office Waste Paper," *Recycling Times*, Jan. 15, 1991.
153. Susan Combs, "James River To Take More Waste Paper at Mich. Plant," *Recycling Times*, May 7, 1991.
154. "Abitibi-Price Receives Energy Grant To Add a Deinking Plant in Ontario," *Recycling Times*, Feb. 26, 1991.
155. Susan Combs, "British Columbia Moves Ahead On Stand-alone Deinking Plant," *Recycling Times*, Aug. 14, 1990; "Paper," *Resource Recovery Report*, September 1990.
156. "Kruger Buys Manistique Papers," *Recycling Times*, April 9, 1991; Kathleen Meade, "Kruger OKs Deinking Expansion; Will Buy ONP, OMG from U.S.," *Recycling Times*, Oct. 23, 1990.
157. Michael Misner, "Railroads Drop Rates to Entice Waste Paper-Hungry Mills," *Recycling Times*, May 7, 1991.
158. See note 157, above.
159. Kathleen Meade, "Wisconsin Recyclers Examine Market Development Issues," *Recycling Times*, April 24, 1990.
160. Susie Thompson, "Stone, Burlington Team Up to Recycle OCC," *Waste Age*, February 1991.
161. Kathleen Meade, "Kruger OKs Deinking Expansion; Will Buy ONP, OMG from U.S.," *Recycling Times*, Oct. 23, 1990.
162. John Burke, James River Corp., presentation at the U.S. Conference of Mayor's "Cloosing the Loop" conference, Washington, D.C., July 11, 1991.
163. See note 18, above.
164. See note 75, above.
165. See note 57, above.
166. Kathleen Meade, "RISI: Deinking Is Not the Best Investment for Canadian Mills," *Recycling Times*, Sept. 11, 1990.
167. Lawrence A. Broeren, "Deinking of Secondary Fiber Gains Acceptance As Technology Evolves," *Pulp & Paper*, March 1990; U.S. Congress, Office of Technology Assessment, *Facing America's Trash: What Next for Municipal Solid Waste*, OTA-0-424, Washington, D.C.: U.S. Government Printing Office, October 1989, p. 142.
168. Paul Kemezis, "The Promise of Newspaper Recycling," *Environment Week*, May 10, 1990.
169. Kathleen Meade, "Good News for Stone Means Less Recycled Newsprint," *Recycling Times*, March 12, 1991.

170. Lawrence A. Broeren, "Deinking of Secondary Fiber Gains Acceptance As Technology Evolves," *Pulp & Paper*, March 1990.

171. See note 71, above; "Recycling Waste to Save Energy," U.S. Department of Energy's Conservation and Renewable Energy Inquiry and Referral Service, FS 227, January 1989; "Recycling Scrap Materials Contributes to a Better Environment," Institute of Scrap Recycling Industries Inc., Washington, D.C., undated fact sheet.

172. Holly Brough, "Why the Recycled Newspaper Bust?," *WorldWatch*, November/December 1989.

173. Kathleen Meade, "API: Recycling Growth Higher Than Expected," *Recycling Times*, Feb. 12, 1991.

174. See note 15, above.

175. See note 29, above; "Recycling Primer," P.H. Glatfelter Co. brochure, undated.

176. See note 57, above.

177. See note 3, above.

178. See note 75, above.

179. Daniel Sandoval, "Paper Industry Reports Success for 40% Recovery Rate," *Recycling Today*, April 15, 1991.

180. James P. Miller, "Waste Management to Form Venture with Smurfit on Paper for Recycling," *The Wall Street Journal*, Jan. 9, 1990.

181. "Newark Buying Eastern," *Recycling Today*, Jan. 15, 1991.

182. Susie Thompson, "Stone, Burlington Team Up to Recycle OCC," *Waste Age*, February 1991; Jerry Powell, "The Big Haulers Are Becoming the Big Recycling Processors," *Resource Recycling*, September 1990.

183. See note 169, above; Kathleen Meade, "De-inking Projects Raise Waste Paper Capacity Across the U.S.," *Recycling Times*, Dec. 31, 1990; Jerry Powell, "The Big Haulers Are Becoming the Big Recycling Processors," *Resource Recycling*, September 1990.

184. See note 3, above.

185. See note 3, above.

186. Michael Misner, "RSC Plans Three SE Mills for OCC," *Recycling Times*, Sept. 25, 1990.

187. See note 173, above.

188. American Newspaper Publishers Association, Reston, Va., personal communication, Aug. 20, 1991.

189. See note 6, above.

190. Robert J. Brennan, "Paper Makers See Slower Growth, More Recycling," *The Wall Street Journal*, Dec. 10, 1990; "How to Recycle Waste Paper," American Paper Institute Inc., New York, N.Y., 1990.

191. Paul J. Schierl, Fort Howard Corp., "Remarks at the 9th Annual Resource Recovery Conference of the United States Conference of Mayors," Washington, D.C., March 29, 1990; "40 Percent Recycling by '95: API," *Recycling Today*, March 15, 1990; "Recycling Waste to Save Energy," U.S. Department of Energy's Conservation and Renewable Energy Inquiry and Referral Service, FS 227, January 1989.

192. See note 59, above.

193. Susan Combs, "Print Communications Associations Form Paper Recycling Council," *Recycling Times*, Jan. 15, 1991.

194. See note 156, above.

195. Letter to membership, National Audubon Society, New York, N.Y., undated.

196. "Paper or Plastic?," *The Washington Post*.

197. Arthur Amidon, "Plastic Grocery Sack Recycling," *Resource Recycling*, November 1990.

198. See note 196, above.

199. "Decisions at the Supermarket Extend Beyond Brand Names," *Chemecology*, November

1990.
200. See note 197, above.
201. See note 84, above.
202. See note 6, above.
203. Jerry Powell, "Quantity and Quality: the Southeast Paper Story," *Resource Recycling,* July 1990.
204. See note 84, above.
205. Jeffrey Bruner, "Post, Canusa to Market D.C.'s ONP," *Recycling Times,* July 17, 1990.
206. See note 6, above.
207. See note 18, above.
208. "Paper," *Resource Recovery Report,* February 1991.
209. "Envision™: Environmentally Friendly Paper Products," Fort Howard Corp. brochure, undated; Susan Combs, "Fort Howard to Increase Capacity by 100,000 Tons," *Recycling Times,* Jan. 15, 1991; Kathleen Meade, "Paper Industry Focuses on MWP Recycling, Content Definitions," *Recycling Times,* April 23, 1991.
210. "Publicly Announced Expansion Plans for Increased Use of Recovered Waste Paper," American Paper Institute Inc., New York, N.Y., July 1991.
211. See note 5, above.
212. See note 210, above.
213. "Is Recycling Important?," *Orion,* Winter 1990.
214. "Recycling Primer," P.H. Glatfelter Co. brochure, undated.
215. See note 210, above.
216. Kathleen Meade, "De-inking Projects Raise Waste Paper Capacity Across the U.S.," *Recycling Times,* Dec. 31, 1990.
217. Kathleen Meade, "International Paper to Use a German Recycling Technology," *Recycling Times,* March 26, 1991.
218. See notes 26 and 29, above.
219. Kathleen Meade, "N.Y.C. Considers Brokering Directly to Newsprint Mills," *Recycling Times,* June 19, 1990.
220. See note 27, above.
221. See note 137, above.
222. See note 27, above.

Notes to Chapter 5

1. "Methods to Manage and Control Plastic Wastes," Executive Summary, (EPA/530-SW-90-051A), U.S. Environmental Protection Agency, Office of Solid Waste and Emergency Response and Office of Water, February 1990, Washington, D.C.
2. Bill Lawren, "Plastic Rapt," *National Wildlife,* October/November 1990.
3. "Industry Outlook," *Environmental Business Journal,* December 1990.
4. "A Right Cross to the Chin," *Bottle/Can Recycling Update,* November/December 1990.
5. "Waste Stream Advertising Hits the Mainstream," *The Soft Drink Recycler,* National Soft Drink Association, Washington, D.C., Winter 1990.
6. Anne E. Nichols, "Plastic Bottle Maker Seeks to Profit from Recycling," *The Wall Street Journal,* Dec. 13, 1990.
7. Emma Chynoweth, "Green Power Drives Recyclers," *Chemicalweek,* Nov. 21, 1990.
8. Kathleen Meade, "Container Wars 1990: The Impure Strikes Back," *Recycling Times,* Dec. 4, 1990.

9. *Franklin's Insight*, Franklin Research & Development Corp., Boston, Mass., Vol. 5, No. 8, August 1988.

10. "GE Plastics' Resource Recovery Strategy," General Electric Co. brochure, January 1990.

11. "Recycling Plastics: A Forum," *Environmental Action*, July/August 1988.

12. "Trade-offs Involved in Beverage Container Deposit Legislation," U.S. General Accounting Office, (GAO-RCED-91-25), November 1990.

13. See note 1, above.

14. U.S. Environmental Protection Agency, Office of Solid Waste and Emergency Response, "Characterization of Municipal Solid Waste in the United States: 1990 Update," (EPA/530-SW-90-042), June 1990, Washington, D.C.

15. See note 14, above.

16. See note 14, above.

17. See note 14, above.

18. "An Industry Tries to Improve Its Record on Plastic," *The New York Times*, March 31, 1991; "Plastics Industry Introduces Blueprint," *Recycling Today*, May 15, 1991.

19. "Programs Now in 450 Communities: Recycling of Plastic Bottles Expands Rapidly," Johnson Controls Inc. press release, Oct. 2, 1990.

20. Susan Vadney, Council for Solid Waste Solutions, personal communication, March 1, 1991.

21. "Market Research on Plastics Recycling," Center for Plastics Recycling Research, The State University of New Jersey, Rutgers, Technical Report #31, February 1989.

22. "Things You've Always Wanted to Know About Soft Drink Container Recycling," National Soft Drink Association, Washington, D.C., 1990.

23. See note 20, above.

24. David Rotman, "No Go for Dow PET Recycling," *Chemicalweek*, April 18, 1990.

25. See note 21, above.

26. "A Few Numbers," *Bottle/Can Recycling Update*, April 1991; "Production by the U.S. Chemical Industry," *Chemical and Engineering News*, June 18, 1990.

27. See note 18, above.

28. See note 21, above.

29. Faye Flam, "Putting a Lid on Throwaways," *Chemicalweek*, July 25, 1990.

30. See note 11, above.

31. Wayne Pearson, Plastics Recycling Foundation, personal communication, Oct. 22, 1990.

32. Jeanne Wirka, "A Plastics Packaging Primer," *Environmental Action*, July/August 1988.

33. See note 31, above; Sherman P. Stratford, "Trashing a $150 Billion Business," *Fortune*, Aug. 28, 1989.

34. U.S. Congress, Office of Technology Assessment, *Facing America's Trash: What Next for Municipal Solid Waste*, OTA-O-424, Washington, D.C.: U.S. Government Printing Office, October 1989, p. 175.

35. See note 31, above.

36. Michael Misner, "Quality Control Considered Key to Use of Post-Consumer HDPE," *Recycling Times*, July 3, 1990.

37. See note 36, above.

38. Susan Combs, "'Recyclepak' Drug Package to Contain Post-Consumer HDPE Layer," *Recycling Times*, June 19, 1990.

39. "New Compounded Resin Developed by Soltex Contains Recycled Content," *The Plastic Bottle Reporter*, Society of the Plastics Industry Inc., Washington, D.C., Fall 1990.

40. David Sheon, representative of the National Polystyrene Recycling Co., personal com-

munication, Oct. 16, 1990.

41. "Recycling PET: A Guidebook for Community Programs," National Association for Plastic Container Recovery, Charlotte, N.C., 1989.

42. "Recovering Plastic Resources For a Better World," Partek Corp. brochure, undated.

43. Jerry Powell, "It's The Real Thing: The Recycled Plastic Soft Drink Bottle," *Resource Recycling*, January 1991.

44. Richard Olson, Dolco Packaging Corp., personal communication, Oct. 25, 1990.

45. "Closing The Loop," *The Soft Drink Recycler*, National Soft Drink Association, Washington, D.C., Spring 1991; "FDA Approves Regenerated PET for Plastic Beverage Bottle," *Bottle/Can Recycling Update*, January 1991.

46. Michael J. McCarthy, "Recycled Plastic Wins Converts: Coke and Pepsi," *The Wall Street Journal*, Dec. 5, 1990; "Plastic Bottle Recycling News," *Bottle/Can Recycling Update*, November/December 1990.

47. "Commodities Focus: Plastics Market," *Recycling Today*, March 15, 1991.

48. "Plastic Bottle Recycling News," *Bottle/Can Recycling Update*, November/December 1990.

49. "News and New Products," *The Green Consumer Letter*, May 1991.

50. "Agenda: Planet Earth," McDonald's Corp. brochure, March 1990.

51. See note 11, above.

52. James S. Hirsch, "Heinz to Unveil Recyclable Bottle for Its Ketchup," *The Wall Street Journal*, April 9, 1990.

53. "PBI Test Shows Ketchup Bottles Recycle as Single Resin," *The Plastic Bottle Reporter*, Society of the Plastics Industry Inc., Washington, D.C., Spring 1990; "Multi-Bottles Recycled," *Recycling Today*, June 1990.

54. "Studies Show Multi-Layer Polypropylene is Recyclable in HDPE Post-Consumer Stream," *The Plastic Bottle Reporter*, Society of the Plastics Industry Inc., Washington, D.C., Winter 1991.

55. See note 6, above.

56. Gordon Graff, "From Bottles to Bathtubs," *The New York Times*, Sept. 25, 1988.

57. See note 11, above.

58. Plastics Recycling Foundation's 1990 Annual Report; "Recycling Technology News," *Bottle/Can Recycling Update*, April 1991.

59. Pure Tech International Inc.'s 1989 Form 10-K; Susan Fine, "The Nine Lives of Plastic," *WorldWatch*, May/June 1989.

60. Wayne Pearson, "Plastics Recycling Foundation: The First Five Years," Plastics Recycling Foundation, Washington, D.C., February 1990; Representative of United Resource Recovery Inc., personal communication, Jan. 23, 1991.

61. Plastics Recycling Foundation's 1990 Annual Report.

62. Susan Fine, "The Nine Lives of Plastic," *WorldWatch*, May/June 1989.

63. David Rotman, "Solid Waste is a Mushy Problem," *Chemicalweek*, Dec. 20/27, 1989.

64. Amal Kumar Naj, "Chemists Seek Ways to Recycle Plastics Before Movement to Ban Products Grows," *The Wall Street Journal*.

65. See note 61, above.

66. "Recycled Plastic Market News," *Bottle/Can Recycling Update*, April 1991.

67. Michele Raymond, "Rutgers Does Research to Refine Commingled Plastics Recycling," *Recycling Times*, Aug. 14, 1990.

68. Thomas J. Nosker, Richard W. Renfree and Darrell R. Morrow, "Recycle Polystyrene, Add Value to Commingled Products," *Plastics Engineering*, February 1990.

69. See note 67, above; "Rutgers Begins New Research Effort," *COPPE Update*, Council on Plastics and Packaging in the Environment, Washington, D.C., August 1987.

70. See note 67, above.

71. See note 64, above.
72. Plastics and the Environment: Progress and Commitment," The Society of the Plastics Industry Inc., Washington, D.C., undated.
73. "States, Bottle Makers and Food Packagers Adopt Plastic Industry's Voluntary Container Code System," The Society of the Plastics Industry Inc.'s Plastic Bottle Institute's press release, Washington, D.C., undated.
74. See note 20, above.
75. Michael Misner, "Plastic Labeling Costs," *Recycling Times*, June 19, 1990.
76. "Misleading Labels," *Garbage*, September/October 1989.
77. Amal Kumar Naj, "GE Pushes to Develop Recyclable Plastic," *The Wall Street Journal*, Aug. 13, 1990.
78. Leslie Harpold, "Polymerland to Market Resin Recycled from Durable Goods," *Recycling Times*, July 17, 1990.
79. Laurie A. Rich, "An Overwhelming Problem Offers Business Opportunities," *Chemicalweek*, July 27, 1988.
80. Wayne Pearson, "Plastics Recycling Foundation: The First Five Years," Plastics Recycling Foundation, Washington, D.C., February 1990.
81. Louis Agnello, Union Carbide Corp., personal communication, Oct. 16, 1990.
82. Dr. Charles Lancelot, Rubbermaid Commercial Products Inc., personal communication, Feb. 22, 1991.
83. See note 34, above, p. 176.
84. See note 34, above, p. 194.
85. "Plastics Recycling: From Vision to Reality," Plastics Recycling Foundation, Washington, D.C., undated.
86. Ellen Goldbaum, "A New Wave of Plastics Recycling, *Chemicalweek*, May 10, 1989.
87. Edmond Carreras, Day Products Inc., personal communication, Oct. 16, 1990.
88. Tom Watson, "Polystyrene Recycling: Big Money, Big Implications," *Resource Recycling*, September 1989.
89. "Association News," *Recycling Today*, April 15, 1990.
90. *Resource Recovery Report*, September 1990.
91. Ann M. Thayer, "Degradable Plastics Generate Controversy in Solid Waste Issues," *Chemical and Engineering News*, June 25, 1990; Amal Kumar Naj, "Big Chemical Concerns Hasten To Develop Biodegradable Plastics," *The Wall Street Journal*, July 21, 1988; John Holusha, "Scientists Are Proving That Natural Plastic Is Not an Oxymoron," *The New York Times*, Oct. 21, 1990; Michael Waldholz, "New Plastic Is Promoted As a Natural," *The Wall Street Journal*, Jan. 24, 1990; Peter Knight, "A Package Deal for Consumer Products," *The Financial Times*, March 28, 1990.; Gwendolyn Cofield, "Warner-Lambert Says New Starch Product is 100% Degradable," *Recycling Times*, March 13, 1990; *Resource Recovery Report*, October 1990.
92. "Industry Outlook," *Environmental Business Journal*, February 1991.
93. Jeanne Wirka, "The Degradable Plastics Hoax," *Environmental Action*, November/December 1989.
94. Ann M. Thayer, "Degradable Plastics Generate Controversy in Solid Waste Issues," *Chemical and Engineering News*, June 25, 1990.
95. See note 93, above.
96. John Holusha, "Recyclable Claims are Debated," *The New York Times*, Jan. 8, 1991.
97. John Holusha, "Mobil Ends Environmental Claims," *The New York Times*, March 30, 1990.
98. Letter to membership, Environmental Defense Fund, New York, N.Y., undated.
99. Amal Kumar Naj, "Big Chemical Concerns Hasten To Develop Biodegradable Plastics,"

The Wall Street Journal, July 21, 1988.

100. See note 94, above; Few large plastic resin manufacturers have become involved in biodegradable plastics, making photodegradable materials instead. Producing photodegradable plastics is well within the expertise of the plastics industry, and the photodegradable materials can be processed on existing equipment. Dow, Du Pont and Union Carbide each produce a photodegradable resin for six-pack holders.

101. William L. Rathje, "Once and Future Landfills," *National Geographic*, May 1991.

102. See note 1, above.

103. See note 40, above.

104. See note 31, above.

105. Sherrie Gruder-Adams, "Residential Polystyrene Recycling," *Resource Recovery*, October 1990.

106. Kathleen Meade, "Hardee's to Use Recycled Polystyrene in Restaurants," *Recycling Times*, April 9, 1991.

107. Donella Meadows, "McDonald's Recycling Is Better Than Nothing, But Just Barely," *The Valley News*.

108. Tom Watson, "Products from Mixed Plastics: Will the Profits Flow?," *Resource Recycling*, July 1990.

109. See note 108, above.

110. Jeffrey M. Schell, "Plastics Recycling Rates Will Rise," *Waste Age*, December 1989.

111. "Recycled Plastics (PET/HDPE) Prices: National Averages—1990," *Recycling Times*, Dec. 31, 1990.

112. "Marketing Post-consumer Recycled Plastic for Reuse in Non-food Bottles, and Other Plastic Markets," Pure Tech International Inc., September 1990.

113. Michael Misner, "Sonoco Inflates HDPE Price," *Recycling Times*, Aug. 14, 190.

114. "Recycle PVC Price List, First Quarter 1991," Occidental Chemical Corp., Jan. 15, 1991.

115. Clark Ray, representative of the National Polystyrene Recycling Co., personal communication, Oct. 16, 1990.

116. Andrew Wood, "Plastics: Can More Be Made into Less?," *Chemicalweek*, May 2, 1990.

117. Bruce F. Greek, "Polystyrene Heads for Down Year in Face of Market Pressures," *Chemical and Engineering News*, Oct. 15, 1990.

118. Representative of United Resource Recovery Inc., personal communication, Jan. 23, 1991.

119. Hannah Holmes, "Recycling Plastics," *Garbage*, January/February 1991.

120. See note 34, above, p. 171.

121. "Export Data Reported," *Plastics Recycling Update*, March 1990.

122. See note 32, above.

123. "Recycling Case Histories Offered," *COPPE Update*, Council on Plastics and Packaging in the Environment, Washington, D.C., June 1987.

124. Ellen Goldbaum, "A Well-coordinated Buy for Wellman," *Chemicalweek*, Sept. 6, 1989.

125. See note 21, above.

126. "Plastic Bottle Recycling News," *Bottle/Can Recycling Update*, November/December 1990.

127. See note 72, above.

128. "Plastics Industry Ponders 'Voluntary' Recycling Plans," *Environment Week*, Oct. 26, 1989.

129. "Plastics," *Resource Recycling*, September 1990.

130. "Plastics Industry Group Asks 25% Recycling by '95," *The Wall Street Journal*, March 29, 1991; "Plastics Recycling Plan Announced," *Chemicalweek*, April 3, 1991; "Plastics Industry Unveils Blueprint," *Resource Recovery Report*, May 1991.

131. See note 80, above.
132. "Polystyrene Packaging and Solid Waste Disposal: Issues and Answers," Polystyrene Packaging Council brochure, Washington, D.C., January 1990.
133. See note 41, above; Allen Giles, National Association for the Plastic Container Recovery, personal communication, Sept. 25, 1990.
134. See note 112, above.
135. Procter & Gamble Co. press release, March 28, 1990; "Plastics Recycling Market News," *Bottle/Can Recycling Update*, November/December 1990.
136. Mark Meade, Embrace Systems Corp., personal communication, Oct. 17, 1990; Embrace Systems Corp. brochure, undated.
137. Michael Misner, "Recycled PET Finds Use on Cars; Auto Supplier Agrees to Purchase," *Recycling Times*, Nov. 20, 1990.
138. See note 80, above.
139. See note 87, above; Barbara Spector, "Firm Recycles NSF-Sponsored Research into New Plant," *The Scientist*, Dec. 11, 1989.
140. See note 19, above; Susan Davis, Johnson Controls, personal communication, Oct. 16, 1990.
141. See note 140, above.
142. Michael Misner, "Pricing Trends," *Recycling Times*, Dec. 18, 1990; "Need for Plastics Converts User to Big Fan of Recycled PET," *Recycling Times*, January 1989; "St. Jude's Goes National," *COPPE Update*, Council on Plastics and Packaging in the Environment, Washington, D.C., February, 1987.
143. Bruce Bond, wTe Corp., personal communication, Feb. 26, 1991; Bruce Bond, presentation at the National Solid Waste Management Association's Waste Expo '91, Atlanta, Ga., May 1, 1990; "Venture Capital Fuels Fast Growth in Waste Recycling," *Environmental Business Journal*, September 1990; "Two on Private List," *Waste Age*, January 1988.
144. David C. Katz, Pure Tech International Inc., personal communication, March 8, 1991; Pure Tech International Inc.'s 1989 Form 10-K; "Pure Tech International Inc. Taiwan Licensee Commences Operations at Recycling Plant," Pure Tech International Inc. press release, Sept. 5, 1990.
145. See note 144, above.
146. See note 126, above.
147. See note 112, above.
148. Elaine Plummer, Procter & Gamble Co., personal communication, Jan. 28, 1991.
149. "Plastics: Seattle Asks for Less; PS Plant Opens," *Waste Age*, July 1989.
150. "Recycled Plastic Market News," *Bottle/Can Recycling Update*, April 1991.
151. "Lever Brothers Will Bottle Liquids in Recycled Plastic," *The Wall Street Journal*, Aug. 8, 1990; "Lever Brothers Announces Start of Nationwide Program to Use Recycled Plastic in Laundry Product Bottles," *The Plastic Bottle Reporter*, Society of the Plastic Industry Inc., Washington, D.C., Fall 1990; Susan Combs, "Jennico Uses 50% Postconsumer HDPE in Fabric Softener Bottles," *Recycling Times*, Dec. 18, 1990.
152. See note 82, above.
153. Martin Forman, Poly-Anna Plastic Products, personal communication, March 1, 1991.
154. Pat Getter, Du Pont Co., personal communication, Oct. 3, 1990; Illinois, Du Pont Announce Partnership in Recycling," Du Pont press release, April 1989; "Industry Outlook," *Environmental Business Journal*, March 1991.
155. Kim Watkins, Graham Packaging Co., personal communications, Oct. 19, 1990, and Jan. 11, 1991; Susan Combs, "Sonoco Graham to Build HDPE Recycling Plant on East Coast," *Waste Age*, March 13, 1990.

156. Robert Gaundet, Partek Corp., personal communications, Sept. 3, 1991, Oct. 19, 1990, and Jan. 11, 1991; Phillips Petroleum Co.'s press release, Sept. 20, 1990.

157. See notes 42 and 156, above.

158. Jill Rea, Wellman Inc., personal communication, Jan. 24, 1991; Wellman Inc.'s 1990 and 1989 annual reports.

159. See note 158, above.

160. Jill Rea, Wellman Inc., personal communication, June 27, 1991.

161. See note 158, above.

162. See note 160, above.

163. See note 158, above.

164. "Nation's Plastic Recycling Effort Gets Boost From New Joint Venture," Plastic Recycling Alliance press release, May 22, 1989.

165. Pat Getter, Du Pont Co., personal communication, Oct. 3, 1990.

166. Du Pont press release, Sept. 25, 1990; Marc Reisch, "Plastics Recycling Expansion Planned," *Chemical and Engineering News*, Oct. 1, 1990.

167. "Plastics Recycling Alliance and OxyChem to Adapt PVC Sortation in Philadelphia Plant," *EcoVinyl Echoes*, an Occidental Chemical Corp. newsletter, First Quarter, 1991.

168. Collingwood Harris, ITC, personal communications, Oct. 22, 1990, and Jan. 16, 1991.

169. See note 168, above; "Closing the Loop," PolySource Mid-Atlantic brochure, undated; "German Technology Called Expensive," *Recycling Times*, July 3, 1990.

170. George Castaneda, Clean Tech Inc., personal communication, Oct. 23, 1990.

171. Jeffrey Smith, Orion Pacific Inc., personal communication, Jan. 11, 1991.

172. Gregory Boguski, Secondary Polymers, personal communication, Jan. 28, 1991.

173. Tom Tomaszek, North American Plastics Recycling Corp., personal communication, June 12, 1991.

174. Michael Kopulsky, Envirothene Inc., personal communication, Jan. 22, 1991.

175. See note 81, above; "Union Carbide Delays Opening Recycling Plant," *Recycling Times*, May 7, 1991; "Carbide Proposes Plant," *Recycling Today*, May 1990.

176. "New Compounded Quantum Chemical to Build Major Recycling Plant in Midwest," *The Plastic Bottle Reporter*, Society of the Plastics Industry Inc., Washington, D.C., Winter 1991; "Thomas Ewing, "Quantum Connects Plastic Recycling Plant to Ohio MRF," *Recycling Times*, Feb. 26, 1991.

177. Hank Gudrian, Quantum Chemical Corp., personal communication, Oct. 19, 1990.

178. "N.Y. Plastics Recycling Facility Planned Next to Yonkers MRF," *Recycling Times*, Feb. 12, 1991.

179. Roger Geyer, M.A. Industries Inc., personal communication, April 10, 1991; Gail Brown, M.A. Industries Inc., personal communication, Jan. 11, 1991.

180. See note 119, above.

181. Paris Wolfe, "From Sortation to Marketing, the Vinyl Loop Gets Stronger," *Recycling Today*, March 15, 1990.

182. "More UBC News," *Bottle/Can Recycling Update*, October 1990; "Foreign News," *Bottle/Can Recycling Update*, September 1990.

183. "High Vinyl Demand Predicted," *Recycling Today*, Oct. 15, 1990.

184. William Carroll, Jr., Occidental Chemical Corp., personal communication, Oct. 3, 1990; *EcoVinyl Echoes*, Occidental Chemical Corp. newsletter, Fourth Quarter 1990.

185. D'Lane Wisner, B.F. Goodrich Co., personal communication, Jan. 23, 1991.

186. *EcoVinyl Echoes* Occidental Chemical Corp. newsletter, Fourth Quarter 1990.

187. "Industry Announces Support for Solid Waste Sortation Program," The Vinyl Institute press release, Wayne, N.J., Dec. 11, 1989.

188. Fred Krause, B.F. Goodrich Co., personal communication, Jan. 23, 1991.

189. William Carroll, Jr., Occidental Chemical Corp., personal communication, Oct. 3, 1990.

190. See note 167, above.

191. Frank Borelli, Georgia Gulf Corp., personal communication, Oct. 3, 1990.

192. See note 188, above.

193. "Recycling Vinyl in the U.S.A.," *Environmental Briefs*, The Vinyl Institute, Wayne, N.J., May 1991.

194. "Zoo Benches Recycled," *Recycling Today*, Oct. 15, 1990.

195. See notes 181 and 187, above; Peter Brown, XL Disposal Corp., personal communication, Aug. 29, 1991; "Automated Sortation Update," *EcoVinyl Echoes*, Occidental Chemical Corp. newsletter, Third Quarter 1991; Paul Kemezis, "Tennessee Company Pushes PVC Recycling Technology," *Environment Week*, Sept. 21, 1989; "Full Scale Pilots Set," *Environmental Briefs*, The Vinyl Institute, Wayne, N.J., January 1991.

196. Susan Combs, "NRT Unveils PVC Sorting Systems: Called Too Costly for MRFS," *Recycling Times*, Nov. 20, 1990.

197. See note 188, above; "Recycling Technology News," *Plastics Recycling Update*, March 1990.

198. "Vinyl Sortation Debuts," *Recycling Today*, July 16, 1990

199. "Dow Forms New Marketing Group," *Recycling Times*, July 3, 1990; "Recycling Venture Abandoned," *Recycling Today*, June 1990; Kathleen Meade, "Dow, Domtar End Venture," *Recycling Times*, April 24, 1990; see note 24.

200. See note 117, above.

201. "Questions & Answers," National Polystyrene Recycling Co. fact sheet, Oct. 26, 1989.

202. See note 82, above; Donald Awbrey, Rubbermaid Inc., personal communication, Feb. 26, 1991.

203. "Acme United Markets Line With 90% Recycled Plastic," *The Wall Street Journal*, Dec. 4, 1990.

204. See note 106, above; "Adam Lashinsky, "Recycled PS is Sandwiched in Burger Box," *Plastic News*, March 25, 1991.

205. Scott Kilman, "McDonald's to Drop Plastic Foam Boxes in Favor of High-Tech Paper Packaging," *The Wall Street Journal*, Nov. 2, 1990.

206. Ken Sternberg, "McDonald's Polystyrene Pullout Draws Mixed Reviews," *Chemicalweek*, Nov. 14, 1990; Susan Combs, "McDonald's Drops polystyrene Clamshells, Recycling," *Recycling Times*, Nov. 20, 1990.

207. Kathleen Meade, "Companies Recycle Polystyrene to Avoid Bans in the Twin Cities," *Recycling Times*, Oct. 10, 1990.

208. See note 40, above.

209. "Polystyrene Added to Curbside Recycling Program," *Solid Waste & Power*, June 1991.

210. Patricia Ireland, Dart Container Corp., personal communication, Sept. 27, 1990.

211. Ellen M. Kosty, National Polystyrene Recycling Co., written communication, July 5, 1991.

212. See notes 40, 115 and 211, above; Ellen M. Kosty, National Polystyrene Recycling Co., written communication, July 5, 1991; Susan Combs, "NPRC to Stop Plastics Again's Polystyrene Recycling in Mass.," *Recycling Times*, May 21, 1991.

213. "Polystyrene Recycling News," *Bottle/Can Recycling Update*, March 1991; Randolph B. Smith, "Plastics Industry, Seeking to Head Off Packaging Bans, Plans Recycling Plant," *The Wall Street Journal*, Aug. 20, 1990; "Big Polystyrene Recycling Plant Started," *Chemical and Engineering News*, Aug. 27, 1990; see note 40.

214. "Recycling and Solid Waste Management Experience: Project Summary," New England CR Inc. fact sheet, undated; "Recycling: PS Plan for Chicago," *Chemicalweek*, March 27, 1991; Bruce Bond, wTe Corp., personal communication, Feb. 26, 1991.

215. See note 210, above.

216. See note 210, above.

217. "Disposable Diapers—Do They Have a Future?," *Waste Age,* May 1991; Kathleen Deveny, "States Mull Rash of Diaper Regulations, *The Wall Street Journal*;" "Benefits of Disposable Diapers," Procter & Gamble Co. fact sheet, undated; "In Vermont, a Prospect to Ban Disposable Diapers," *The New York Times,* Dec. 31, 1989.

218. "Day-Care Centers Stick With Disposables," *The Wall Street Journal,* May 17, 1990; Kathleen Deveny, "States Mull Rash of Diaper Regulations," *The Wall Street Journal.*

219. Kathleen Deveny, "States Mull Rash of Diaper Regulations," *The Wall Street Journal.*

220. "Diapers Restudied," *Resource Recovery Report,* February 1991.

221. "P&G Commits $20 Million to Advance Composting as a Solid Waste Solution; Will Develop New Compostable Materials for Diapers," Procter & Gamble Co. press release, Oct. 9, 1990; Alecia Swasy, "Procter & Gamble Hopes to Recycle Disposable Diapers," *The Wall Street Journal,* June 21, 1989.

222. See note 88, above; "Amoco Closes PS Recycling Unit," *Chemicalweek,* July 24, 1991; Bruce Bond, wTe Corp., personal communication, March 29, 1990; John Holusha, "Plastic Trash: 'Silk Purses' Sought," *The New York Times,* May 3, 1989.

223. See note 88, above; Lee Messer, Polystyrene Recycling Inc., personal communication, Sept. 27, 1990.

224. See note 63, above.

225. "Recycling Collection News," *Plastics Recycling Update,* March 1990.

226. See note 119, above.

227. "Recycling Mixed Plastics: New Markets," The Council for Solid Waste Solutions and the Plastics Recycling Foundation, Washington, D.C., undated.

228. See note 21, above.

229. See notes 108 and 227, above.

230. Carl Lanza, National Waste Technologies Inc., personal communications, Oct. 26, 1990 and Feb. 26, 1991; Roger Many, ARW Polywood, personal communication, Feb. 26, 1991; Susan Combs, "Plastics Recycling Takes Off with New Facilities, Methods," *Recycling Times,* Dec. 31, 1990.

231. Carl Lanza, National Waste Technologies Inc., personal communications, Oct. 26, 1990 and Feb. 26, 1991.

232. See note 21, above.

233. See note 108, above.

234. Advanced Environmental Recycling Technologies Inc.'s 1989 annual report.

235. See note 108, above.

236. Susan Combs, "Hammer to Build 16 New Mixed Plastic Recycling Plants," *Recycling Times,* Sept. 11, 1990.

237. "Plastics," *Resource Recycling,* September 1990.

238. Mark Nesbitt, Hammers Plastic Recycling Corp., personal communication, Feb. 26, 1991.

239. See note 108, above.

240. "Plastic Recycling Joint Venture," *Chemicalweek,* Feb. 21, 1990.

241. See note 236, above.

242. See note 234, above; Douglas Brooks, Advanced Environmental Recycling Technologies Inc., personal communication, March 1, 1991; "Doors Use Wood, Plastic Waste," *Recycling Times,* May 21, 1991; "Dow, AERT to Recycle Plastics," *Recycling Times,* Oct. 23, 1990.

243. Douglas Brooks, Advanced Environmental Recycling Technologies Inc., personal communication, March 1, 1991; Paul Kemezis, "U.S. Firm Pushes Plastic-Based

Wood," *Environment Week*, Dec. 21, 1989; Primary and secondary paper fiber recovery mills hydropulp recycled paper and polyethylene-coated paperboard to recover the paper fiber. The by-product is a water-saturated composite of polyethylene and unrecovered paper fiber, which most mills dispose of without further processing. AERT recovers the polyethylene from this byproduct to produce Moistureshield.

244. "Demand for Plastic Lumber Steadily Expands," *BioCycle*, November 1990.

245. Jeffrey Bachrach, Polymerix Inc., personal communication, March 1, 1991.

246. "Plastic Lumber in Florida," *Recycling Today*, Jan. 15, 1991.

247. See note 245, above; Polymerix Inc.'s 1990 annual report and Jan. 8, 1990, prospectus.

248. Carl Lanza, National Waste Technologies Inc., personal communications, Oct. 26, 1990, and Feb. 26, 1991; *Resource Recovery Report*, September 1989.

249. See note 108, above; Superwood International Ltd. brochure, undated.

250. "Post Consumer Plastic Bottle Recycling with Eaglebrook," Eagle Plastics brochure, undated; Ann MacDonald, "From Old Plastic, a New Playground," *The New York Times*, June 28, 1990; V. Elaine Gilmore, "Home Newsfront," *Popular Science*, 1989.

251. Mark Rogers, Duratech Industries Inc., personal communication, March 1, 1991.

252. Susan Combs, "Wis. Plastic Lumber Co. Uses 100% Post-Consumer HDPE," *Recycling Times*, March 12, 1991.

253. Roger Many, ARW Polywood, personal communication, Feb. 26, 1991.

254. Robert Riber, BTW Industries Inc., personal communication, June 11, 1991; Susan Combs, "Fla. Company's Plastic Lumber is Called 'Better Than Wood,'" *Recycling Times*, April 9, 1991.

255. See note 227, above.

256. Kathleen Meade, "CSWS Announces 25% Recycling Goal for Plastics," *Recycling Times*, April 9, 1991.

257. See note 79, above.

258. See note 256, above.

259. See note 31, above.

260. "Council Announces Blueprint," *Bottle/Can Recycling Update*, April 1991.

261. Bruce Bond, presentation at the National Solid Wastes Management Association's Waste Expo '91, Atlanta, Ga., May 1, 1990.

262. See note 256, above.

263. See note 80, above.

264. Roger Geyer, M.A. Industries Inc., presentation at the National Solid Wastes Management Association's Waste Expo '91, Atlanta, Ga., May 1, 1990.

265. Geoffrey Place, Procter & Gamble Co., presentation at "Building Confidence in Recycling" conference sponsored by the U.S. Conference of Mayors, Washington, D.C., March 29, 1990.

Notes to Chapter 6

1. Eugene Wingerter, "Keeping Up With the Changes," *Waste Age*, September 1990.

2. Susan Combs, "...Enter the MRF," *Waste Age*, October 1990.

3. Peter Grogan, "A 'Multiplexed' Future for MRFs," *Waste Age*, December 1989.

4. "The Municipal Solid Waste Dilemma: Challenges for the 90's," U.S. Environmental Protection Agency, January 1991, Revised Draft.

5. "Leading Companies in the Municipal Solid Waste Market," *Recycling Today*, May 15, 1991.

6. See note 5, above; Martha Hamilton, "Turning Trash Into Cash," *The Washington Post*, July 8, 1990.

7. Thomas Naber, "A New Chairman's Perspectives on the Nineties," *Waste Age*, June 1990.

8. Richard Widrig and Craig Osepian, Western Waste Industries, personal communication, May 29, 1991.

9. Kathleen Meade, "Minnesota Teaches By Doing," *Waste Age*, November 1989.

10. See note 9, above.

11. See note 8, above.

12. Richard Riley, Laidlaw Inc., personal communication, May 29, 1991.

13. Joseph Ruiz, Attwoods Inc., personal communication, Oct. 22, 1990.

14. "Comprehensive Curbside Recycling: Collection Costs and How to Control Them," Glass Packaging Institute, Washington, D.C., 1988.

15. Scott Bronstein, "Where, Oh, Where To Empty the Trash?," *The New York Times*, Sept. 14, 1986.

16. Mary-Lane Kamberg, "Recycling Cuts Disposal Costs in Seattle," *Solid Waste & Power*, August 1990.

17. "Plastics Recycling: From Vision to Reality," State University of N.J., Rutgers, Center for Plastics Recycling Research, Piscataway, N.J., undated.

18. See note 17, above.

19. Jane Witheridge, Waste Management Inc., personal communication, Oct. 22, 1990.

20. See note 5, above.

21. Robert Morris, Waste Management Inc., personal communication, July 18, 1991.

22. Waste Management Inc.'s 1990 annual report.

23. See note 19, above.

24. Randy Woods, "WMI Introduces Brini," *Waste Age*, September 1990.

25. Paul Aeschleman, Waste Management Inc., personal communication, May 21, 1991.

26. Susan Combs, "BRINI Technology Lets WMI Try Wet/Dry Collection," *Recycling Times*, Dec. 4, 1990.

27. "Project Profiles: Recycle America[R] Processing Facilities," Waste Management of North America Inc. fact sheet, March 1991.

28. See note 26, above.

29. Steve Apotheker, "Curbside Collection: Complete Separation Versus Commingled Collection," *Resource Recycling*, October 1990.

30. See note 25, above.

31. See note 22, above.

32. See note 22, above.

33. Fletcher Thorne-Thomsen, Browning-Ferris Industries Inc., personal communication, May 30, 1991.

34. See note 33, above.

35. Susan Combs, "New MRFs from Texas Firms," *Recycling Times*, March 26, 1991; Joseph T. Sedlock, "Curbside Sorting or Source Separation," *Waste Age*, October 1990.

36. Susan Combs, "BFI's Biggest in San Jose," *Recycling Times*, April 23, 1991.

37. See note 33, above; "Waste-by-Rail System To Serve Southern California," *Solid Waste & Power*, December 1990.

38. Laidlaw Transportation Ltd.'s 1989 annual report.

39. See note 12, above.

40. See note 13, above; Guada W. Lueck, Michael Misner and Randy Woods, "Big Six Prosper in FY 1989," *Waste Age*, June 1990; Steve Apotheker, "Mindis Recycling: Moving Beyond Metals," *Resource Recycling*, February 1991; Guada W. Lueck, "Recycling Among the Palms," *Waste Age*, May 1991.

41. Guada W. Lueck, Michael Misner and Randy Woods, "Big Six Prosper in FY 1989," *Waste Age*, June 1990.
42. Paris Wolfe, "Mindis International: Beyond Tradition," *Recycling Today*, May 15, 1991.
43. Steve Apotheker, "Mindis Recycling: Moving Beyond Metals," *Resource Recycling*, February 1991.
44. Frank Pietron, Chambers Development Co., personal communication, Oct. 18, 1990; Chambers Development Co.'s 1990 and 1989 annual reports.
45. See note 44, above.
46. "Bottle Battles," *Congressional Quarterly*, April 20, 1991.
47. "Trade-offs Involved in Beverage Container Deposit Legislation," U.S. General Accounting Office, (GAO-RCED-91-25), November 1990; Paris R. Wolfe, "The Troops are Organized for the Bottle Bill Battle," *Recycling Today*, March 15, 1990.
48. "Characterization of Municipal Solid Waste in the United States: 1990 Update," EPA/530-SW-90-042, U.S. Environmental Protection Agency, Office of Solid Waste and Emergency Response, Washington, D.C., June 1990.
49. "Trade-offs Involved in Beverage Container Deposit Legislation," U.S. General Accounting Office, (GAO-RCED-91-25), November 1990.
50. See note 48, above.
51. Patricia F. Franklin, "Bottle Bill: Litter Control Measure in a New Role?," *Solid Waste & Power*, February 1991.
52. See note 49, above.
53. Rep. Paul B. Henry, "A National Bottle Bill? Yes," *Waste Age*, December 1989.
54. Reclaiming a Valuable Resource," National Container Recycling Coalition brochure, Washington, D.C., undated.
55. See note 53, above.
56. "National Bottle Bill Includes a New Twist," *Solid Waste & Power*, February 1991.
57. Joseph T. Sedlock, "Bottle Bills: Recycling's Boon or Doom?," *Waste Age*, October 1990.
58. "Curbside Recycling 'Not Compatible,'" *Independent Energy*, November 1989.
59. "Recycling Ad Targets State Legislators," *The Soft Drink Recycler*, National Soft Drink Association, Washington, D.C., Fall 1990.
60. See note 57, above.
61. "Groups Endorse Curbside," *Recycling Today*, Sept. 15, 1990.
62. See note 51, above.
63. See note 8, above.
64. Western Waste Industries' 1990 and 1989 annual reports; Western Waste Industries brochure, undated.
65. Susan Combs, "WMI, American National Can To Market Glass and Metal," *Recycling Times*, Oct. 9, 1990.
66. "Recycling Venture Is Set with Waste Management," *The Wall Street Journal*, July 18, 1990; "Waste Management, Stone Form Company To Market, Use and Trade Waste Paper," *Recycling Times*, July 31, 1990; "WMI, Smurfit End Paper Deal," *Recycling Times*, April 24, 1990.
67. William Moore and Linda Koffenberger, "Giants Team Up on Plastics," *Waste Age*, August 1989.
68. Browning-Ferris Industries Inc.'s 1989 annual report.
69. Kathleen Meade, "BFI Agrees to Market All of Its Aluminum Cans to Alcoa," *Recycling Times*, July 17, 1990.
70. "BFI To Provide Waste Paper to Weyerhaeuser's New Mill," *Recycling Times*, June 19, 1990.
71. Susan Combs, "Augusta Newsprint Will Buy BFI's ONP and OMG," *Recycling Times*, April 23, 1991.

72. Susan Combs, "BFI's New Recycling VP is Confident About Markets," *Recycling Times*, Oct. 9, 1990.

73. See note 12, above.

74. Frank Pietron, Chambers Development Co., personal communication, Oct. 18, 1990.

75. See note 13, above.

76. See note 8, above.

77. "BFI Acquires Paper Processor," *Resource Recovery Report*, August 1990.

78. Jerry Powell, "The Big Haulers Are Becoming the Big Recycling Processors," *Resource Recycling*, September 1990; Susan Combs, "WMI Buys Durbin Paper Stock; Increases International Markets," *Recycling Times*, Nov. 20, 1990.

79. Gwen Cofield, "Ripe for Integrated Management," *Waste Age*, September 1990.

80. Jay Mathews, "California Embarks on Complex Bottle-Recycling Program," *The Washington Post*, Oct. 18, 1987.

81. "State/Province Watch," *Bottle/Can Recycling Update*, October 1990.

82. Jill Simons, California Department of Conservation, personal communication, Aug. 29, 1991.

83. See note 80, above.

84. See note 80, above.

85. "State Watch," *Bottle/Can Recycling Update*, November/December 1990.

86. Kathleen Meade, "Glass Manufacturers Can't Use California's Recycling Incentive," *Recycling Times*, Jan. 15, 1991.

87. See notes 81 and 86, above.

88. "Rigid Containers," *Bottle/Can Recycling Update*, March 1991.

89. "PRCC Files Lawsuit Against California," *Recycling Today*, May 15, 1991.

90. "Bottle Collection Hits 72%," *Recycling Today*, Oct. 15, 1990; "$1.00/Container Possible in California," *Resource Recovery Report*, October 1990.

91. Michael Misner, "Reynolds Slams California Law by Refusing Glass and Plastic," *Recycling Times*, Aug. 28, 1991.

92. Lee Wiegandt, California Glass Recycling Corp., personal communication, June 20, 1990.

93. Peter Karter, Resource Recovery Systems Inc., personal communication, May 20, 1991.

94. Anton J. Finelli, "Secondary Materials Markets: A Primer," *Solid Waste & Power*, August 1990.

95. "Recycling Centers," RecycleNOW™ brochure, Browning-Ferris Industries Inc., July 1989.

96. "1991 Directory of Materials Recovery Facilities," *Waste Age*, May 1991.

97. "MRFS to Double in 1990," *Waste Age*, April 1990.

98. Dan Goldberg, "MRFS Thrive on the East Coast," *Waste Alternatives*, June 1989.

99. See note 2, above.

100. Wayne P. Pferdehirt, "Planning Bigger, Faster, More Flexible MRFS," *Solid Waste & Power*, October 1990.

101. Bill Paul, "New Methods May Help U.S. Recycle More Plastics, a Scourge of Landfills," *The Wall Street Journal*, Feb. 9, 1989; William K. Stevens, "When the Trash Leaves the Curb: New Methods Improve Recycling," *The New York Times*, May 2, 1989.

102. See note 100, above.

103. See note 17, above.

104. Prall Culviner, "McMRFs: Mobile Recycling," *Waste Age*, May 1991; Susan Combs, "McMRFS and MRFS on Wheels," *Recycling Times*, Sept. 25, 1990.

105. David Stipp, "Consumers' Improper Sorting of Trash Is a Messy Problem for Recycling Industry," *The Wall Street Journal*, May 9, 1991.

106. Eugene J. Wingerter, "Serious New Safety Concern," *Waste Age*, September 1989.
107. See note 100, above.
108. See note 106, above.
109. Aluminum Association Inc., Report to the Coalition of Northeastern Governors on Aluminum Recycling Rates and Recycled Content, Washington, D.C., Aug. 27, 1990.
110. See note 100, above.
111. Steve Apotheker, "David Buckner and Browning-Ferris Industries See Recycling As a Business Opportunity," *Resource Recycling*, December 1990; Jamie Hill, "Large Cities Try to Cut Collection Costs with Blue Bag Systems," *Recycling Times*, Jan. 15, 1991.
112. "MSW Compaction Studied," *Recycling Today*, Oct. 15, 1990.
113. Joseph T. Sedlock, "Curbside Sorting or Source Separation," *Waste Age*, October 1990.
114. Robert N. Gould, "MRFS, Past and Future," *Waste Age*, July 1990.
115. See note 114, above.
116. Dexter Ewel and Frank C. Shaw, "Risk Allocation in a Changing MRF Industry," *BioCycle*, April 1990.
117. Robert E. Randol and Walter J. Kulakowski, "The System Approach: A Way to Better Credit and Lower Costs," *Solid Waste & Power*, October 1990.
118. Richard N. McCarthy, "Financing Recycling Facilities," *Waste Age*, March 1991.
119. See note 118, above.
120. Mark B. Shufro, GE Capital, "Financing the Recycling Industry," presentation at "Building Confidence in Recycling" conference sponsored by the U.S. Conference of Mayors, Washington, D.C., March 29, 1990.
121. Roger D. Stark and Mary Ellen Hogan, "Recycling: California's Market Approach," *Transactional Finance*, June 1990.
122. Susan Combs, "RRT Uses Tax-Exempt Leasing to Finance N.Y. County's MRF," *Recycling Times*, May 7, 1991.
123. See note 118, above.
124. See notes 116, 117 and 118, above.
125. Stephen A. Katz, New England CRInc., written communication, May 23, 1991.
126. James Luci, Anchor Glass Container Corp., personal communication, June 18, 1990.
127. See note 125, above.
128. Wellman Inc.'s 1990 annual report.
129. "Balanced and Integrated Solid Waste Management Systems," New England CRInc. brochure, 1989.
130. "Wellman Inc. Announces Plans to Acquire New England CRInc.," Wellman Inc. press release, April 26, 1990.
131. Stephen A. Katz, New England CRInc., written communication, July 11, 1991.
132. See note 128, above.
133. "CRInc. Construction Contracts," *Resource Recovery Report*, April 1990.
134. "Recycling and Solid Waste Management Experience: Project Summaries," New England CRInc., undated.
135. See note 93, above.
136. See note 93, above.
137. Resource Recycling Technologies Inc.'s 1990 annual report.
138. See note 137, above; Resource Recycling Technologies Inc.'s "Plant Presentation" video; Resource Recycling Technologies Inc.'s 1989 annual report and Form 10-K.
139. Lawrence J. Schorr, Resource Recycling Technologies Inc., personal communication, June 11, 1991.
140. See note 139, above.
141. David Weisman, Resource Recycling Technologies Inc., personal communication, May 28, 1991.

142. Resource Recycling Technologies Inc.'s 1990 and 1989 annual reports.

143. Mark McIntyre, Omni Technical Services Inc., personal communication, May 2, 1991.

144. Edward J. Rutkowski and Jack Quigley, Integrated Waste Services Inc., personal communication, May 23, 1991; "The Best Small Companies," *Business Week*, May 27, 1991.

145. See note 29, above; Michael Misner, "Seattle's Centerpiece MRF," *Waste Age*, August 1990.

146. Robert Blenden, Automated Recycling Technology, personal communication, May 22, 1991.

147. Wes Constable, Commercial Metals Co., personal communication, May 31, 1991; Commercial Metals Co.'s 1990 annual report.

148. Susan Combs, "Wheelabrator Builds a MRF with Waste-to-Energy Plant," *Recycling Times*, April 9, 1991.

149. "Westinghouse To Build Recycling Facility," *Environment Week*, April 12, 1990; "Beyond the Beltway: News from the States," *Environment Week*, Jan. 25, 1990.

150. John Phillips, Ogden Martin Systems Inc., personal communication, June 4, 1991.

151. See note 8, above.

Notes to Chapter 7

1. Steve Apotheker, "Garbage In, But What Comes Out?," *Resource Recycling*, September 1990.

2. See note 1, above.

3. Joe Schwartz, "Squeezed Out," *Environmental Action*, January/February 1991.

4. John Holusha, "In Solid Waste, It's the Breakdown That Counts," *The New York Times*, March 31, 1991.

5. Steve Apotheker, "David Buckner and Browning-Ferris Industries See Recycling As A Business Opportunity," *Resource Recycling*, December 1990.

6. James Eckar, Resource Conservation Services Inc., personal communication, May 23, 1991.

7. See note 3, above.

8. Susan Combs, "Orfa Files Chapter 11," *Waste Age*, August 1990; Orfa Corp. brochure, undated.

9. Randy Woods, "Can RDF Pass the Test?," *Waste Age*, August 1990.

10. Reuter Inc.'s 1990 and 1989 annual reports.

11. See note 10, above.

12. John Holusha, "The Packaging Industry's New Fancy—Composting Garbage," *The New York Times*, Feb. 24, 1991.

13. See note 12, above.

14. See note 12, above.

15. Jackie Prince, Environmental Defense Fund, written communication, July 23, 1991.

16. Wayne Trewhitt, "Commitment Is Part of the Success," *Waste Age*, October 1990.

17. Susan Combs, "EPA: More Than Half of MSW Will Be Recycled by 2000," *Recycling Times*, Sept. 11, 1990.

18. See note 12, above.

19. John Holusha, "Using Biological 'Fire' to Turn Waste into Fertilizer," *The New York Times*, Feb. 3, 1991.

20. Janet Marinelli, "Composting: From Backyards to Big-Time," *Garbage*, July/August 1990.

21. "Characterization of Municipal Solid Waste in the United States: 1990 Update," EPA/ 530-SW-90-042, U.S. Environmental Protection Agency, Office of Solid Waste and Emergency Response, Washington, D.C., June 1990.

22. Richard M. Kashmanian and Alison C. Taylor, "Designing Yard Waste Composting Programs," *Waste Age*, October 1990.

23. See note 21, above.

24. See note 21, above.

25. "Bedminster Bioconversion Corp. Background Information," undated report.

26. Solid Waste Composting Council brochure, undated; Aga S. Razvi, Philip R. O'Leary and Patrick Walsh, "Composting Municipal Solid Wastes," *Waste Age*, August 1989; Aga S. Razvi, Philip R. O'Leary and Patrick Walsh, "Basic Principles of Composting," *Waste Age*, July 1989.

27. "64 Questions about Composting," Buhler Inc. brochure, undated; "Compost: Natural Recycling of Organic Household Garbage," *The Resource*, Minnesota Office of Waste Management, March 1991.

28. See note 20, above.

29. "Agripost: At Peace with the Environment," Agripost Inc. brochure, undated.

30. Aga S. Razvi, Philip R. O'Leary and Patrick Walsh, "Composting Municipal Solid Wastes," *Waste Age*, August 1989.

31. See note 30, above.

32. See note 30, above.

33. See note 30, above; "64 Questions about Composting," Buhler Inc. brochure, undated; Luis F. Diaz and Clarence G. Golueke, "Status of Composting in the United States," *Resource Recycling*, February 1990.

34. See note 30, above; "64 Questions about Composting," Buhler Inc. brochure, undated.

35. See note 30, above.

36. See note 30, above; "What is Composting?," Procter & Gamble Co. fact sheet, undated.

37. See note 29, above; Richard M. Kashmanian, H. Clark Gregory, and Steven A. Dressing, "Where Will All the Compost Go?," *BioCycle*, October 1990; Aga S. Razvi, Patrick Walsh and Philip R. O'Leary," Marketing Composts," *Waste Age*, March 1990; Michael Misner, "How to Avoid A Compost Glut," *Waste Age*, December 1989; William D. Gibson, "The Nature of Compost," Resource Systems Corp. brochure, October 1988.

38. Aga S. Razvi, Patrick Walsh and Philip R. O'Leary, "Marketing Composts," *Waste Age*, March 1990.

39. Bruce Fulford, Tellus Institute, personal communication, May 17, 1991; Tom Watson, "Solid Waste Composting Aims for the Mainstream," *Resource Recycling*, July 1990.

40. Tom Watson, "Solid Waste Composting Aims for the Mainstream," *Resource Recycling*, July 1990.

41. "Portland Metro Pursues Plans for Mixed Waste Composting," *Waste Age*, November 1989.

42. "1990 Farm Bill Supports Composting Research," *BioCycle*, November 1990.

43. Randall Monk, Solid Waste Composting Council, personal communications, April 12 and 29, 1991.

44. Elizabeth Voisin, "Yard Waste a Natural for Recycling," *City & State*, Aug. 1, 1988.

45. Michael Simpson, "Integrating Leaf and Yard Waste Composting with Waste-to-Energy Facilities," *Resource Recycling*, September 1990.

46. See note 45, above; "The Municipal Solid Waste Dilemma: Challenges for the 90's," U.S. Environmental Protection Agency, January 1991, Revised Draft.

47. Luis F. Diaz and Clarence G. Golueke, "Status of Composting in the United States," *Resource Recycling*, February 1990; "The Agripost," Agripost Inc. newsletter, Summer 1989.

48. Patrick Walsh, Aga S. Razvi and Philip R. O'Leary, "Yard Waste Composting: A Management Challenge," *Waste Age*, September 1989.

49. *The Wall Street Journal*, March 23, 1990.

50. See note 22, above.

51. U.S. Congress, Office of Technology Assessment, *Facing America's Trash: What Next for Municipal Solid Waste*, OTA-0-424, Washington, D.C.: U.S. Government Printing Office, October 1989, p. 188.

52. See note 48, above.

53. "Spores from Compost Blamed for Illness," *Recycling Times*, January 1989.

54. See note 48, above; Luis F. Diaz and Clarence G. Golueke, "Status of Composting in the United States," *Resource Recycling*, February 1990.

55. William E. Schmidt, "Beyond Dumps: What to Do With the Grass," *The New York Times*, June 11, 1989.

56. See note 48, above.

57. Dan Goldberg, "Can Grass Clippings Be Composted?," *Waste Age*, April 1990.

58. See note 20, above.

59. Nora Goldstein and Robert Spencer, "Solid Waste Composting in the United States," *BioCycle*, November 1990.

60. See note 20, above.

61. "Compost Applications, Benefits and End-Market Potential," Procter & Gamble Co. fact sheet, undated.

62. See note 20, above.

63. See note 20, above.

64. See note 38, above.

65. See note 22, above.

66. Randall Monk, Solid Waste Composting Council, personal communications, April 12 and 29, 1991; Tom Arrandale, "A Rotten Solution for our Solid Waste Woes," *Governing*, April 1991.

67. See note 43, above.

68. "The Municipal Solid Waste Dilemma: Challenges for the 90's," U.S. Environmental Protection Agency, January 1991, Revised Draft.

69. Tom Arrandale, "A Rotten Solution for our Solid Waste Woes," *Governing*, April 1991.

70. See note 43, above.

71. See note 68, above.

72. See note 43, above.

73. See note 38, above.

74. See note 43, above.

75. See note 51, above, p. 189; "Yard Waste Composting," *Solid Waste and Power*, August 1990.

76. Robert Spencer and Nora Goldstein, "Operational Challenges at MSW Composting Facilities," *BioCycle*, November 1990.

77. Gary Breedon, Sumter County, Fla., personal communication, May 15, 1991.

78. Diane D'Angelo, Agripost Inc., personal communications, March 29 and May 13, 1991.

79. Karen Hyndman, Recomp Inc., personal communication, April 1 and May 29, 1991.

80. Dr. Eliot Epstein, E&A Environmental Consultants, undated fact sheet.

81. "Compost Projects: A New Model for Project Finance," *Finance Alert*, Nixon, Hargrave, Devans & Doyle, Washington, D.C., Spring 1990.

82. See note 81, above.

83. See note 81, above.

84. Paul Atanasio, "Financing an MSW Composting Facility," *BioCycle*, May 1990.

85. Jerome Goldstein, "Investors Discover 'A Sleeping Giant'," *In Business*, July/August

1990. "Construction To Begin On MSW Composting Plant," *BioCycle*, October 1990.

86. "Construction to Begin on MSW Composting Plant," *BioCycle*, October 1990.

87. Timothy Wiens, Environmental Recovery Systems Inc., personal communication, March 29, 1991.

88. See note 29, above.

89. Gwen Cofield, "Composting Mixed Waste," *Waste Age*, January 1990.

90. See notes 59 and 76, above.

91. See note 59, above.

92. See note 59, above.

93. See note 76, above.

94. See note 76, above.

95. Ted Gentile, Daneco Inc., personal communication, April 1, 1991.

96. Guada Lueck, "Compost Project Funded by Revenue Bonds," *Waste Age*, May 1990.

97. "Tipping Fees at Composting Facilities," *BioCycle*, February 1991.

98. "64 Questions about Composting," Buhler Inc. brochure, undated.

99. See note 80, above.

100. See note 40, above.

101. See note 76, above.

102. "Daneco Composting Systems," Daneco Inc. brochure, undated.

103. See note 43, above; Solid Waste Composting Council brochure, undated.

104. Kathleen Meade, "P&G Commits $20 Million to MSW Compost Project," *Recycling Times*, Oct. 23, 1990.

105. "Procter & Gamble Composting Fund," Procter & Gamble Co. fact sheet, undated; "P&G Commits $20 Million to Advance Composting as a Solid Waste Solution: Will Develop New Compostable Materials for Diapers," Procter & Gamble Co. press release, Oct. 9, 1990.

106. See note 78, above; "Waste Deliveries are Halted to MSW Compost Facility," *BioCycle*, February 1991.

107. See note 29, above.

108. See note 89, above; "The Story of the Burr Process," Burr Universal Resource Recovery Inc. brochure, undated.

109. See note 78, above.

110. Don Rondeau, Approved Waste Recycling Corp., personal communication, May 2, 1991.

111. See note 25, above.

112. See note 25, above; Hugh Ettinger, Bedminster Bioconversion Corp., personal communication, March 14, 1991.

113. See note 25, above.

114. See note 79, above.

115. Hugh Ettinger, Bedminster Bioconversion Corp., personal communication, March 14, 1991.

116. "The Daneco Group," Daneco Inc. brochure, undated; *Resource Recovery_Report*, January 1990.

117. See notes 95 & 102, above; "East Central Solid Waste Commission," Daneco Inc. brochure, undated; "Materials Recovery Facilities," Daneco Inc./Horstmann Foerdertechnik GmbH & Co. brochure, undated.

118. See note 95, above.

119. See note 95, above; "The Daneco Group," Daneco Inc. brochure, undated.

120. "Denver Recycler Gets Support for Connecticut Facility," *Waste Age*, August 1990.

121. See note 87, above.

122. See note 120, above.

123. See note 87, above; Timothy Wiens, Environmental Recovery Systems Inc., written communication, March 29, 1991; Environmental Recovery Systems Inc. brochure, undated.

124. Paul Utterback, F&E Resource Systems Technology Inc., personal communication, May 2, 1991.

125. See note 124, above.

126. "Fast-growing Recycling Companies," *Resource Recycling,* January 1991.

127. Mark McIntyre, Omni Technical Services Inc., personal communication, May 2, 1991.

128. Norman Schenck, OTVD Inc., personal communication, May 20, 1991; Randy Woods, "A French 'Revolution' Comes to Minnesota," *Waste Age,* January 1991.

129. Recomp advertisement in *Waste Age,* January 1990.

130. See note 79, above.

131. See note 79, above; "Processing Today's Waste into Tomorrow's Resources," Recomp Inc. brochure, undated.

132. See note 131, above.

133. *Resource Recovery Report,* March 1991.

134. See note 79, above.

135. See note 79, above; "Bonneville Acquires Super Cycle Inc.," *Independent Energy,* November 1989.

136. "P&G Commits $20 Million to Advance Composting as a Solid Waste Solution: Will Develop New Compostable Materials for Diapers," Procter & Gamble Co. press release, Oct. 9, 1990.

137. Leopold F. Schmidt, Resource Systems Corp., written communication, June 6, 1990.

138. Reidel Environmental Technologies Inc.'s advertisement in *Waste Age,* January 1990.

139. See notes 41 and 84, above.

140. See note 96, above.

141. "Reidel Environmental Technologies Inc.," Resource Systems Corp. brochure, undated.

142. See note 96, above.

143. John Boquist, Reuter Inc., personal communication, May 31, 1991.

144. "Proven, Practical Waste Processing Systems," Buhler Inc. brochure, undated.

145. Urs Maire, Buhler Inc., personal communication, May 3, 1991.

146. William Chiles, TRS Industries Inc., personal communication, May 2, 1991.

147. See note 146, above.

148. Larry Tyson, Tyson Environmental Systems & Services Inc., written communication, May 13, 1991.

149. John Nutter, American Recovery Corp., personal communication, May 2, 1991; John Nutter, American Recovery Corp., written communication, Feb. 23, 1991; "Conserving the Nation's Resources with Proven Technology," American Recovery Corp. brochure, undated; American Recovery Corp./Sorain Cecchini Technology fact sheet, undated.

150. Erik Hansen, Burr Universal Resource Recovery Inc., personal communication, March 29, 1991; "The Story of the Burr Process," Burr Universal Resource Recovery brochure, undated; "Burr: The Pollution-free Solution to the Waste Problem," Burr Universal Resource Recovery brochure, undated.

151. *Resource Recovery Report,* May 1989.

152. Peter Karter, Resource Recovery Systems Inc., personal communication, May 20, 1991.

153. "Plants Designed and Built by Triga," Harbert/Triga fact sheet, 1990.

154. Susan Combs, "Wheelabrator Technologies Buys International Composting Company," *Recycling Times,* March 12, 1991.

155. "MRF/Composting Plant Under Development," *BioCycle,* November 1990.

156. "Yard Waste Composting News," *Resource Recycling,* January 1991.

157. Fletcher Thorne-Thomsen, Browning-Ferris Industries Inc., personal communication, May 30, 1991.
158. See note 6, above.
159. Frank Pietron, Chambers Development Co., personal communication, Oct. 18, 1990.
160. "Project Profiles: Yard Waste and Composting," Recycle America[R] fact sheet, March 1991.
161. Joseph Ruiz, Attwoods Inc., personal communication, Oct. 22, 1990.
162. Richard Riley, Laidlaw Inc., personal communication, May 29, 1991.
163. Lewis Shuster, Ebara Environmental Corp., personal communication, May 3, 1991; "Ebara Demonstration Compost Facility," Ebara Environmental Corp. fact sheet, July 6, 1990.
164. Kathleen Meade, "Food Composting: No Small Potatoes," *Waste Age*, April 1990.
165. "Pilot Project Planned for Food Waste Composting," *BioCycle*, February 1991.
166. Frank Howard Allen, "Big Apple Takes a Look at the Compost Heap," *The Wall Street Journal*, April 10, 1991.
167. Susan Combs, "New York City's Budget Could Suspend Recycling," *Recycling Times*, May 21, 1991.
168. *Resource Recovery Report*, April 1991.
169. See note 9, above.
170. Stuart H. Russell, "Pre-Processing, Not RDF," *Waste Age*, August 1989.
171. See note 9, above.
172. See note 143, above.
173. See note 9, above.
174. See notes 9 and 143, above; Reuter Inc.'s 1990 annual report; Jeffrey Bruner, "Metropolitan Council Revokes Reuter's Minnesota RDF Plant," *Recycling Times*, Aug. 28, 1990.
175. See note 143, above.
176. Steve Paulsen, Lundell Manufacturing Co., personal communication, May 15, 1991.
177. *Sorting It Out*, National Recovery Technologies Inc. newsletter, Vol. 1, Nos. 1 & 2.
178. Paul Kemezis, "Tennessee Company Pushes PVC Recycling Technology, *Environment Week*, Sept. 21, 1989.
179. See note 177, above; "City of Nashville Approves Expansion of WTE Facility," *Solid Waste & Power*, June 1991.
180. Peter Brown, XL Disposal Corp., personal communication, Aug. 29, 1991; Peter Brown, XL Disposal Corp., presentation at *Resource Recovery Report's* "Pro-Cycle II" automated solid waste processing conference, July 10, 1991; "XL Disposal—Recycling: The High-Tech Way," Xl Disposal Corp. video, Dec. 12, 1990.
181. Louisville Energy & Environment Corp. fact sheet, undated; Ventech Energy & Development Corp. fact sheet, undated.
182. Robert Merdes, Neutralysis Industries Inc., personal communication, May 28, 1991; Robert Merdes, Neutralysis Industries Inc., presentation at *Resource Recovery Report's* "Pro-Cycle II" conference, July 10, 1991.
183. See note 182, above.
184. Thomas Naber, "Recycling Evolution," *Waste Age*, July 1990; Joe Salimando, "The 'Allied' Lomanginos Are 'Star' Recyclers," *Waste Age*, July 1990.
185. See note 170, above; "Mixed Waste Processing News," *Resource Recycling*, March 1991.
186. See note 1, above.
187. R. Vance Howard, Delta Waste Services Inc., personal communication, June 3, 1991.
188. *Sorting It Out*, National Recovery Technologies Inc. newsletter, Vol. 1, No. 2.
189. Eliot Epstein and T. O. Williams, "Are There Markets for Compost?," *Waste Age*, April 1991.
190. Solid Waste Composting Council brochure, undated.

191. Susan Combs, "California Considers Compost to Meet 50% Recycling Law," *Recycling Times*, May 7, 1991.

192. See note 25, above.

193. Geoffrey Place, Procter & Gamble Co., presentation at "Building Confidence in Recycling" conference sponsored by the U.S. Conference of Mayors, Washington, D.C., March 29, 1990.

194. "MSW Composting: What's In the Mix?," Environmental Action Foundation, Washington, D.C., undated.

195. See note 193, above.

Notes to Chapter 8

Much of the information contained in this chapter is derived from a 1989 IRRC report: *Power Plays: Profiles of America's Independent Renewable Electricity Developers*, Investor Responsibility Research Center Inc., Washington, D.C., 1989. Updated information is otherwise footnoted.

1. Jonathan V.L. Kiser, "A Comprehensive Report on the Status of Municipal Waste Combustion," *Waste Age*, November 1990.

2. "The Municipal Solid Waste Dilemma: Challenges for the 90's," U.S. Environmental Protection Agency, January 1991, Revised Draft.

3. Richard J. Sweetnam Jr. and Marc H. Sulam, "Waste-to-Energy Industry: 1990 Awards: Business Remains Sluggish," Executive Summary, Kidder, Peabody & Co. Inc., Jan. 10, 1991.

4. Michael T. Burr, "Slow Growth in Waste-to-Energy," *Independent Energy*, February 1991.

5. Richard J. Sweetnam Jr., Kidder, Peabody & Co. Inc., personal communication, Aug. 26, 1991.

6. See note 1, above.

7. See note 1, above.

8. "Uncertainties Buffet Market," *Engineering News-Record*, Jan. 14, 1991.

9. See note 1, above.

10. See note 1, above.

11. "EPA Issues New Combustion Regs," *Waste Age*, March 1991; "Clean Air Regs Published by EPA," *Resource Recovery Report*, February 1991.

12. "EPA Answers Questions on New Air Emission Rules," *Solid Waste & Power*, April 1991; Jonathan V.L. Kiser, "Clean Air Act Amendments to Impact Medical Waste Combustors," *Infectious Waste News*, Feb. 19, 1991.

13. "Clean Air Regs Published by EPA," *Resource Recovery Report*, February 1991.

14. John Phillips, Ogden Martin Systems Inc., presentation at the New England Resource Recovery Conference & Exposition, June 4, 1991.

15. See note 1, above.

16. Carl Vansant, "WTE Equipment: Big Gains in a Short Time," *Solid Waste & Power*, June 1991.

17. "Recycling Requirements Dropped From New EPA Standards," *Resource Recovery Focus*, Institute of Resource Recovery, Washington, D.C., Fall 1990.

18. Susan Combs, "NRDC, States Sue EPA to Force Combustor Recycling Requirement," *Recycling Times*, May 7, 1991.

19. See note 2, above.

20. "EPA Introducing New Toxicity Test for Waste," *Solid Waste & Power*, June 1990.

21. Matthew Root, Ogden Martin Systems Inc., presentation at the National Solid Wastes Management's WasteExpo '91, April 9, 1991.
22. Michael Booth, "Incinerator Gives Officials Heartburn," *The Washington Post*, Aug. 11, 1991.
23. "New York Study Sees WTE Ash Potential," *Waste Age*, May 1991.
24. Wheelabrator Technologies Inc.'s 1990 annual report.
25. "ABB To Market Ash Technology for MWS," *Resource Recovery Report*, September 1990.
26. See note 24, above.
27. See note 4, above.
28. "Waste-to-Energy: It Helps Keep Paradise Paradise," Asea Brown Boveri Resource Recovery Systems Inc. brochure, undated.
29. Foster Wheeler Power Systems Inc. brochure, undated.
30. Patrick J. Scanlon, "Trash-to-energy Plants: A Multi-dimensional Approach to Solid Waste Management," *Resource Recycling*, April 1991.
31. See note 28, above.
32. See note 30, above; Michael Simpson, "Integrating Leaf and Yard Waste Composting with Waste-to-Energy Facilities," *Resource Recycling*, September 1990.
33. John Shortsleeve and Robert V. Roche, "Making WTE and RecyclingWork Together," *Solid Waste & Power*, October 1990.
34. Plastics and the Environment: Progress and Commitment," The Society of the Plastics Industry Inc., undated brochure, Washington, D.C.
35. See note 30, above.
36. See note 28, above.
37. John Shortsleeve and Robert Roche, "Integrated Solutions That Work," *Waste Age*, January 1991.
38. See note 3, above.
39. See note 24, above.
40. See note 3, above.
41. Waste Management Inc.'s 1990 annual report.
42. Susan Combs, "Wheelabrator Builds a MRF with Waste-to-Energy Plant," *Recycling Times*, April 9, 1991; "Top of the Heap," *Solid Waste & Power*, April 1991.
43. Susan Combs, "Wheelabrator Technologies Buys International Composting Company," *Recycling Times*, March 12, 1991.
44. "Performance Update," *Forbes*, Oct. 30, 1989.
45. "Ogden Corp.," *The Wall Street Journal*, May 30, 1991.
46. See note 3, above.
47. See note 3, above.
48. "Westinghouse To Build Recycling Facility," *Environment Week*, April 12, 1990.
49. "Beyond the Beltway: News from the States," *Environment Week*, Jan. 25, 1990.
50. Asea Brown Boveri Resource Recovery Systems fact sheet, undated.
51. "Asea Brown Boveri Agrees to Acquire Combustion Engineering for $1.6 Billion," *The Wall Street Journal*, Nov. 15, 1989.
52. "ABB Prospective Major Developer," *Resource Recovery Report*, October 1990.
53. Noel D. Hazzard, ABB Resource Recovery Systems Inc., personal communication, July 24, 1991.
54. See note 3, above.
55. Foster Wheeler Corp. brochure, undated.
56. "An Integrated Plant for Montreal," *Waste Age*, February 1990.
57. Michael T. Burr, "Snapshot: Ogden Projects," *Independent Energy*, April 1991.
58. *National Energy Strategy: Powerful Ideas for America*, (061-00-00754-7), U.S. Department of Energy, Washington, D.C., February 1991.

59. "Characterization of Municipal Solid Waste in the United States: 1990 Update," EPA/ 530-SW-90-042, U.S. Environmental Protection Agency, Office of Solid Waste and Emergency Response, Washington, D.C., June 1990.
60. See note 1, above.
61. "Top of the Heap," *Solid Waste & Power*, June 1990.
62. "Top of the Heap," *Solid Waste & Power*, October 1990.
63. See note 28, above.
64. "Waste-to-Energy: What's Happening Today," *Solid Waste & Power*, August 1990.

Notes to Conclusions

1. John Holusha, "In Solid Waste, It's the Breakdown that Counts," *The New York Times*, March 31, 1991.
2. Donella Meadows, "It Will Take Time to Perfect Recycling," *The Valley News*.
3. "Va. Authority Signs Long-Term Market Contract with Recycler," *Recycling Times*, Sept. 25, 1990.
4. Susan Combs, "Southeast Paper Recycling Processes Other Materials," *Recycling Times*, May 21, 1991.
5. Kathleen Meade, "Weyerhaeuser Buys Kansas Recycler of Paper, Containers," *Recycling Times*, March 26, 1991; Weyerhaeuser to Recycle Paper And More at New Denver Plant," *Recycling Times*, Nov. 20, 1990.
6. Michael Selz, "Glut of Garbage Leaves Recycler Groping for a Market," *The Wall Street Journal*, May 17, 1991; Susan Combs, "Denver Recycler Files Chapter 11," Recycling Times, May 21, 1991; "Around the Country," *Resource Recycling*, September 1989.

COMPANY INDEX